GOSSIP

GOSSIP

A HISTORY OF HIGH SOCIETY FROM
1920 to 1970

Andrew Barrow

Pan Books London and Sydney

First published 1978 by Hamish Hamilton Ltd
This edition published 1980 by Pan Books Ltd,
Cavaye Place, London SW10 9PG
9 8 7 6 5 4 3 2
© Andrew Barrow 1978
ISBN 0 330 26223 8
Design by Don Macpherson
BAS Printers Limited, Over Wallop, Hampshire

Printed and Bound in Great Britain by
R. J. Acford, Chichester, Sussex, England.

INTRODUCTION

To cram into a single volume the day-by-day story of high society over fifty action-packed years has been no mean task. In order to do so, I have based my narrative on London, with occasional excursions into the English and Scottish countryside and, as a rule, have only ventured further afield when the activities of English social figures have made news. Thus, I have included Winston Churchill's accident in a New York street in 1931 but excluded the weighing of the Aga Khan in diamonds in Bombay in 1946. Similarly, I have fully documented the activities of American multi-millionairess Miss Barbara Hutton while she was living in London in the 1930s and building Winfield House, but have not pursued her when she sailed away to California in October 1939.

In the pages that follow, the major and minor social incidents of the period will be found in strict chronological order. It will be seen that sometimes three entirely separate incidents have occurred on one day while rarely has a month gone by without something occurring which seemed to demand inclusion. The major society dramas have been recorded where they occurred, often interspliced with extremely minor events. Thus the reader will be swept from a major landmark like the death of Queen Alexandra to eleven year-old Sarah Churchill finding a pearl necklace in a Chelsea street. Some readers may also be tantalized to find famous episodes, which have inspired whole books and films, such as the Commander Crabb affair of 1956, dismissed in a few lines.

To shorten the story, I have on the whole ignored the artistic and literary worlds, especially the already well-documented Bloomsbury group, and have concentrated instead on more philistine and headline-grabbing figures such as Lady Docker, Princess Margaret, Nubar Gulbenkian, Charles Clore and attendant millionaires and millionairesses, dukes, duchesses and playboys.

I have also omitted show-business stars except where, like Tallulah Bankhead, Noel Coward, Elizabeth Taylor, Danny Kaye or Douglas Fairbanks Junior and Senior, they have been adopted by high society or, in the case of Liberace, paid controversial visits to England. On the other hand, several bishops and clergymen, though not strictly part of Society, have been included, both for their outraged pronouncements on the changing morals of the time and for their own personal misdemeanours. I think about two or three de-frockings are featured in this book and I have included Archbishop Temple's comments on venereal disease in 1943, though the direct bearing of his remarks on the rest of the narrative may be questioned.

Some of the characters in this story explode just once onto the scene, such as wealthy stockbroker's daughter Elvira Barney, whose Old Bailey murder trial was the sensation of 1932, or handsome playboy Edward Langley, whose elopement with the daughter of a millionaire shipbuilder filled the news-papers in the summer of 1959. Others remain present throughout the entire fifty years and are followed through many different stations in life. For example, I have traced the activities of the Prince of Wales from the age of twenty-five, through his short period as King to his long years of exile as Duke of Windsor, while his old friend Lord Louis Mountbatten enters the narrative as a nineteen-year-old lieutenant in the Royal Navy and finishes up as the venerable, much-decorated Royal uncle, Earl Mountbatten of Burma. The beautiful Lady Diana Cooper also reappears constantly throughout the story, from her days as an actress in *The Miracle* in the early Twenties right through to an incident in 1968 when she receives apologies from the Deputy Commissioner of the Metropolitan Police after a midnight raid on her house by policemen seeking cannabis in a hat box. Miss Margaret Whigham is another famous beauty who will be followed from her debut in 1930, when she was named Deb of the Year, through her marriages with Mr. Charles Sweeny and the Duke of Argyll, retaining her swan-like good looks well into middle age. Sir Oswald Mosley is yet another formidable survivor, whose political activities will occasionally intrude upon the social events of the period.

As well as following certain individuals through, it will be observed that certain leading families dominate the social scene. Five generations of the Royal Family are featured in the pages that follow, from Queen Alexandra, who died in 1925, to her great-great-granddaughter Princess Anne, who in 1968 meets her future husband Olympic equestrian Mark Phillips for the first time. Three utterly different Dukes of Bedford are featured, and in the course of this narrative Woburn Abbey changes from being an impenetrably grand feudal retreat, staffed by more than sixty liveried servants, to become the great Show Place of the Midlands and the setting for scenes in a nudist film. As the story unfolds, it will be found that many of the leading figures of the later years are the children or grandchildren of those who have featured prominently in the earlier pages of the book. A remarkable instance is presented by the young Lady Annabel Birley, after whom London's most fashionable new nightclub was named in 1962, whose grandmother, the great Marchioness of Londonderry, was indisputably the leading political hostess of the Twenties and Thirties.

Although I have avoided cluttering the text with social analysis, I have deliberately selected items which illustrate changes in taste, fashion, morals as well as other items to show how much anachronistic grandeur still existed right up to the end of the period. I have also chosen incidents to show the changing face of London, and England, against which the dramas of the period have been played out. I have noted the demise of great town-houses (from Devonshire House in 1920 to Londonderry House in 1962), the erection of hotels or blocks of flats on their sites and the gradual transition of emphasis from old to new money. I have also noted various pieces of legislation which may have had some bearing on the social climate. Although I have tried to avoid referring directly to major political events, the general course of history may be sensed beneath the social parade.

I have drawn my material from the newspapers and magazines of the period, as well as autobiographies, biographies and published diaries. Of newspapers, the Court Circular of *The Times* proved unexpectedly useful with its announcements of the comings and goings of celebrities and its comprehensive lists of those attending parties, weddings, funerals and christenings. The gossip columns of the *Daily Express* and *Daily Mail* have borne much fruit and the news-packed *Daily Telegraph* was particularly helpful during the war years. The *Evening Standard*'s Diary page furnished me with many items not the least of which were details of the refreshments served on the aeroplane carrying Neville Chamberlain to and from Berchtesgarten on September 15, 1938. The *Tatler* provided a useful pictorial record of social events throughout this period, though some of its items are a little difficult to give an exact date to. Of the many books I have found helpful, I must acknowledge my debt to *The Diaries of Sir Henry Channon* which span the years 1934–1953 and provide an unrivalled record of social life in London during the Blitz, *Edward VIII* by Frances Donaldson, *The Secrets of the 43 Club* by Mrs. Meyrick, *In Vogue: Six Decades of Fashion* edited by Georgina Howell, *My Life* by Sir Oswald Mosley, *The Savoy: The Romance of a Great Hotel* by Stanley Jackson, *Forget Not* by Margaret Duchess of Argyll, *A Silver-plated Spoon* by the Duke of Bedford, *The Wandering Years* by Cecil Beaton, *Winston Churchill: the Struggle for Survival* by Lord Moran, *The Life and Times of Private Eye* edited by Richard Ingrams, *The Aga Khans* by Willi Frischauer, *Queen Mary* by James Pope-Hennessy, *Unity Mitford: A Quest* by David Pryce-Jones, and *Mick Jagger* by Anthony Scaduto.

I would also like to thank Hugo Vickers, who has helped to put an exact date to many of the incidents and obligingly worked out the age, at various stages, of the personalities involved. I must also thank Caroline Tonson Rye for her industry in gathering the photographs, Dana Turner for typing the manuscript and John Henderson for his editorial skills and suggestions. Others who have helped or encouraged me in one way or another include Gillon Aitken, Beatrix Miller, Hugh Montgomery-Massingberd, Annette Worsley-Taylor, Ann Barr, Philippa Pullar, Jonathan Gathorne-Hardy, Guy Hungerford, Isobel Strachey, Viva King, Peter O'Connor, Diana Holman-Hunt, Bryony Edmunds, Quentin Crisp and Michael Holroyd. The incidents which follow are, however, entirely of my own choosing and no one but me should be held responsible for the constant emphasis that has been placed on seemingly trivial events.

THE TWENTIES
1920–1929

At the beginning of the Twenties, high society showed few superficial signs of the ravages of the ghastly war through which it had recently passed. Mayfair was still full of great town mansions occupied by the families who had built them and run by staffs of thirty or forty servants, and the governing class was still drawn mainly from a handful of historic families, presided over by an old-fashioned monarch, whose fear of any threat to old-fashioned values was frequently echoed from the pulpit by the leading churchmen of the day. During this decade, Society reluctantly underwent many changes. Several of the great town mansions were sold and demolished, the barriers between stage and Society and between Society and the business world were shattered and socialites resigned themselves to the idea of a Labour government. The old order was also disturbed by the emergence of wealthy and resourceful American hostesses such as Mrs. Laura Corrigan and the acquisition by American collectors of some of England's finest works of art. By the end of the Twenties, while politicians wrestled with the coming economic catastrophe, a new social group had appeared, dubbed the Bright Young Things, who seemed more at home in Mrs. Meyrick's expanding chain of Soho nightclubs than in the Mayfair drawing-rooms where they had been brought up and whose extravagant and reckless behaviour suggested that they were social butterflies without a serious thought in their closely-shingled heads.

1920

Over 5,000 people greeted the New Year at the Chelsea Arts Ball at the Albert Hall. Among the revellers were nineteen-year-old Lord Louis Mountbatten, Major Harold and Lady Zia Wernher and thirty-one-year-old actress Gladys Cooper. Many of the men present were daubed in make-up.

Alas, the ball had a tragic sequel. The following morning, one of the revellers, wealthy Captain Alexander Mitchell, was found dead at the foot of the staircase of his mansion in Berkeley Square. 'We do not know if he was going downstairs in the dark or whether he intended to turn off the lights in the lower rooms' said a friend staying at the house.

On January 2, interest turned to the London Homeopathic Hospital in Great Ormond Street where a much-wrinkled man of eighty-five lay desperately ill following a fall on an Underground station. He had been booked in under the name of Norris Redmond but staff at the hospital were convinced that their patient was really a certain Louis de Rougemont, a famous adventurer who twenty years earlier had amazed the world with stories of his life among the Australian Aborigines. One of his many claims was that he had ridden across the sea on turtles.

On January 8, the news broke that Lady Dorothy Cavendish, nineteen-year-old daughter of the Duke of Devonshire, was engaged to her father's ADC, Captain Harold Macmillan. Much regret was expressed in certain quarters that all the Duke's daughters were marrying commoners.

Meanwhile, the hard-worked twenty-five-year-old Prince of Wales had returned to London from Sandringham. On January 12 at a banquet at the Savoy Hotel, he shook hands with 500 people. His hand had still not recovered from the ordeal of his Canadian tour the previous year and he was obliged to switch to his left hand half-way through the evening.

On January 13, famous sporting peer Lord Lonsdale was seriously injured out hunting with the Cottesmore Hounds. His horse caught its legs in some rabbit wire and off came Lord Lonsdale, breaking several ribs.

In the middle of the month, it was revealed that Colonel T. E. Lawrence, said to have recently turned down the Crown of Arabia, had lost the 200,000 word manuscript of his book *Seven Pillars of Wisdom*. It had been snatched from his compartment on the Paddington to Oxford train when he went to buy a newspaper. 'I regard the loss as catastrophic' said Lawrence's friend American lecturer Lowell Thomas. 'I really do not see how such voluminous material can be re-written.'

Meanwhile, Mrs. Kate Meyrick had got her name in the papers for the first time. Mrs. Meyrick, a Brighton doctor's wife, had recently taken up night-club work to pay for her daughters' education. On January 28, she heard a magistrate describe a club she had helped to run in Leicester Square as 'a sink of iniquity'. Its licence was removed and Mrs. Meyrick was fined £25.

On February 1, wealthy American Mrs. William B. Leeds, who had settled in England shortly before the war in order to see her son Billy through Eton, announced her engagement to thirty-one-year-old Prince Christopher of Greece. The glory of this engagement was somewhat tarnished when it was announced that Mrs. Leeds would not be permitted to use the title Princess and was thus excluded from even the humblest court in Europe.

On February 15, 7,000 people packed into Durham Cathedral to hear a sermon by Dr. J. H. Jowett, the famous Congregational divine. As the eminent visitor ascended to the pulpit, a vicar in the congregation leapt to his feet and started to hurl abuse. The irate clergyman was first asked to leave by the head verger and then physically ejected by three uniformed police officers supervised by the Chief Constable of Durham. Dr. Jowett remained unperturbed during this commotion and then pressed on with his sermon.

On February 27, Prince Jaime, eleven-year-old deaf-and-dumb son of the King of Spain, arrived in London to receive treatment from Mr. Johnson May, the 'physiological adjuster' of Park Lane. Mr. May, who was not a qualified doctor but always dressed in reassuring white or cream-coloured suits, believed that all human ailments were caused by lack of nourishment owing to misplaced bones.

On March 4, Viscountess Grimston was the victim of a daring robbery in the refreshment rooms at St. Pancras Station. While she was waiting for a train to St. Albans, a small attaché case containing a pearl and diamond necklace valued at £1,000 was snatched from her.

Captain Harold Macmillan and his fiancée Lady Dorothy Cavendish

Meanwhile, the Duchess of Marlborough, formerly Consuelo Vanderbilt, had begun divorce proceedings against her husband. The marriage, which had been arranged by the Duchess's mother back in the 1890s, had never been a happy one and the couple had lived apart since 1907. The hearing took place in the High Court on March 19. The Duchess, dressed in black with several strings of pearls enveloping her long neck, answered her counsel's questions in a soft, mournful voice. After the proceedings were over, she drew a black chiffon veil from her muff and tied it over her head, completely covering her face and hat.

On March 23, the Vicar of All Saints, Cheltenham, was preaching by candlelight when the horrified faces of his congregation drew his attention to the fact that his surplice was on fire. A short while after the flames had been extinguished, it was discovered that the garment was again alight.

On April 14, the Duke of Devonshire lent Devonshire House, his palatial early eighteenth-century house in Piccadilly for a charity ball. The Duchess of Albany, organiser of the event, greeted guests at the head of a sweeping staircase with rock crystal balustrades. One of the star guests was Lady Cynthia Curzon, daughter of Lord Curzon, who had recently announced her engagement to dashing young Conservative MP, Mr. Oswald Mosley. Also there was Lady Diana Cooper, beautiful twenty-seven-year-old daughter of the Duke and Duchess of Rutland, who had recently married a young Foreign Office official, Duff Cooper.

On April 21, Captain Harold Macmillan and Lady Dorothy Cavendish were married at St. Margaret's, Westminster. Most of the Royal Family were present and a reception was held afterwards at Lansdowne House, stately Adam house at the corner of Berkeley Square belonging to Lord Lansdowne.

On April 29, disgraceful scenes greeted the opening night of a play at the Garrick Theatre, starring American actress Miss Laurette Taylor. Stink bombs and snuff were thrown from the gallery and pandemonium broke out. Eventually, the play's producer, Mr. Charles B. Cochran, made his way onto the stage. 'I have brought Miss Taylor three thousand miles to appear here tonight. I will not allow her to appear amid this scene of disorder' he said, before ordering the curtain to be run down. In her dressing-room, the star was in tears. 'I cannot imagine what I have done to deserve this. I am absolutely at sea about it all.'

Meanwhile, motor-vans and messengers bearing wedding gifts for Lady Cynthia Curzon and Mr. Oswald Mosley converged on 1 Carlton House Terrace, home of the bride's father. On May 11, the marriage took place at the Chapel Royal, St. James's Palace. Lunching at the Ritz before the ceremony, the twenty-one-year-old bridegroom was suddenly approached by Lady Cunard, one of London's leading hostesses. 'Were you not being married five minutes ago?' she wanted to know. Mosley jumped up without his hat and hurried down St. James's Street to the Chapel Royal.

On May 18, the news broke that Devonshire House had changed hands for one million pounds. The purchasers, a Liverpool ship-owner named Harris and a London financier named Sibthorp, planned to build an entertainment centre on the site. 'I may be called a vandal for pulling down Devonshire House' said Mr. Sibthorp 'but personally I think the place is an eyesore. My new super-cinema restaurant, dance hall and tea rooms will be far more beautiful and are much needed.'

The Duke and Duchess of Devonshire were to move into a mansion in Carlton Gardens. 'It will be interesting to see what the pictures look like in a small house' remarked the Duchess.

On June 3, Isobel Law, daughter of the Lord Privy Seal, Andrew Bonar Law, was married to bald-headed soldier Sir Frederick Sykes. Lord Beaverbrook's daughter Janet was a bridesmaid and the Prime Minister, Mr. Lloyd George, was in the congregation. Members of Parliament clubbed together to give the bride a silver tea and coffee service in the style of George I.

On June 10, the first daylight court of the season was held. For several hours the Mall was jammed with large black cars carrying débutantes in tiaras. One girl was noticed smoking a cigarette.

A few days later, there was a gala at Covent Garden Opera House. The Marchioness of Londonderry, leading political hostess of the day, wore her famous diamond and ruby tiara, Lady Lavery, beautiful American wife of painter Sir John Lavery, was in flaming pink, and Lady Cunard, who had recently moved into a huge house in Carlton House Terrace, was in mauve and gold.

On June 21, newly-married couple Douglas Fairbanks and Mary Pickford arrived in London and were safely installed in the Ritz Hotel. Crowds around the hotel were so dense that buses were delayed for up to twenty minutes.

On June 26, the death of the beautiful Countess of Dudley, wife of the former Governor General of Australia, made headline news. She had died while bathing with the aid of swimming wings, in Camus Bay, County Galway. Her maid had seen that her mistress was in distress but was unable to give her assistance.

On July 3, there were gasps in court in Kidwelly in Wales when one of the leading local inhabitants, solicitor Arthur Greenwood, was charged with murdering his wife by putting poison in her port. Greenwood, an imposing figure in tweed cap, knee-breeches and leggings, was committed for trial at Carnarvon Assizes.

On July 24, the Earl of Clancarty was sentenced to three months' imprisonment for obtaining credit without disclosing that he was an undischarged bankrupt. The immaculately dressed peer, the head of a famous Irish house, remained unruffled throughout the proceedings. He had been offered a seat beside his solicitor but said he would prefer to take his place in the dock.

At the beginning of August, music-hall star Vesta Tilley, wife of Conservative MP Sir Walter de Frece, announced that half her collection of valuable china had been smashed when the cupboard containing it, insecurely fixed on its brackets, had fallen to the floor.' Sir Walter and I had been making this collection for years. What we have lost is worth about ten thousand pounds. Unfortunately none of it is insured.'

On August 14, it was announced that the twenty-four-year-old Duke of York had arrived in Scotland for several weeks shooting with Lord and Lady Ancaster at Drummond Castle. During the course of his holiday, the Duke re-met the beautiful Lady Elizabeth Bowes-Lyon, whom he had not seen since childhood.

At the beginning of September, attention turned to Deauville, where the bulky forty-three-year-old Aga Khan and monocled Jimmy de Rothschild were taking their turns in the baccarat rooms along with racehorse owner Solly Joel, resplendent in a natty yachting suit.

Multi-millionaire Jimmy de Rothschild

Meanwhile, the strange behaviour of the elderly President of France, M. Deschanel, had excited much interest and gossip throughout Europe. Earlier in the year he had fallen from the presidential train and been found wandering about the countryside in his pyjamas. Now, on September 16, it was announced that he had fallen into a lily pond in the grounds of his château, remaining there for several hours before being fished out by a gardener.

On September 30, Lord Hamilton of Dalzell appeared before a committee on Smoke and Noxious Vapours at Glasgow brandishing a blouse worn by his wife while harvesting. Lord Hamilton said the blouse could not have been dirtier if his wife had been working as a chimney sweep. He blamed the thick black smoke pouring from the pits near his estate.

On October 9, the public were shocked to hear that Augustus John's recent portrait of soap magnate Lord Leverhulme had been severely mutilated by the sitter. The multi-millionaire had snipped out only the head, returning the rest of the portrait and frame to the artist's Chelsea studio. In the furore that followed, he attempted to justify his vandalism by saying that he wished to fit the portrait into a small safe. 'I did not want this publicity' said Augustus John, who was staying with Lady Tredegar at Broadstairs when the news broke. 'I get too much advertisement as it is. The artistic ethics of the operation performed by Lord Leverhulme is a question I must leave people to decide for themselves.'

On November 13, it was announced that twenty-eight-year-old Lady Diana Cooper, the most beautiful woman of the day, had at last agreed to appear as a film actress. A handsome offer had been made to her by a film director named J. Stuart Blackton. Rumours of this venture had been circulating for some time.

On November 19, Miss Marguerite Radclyffe Hall brought a slander action against Mr. St. George Fox-Pitt. It was alleged that he had described her as 'a grossly immoral woman' and accused her of coming between Admiral Sir Ernest Troubridge and his wife, wrecking their marriage. The Lord Justice decided in favour of Miss Radclyffe Hall, who wore male attire in court, and awarded her £500 damages.

On November 26, there was much excitement over the marriage of the fabulously wealthy Duke of Westminster, owner of much of Mayfair and Belgravia and vast estates in Scotland and Cheshire. His bride was Mrs. Violet Rowley, who was said to be passionately fond of outdoor sports. At the wedding ceremony, she wore a sage green outfit with brown spats.

Meanwhile, the financial affairs of conductor Sir Thomas Beecham had come under the scrutiny of the London Bankruptcy Court. On December 6, Lady Beecham, in a purple velvet coat trimmed with dark green fur, assured the court that she would do everything in her power to see that her husband's debts were paid. Liabilities of £105,000 had been mentioned by the Official Receiver.

At Christmas, the Prime Minister Lloyd George was to be found alone at 10 Downing Street with only his secretary Miss Frances Stevenson as a companion. After lunch on Christmas Day, the organist at Westminster Cathedral came in to play the piano for them.

On December 28, Lloyd George left to spend the weekend at Sir Philip Sassoon's lavishly appointed home at Lympne in Kent. Here, he was reported to have joined in the New Year's Eve celebrations with relish, singing 'Cockles and Mussels' at the top of his voice. Also staying at the house was the forty-six-year-old Secretary of State for War, Mr. Winston Churchill.

New Year celebrations at the Savoy Hotel, where a red-coated orchestra played cheerful foxtrots, were disturbed when one of the guests, a wealthy Greek woman named Mrs. Mango, raised her hand to her throat and found that her £40,000 pearl necklace was missing.

On January 8, Lord Lee of Fareham formally presented Chequers to the nation as a residence for the exclusive use of its Prime Ministers. A party was held at the house that evening which was attended by Lloyd George and the American Ambassador, Mr. Davis. Afterwards, Lord Lee drove off into the night shouting 'Take good care of her!'

On January 24, Mr. Winston Churchill arrived at Victoria Station following a short painting holiday in the South of France. He was driven away by a soldier-chauffeur and followed by another vehicle carrying a vast quantity of luggage.

On January 26, Mrs. Mary Nolan, the owner of a two-room massage parlour in Jermyn Street where men were massaged by women, was refused a licence at Bow Street. 'I cannot imagine any decent man consenting to it' said the magistrate. 'And I do not think any respectable woman would engage in massaging men.'

Early in February, a major ecclesiastical scandal gripped the public's attention. It was said the sixty-one-year-old Archdeacon John Wakeford, precentor of Lincoln Cathedral, had been staying at the Bull Hotel, Peterborough, with a young woman. At a consistory court hearing, Wakeford vigorously denied these charges and claimed that he was the victim of a plot engineered by his brother-in-law and another clergyman.

Archdeacon John Wakeford, who was found guilty of grave misconduct at the Bull Hotel, Peterborough

On February 5, after sensational evidence from chambermaids at the hotel, the court decided that Mr. Wakeford had been guilty of grave misconduct though the woman involved had failed to make an appearance. Wakeford, who was said to be one of the best preachers in the country, immediately announced that he would appeal against the verdict and asked for financial assistance from the public. 'Some of you can help me and I know you will' he said.

On February 17, twenty-year-old Prince Henry was injured while hunting with the South Berkshire Hounds. His horse fell at a hedge and as the Prince was struggling to his feet, he received a kick on the back of his head. 'The spill was certainly a very nasty one' said the Master of the Hunt afterwards. 'It occurred just as we were in the midst of a particularly fine piece of sport.'

On February 25, Lady Cynthia Mosley gave birth to a baby girl, later named Vivien. One of the first visitors to her bedside was Mrs. Margot Asquith, wife of the former Liberal Prime Minister. 'Dear child, you look very pale' she said. 'You must not have another child for a long time. Herbert always withdrew in time, such a noble man.'

At the beginning of March, Kathleen Countess of Drogheda was fined twenty shillings for driving her motor-car through the London streets in a dangerous manner. On being reprimanded by a policeman, she had declared 'Nonsense. Do you know who I am? I can't stop, I'm in a hurry.'

On March 21, vivacious American-born MP Lady Astor faced an intruder at her Devonshire home threatening to kill her. After coaxing him into a calmer frame of mind, Lady Astor got him out of the house. She then gathered up her skirts and chased him through the surrounding lanes.

On April 5, it was announced that the bodies of eighteen dukes, marquesses and barons were to be disinterred from a mausoleum adjoining Hamilton Palace. Coal mines near the palace had created subsidences and a safer sepulchre for the bodies had to be found.

On April 7, Archdeacon Wakeford's appeal against conviction on immorality charges opened in the Privy Council room in Downing Street. It was attended by the Bishops of London, Ely, Gloucester and Rochester and a large number of other clergy, many of whom were in top-hats and gaiters. Women fought for seats in the crowded room and dresses were torn. It was said that during the course of the proceedings, which dragged on for several weeks, the Bishop of London's gaze hardly ever wandered from the face of the grey-haired Archdeacon. On April 26, Wakeford took the failure of his appeal in heroic spirit. 'I am still a priest and shall remain a priest' he said. 'I look forward to the future with supreme confidence.'

On May 24, the King and Queen spent an hour and a half at the Chelsea Flower Show. Queen Mary wore a toque brimmed with pink and mauve flowers and a spray of long-bearded wheat. She and the King sampled a new strawberry named 'Sir Douglas Haig'.

On May 30, the Crown Prince Hirohito of Japan left London after a brief visit. At eight o'clock that morning, he called at the Chelsea studio of Mr. Augustus John and sat for a quick portrait. 'I was very much impressed by his tranquil personality and natural dignity' said the artist. 'He sat through the hour with complete ease.'

On June 7, Lord and Lady Curzon gave a dinner-party for the King and Queen at 1 Carlton House Terrace. The table was heavily laden with gold and silver plate and decorated with roses and sweet-peas from Montacute and Hackwood, Lord Curzon's country houses. After dinner, the party was entertained by comedian George Robey.

Meanwhile, the recently divorced Duke of Marlborough had announced his engagement to Miss Gladys Deacon, beautiful daughter of a Boston millionaire and a well-known figure in English and French society. The marriage took place in Paris on June 24 and was attended by Marshal Foch and M. Anatole France. Five clergymen had refused to officiate at the ceremony and a chaplain was summoned from Blenheim at the eleventh hour. Afterwards, the bride and groom faced a battery of cameras and cine-cameras. 'Oh, is that a cinema?' asked the new Duchess. 'I shall come out something frightful.'

On June 29, Lady Randolph Churchill, mother of Winston, died following an accident. It was revealed that while staying at Mells Manor near Frome in Somerset with Sir John and Lady Horner, she slipped on the staircase. 'I didn't actually see what happened' said Lady Horner. 'But I heard her fall and cry out and I ran to her assistance. A doctor came from Frome within fifteen minutes and said it was a bad fracture of the leg near the ankle.'

On July 4, Consuelo Vanderbilt, former Duchess of Marlborough, married Colonel Jacques Balsan, a well-known figure in French sporting circles and a close friend of the Duchess for several years. The ceremony took place at nine o'clock in the morning at the Chapel Royal of the Savoy. The new American Ambassador, Mr. George Harvey, was present and the Duchess walked up the aisle on the arm of her son, the commandingly tall Marquess of Blandford.

On July 7, the first State Ball since 1914 was held at Buckingham Palace. Among the motor-cars converging on the Palace there were still a few horse-drawn broughams. The waiting crowds peered inside these vehicles and saw beautiful young girls with ostrich feather fans and white-haired dowagers covered in ropes of pearls. Queen Mary received her guests, wearing a dress of sapphire blue brocade and a diamond tiara.

On July 10, the fifty-two-year-old Earl of Craven disappeared from the deck of his yacht while it was anchored at Cowes. He was later found drowned, dressed in a dinner-jacket, silk shirt and pearl cuff-links, and was succeeded by his son, one-legged Viscount Uffington.

In the middle of July, a blaze of publicity surrounded the wealthy Mrs. Smith-Wilkinson, owner of a chain of hydropathic hotels. It was stated that over the past eighteen months, she had spent £200,000 on clothes and jewellery. Her wardrobe now included the Romanoff jewelled crown, a head-dress incorporating twelve birds of paradise and a silk dress that had once belonged to the Empress of China. Mrs. Smith-Wilkinson lived in a bungalow on the outskirts of Nottingham, where the bath-tubs were said to be made of solid gold, and had recently married a young Grenadier Guardsman, whose name she had taken.

On July 28, thousands of people packed into the Queen's Hall in London to hear ex-Archdeacon Wakeford plead his innocence. At first, he held the audience in the palm of his hand but later, when he showed some slides of the night-gown he was supposed to have worn on the night in question, there were bursts of laughter and sniggers.

On August 3, Field Marshal Sir Henry Wilson, Chief of the Imperial Staff during the war, fell off his yacht at Cowes and was weighed down in the water by his heavy rubber sea-boots and oilskins. Another boat sailing nearby, with Royal Academician Sir Arthur Cope on board, went to his assistance and Sir Henry was fished out of the sea. That evening, he was reported to be none the worse for his adventure.

On August 5, the Duke of Portland announced that he might have to leave Welbeck Abbey, his vast Nottinghamshire mansion, famous for the underground ballroom and library created by the Duke's predecessor in order to hide away from the world. 'With the present enormous weight of taxation and the extremely onerous incidence of death duties, the future has become uncertain for all landed proprietors' the Duke told a gathering of his tenants.

The same day, the Earl of Powis was giving a party at Lymore Hall, Montgomeryshire when part of the floor gave way. Thirty people, including the Earl and the local vicar, went through to the cellar.

On August 8, a huge brown Daimler carrying the King's mother, Queen Alexandra, broke down at Holborn in the middle of London. A crowd of several hundred people quickly formed round the motor-car, which also contained Queen Alexandra's shy, unmarried daughter, Princess Victoria. The car was then jacked up and given a new wheel. Forty minutes later, it drove off to a chorus of rousing cheers.

On August 27, details were released of a huge dolls' house being made for Queen Mary. The house, designed by architect Sir Edwin Lutyens, would be eight foot high and would be fitted with a small furnace to provide hot and cold water in all rooms and a working sanitary system. The house would also have a wine cellar, stocked with miniature bottles of wines and spirits.

On September 3, the eightieth birthday of famous twin sisters, the Dowager Lady Lytton and the Dowager Lady Loch, was celebrated with a tea-party for villagers at Knebworth in Hertfordshire. The two sisters still looked remarkably alike and were frequently mistaken for each other.

Meanwhile, Charles Chaplin was sailing towards England on board the White Star liner *Olympic*, breakfasting on a glass of water and a pinch of salt. He arrived on September 10, after an absence of nine years during which he had risen from being totally unknown to become a millionaire. Armistice Day-size crowds greeted him at Waterloo Station and forty police were needed to get him into the Ritz Hotel where the first-floor Regal Suite had been prepared for him. Later he appeared at a window and threw carnations to the crowds below.

On September 11, the Marquess of Milford Haven died suddenly at the Naval and Military Club in Half Moon Street. He was found by a housekeeper clutching a silver cross. Telegrams were immediately sent to his sons, Lord Louis Mountbatten, now serving on the *Repulse*, and the Earl of Medina, now the new Marquess.

A few days later, Sir Ernest Cassel was found dead in his library at Brook House, Park Lane. Sir Ernest, a famous financier who had become a close friend of Edward VII, had spent the last few years of his life alone in his elaborate Victorian mansion overlooking Hyde Park. Attention immediately turned to his wealthy grand-daughter, nineteen-year-old Edwina Ashley, fair-haired, studious and said to be fond of golf.

At the beginning of October, there was an outcry following rumours that the Duke of Westminster had sold Gainsborough's *Blue Boy* to an American collector. A figure of 620,000 dollars was quoted.

On October 9, eighteen-year-old Old Etonian Billy Leeds was married to Princess Xenia of Russia, first cousin of Lady Zia Wernher. The King and Queen sent the bride a diamond and ruby pendant. The bridegroom's mother, who had recently married the brother of the King of Greece, had meanwhile moved into Spencer House, St. James's, rented from Earl Spencer.

Horatio Bottomley arrives at Bow Street. He later parted company with his silk top hat

On October 11, Horatio Bottomley, genial seventeen-stone MP for Hackney, appeared as a witness at Bow Street Magistrates Court in the prosecution of a certain Mr. Reuban Bigland who had published a pamphlet attacking Bottomley. Hostile members of the crowd separated Mr. Bottomley from his silk top-hat after the case.

At the end of October, it was revealed that the new Duchess of Marlborough had been working among the potato-pickers on the Blenheim estate. The object of the exercise was to find out how arduous the work was – so that she could advise her husband about fair rates of pay.

On November 7, Kinnaird Castle, the Earl of Southesk's home near Brechin, was damaged by fire. The library, full of priceless first editions, was reported to have been burnt out. Hero of the evening was the Earl's daughter, twenty-nine-year-old Lady Katherine Bosanquet, who dashed through the flames to rescue a picture by Raeburn.

In the middle of the month, Mrs. Kate Meyrick, the Brighton doctor's wife who had taken up night-club work to make ends meet, opened a club of her own in the damp, ill-lit cellar of 43 Gerrard Street, a house once occupied by Dryden. Shortly afterwards, Mrs. Meyrick made the aquaintance of a handsome Chinaman named Brilliant Chang, who was said to be the mastermind behind the city's drug traffic.

On November 23, the public were delighted to learn of the engagement of Princess Mary and Viscount Lascelles, son and heir to the Earl of Harewood. It was revealed that the couple had ridden together in Rotten Row and walked together in London. Thirty-nine-year-old Viscount Lascelles had recently purchased Chesterfield House in Mayfair and filled it with art-treasures he had inherited from his great-uncle, the Marquess of Clanricarde, who had altered his will in the Viscount's favour after a chance meeting at his club.

On December 10, Mr. Edward Weiner, son of a naturalised Englishman, sued Lord Wavertree for describing him at a lunch-party as a German. Lord Wavertree denied that the statement had ever been made and amid much fuss and bother, the case went to the High Court.

On December 21, the Lord Chancellor, Lord Birkenhead, put on a blue overcoat and bowler-hat and left for Switzerland with his wife and daughter. Confronted by the Press at Victoria Station, he said 'Yes, I'm off for a holiday and frankly I feel I need one.' A few days later, the handsome peer was found skating in St. Moritz, wearing a white polo-neck sweater.

1922

At the beginning of January, hundreds of people hurried to the National Gallery to have a last look at Gainsborough's *Blue Boy*, soon on its way to the home of its new American owner, Mr. Henry E. Huntington.

On January 10, the Marquess of Linlithgow announced that he was closing his home, Hopetoun House, owing to the new levels of taxation. 'I do not care to dwell on the personal aspects of the case,' he told estate workers, 'though obviously to leave a house which has been in continuous operation from father to son since 1705 is a terrible wrench.'

Meanwhile, Richard Strauss, the world's greatest living composer, had arrived in London and was installed at the Savoy Hotel, where he soon complained that his suite was overheated. A window was opened and in came thick, yellow fog. 'I have represented fog musically' remarked Strauss cheerfully.

On January 16, there was a warm reception at the Covent Garden Theatre for Lady Diana Cooper's first film, *The Glorious Adventure*, set in the days of King Charles. 'I am so happy' said Lady Diana. 'A good many people thought I was not interested in undertaking film work but they little knew how really interested in acting I have been for years.'

At the end of the month, Mrs. Margot Asquith set off for America for a series of public readings from her autobiography. She explained that the reasons for her tour were purely financial. 'England does not provide a pension or any other means of support for ex-Prime Ministers.' During his wife's absence, sixty-nine-year-old Herbert Asquith fell and sprained his knee. One story was that he had slipped on a mat on a polished floor. Another theory was that he had tripped on a rolled-up carpet in a darkened room.

On February 11, strange rumours surrounded the City Equitable Fire Insurance Company. The Chairman of the company, Old Etonian Gerard Bevan, was said to have fled the country on board a French Farman Goliath plane, taking with him £80,000 in cash and a large quantity of luggage.

Meanwhile, more than a thousand wedding gifts flooded in for Princess Mary and Viscount Lascelles. Harrow School's gift to the couple was a pair of mahogany dressing-tables, which were delivered to Buckingham Palace by three senior pupils.

The marriage on February 28 was said to be the first big State pageant since before the war. Queen Alexandra, glamorous grandmother of the bride, wore purple velvet, the Order of the Garter and many jewels.

On March 6, a twenty-five-year-old woman was found brutally murdered in her flat in Finborough Road, Chelsea. The following day, wealthy Mr. Ronald True, a former officer in the Royal Air Force, was arrested in a private box at the Hammersmith Palace of Varieties and taken to Walton Street police station, where he was charged with the murder.

On March 19, the eighty-seven-year-old Earl of Ducie arrived in England after a sixty-seven year absence sheep-farming in Australia. 'I expect to find great changes in the old country' he said, stepping nimbly off the Boat Train. 'I expect I shall have a few shocks while I am in London.' The white-bearded Earl soon set off for his 100-room family seat in Gloucestershire, Tortworth Court, where his two ancient sisters, Lady Eleanor Brodie and Lady Alice Havelock-Allan, were waiting to receive him.

At the end of the month, the Earl of Derby attempted to quell the controversy currently raging about the Grand National. 'I consider the suggestion that the Grand National is a cruel race is a very ridiculous one' he said. 'I hope that it will continue and that the fences will in no way be altered.'

On April 1, it was announced that a wealthy American, Mrs. James Corrigan, had arrived in England and rented 16 Grosvenor Street from Mrs. George Keppel, one-time mistress of the late King Edward VII. Rumours circulated that Mrs. Corrigan, a former telephone-operator from Cleveland, Ohio, U.S.A., who had married a multi-millionaire, had asked for Mrs. Keppel's guest-list to be included in the lease.

On April 12, the news broke that twenty-one-year-old Lord Louis Mountbatten was to marry Miss Edwina Ashley, whose wealthy grandfather, Sir Ernest Cassel, had died the previous year.

On April 16, Easter Day, the Dean of St. Paul's, Dr. Inge, preached a characteristically gloomy sermon at

Lord Derby, King of Lancashire

the Cathedral. 'The war has not improved the moral tone of our people' he declared. 'In some ways it has made it worse. I cannot doubt that we are threatened with a great outburst of licentiousness such as that which disgraced the country in the reign of Charles II and again during the Regency.'

On May 2, the trial of thirty-one-year-old Ronald True opened at the Old Bailey. The debonair former Air Force officer was found guilty of murder and sentenced to death. Shortly before his execution, he was suddenly declared insane and removed to Broadmoor Prison in the midst of exciting rumours that he was the son of a famous peeress by her first marriage who, it was suggested, had intervened on his behalf.

Meanwhile, the wealthy Mrs. Corrigan had begun entertaining at 16 Grosvenor Street, assisted by a social secretary, Mr. Stirling, who had for many years worked for the great Lady Londonderry. On May 17, dressed in gown of white crêpe embroidered with opalescent pearls, she gave a dinner-party at which Princess Marie Louise, cousin of the King, was guest of honour.

On May 25, seventeen-stone Member of Parliament, Horatio Bottomley, one of the most outstanding orators of his day, climbed into the dock at the Old Bailey and pleaded 'decidedly not guilty' to charges of converting vast sums of money entrusted to him by the public to his own use. Four days later, he was sentenced to seven years' penal servitude and removed to Brixton Prison, where for the first few weeks he required the assistance of several warders to help him get dressed and undressed.

On June 2, Princess Mary made her debut as a hostess. She and Lord Lascelles gave a dinner-party at Chesterfield House which was attended by the King and Queen and the Duke of York. The men wore breeches and decorations and the table was adorned with sweet-peas, the Princess's favourite flower.

On June 19, Old Etonian financier Gerard Bevan, who had fled from London following the failure of his companies, was found in Vienna. He was arrested after a fight with armed detectives during which he attempted to swallow the contents of a phial. After a period in a padded cell, he was transferred to a special cell 'for prisoners of refinement and education', in which to await extradition proceedings. It was noted that he was allowed to send out for his favourite marmalade and ample supplies of fresh underclothing were brought in.

On June 22, there was a storm in the House of Lords over a proposal to give a peerage to Sir Joseph Robinson, a South African millionaire who had recently been fined £500,000 for fraud. The debate led to a major outcry about the sale of honours. It was said that knighthoods were selling for £10,000, peerages for £30,000. Lord Selborne stated that the country faced 'a public scandal of the first magnitude'.

The same day, Field Marshal Sir Henry Wilson, recently appointed supremo in Northern Ireland, was shot dead on the doorstep of his home, 36 Eaton Place, Belgravia. He had been attending an official function and was in full dress-uniform. While he was fumbling with his latch-keys, two assassins opened fire. 'I was in my pantry when I heard four distant shots' said the butler at the house next door. 'I rushed upstairs and out into the street. I saw Sir Henry lying half on the pavement, half on the street. I picked up Sir Henry's sword. It was out of its scabbard.'

On July 5, the thirty-year-old Duke of Leinster won a £3,000 wager by driving his Rolls Royce from London to Aberdeen in fourteen and a half hours. He was accompanied during his journey by a huge wolf-hound. The Duke's achievement prompted Mr. Morgan Jones, Labour MP for Caerphilly, to ask if the young peer would be prosecuted for speeding.

On July 8, attention turned to the divorce courts where the strange marriage of Mr. and Mrs. John Russell came under public scrutiny. It was stated that the day before her wedding, Christabel Russell had obtained a promise from her future husband that there should be no question of their having children, at least to begin with. Having apparently complied with this request, Mr. Russell was shaken by the arrival of a child and thus was suing his wife for adultery. After a lengthy hearing, which created feverish public interest, it was decided that there was no evidence of adultery and Mr. Russell, heir to Lord Ampthill, had lost the case.

On July 13, Lady Beatty, wife of the First Sea Lord, announced that she had lost a beautiful old pearl brooch during the course of a long evening's dining and dancing. Detectives joined in the search and a reward of £200 was offered. A few days later, Lady Beatty's maid found the gem caught inside the lower part of her mistress's ball-gown.

On July 18, high society flocked to the marriage of Lord Louis Mountbatten and heiress Edwina Ashley. After the ceremony at St. Margaret's, Westminster, at which the Prince of Wales was best man, thirty sailors pulled the bride and bridegroom's motor-car to a reception at Brook House, Park Lane, where ten-foot-high orange trees had been imported to create an artificial orangerie.

On July 28, American-born Adela Countess of Essex was found dead in her bath at her house in Bruton Street. The cord of the electric bell had been torn from the ceiling and was lying in the bath. At the inquest a few days later, Mrs. Asquith, who had seen the Countess on the night of her death, created a sensation giving evidence in a jet-black dress and an enormous pair of tortoiseshell-framed spectacles.

Meanwhile, financier Gerard Bevan was on his way back from Vienna accompanied by Detective-Inspector Hubert Smith and Serjeant Hippisley of the City of London police. They travelled on the Budapest–Ostend express in a compartment marked 'Reserved for English Prisoner'. Inside, Old Etonian Bevan was heard laughing heartily with his captors.

Back in England, the mental and physical health of Lord Northcliffe was giving rise to anxiety. For some weeks, the famous newspaper proprietor had been living in a small wooden hut on the roof of the Duke of Devonshire's house in Carlton Gardens. On August 14 he died there, surrounded by his family. Telegrams of sympathy poured in from all over the world and his famous stately home, Sutton Place in Surrey, was soon acquired by the Duke of Sutherland.

On September 1, it was suggested that there was a mastermind behind the crop of recent jewel robberies. A leading London assessor, Mr. J. W. Bell, suggested that the criminal was a man of good social position. 'This man has two powerful motorcars, an address in town and a house on the South Coast' said Mr. Bell.

On September 5, Greatford Hall, Lincolnshire, sixteenth-century home of Major C. G. L. Fitzwilliam, was completely destroyed by fire. The blaze started in the East Wing of the house, near the gun-room. Mr. Darcy Braddell, a London architect staying at the house, was woken up by the sound of cartridges exploding. At first he thought he was trapped in his room. Then he remembered a secret panel through which he escaped to raise the alarm. 'Everything has been lost' said Major Fitzwilliam the following day. 'I have just had a suit sent down from London. My wife is still in her nightdress.'

Meanwhile, poet and traveller Wilfrid Scawen Blunt had died leaving strict instructions that his body should be buried without religious ceremony. Instead of a casket or coffin, Blunt ordered that his body should be wrapped in his old oriental travelling-rug. On September 12, his daughter, Lady Wentworth, faithfully carried out these instructions.

On September 26, burglars broke into Middleton Park, Oxfordshire, home of the Earl of Jersey, and stole eighteen gold rings, four gold watches, four snuff-boxes and an ivory eye-glass bearing the initials of the late Duke of Wellington. They also helped themselves to some of the Earl's wine. Several bottles were found open in the dining-room.

At the end of the month, it was reported that forty-seven-year-old Mr. Winston Churchill was in the process of buying an old manor-house, high on the Kentish hills. Known as Chartwell, it was said to be an ideal spot for an artist.

On October 7, seventy-year-old Sir Almeric FitzRoy, Clerk to the Privy Council since 1898, was arrested and charged with 'annoying persons in Hyde Park'. He was fined £5 but later appealed successfully against the conviction, leading many people to question the judgment of the elderly and autocratic Marlborough Street magistrate, Mr. Mead. 'My experience has shown that a perfectly innocent person may unwittingly find himself in a very serious position' said Sir Almeric, great-grandson of the 3rd Duke of Grafton.

On October 23, Lloyd George's long olive-green Rolls-Royce left 10 Downing Street for the last time. After a series of failures, the Welsh Wizard had been replaced as Prime Minister by Mr. Andrew Bonar Law. The new hostess at Number 10 would be Bonar Law's newly-married daughter, Lady Sykes.

The same day, the Bishop of Oxford announced that he had banned the Duke of Marlborough from attending the Oxford Diocesan Conference – on the grounds that the Duke had been divorced and re-married. This was a curious announcement as the Duke had at no time expressed any desire to attend the conference.

On November 1, a bull galloped down the village street at Hatfield Peverel in Essex and charged at a car driven by Lady Curtis-Bennett and carrying two women passengers. Lady Curtis-Bennett swerved and knocked the local blacksmith off his bicycle.

Meanwhile, the sixty-three-year-old ex-Kaiser, living in style and comfort at Doorn in Holland, had announced his engagement to Princess Hermine of Reuss. The marriage took place on November 5. 'The Kaiser is one of the most generous and kind-hearted men in the world' said the happy bride.

In the middle of November, the world's attention was concentrated on the ancient tomb of Tutankhamen in Egypt. An expedition led by the Earl of Carnarvon and financed by Lady Carnarvon, had been working on the site for several months.

On November 19, the 3,000-year-old tomb was opened, causing murmurs of disapproval in many corners of the globe. In London, the brother of King Fuad of Egypt, complained to night-club proprietor Mrs. Meyrick in the following words: 'It is ill work. The dead must not be disturbed. Only evil can come of it. Those who desecrate the resting places of the ancient dead do so at their peril. You will see.'

On December 5, financier Gerard Bevan, head of one of the oldest firms of stockbrokers in London, was sentenced to seven years penal servitude for fraud. In the meantime, it was noted that Mrs. Bevan had purchased Wickhurst Manor, a beautiful old Tudor house near Sevenoaks, along with an estate of 112 acres.

On December 9, the new Italian dictator, Benito Mussolini, arrived in England for an Allied Premiers conference on German reparations. He was met at Victoria Station by cheering London fascists and escorted to Claridge's Hotel. He later dined at Buckingham Palace where he was described as being 'in fine fettle'.

On December 13, the Prince of Wales dined with Lady Cunard at 5 Carlton House Terrace and went on afterwards to a dance at 16 Charles Street, London home of Mrs. Ronnie Greville, the wealthy daughter of a Scottish brewer who had become an intimate friend of the Royal Family. Also there were Lord and Lady Louis Mountbatten, just back from a long honeymoon in California where Lord Louis had appeared in a short film with Charlie Chaplin.

On December 27, the public were astounded to learn that Colonel T. E. Lawrence, uncrowned King of Arabia, had joined the ranks of the Air Force under an assumed name. It was revealed that he had signed on as a volunteer at a depot near Uxbridge and had been enduring the agonies of barrack-room life. An officer there had leaked the story to the press in return for £30.

1923

On New Year's Day, it was revealed that the young Marchioness of Queensberry was driving herself to Rome in a two-seater sports car. During the journey, the car lost its horn and left mudguard and the Marchioness, a former Gaiety girl, ran out of money and had to live on buns.

On January 15, the public were thrilled to hear of the betrothal of the twenty-seven-year-old Duke of York and Lady Elizabeth Bowes-Lyon, daughter of the Earl and Countess of Strathmore and a descendant of the ancient Kings of Scotland. The following day, the engaged couple lunched at 17 Bruton Street, London home of the Strathmores, went shopping and had tea at Buckingham Palace. 'I have not yet got my engagement ring but I am blissfully happy' said twenty-two-year-old Lady Elizabeth.

On January 18, there was a ball at Arundel Castle in honour of seventeen-year-old Lady Rachel Howard ; 800 guests were waited upon by footmen in white coats and scarlet breeches. It was noted that Lady Rachel's brother, the fourteen-year-old Duke of Norfolk, wore a dinner-jacket.

On January 29, the King was involved in a scuffle at St. Pancras Station. A small man with a club-foot attempted to strike the monarch with his crutch. 'If I had a revolver I would shoot you all' he shouted, as police dragged him away from the red carpet. 'I expect the poor fellow is suffering from shell shock' said the King.

The following day, the white-bearded eighty-eight-year-old Earl of Ducie, who had arrived in England the previous March after an absence of sixty-seven years, set off again for his Australian sheep-farm, complaining that the English climate had not suited him. 'I have suffered in health from the cold and wet' he said before stepping on board the liner *Themistocles*.

At the beginning of February, Sir William Forwood, Commissioner of the Metropolitan Police, received a box of chocolates through the post, accompanied by a note saying: 'A good lunch and a hearty appetite.' After eating one of them and offering one to his secretary, Sir William began to feel sick. Turning to examine the chocolates more carefully, he discovered they had been tampered with. A public-school boy was later arrested and charged with attempted murder of the police chief. 'When he was at college, he got sun-stroke on the playing fields' explained the accused boy's parents.

On February 15, an American Senator's daughter named Tallulah Bankhead, who had recently arrived in England keen to make her name as an actress, opened in a play called *The Dancers* at Wyndham's Theatre. Miss Bankhead's part was a small one but her husky voice and vitality appealed to several critics.

At the end of February, it was announced that Westminster City Council had appointed a certain Captain W. H. Hainsworth to watch over the West End and report on the existence of 'undesirable houses'. 'Most of my work will of course be done at night' the genial Captain Hainsworth told reporters.

On March 5, Lady Diana Cooper was fined forty shillings for allowing her car to cause an obstruction outside a West End theatre where she was attending a rehearsal. 'We are not all lucky enough to have chauffeurs' remarked Lady Diana, who was said to have five previous convictions for similar offences.

Meanwhile, the famous Russell divorce case was being tried again. On March 17, after an arduous eleven-day hearing during which the Russell baby was brought into court and scrutinized by the judge and jury, Mrs. Christabel Russell was found guilty of adultery 'with an unknown man'.

On March 19, the Countess of Carnarvon chartered a tiny three-seater De Havilland aeroplane to fly to Egypt where her husband, discoverer of Tutankhamen's tomb, had been struck down by severe blood poisoning following a mosquito bite on his face. When she arrived in Cairo, Lord Carnarvon was already delirious and had not long to live.

A few days later, the Hon. Ernest Guinness, younger son of wealthy brewer Lord Iveagh, left on a 40,000-mile world cruise on his 600-ton motor-yacht *Fantome II*, accompanied by a party of his friends.

On April 10, Sir John Dimsdale, son of a former Lord Mayor of London, shot himself in a Kent churchyard following a series of financial difficulties. He was found lying face downwards near the grave of his first wife.

Lady Diana Cooper, the most beautiful woman of the age

The Duke and Duchess of York after their wedding

On April 26, the Duke of York and Lady Elizabeth Bowes-Lyon were married in Westminster Abbey. The bride wore a medieval-style chiffon moiré wedding dress embroidered with silver thread and pearls and incorporating sleeves of Nottingham lace. Afterwards, the happy couple left to spend their honeymoon at Polesden Lacey, country home of the Royal Family's intimate friend, Mrs. Ronnie Greville.

On April 30, the strange burial of Lord Carnarvon made headline news. A grave was cut into a chalk hillside in Hampshire, said to be an ancient burial place that had not been used for the purpose since Roman times. Lady Carnarvon was present at the ceremony and sightseers were held back by a cordon of police and local villagers.

In early May, the King and Queen left for a State visit to Italy. On May 9, they were received by the Pope. The King looked spruce in the uniform of an Admiral of the Fleet, but the Queen, in dazzling white, appeared tired and pale.

Back in London, one of the King's first duties was the appointment of a successor to Mr. Bonar Law, who had resigned as Prime Minister on May 20, owing to ill health. Old Harrovian steel magnate Stanley Baldwin was eventually chosen for the task.

On May 29, eighty-two-year-old Lord Chaplin, father of Lady Londonderry, died at his daughter's home in Park Lane. Sir Thomas Horder, the leading doctor of the day, was in constant attendance on the aged statesman through his final illness. Much surprise was expressed when a few days later it was announced that Lord Chaplin, supposedly a man of great wealth, had left only £4,800.

On June 14, Lady Mary Cambridge, niece of the Queen, was married to the tall young Marquess of Worcester, son and heir to the Duke of Beaufort. Wedding programmes and souvenir handkerchiefs were sold in the street and Lord Lonsdale lent the young couple Lowther Castle, his stately home in Cumberland, for the honeymoon.

On the night of July 10, shots rang out in a corridor of the Savoy Hotel and Prince Ali Kamel Fahmy, one of Egypt's richest princes, fell dead. His beautiful French-born wife was arrested and later appeared at Bow Street, diamond and emerald rings flashing on her fingers.

Meanwhile in New York, the young Earl of Northesk had applied for a licence to marry high-kicking Ziegfeld Follies dancer, Miss Jessica Brown. The ceremony took place on July 19 and was followed by a nasty scene with a photographer. 'Don't you dare take a photograph of me' said the new Lady Northesk. 'I am through with the stage now.'

On July 23, Princess Catherine Yourievsky, daughter of Alexander II of Russia, made her debut as a music-hall singer. She sang a verse from 'Down in the Forest' at the Coliseum Theatre. 'I am delighted by my reception' she said. 'Singing has become my sole means of maintenance.'

At the end of the month, it leaked out that the fifty-four-year-old Duke of Orleans, head of the House of Bourbon and Pretender to the French throne, was living at a doctor's house in Roehampton watched over by male attendants. It was said that the tall, distinguished Duke, with a short Imperial beard, suffered from wild deliriums.

On August 7, the Prince of Wales was back in London after a short holiday in Le Touquet during which the dye had come out of his red bathing-costume, giving him the temporary appearance of a Red Indian.

On August 14, the public's attention turned to Arundel Castle, where the fifteen-year-old Duke of Norfolk was the central figure in a lavish and spectacular pageant. Before an audience of 4,000 people, the young Duke, in a peacock-blue Elizabethan doublet, paraded on a thoroughbred grey pony. The Duke's mother was among the spectators, wearing a black hat wreathed with white flowers.

On August 29, American millionairess Mrs. William B. Leeds, wife of Prince Christopher of Greece, died at Spencer House, St. James's, leaving the famous Leeds jewels, said to be worth £250,000, to her daughter-in-law, Princess Xenia of Russia. Princess Xenia soon refused to wear the jewels following her husband's insistence that they were unlucky and must be stored at a jeweller's.

On September 1, there was much excitement over the elopement of the one-legged Earl of Craven, whose father had drowned at Cowes in 1921, and the Countess Cathcart. It was revealed that they had left for South Africa on board the *Balmoral Castle*. They took with them thirty-six cases of antiques from Combe Abbey, the Earl's famous home near Coventry, which was now said to be on the market.

A few days later, the Duchess of Leinster, whose husband was in custody following his attempt to obtain credit without disclosing that he was an undischarged bankrupt, was found living in poverty in a tiny flat in Eastbourne. She complained that she could not afford the fare to visit her son, nine-year-old Marquess of Kildare, who was being brought up by relations at Johnstown Castle, County Wexford. 'It is a struggle to buy a pair of shoes' said Ireland's premier Duchess, 'and luxuries are out of the question.'

On September 15, the beautiful Madame Fahmy was acquitted of murdering her husband at the Savoy Hotel. Much speculation followed the verdict about whether or not Madame Fahmy would now inherit her husband's vast fortune and Egyptian palace. To make matters more complicated, it was revealed that Madame Fahmy was expecting a baby.

On September 27, the death of Lord Carnarvon was followed by that of his half-brother, the Hon. Aubrey Herbert. Mr. Herbert had been present at the opening of the Tutankhamen tomb and was reported to have remarked to a bystander, 'Something dreadful is going to happen to our family.'

Early in October, a certain Mrs. Travers-Smith of Cheyne Gardens, Chelsea, announced that she was receiving spirit messages from the late Oscar Wilde. She explained that the famous playwright was engaged on another dramatic work and she was writing down the dialogue. 'A week ago he gave me the characters and the plot but the dialogue is coming slowly because he re-writes almost every sentence' said Mrs. Travers-Smith, adding that Mr. Wilde did not appear to be aware of the progress of the world since his death twenty-three years earlier.

Later in the month, attention was focused on the Warwickshire and Leamington by-election. The Countess of Warwick, a former mistress of King Edward VII, was standing as Labour Candidate while most of her relations supported the Conservative candidate, handsome twenty-six-year-old Captain Anthony Eden. 'It was the last place in the world she should have stood for' said Lady Warwick's son when Captain Eden was duly elected to Parliament.

On October 22, Lady Dimsdale, whose husband had committed suicide earlier in the year, was found soaking wet on the shore at Whitstable. 'I walked into the sea and tried to sink but the waves washed me ashore again. I have nowhere to go and not a friend in the world.' This sad creature was put into a home in Maidstone, but discharged herself after twenty-four hours complaining that she had not been allowed to wear face-powder and had been put into a cap and apron and made to do kitchen work.

Meanwhile, a fascinating sequel to the Tichborne case, which had enthralled the public some fifty years earlier, was being played out at the Old Bailey. Miss Theresa Tichborne, stout daughter of the Wapping butcher who had claimed to be the heir to the Tichborne baronetcy, appeared in the dock accused of threatening to kill solicitor Sir George Lewis and libelling Sir Joseph Tichborne, the present baronet. She was described in court as a woman with a grievance.

On November 3, high society gathered at the Chapel Royal, St. James's Palace, for the marriage of Lady Louise Mountbatten and the Crown Prince of Sweden. Among the many wedding-gifts that had been sent to the couple were a set of blue enamelled teaspoons and a gold tea-strainer from the King and Queen of Norway. After the ceremony, the couple left for their honeymoon at a house at Sandwich, lent by Lord and Lady Astor.

On November 22, a theatrical agent named Mr. J. Tysoe-Smith shot himself in the Golden Gallery at the top of the dome of St. Paul's Cathedral. Police and doctors had great difficulty getting his body down the narrow, winding staircase and Mr. Tysoe-Smith died soon after he was outside the cathedral walls. A colleague explained that his business had been badly affected by the advent of the cinema.

At the end of November, the beautiful Lady Diana Cooper sailed for New York, where she had agreed to appear in a play called *The Miracle*.

Back at the Old Bailey, Lord Alfred Douglas, the fifty-three-year-old poet, was charged with criminally libelling Mr. Winston Churchill in a pamphlet entitled 'The Murder of Lord Kitchener and the Truth about the Battle of Jutland and the Jews'. On December 19, the jury took only eight minutes to find Lord Alfred guilty. 'It is to be regretted that your undoubted literary abilities have been degraded to such purposes as this' said Mr. Justice Avory, passing sentence of six months imprisonment.

On December 22, the King and Queen left for Sandringham, where the King was soon reported to be shooting over his preserves, along with the Prince of Wales, the Duke of York and the King of Norway.

On December 27, it was announced that two warders at Wormwood Scrubs had been dismissed from the prison service following an enquiry into how articles by Horatio Bottomley, the swindler, had been smuggled out of the gaol. It was noted that the former MP was now in Maidstone Prison.

On December 30, the stocky new American Ambassador, Mr. Frank B. Kellogg, arrived in England with his wife. A special train was laid on to carry the couple from Plymouth to London. 'I want to select a house as soon as I can' said Mrs. Kellogg. 'I believe several possibles are ready for me to see.'

1924

The New Year began with rumours of fierce rivalry between Lady Diana Cooper and her co-star, Princess Matchabelli, about who should play the leading role in the New York production of *The Miracle*. Eventually, it was decided that the co-stars should draw lots. Lady Diana won – confessing afterwards that the ballot had been rigged in her favour.

On January 15, the play opened and Lady Diana received rave reviews. Impresario Charles Cochran telegraphed Mr. Duff Cooper in London: 'Wife's performance exquisitely beautiful unquestionable work of sensitive artist.'

On January 22, a Labour Government was sworn in for the first time in history. Socialites wondered what sort of entertaining the new Prime Minister, Ramsay MacDonald, would do. Soon Co-op vans were seen delivering provisions at 10 Downing Street.

At the end of the month, Maureen, Oonagh and Aileen, vivacious young daughters of Ernest Guinness, left Socialist Britain to join their father's yacht *Fantome II* on its leisurely world cruise.

On February 6, whisky distiller Sir John Stewart was found dying in the hall of Fingask Castle, Perthshire, a revolver in his hand. This was one of the first of many suicides by failing businessmen during this period.

On February 9, the Prince of Wales was injured during an exercise gallop at Leighton Buzzard while staying with Lord Dalmeny at Mentmore Towers. 'I'm afraid your collarbone must be broken, Sir' said his Equerry, Major 'Fruity' Metcalfe. 'I believe it is' replied the Prince.

On February 11, Lady Londonderry gave a reception at Londonderry House, Park Lane, in honour of the defeated Conservative Party. The hostess wore her famous tiara and long, antique earrings and there was a scent of mimosa throughout the great house.

On February 19, Winston Churchill hurried home from a holiday with the Duke of Westminster in France to inspect the work being done on his newly-acquired country house, Chartwell, now in the process of reconstruction.

On March 15, another riding accident befell the Prince of Wales. He was unconscious for half an hour after a head injury sustained in the last race at an Army point-to-point at Arborfield Cross near Wokingham. This mishap caused a surge of public anxiety and the King commanded that the heir to the throne should give up steeplechasing for good.

On March 19, the Duchess of Hamilton received guests at a dinner of the London Vegetarian Society. 'Not only do I cordially dislike the taste of meat,' said the Duchess, 'but I believe it to be unhygienic to eat any animal flesh.'

At the end of the month, it was announced that Mr. Oswald Mosley, brilliant young Conservative MP for Harrow, had joined the Labour Party. 'I have had an interview with the Prime Minister and he has welcomed me into the Party' he explained. 'The government has clearly emerged as the effective champion of progress and sanity.' It was rumoured that Lady Cynthia Mosley, beautiful daughter of Lord Curzon, had also embraced the Socialist cause.

On April 8, a warrant was issued in Montreal for the arrest of the Duke of Manchester on a false pretences charge. It was said that the Mount Royal Hotel were holding his suitcases. Since his marriage in 1900 to the daughter of a wealthy railway director from Cincinnati, it was said that the Duke had devoted his life to selfish pleasures.

On April 10, Chang, the notorious London dope king, was sentenced to fourteen months imprisonment followed by deportation, following the disclosure of his drug-trafficking activities. The conviction drew grim comments from the Bishop of Willesden about conditions prevailing in London's West End: 'I know of no place today to compare with Piccadilly and Leicester Square for vice and temptation to the youth of England and the Dominions.'

Meanwhile, Lady Louis Mountbatten had given birth to a girl at Brook House, Park Lane. On April 22, the child was christened Patricia Edwina Victoria and pronounced by the Press to be 'the richest baby girl in England'.

Up and coming MP, Oswald Mosley

On April 30, the Earl of Dudley married musical-comedy actress Gertie Millar. Among the guests at the ceremony, which took place in Paris, were artist Sir William Orpen and singer Dame Clara Butt. The bride wore a grey cloche hat.

At the beginning of May, a baby girl was born to a passenger on the Bakerloo Line – thought to be the first baby to be born on the Underground system. Lord Ashfield, Chairman of the Underground Railways Company, gladly consented to be a godfather to the little girl, who was subsequently christened Marie Ashfield Elena Hammond.

Missing from official ceremonies at the opening of the Season was Queen Alexandra. It was announced that the seventy-nine-year-old Queen, now stone deaf, had retired from public life.

On May 12, Lord Alfred Douglas was released from Wormwood Scrubs and hurried to the office of a friend to write out a long poem called 'In Excelsis', which he had written in prison and committed to memory.

In the middle of the month, the Duke of Westminster suddenly withdrew permission for Grosvenor House, his vast house in Park Lane, to be used for a ball in aid of the Italian Hospital. Society hostess, Mrs. Ronnie Greville, immediately offered the use of 16 Charles Street. On the night of the dance, the house was so packed that the King and Queen of Italy had to sit waiting in their car while footmen cleared a pathway through the crowds and upstairs to the ballroom.

Meanwhile, Norfolk House, in St. James's Square, had been let to American millionairess Mrs. Harry Brown for £1,000 a week for the course of the Season. 'I do not know whether I shall be entertaining much' said Mrs. Brown. 'My plans are not yet complete.'

*Master Geoffrey Russell, central
figure in the Russell Baby Case,
playing in Kensington Gardens*

On May 30, Mrs. Christabel Russell took her long-disputed divorce case to the House of Lords. After some deliberation, a majority of the noble Lords decided that Mrs. Russell's husband's evidence was inadmissible and she had thus, at last, won her case. Jubilant scenes followed at Mrs. Russell's dressmaking establishment in Curzon Street, where she arrived later in the day by taxi cab.

On the night of June 12, £250,000-worth of jewellery was stolen from Bath House, the Piccadilly residence of Lady Ludlow, former wife of Sir Julius Wernher, the multi-millionaire diamond king. The jewels were part of a collection of ancient royal jewels painstakingly assembled by Sir Julius, who had died in 1912 leaving twelve million pounds. It was obvious that the thieves knew the house well. Security arrangements

Margot Asquith arrives at a society wedding

were very strict, the house being known among Lady Ludlow's friends as 'The Fortress'.

On June 20, Queen Alexandra's devoted secretary, Sir Dighton Probyn, died aged ninety-one. This venerable, white-bearded man had been in Her Majesty's entourage for over fifty years. Recently his duties had been limited to opening her private door to Sandringham Church and escorting Her Majesty to her pew each Sunday.

At the beginning of July, Mrs. James Corrigan entertained 104 guests to dinner at 16 Grosvenor Street. The house, rented from Mrs. George Keppel, was converted for the evening into a 'Jardin des perroquets verts'.

On July 11, Mrs. Harry Brown put on a white dress decorated with diamanté and crystal trimmings and gave a dance at Norfolk House, St. James's Square, which she had rented from the Duchess of Norfolk. The mansion, built in 1748, was filled with red and white roses.

Meanwhile, the Dowager Countess of Warwick, former mistress of the late King Edward VII, had thrown open her stately home in Essex, Easton Lodge, for the use of the Labour Party. Members of Parliament and trade-union leaders were found installed in gilt armchairs and egg-and-spoon races were run on the great lawns. Many visitors were perplexed to find photographs of the late King in their rooms. Occasionally, the hostess, who remained in her own lavishly-equipped private wing, pointed out the bed in which she had slept with the late King.

On July 24, twenty-one-year-old Alice Astor, who had inherited £1,000,000 following her father's death on the *Titanic* in 1912, married poverty-stricken Prince Serge Obolensky, in spite of the objections of her formidable mother, now Lady Ribblesdale. Soon afterwards, the newly-married couple moved into Hanover Lodge, Regent's Park, former home of Admiral of the Fleet Lord Beatty. It was said that the Beattys had second thoughts about the sale and offered to buy the house back at a higher price.

On August 7, it was revealed that a controversial painting of Lady Astor had been defaced at the House of Commons. Dark green canvas was at once placed over the portrait and it was later removed to a safer place.

On August 27, it was announced that the Duchess of Westminster was taking action in the High Court to prevent her husband ejecting her from Bourdon House, her home in Davies Street, Mayfair. A few days later, she also filed a petition for divorce, claiming that the Duke had misbehaved with a number of women on board his yacht and in hotels in Monaco and Biarritz.

In the middle of September, Prime Minister Ramsay MacDonald answered criticism regarding his holding of 30,000 £1 shares in the McVitie and Price biscuit business. He explained that the previous year, Sir Alexander Grant, head of the firm, had presented him with a Daimler motor-car. He had refused this generous gift saying that he could not afford to pay for its upkeep. Sir Alexander had promptly 'endowed' the car with a block of shares.

On September 20, the Dean of St. Paul's, Dr. Inge, famous for his pessimistic pronouncements about the future of mankind, walked through the streets of London flourishing a fancy, coloured umbrella of the sort carried by stage comedians.

On September 30, the Bishop of Woolwich denounced the use of birth-control. 'The use of all artificial contrivances is clearly opposed to Christian conduct' he said. 'The sex instinct is a sacramental thing.'

On October 2, financier Mr. John Quiller-Rowett was found hanging by a sash-cord in the billiard room of his house in Hyde Park Terrace. It was said that Mr. Quiller-Rowett, who had made his money selling rum to the Army during the war, had suffered heavy losses following the crash of whisky distiller, Sir John Stewart. He had also been upset by the recent death of Sir Ernest Shackleton, whose famous expedition he had helped finance.

Meanwhile, the police forces of Europe were hunting a well-dressed Englishman by the name of Gerald Hamilton in connexion with an attempt to swindle a Milan jeweller out of a £1,500 necklace. On October 17, he was arrested at Marseilles station as he stepped off a train from Paris, accompanied by his valet and a small dog, and was thrown into a communal cell. Hamilton, who was educated at Rugby and claimed to be a relation of the Duke of Abercorn, revealed afterwards that he kept two cyanide capsules hidden in a tiny chamois leather pad under his wig which he was prepared to swallow if things got too tough.

On October 20, thirty-three men and eight women appeared at Bow Street Court following a raid on Mrs. Meyrick's fashionable basement club at 43 Gerrard Street. Each was fined forty shillings. Mrs. Meyrick, whose customers included the Prince of Wales, was charged with selling intoxicating liquor without a licence and was sentenced to six months imprisonment.

On October 22, it was announced that grocer's son, Lord Leverhulme, had purchased Grosvenor House in Park Lane, originally built for a brother of George III and said to have the largest private ballroom in London. It was explained that Lord Leverhulme had no intention of living in the house himself.

Meanwhile, the country was preparing itself for another General Election. Lady Diana Cooper, fresh from her triumphs in America, was helping her husband fight for the Oldham seat. Many of her relations were also there to lend their support, occupying several suites at the luxurious Midland Hotel, Manchester.

On October 29, the Labour Party was swept out of office and the defeated Prime Minister, Ramsay MacDonald, left for a walking tour of the West Country. The new Prime Minister, Stanley Baldwin, spent his first weekend in office staying with Mr. and Mrs. Geoffrey Fry at their house near Reading, pondering over the composition of his Cabinet.

On November 5, it was revealed that Lord Lonsdale's niece, Mrs. Barbara Innes, daughter of the Hon. Lancelot Lowther, was selling motor-cars in a Bond Street showroom. 'I intend to specialise in salesmanship' she said. 'I shall drive for the firm as well as demonstrating to customers. I shall miss a certain amount of hunting but foot-and-mouth disease has stopped most of that so I really cannot grumble.'

In the middle of November, the public's attention turned to the High Court where a former bookmaker attempted to obtain £125,000 which he claimed was owed to him in return for not bringing a divorce action against his wife, naming an oriental potentate as co-respondent. In the course of the hearing, it emerged that there had been an ingenious plot to blackmail the potentate, referred to in court as 'Mr. A', and the outcome was a long prison sentence for an elderly solicitor's clerk. Sir Ernest Wild, QC, suggested that the plot was 'as monumental and impudent a fraud as perhaps has ever been perpetuated in our criminal history.' Shortly afterwards, it was revealed that 'Mr. A' was Sir Hari Singh, heir to the Maharajah of Kashmir.

On November 25, it was announced from Badminton in Gloucestershire that the seventy-seven-year-old Duke of Beaufort was seriously ill. His hounds had been 'called back' and future fixtures cancelled. The Duke died two days later and was succeeded by his son, the Marquess of Worcester, who had recently married the Queen's niece and was said to be as keen on foxhunting as his father.

On December 1, Queen Alexandra celebrated her eightieth birthday at Sandringham. To mark the occasion, a two-foot high cake had been made which was an exact replica of the thatched house in the grounds of Sandringham. Joining in the celebrations was the Queen's eighty-three-year-old hairdresser, Mr. Charles Howlett, who travelled to Sandringham each week in a pony-cart to attend to the Queen's coiffure. 'The youngest barber alive hasn't a steadier hand than mine' he boasted.

On December 16, the £250,000 worth of antique jewels stolen from Lady Ludlow six months earlier were mysteriously returned to her, wrapped in cushion covers. The mystery deepened when it was revealed that the jewels had been retrieved without the assistance of the police.

That evening, *The Vortex* opened at the Royalty Theatre with the author, Noel Coward, in a starring role. It was enthusiastically received and twenty-five-year-old Coward celebrated by buying new suits, pyjamas, dressing-gowns and silk shirts. Among those who did not care for the play was veteran actor Sir Gerald du Maurier. 'The public are asking for filth' he declared. 'The younger generation are knocking at the door of the dustbin.'

On December 23, housebreakers began work on Devonshire House, built in 1733 and one of the grandest of all ducal town houses. The Duke of Devonshire, who had sold the house for £1,000,000 in May 1920, watched the demolition work in progress.

On Boxing Day, sixty-eight-year-old white-bearded Bernard Shaw left England on board the liner *Olympic* for 'a sun bath' in Madeira. He later transferred to the *Edinburgh Castle* from which reports emanated that the famous playwright was learning the tango.

On New Year's Day, Old Rugbeian Gerald Hamilton was removed to the bug-infested prison at San Remo to await his trial on charges of swindling a Milan jeweller out of a pearl necklace.

Meanwhile in London, another member of the Hamilton clan was in hot water. On January 3, Percy Milnwood McNeil Hamilton, rumoured to be a close relative of a famous Scottish Duke, was sentenced to twelve months hard labour for stealing overcoats from the Savoy Hotel. The court was told that he had already spent more than twenty years in prison.

On January 9, it was announced that Arundel Castle, 120-room home of the sixteen-year-old Duke of Norfolk would be closed for the next five years. The indoor staff had already been discharged and the forty outdoor staff were to be found other work. It was stated that the Duchess of Norfolk and her family would be living in Italy, for financial reasons.

On January 11, the crippled Duke of Newcastle invited a dozen boys from Hoxton, East London, to a belated Christmas dinner at his comfortable flat in Mayfair's Hay Hill. 'I asked a friend of mine to find twelve of the poorest boys from the poorest part of London' the Duke explained afterwards. The Newcastle family were no strangers to charitable work. The Duke's mother had spent the last few years of her life living and working in the slums of Whitechapel.

On January 13, the coming-of-age of Cambridge undergraduate Cecil Beaton, who had already made a name for himself designing scenery and costumes for the university amateur dramatic productions, was celebrated with a dance at his parents' home, 3 Hyde Park Street.

Meanwhile, the Hon. Gwyneth Morgan, thirty-year-old daughter of Lord Tredegar, had gone missing from her London home. She had vanished dressed only in her pyjamas but was said to have at least £50 in cash on her. 'It is quite true my daughter has disappeared' said Lord Tredegar, one of Wales's wealthiest peers. 'Enquiries have been instituted without effect.'

On February 6, the retiring American Ambassador, Mr. Kellogg, gave a dinner-party for the King, Queen and Archbishop of Canterbury at Crewe House in Curzon Street. The house was stuffed with lilies, lilac and azaleas, some of which were later taken to decorate Mr. and Mrs. Kellogg's suite on the ship which took them back to America.

On February 10, the news came from Africa that the twenty-four-year-old Duchess of York had shot a rhinoceros.

Later in the same month, it was revealed that the floor of the drawing-room at 11 Downing Street, official home of Chancellor of the Exchequer Winston Churchill, was being strengthened with a steel joist in order that large receptions might be given there later in the year.

On March 20, the great Lord Curzon died at his home in Carlton House Terrace. He had recently returned from a fortnight's holiday with the former Duchess of Marlborough, Madame Consuelo Balsan, at her home in the South of France where he had sat up at night editing his memoirs.

On April 7, twenty-one-year-old Evelyn Waugh, currently working as a schoolmaster, was fined 15s.6d. for being drunk and incapable in Oxford Street following a pub-crawl to Golders Green and back.

At the end of April, Noel Coward's *Fallen Angels* opened at the Globe Theatre with husky-voiced Tallulah Bankhead in one of the leading roles. Tallulah got her part just five days before the play was to open when another actress had fallen ill. The play was immediately described as 'vulgar, obscene and degenerate' and became the talk of London.

On May 5, the Queen, in a grey sequinned toque trimmed with grey ostrich feathers, attended a charity matinée performance of *No No Nanette!* at the Palace Theatre. During one scene, the chorus appeared in bathing-costumes and the Queen turned her head away from the stage.

On May 7, soap magnate Lord Leverhulme died at his home in Hampstead. His coffin later went on show at his art-gallery at Port Sunlight and 30,000 people filed past to pay their last respects.

On May 8, the Duke of Rutland died at his London home, 16 Arlington Street. His body was removed to the guardroom at Belvoir Castle where his artistic widow covered the coffin with bay-leaves and set about designing a tomb.

On May 21, the Home Secretary Sir William Joynson-Hicks fainted at a reception at Buckingham Palace. It was said that he had been overworking recently. One of his major aims was to crush Mrs. Meyrick and her expanding chain of nightclubs.

Four days later, the body of Lord Tredegar's daughter Gwyneth was found in the Thames at Wapping Reach. Detectives wondered if the body, on which only one penny was found, could have floated all the way from her home near Battersea Bridge or whether she had fallen into the river from the Chinese Quarter of Limehouse, where she was known to be a regular visitor.

On the morning of June 10, the Chancellor of the Exchequer Winston Churchill was riding in Rotten Row when he was confronted with a Rose Day girl. The Chancellor felt in all his pockets and found he was penniless. A passerby came to his rescue and purchased a rose for him.

On June 25, it was announced that the recently widowed Duchess of Rutland, mother of Lady Diana Cooper, would be moving out of the mansion at 16 Arlington Street into the lodge, said to be the former laundry.

This year, American millionairess Mrs. Harry Brown had taken Spencer House in St. James's for the summer. On July 4, she gave a musical party there, which was attended by Princess Louise, Duchess of Argyll, and at which Lady Dean Paul, a Polish-born composer, sang some of her own compositions.

Meanwhile, Mrs. Audrey Coats, close friend of the Prince of Wales and Lord Louis Mountbatten, opened a shop in Davies Street. She called it 'Audrey' and sold non-staining scents and embroidered handbags made out of eighteenth-century materials.

On July 21, Major 'Fruity' Metcalfe, close friend and former Equerry to the Prince of Wales, married Lady Alexandra Curzon, whose father, Lord Curzon, had died earlier in the year. The ceremony took place at the Chapel Royal, St. James's Palace. One of the pages was the bride's two-year-old nephew, Nicholas Mosley.

The following day, Anne Messel, beautiful sister of stage designer Oliver Messel, was married to Old Etonian barrister Ronald Armstrong-Jones. After the ceremony at St. Margaret's Westminster, at which the Archbishop of Wales officiated, a troupe of Girl Guides from the bride's Sussex home formed a guard of honour.

Meanwhile, hundreds of people began to tramp through the stately rooms of 16 Arlington Street, home of the late Duke of Rutland, where most of the contents were for sale. 'This house has not been touched since 1725' said the Duchess. One of the sensations of the sale, which took place on July 27, was that a painting described in the catalogue as a portrait of a child by Sir Joshua Reynolds fetched only £42. Lady Diana Cooper's Italian bedstead went for £58.

On August 1, the Maharajah of Patiala arrived in England and took over the entire fifth floor of the Savoy Hotel – comprising thirty-five suites. This wealthy Prince was said to have a private income of £640,000 a year and wear special underpants costing £200 a pair. During his three-week stay at the Savoy, the Maharajah and his wife dined off solid silver dishes, eating food prepared by their own chefs.

On August 4, Colonel Freyberg, VC, hero of Gallipoli, attempted to swim the Channel. He got within fifty-five yards of the English coast before giving up and being fished out of the sea purple with cold. It was noted that he had been wounded nine times during the war.

Meanwhile, Noel Coward's *Fallen Angels*, starring Tallulah Bankhead, had created a considerable sensation at the Globe Theatre. On August 29, the last night of the run, notorious public protestor Mrs. Charles Hornibrook visited the theatre. This odd lady had recently parted company with the London Council for the Promotion of Public Morality and was operating on her own. At the end of the second act, she stood up in her box. 'Ladies and Gentlemen, I wish to protest. This play should not go unchallenged.' In the disturbance that followed, there were hoots from the gallery, the orchestra struck up with 'I Want To Be Happy' and Mrs. Hornibrook was gently guided out of the theatre.

On August 31, Lord Oxford and Asquith was stung by a wasp on his way to open a fête at Faringdon,

The Maharajah of Patiala, who was said to wear underpants costing £200 a pair

Berks. His chauffeur turned round and raced the former Prime Minister back to his Thames-side home, The Wharf, Sutton Courtenay, where he was treated by a doctor.

On September 1, Prince Ahmed Sief-el-did escaped from a private lunatic asylum at Ticehurst, Sussex. He had been interned there for the past twenty-four years following a murderous attack on his brother-in-law, the King of Egypt. A few days later, the Prince was seen in the Forest of Fontainebleau outside Paris and said to be dressed as a woman.

On September 21, Lady Cynthia Mosley, beautiful daughter of the late Marquess Curzon, was adopted as Labour candidate for Stoke-on-Trent, thus joining an illustrious group of Society women now working for the Socialist cause, who included the Countess of Warwick and the Marchioness of Tavistock. 'I am heart and soul behind my husband in this matter' said Lady Cynthia.

Meanwhile, a group of bright, young socialites had emerged whose activities were constantly in the news. On October 3, they staged a treasure-hunt which involved a young man scaling Cleopatra's Needle and brought traffic chaos to Sloane Square in the small hours of the morning.

On October 16, the Prince of Wales returned from an overseas tour during which he had visited forty-five countries. Lunch on the Royal train carrying the Prince from Portsmouth to London consisted of suprême de sole chablis, poularde rôtie à la broche and Charlotte Russe à la chantilly. On arrival at Victoria Station, he kissed his mother on both cheeks.

On October 21, Lord Ribblesdale, a former Lord-in-Waiting to Queen Victoria, died at his home in Grosvenor Square. This old-fashioned man had been nicknamed 'The Ancestor' by Edward VII because he looked as if he had walked out of the frame of an old family-portrait. Following his death, his widow, the former Mrs. Astor who had lost her first husband on the *Titanic*, plunged back into high society with a vengeance. She was soon seen everywhere, heavily scented and followed by half a dozen yapping Cairn terriers.

On October 27, Alexander Grant, a retired elderly tutor living in Cromwell Road, challenged the nineteen-year-old Countess of Seafield's right to her title. Mr. Grant, who had been brought up in mysterious circumstances by the gardener at Gordon Castle, claimed to be the rightful 8th Earl of Seafield. This claim was successfully refuted by the Countess's representatives and Grant entered into an agreement not to repeat the slander.

On November 4, the Cunard liner *Berengaria* arrived at Southampton after an extremely rough crossing during which £2,000-worth of crockery had been broken and twenty-six passengers injured. 'Crockery and furniture were thrown about like feathers' said a First Class passenger.

On November 16, Mrs. Wakeford, whose husband had been at the centre of a major ecclesiastical scandal in 1921, was fined £2 for failing to look after ten dogs in her care. Inspector Drake of the RSPCA said he had visited the bungalow in Kent where Mr. and Mrs. Wakeford were now living and found the dogs in a filthy, ill-ventilated shed. Mrs. Wakeford denied that the shed was filthy and said that she had a big stock of prize-winning cats, dogs and poultry.

On November 19, news came from Sandringham that Queen Alexandra was critically ill following a heart-attack. The King, Queen, Prince Henry, the Princess Royal and Princess Victoria were at her bedside. Thick fog surrounded the house when she died the following day.

On November 21, Winston Churchill's eleven-year-old daughter Sarah, found a pearl necklace lying in a Chelsea street. She was later given a £50 reward by the grateful owner.

At the beginning of December, famous Society beauty Mrs. Richard Norton, close friend of Lady Louis Mountbatten, announced that she would shortly be taking over as manageress of the New Gallery Cinema in Regent Street.

Meanwhile, a reconciliation had taken place between Lord and Lady Craven and their divorce proceedings had been scrapped. On December 14, the couple were off for a holiday in Bermuda. 'We are looking forward to a very happy time' said the one-legged peer. 'It is just like a second honeymoon.'

On December 23, flamboyant Old Rugbeian Gerald Hamilton was released from prison in Milan, his conviction for swindling a local jeweller out of a pearl necklace having been finally quashed by the Genoa Court of Appeal.

That Christmas, the Duke of Devonshire had a large house-party at Chatsworth. Among the guests were the Duke's daughter, Lady Dorothy, and her young husband, Captain Harold Macmillan, who had recently been elected Conservative MP for Stockton-on-Tees. After Christmas, the party was reported to have enjoyed some 'excellent sport' over the local moors.

1926

The New Year was greeted with the usual tumultuous scenes at the Albert Hall. Among the revellers were Mr. Houghton, the new American Ambassador, Mr. Gordon Selfridge, whose Oxford Street store was now in its seventeenth year, Prince and Princess Arthur of Connaught and the much-fêted Prince Chichibu of Japan. In Prince Chichibu's box was Lord Churston's beautiful daughter, seventeen-year-old Joan Yarde-Buller.

On January 4, sixty-four-year-old Sir Basil Thomson, former Assistant Commissioner of the Metropolitan Police, appeared at Marlborough Street Court accused of 'committing an act in violation of public decency in Hyde Park'. Sir Basil, said to be a world expert on criminal investigation, was found guilty of the offence and fined £5.

Meanwhile, there had been an outcry over a play called *Scotch Mist* in which Tallulah Bankhead played the promiscuous wife of a British Cabinet Minister. The bachelor Bishop of London was particularly incensed by the play and on January 15 wrote to the Prime Minister Stanley Baldwin on behalf of the London Public Morality Council urging stricter theatre licensing laws. The resulting publicity helped make the play into a great commercial success. With her share of the proceeds, Miss Bankhead bought the lease of a house in Mayfair – 1 Farm Street – where she soon held cocktail parties in her bathroom and opened the door to callers stark naked.

On January 18, there was much excitement over the runaway marriage of the Marchioness of Queensberry and wealthy Canadian financier Sir James Dunn. After the ceremony in Paris, attended by Lord Beaverbrook, the couple returned to England to live at Templeton, Sir James's vast house at Roehampton where floodlit parties were held in the garden.

Early in February, Vera Lady Cathcart set off for America where she hoped to stage a play she had written about her relationship with the one-legged Earl of Craven. On February 10, she was forbidden to land at New York on the grounds that having been involved in a divorce case, she was guilty of 'moral turpitude'. While the authorities deliberated about what action to take, she was removed to Ellis Island where she joined other unwelcome immigrants and was stripped to the waist and examined by sneering officials. 'I will fight until I jolly well have to give in' she said valiantly. Back in England, her ex-lover Lord Craven joined in the chorus of criticism of the American authorities. 'It is disgusting the way Lady Cathcart is being treated' he declared.

On February 15, Oulton Park, Cheshire was burnt to the ground. Five people died in the blaze and damage was estimated at £400,000. The house was the seat of Sir Philip Grey Egerton, a well-known host, famous for his habit of handing round the Cheshire cheese himself at the end of his dinner-parties.

On February 22, police were called to the Eaton Square home of Health Minister Neville Chamberlain. A small, elderly French woman named Madame Juro had thrust her way in and, in a frenzy of religious mania, had attempted to enter Mr. Chamberlain's study.

On March 5, Countess Cathcart was at last permitted to enter the United States and set about the staging of her autobiographical play, *Ashes*. A few days later, it opened simultaneously in London and Washington, being described in *Punch* as a 'sentimental tragi-farce'.

On March 16, the news broke that nineteen-year-old Lord de Clifford, said to own large tracts of land in Ireland, had secretly married Dorothy Meyrick, daughter of nightclub-owner Mrs. Meyrick. 'I am astonished at the news' said a friend of the young peer. 'He is one of the most serious-minded boys of my acquaintance.' At her club in Gerrard Street, the famous Mrs. Meyrick had no comment to make.

On March 26, the Prince of Wales was suddenly struck down by earache and had to cancel his plans to attend the Grand National. His Equerry, one-armed General Trotter, was sent to Euston to inform Prince Henry and others in the party that the Prince was not well and must remain at York House.

Early in April, American multi-millionaire James Stillman and his wife arrived in London to see if psychoanalytic help could solve their marital problems. Staying in a quiet hotel, they were both to receive treatment from Dr. H. G. Baynes, a friend of the famous Swiss psychoanalyst, Jung. 'It is a pity that so little is known of this science which might prove a great benefit to mankind' said Mrs. Stillman.

On April 6, the Duke and Duchess of York arrived at 17 Bruton Street, fine eighteenth-century town house of the Earl and Countess of Strathmore, where the Duchess had spent a great deal of her childhood. Here, at 2.40 am on April 21, she gave birth to a baby girl.

A few hours later, the King and Queen arrived from Windsor Castle to see their first granddaughter. A liveried footman, carrying a huge spray of purple lilac and a smaller sheaf of pale pink carnations, followed them into the house. That day there were so many callers at 17 Bruton Street that in the afternoon, the Visitors Bell broke down. The large crowd of bystanders watched the mending operation with interest.

On April 30, Lady Oxford and her daughter Princess Bibesco were among the celebrities at the opening of the Summer Exhibition at the Royal Academy. Much controversy surrounded a painting by Mr. John B. Souter of a nude woman dancing to a saxophone played by a negro. It was soon withdrawn at the request of the Colonial Office.

On May 4, the country plunged into the General Strike. For the next ten days innumerable high society figures helped to keep essential services running. Lady Louis Mountbatten and her friend, Mrs. Richard Norton, operated the switchboard of the *Daily Express* and Lady Diana Cooper sat up all night folding an abbreviated version of copies of *The Times*.

In the middle of the commotion, twenty-year-old heiress Thelma Hays Morgan arrived from New York. She was met at Southampton by shipping magnate, Lord Furness, with a fleet of Rolls-Royces to bear her to Claridge's. During the journey to London, the forty-two-year-old peer kept a loaded revolver on his lap. 'I'd like to see any bastard try and stop this car' he said.

On May 19, six days after the strike was over, the wealthy Duke of Bedford travelled from Woburn Abbey to his large establishment in Belgrave Square, where, it was said, eight chauffeurs were kept permanently on call though the Duke was only in London two or three times a year.

On May 24, the King and Queen were present at the opening of the Italian opera season at Covent Garden. Puccini's *La Bohème* was slightly spoilt on this occasion by the extremely audible hissing of the prompter. He explained afterwards that he had been over-excited by the presence of Royalty in the audience.

Five days later, the Duchess of York's baby was christened Elizabeth Alexandra Mary at a service in the chapel at Buckingham Palace. During the ceremony, the baby cried so much that her nurse, Mrs. Knight, was obliged to dose her with dill water.

On June 17, nineteen-year-old Lord de Clifford was fined £50 at Mansion House for making a false declaration about his age in order to marry Miss Dorothy Meyrick. After explaining that he was not yet a man of means, the young peer was given two weeks to find the money. 'Elsewhere' said the Lord Mayor, 'the penalty would be seven years.'

On June 27, the marriage took place of bluff shipping magnate Lord Furness and twenty-year-old American heiress Thelma Hays Morgan. Lord Furness, said to be one of Britain's richest men, was described by his friends as 'a lucky dog'.

On July 7, the new Viscountess Leverhulme was present at the third court of the Season at Buckingham Palace. She wore a dress of green crêpe embroidered in diamanté and silver. It had recently been announced that her father-in-law's executors had disposed of Grosvenor House, Park Lane. The mansion would be pulled down and a block of flats erected on its site.

The following day, the widowed Marchioness Curzon gave a dance in the garden of 1 Carlton House Terrace. The King and Queen of Spain, Lord and Lady Londonderry and the Duchess of Sutherland, in a helmet of diamonds, packed into a tent lined with tapestries.

On July 16, the Duchess of Sutherland threw a fancy-dress party at Hampden House, Green Street. The tall Lord Blandford, heir to the Duke of Marlborough, came as a female cross-Channel swimmer and Lady Diana Cooper was a French revolutionary. Highlight of the evening was the arrival of a team of fashionable young women dressed as an Eton College eight and 'coxed' by Duff Cooper.

On July 21, Mrs. Corrigan gave a party at 16 Grosvenor Street at which the guests provided the cabaret. Lady Lettice Lygon, daughter of Earl Beauchamp, performed a comic cycling act and the hostess herself, in top-hat and red shoes, gave a demonstration of the Charleston. Lady Maud Warrender, daughter of the Earl of Shaftesbury, was to do a plate-breaking turn but decided to call it off, fearing that the parquet floor would be damaged.

The month ended with festivities at Longleat to celebrate the coming-of-age of Lord Bath's son and heir, the raffish-looking Viscount Weymouth. Among the thirty people staying at the house, said to be Britain's earliest unfortified dwelling, was young Maureen Guinness, whose current nickname was 'Teapot'.

Early in August, it was revealed that the sixty-one-year-old Duchess of Bedford had taken up flying. She had already flown between London and Woburn Abbey several times and it was said that she found the experience helped to relieve a buzzing sound in her ears.

On August 23, the Duke and Duchess of Sutherland left London for Dunrobin Castle. They travelled in their own luxurious green railway-coach which was attached to a scheduled express train. This very special privilege had been granted to the Duke's grandfather in return for a long stretch of railway-line in Scotland.

Early in September it was revealed that the Duke and Duchess of York had purchased 145 Piccadilly, a large house overlooking Hyde Park Corner, where the nearest neighbours were the Duke of Wellington, Lord Rothschild and Lord Allendale. Central-heating was now being installed and the Duke and Duchess's furniture was brought from Bruton Street.

On September 20, twenty-two-year-old baronet Sir Francis Laking, part-time secretary to Tallulah Bankhead, appeared at a party of 'Bright Young People' dressed as a woman. Later in the evening he stripped and attempted to Charleston stark naked.

On October 1, pioneer aviator Alan Cobham landed on the Thames in front of the Houses of Parliament following a 28,000-mile flight from Australia. He had coped with many difficulties during the flight, not the least of which was a colony of wasps landing in the fuselage. A wet towel had been used to drive them out. Asked if he was going away for the weekend, Cobham replied: 'Good heavens, no. I have far too much work to do. I have long reports to write for the Air Ministry and the De Havilland Company.'

On October 8, twenty-one-year-old Viscount Weymouth and the Hon. Daphne Vivian side-stepped parental opposition and married secretly at St. Paul's, Knightsbridge. Two charladies acted as witnesses and the young couple did not reveal their parents' identity on the marriage certificate. For the next year, the new Lady Weymouth wore her wedding-ring on a chain round her neck.

The same day, Lady Dimsdale, daughter-in-law of a former Lord Mayor of London, committed suicide at the Great Western Hotel in Paddington by swallowing a large quantity of carbolic disinfectant. Nothing had been heard of this unfortunate woman since her attempt to walk into the sea at Whitstable three years earlier.

On Sunday October 17, an anonymous worshipper put a £1,000 banknote into the collection at Salisbury Cathedral. The Bishop of Aberdeen and Orkney, who was present at the service, spoke of the 'extraordinary generosity' of the mystery donor.

On October 28, the Marquess of Tavistock, eccentric pacifist heir to the Duke of Bedford, upset a crowded lunchtime audience in Birmingham by defending the ex-Kaiser and attacking England. Several ex-servicemen walked out. It was said that the Marquess and his father had not seen each other since before the Great War.

On November 16, Lady Michelham sold her thirty-bedroom mansion in Arlington Street. The house was considered too large for present-day use and was knocked down to Mr. Jefferson Cohn, former son-in-law of Horatio Bottomley, for only £75,000. At a sale a few days later, the contents of the mansion raised £596,000. Art dealer Sir Joseph Duveen purchased a number of pictures. Among the last items sold were several half-bottles of Pommery champagne. These fetched sixteen shillings each.

At the end of November, it was revealed that well-to-do murderer Ronald True, detained at Broadmoor for the past four years, had undergone an operation at the prison. It was stated that True had paid the £70 specialist fees with his own money.

On December 3, there was great excitement over the disappearance of thirty-five-year-old Mrs. Agatha Christie, novelist wife of Colonel Archibald Christie. The following day, her two-seater motor-car was found crashed and abandoned near her home at Newlands Corner, Surrey and one of her gloves was found in a bush. 'She was in a very peculiar state' said a man who had seen her after the crash. 'Her teeth were chattering and she kept putting her hands to her head.' Soon, the entire country joined in the search. One report was that she had been seen on a London bus disguised as a man. On December 14 much indignation was expressed when she was discovered fit and well and staying a hotel in Harrogate.

Meanwhile, wealthy Mr. Oswald Mosley was campaigning as Socialist candidate in the Smethwick by-election assisted by his wife, Lady Cynthia, and Oliver Baldwin, Socialist son of the Prime Minister. Wild rumours were circulated about Mosley's luxurious life-style. It was said that Mosley had left his Rolls-Royce on the outskirts of the constituency and transferred to a Ford, while Lady Cynthia, said to have a private income of £28,000 a year, had climbed out of a dress embroidered with diamonds into more modest attire. In spite of this unfavourable gossip, Mosley was elected MP on December 21.

On December 24, socialites gathered in London for christening of the Hon. Colin Tennant, infant son of Lord and Lady Glenconner. The font at Holy Trinity Church, Sloane Street was decorated with white heather and the baby wore an old family christening-robe adorned with Valenciennes lace. Among those present was Violet Wyndham, daughter of Oscar Wilde's friend, Ada Leverson.

At the beginning of January, Mr. Oswald and Lady Cynthia Mosley left for the South of France. Both needed a holiday after the strain of the Smethwick by-election. On their way south, they stopped in Paris where they stayed at the Ritz Hotel and Lady Cynthia visited some dressmakers.

On January 6, the Duke and Duchess of York left for a tour of Australia and New Zealand leaving Princess Elizabeth in the care of her grandmother. The couple's suite on board the battle-cruiser *Renown* was fitted with blazing log-fires.

On January 11, Richard Inge, eleven-year-old son of the famous Dean of St. Paul's, went to the Lord Mayor's fancy-dress party dressed as his father in miniature frock-coat and gaiters.

At midnight on January 13, baronet's son Victor Chetwynd removed his wife's coffin from a parish church in Worcestershire and took it by hearse to London. The following morning, the Dean of Worcester arrived to take the funeral and found the church empty. Mr. Chetwynd, who had a house in Curzon Street, Mayfair, later issued a statement via his solicitors that he had decided at the last moment that he would prefer his wife to be buried nearer London.

On January 25, the Dowager Marchioness of Bristol was knocked down by a car in Hyde Park and died afterwards in St. George's Hospital. It was noted that Lady Bristol had been a skilled embroideress in her day and in 1910 had won the Gold Medal of the Fan Makers Company.

At the end of the month, the reputation and character of the late Mr. Gladstone came under scrutiny in the High Court. Seventy-three-year-old Lord Gladstone fiercely rejected a suggestion by author Peter Wright that his father used to 'pursue and possess every sort of woman'. Gold-monocled Mr. Wright counter-attacked by describing Lord Gladstone as an arch-humbug. After several days of legal argument, the court decided that the great Liberal statesman's high moral character had been vindicated. Telegrams of congratulations poured in for Lord Gladstone and several people suggested that Mr. Wright should leave the country.

On February 2, the Earl of Shaftesbury vigorously denied that his twenty-six-year-old son, Lord Ashley, was on the point of marrying actress Sylvia Hawkes, who had recently starred in a show called *Midnight Follies* and was said to be the daughter of a footman. 'My son is not engaged to Miss Hawkes, nor is there any question of his marrying her' he declared. The following day, the couple were married by special licence and a lively reception was held at the Hyde Park Hotel. Among the many young men who had pursued the beautiful young bride was the precocious sixteen-year-old Randolph Churchill.

On February 11, it was rumoured that former Liberal MP and self-confessed master-spy Mr. Trebitsch Lincoln was in Europe trying to raise four million pounds for the Cantonese Army. This shady figure had announced some time ago that he had given up political work for good.

Meanwhile, twenty-three-year-old Cecil Beaton had begun to make a name for himself as a photographer using a tiny box-camera given to him by his mother on his tenth birthday. Among those who had already sat for him were Prince George of Russia and poet Edith Sitwell. 'I only started to take photographs a few weeks ago to pay off my Cambridge debts' he explained on February 24, before leaving for the South of France where he had been invited to stay by Lady Grey of Fallodon at her villa at Cap Ferrat.

On March 27, the public's attention was diverted by a shooting incident at the Gare du Nord in Paris. Sir Humphrey de Trafford's son, Raymond, was on the point of departing for England when the American-born Countess de Janzé plunged into his First Class compartment armed with a gun. After firing at him, she turned the gun on herself. Both were now said to be dangerously ill. 'It is my secret' murmured the Countess when asked to explain her actions.

Back in England, early the next month, Tallulah Bankhead and her young friend, Sir Francis Laking, were involved in a car-crash and had to wander for miles along lonely lanes in Kent.

On April 20, a bearded Dorset farmer named Trelawney Dayrell Reed, appeared in court accused of firing with a double-barrelled shotgun at an aeroplane flying over his land. Forty-eight bullet marks were found in

The young Cecil Beaton with Miss Peggy Broadbent and Miss Joyce Grieg at Leicester Races

the left wing of a machine flown by a certain Squadron Leader W. H. Longdon.

At the end of the month, the wounded Raymond de Trafford was released from hospital in Paris and on his way home to England. His attacker, the Countess de Janzé, had meanwhile been charged with attempted murder and taken to the famous St. Lazare gaol where it was said she was placed in the cell once occupied by the notorious Mata Hari.

On May 5, details were released of the gigantic blocks of service flats which were to be erected on the site of Grosvenor House. This announcement was followed by rumours that Dorchester House, palatial home of the Earl of Morley further down Park Lane, was also to be demolished. 'It is too terrible to contemplate', said Lady Beecham, wife of Sir Thomas. 'If the public wish to save the house for London they must make a strong protest before the completion of the sale.'

On May 18, millionaire Old Etonian Billy Leeds Jr., husband of Princess Xenia of Russia, arrived at Southampton after crossing the Atlantic in a small boat. He brought no clothes with him and immediately ordered sixteen suits.

On May 20, there was a coming-out dance for scientifically-minded Miriam Rothschild. Throughout the Season seventeen-year-old Miriam was to divide her time between the events of high society and her laboratory. Her special subject was parasitology – the study of internal parasites of birds and animals.

On May 22, a new Cochran revue opened at the London Pavilion. Jazz pianist Edyth Baker, rumoured to be a close friend of Prince George, had such an impact that the Earl of Lonsdale dropped his cigar. Also there was the Prince of Wales, slipping out halfway through to join Lady Diana Cooper and others at the Embassy Club in Bond Street.

On May 31, American airman Charles Lindbergh, whose recent solo flight across the Atlantic had amazed the world, was a guest of honour at the Eve of Derby Ball at the Albert Hall. It was observed that the lanky young aviator did not venture on to the dance-floor.

Early in June, an elderly well-dressed man named Arthur Loftus created a stir by claiming to be the rightful Marquess of Ely. In the face of this attack, the real Marquess remained calmly confident, even offering to give £1,000 to charity if Mr. Loftus's claim could be substantiated. 'Why should I be badgered with questions about my birth certificate?' said Mr. Loftus angrily.

On June 15, Mrs. Winston Churchill, wife of the Chancellor of the Exchequer, was knocked down by a bus in Brompton Road. She was able to return to 11 Downing Street by taxi but had to cancel an appointment to open a bazaar that afternoon.

Meanwhile, the Duke and Duchess of York were sailing home after their tour of Australia during which they had been presented with three tons of toys for the infant Princess Elizabeth. They arrived in England on June 27 and moved into 145 Piccadilly at last. It was said to be the first time in history that members of the Royal Family had lived in a house without a name.

On the morning of June 30, millionaire financier Jimmy White was found dead at his racing stables at Foxhill. Rumoured to have been severely hit by the return to the Gold Standard, he had swallowed diluted prussic acid and then pressed a sponge soaked in chloroform to his face. News of his death caused consternation among businessmen lunching at the Savoy Grill that day. In a suicide note, White had written: 'The world is nothing but a human cauldron of greed. My soul is sickened by the homage paid to wealth.'

On July 4, King Fuad of Egypt arrived – his first visit to the country for seventeen years. It was announced that, while in England, the teetotal monarch hoped to meet Bernard Shaw. On July 8, he was present at the Eton-Harrow match at Lords, where spectators ranged from Prime Minister Stanley Baldwin to young photographer Cecil Beaton and on July 12, he dined with the wealthy Mrs. Ronnie Greville at 16 Charles Street.

Another visitor at this time was Madame Consuelo Balsan, former Duchess of Marlborough, who had rented the Inverness-shire estate of the Mackintosh of Mackintosh. In the middle of July, Madame Balsan and her son, Lord Ivor Churchill, were found dining with Lady Cunard at her new house in Grosvenor Square. The American millionairess wore a pearl necklace that had once belonged to Catherine the Great. After dinner, Sir Thomas Beecham, to whom Lady Cunard was devoting much time and energy, conducted a small chamber-orchestra. It was noted that Lady Cunard had recently adopted the Christian name 'Emerald'.

On July 20, it was revealed that Mr. Lionel de Rothschild was moving into 18 Kensington Palace Gardens, the former home of Lord Lee of Fareham. Panelling from Mr. de Rothschild's house in Park Street would be moved to his new forty-bedroom mansion.

On July 29, swindler Horatio Bottomley was released from Maidstone Prison after five years' incarceration. He was driven straight to his large red-brick mansion in Sussex, known as 'The Dicker'. Flags were out in the village and his wife and daughter were there to greet him. It was revealed that the former MP had signed a contract to write a series of articles for the *Weekly Despatch* for £12,000.

A day or two later, Mrs. Reginald Coke gave a party at her house in Carlisle Square, Chelsea, at which guests were asked to dress as tramps. Sybil Thorndike and Osbert Sitwell were among those who attended.

On August 6, Lord Herbert's coming-of-age was celebrated with a spectacular dance at Wilton. Among the 600 guests were writer Rudyard Kipling, ablaze with decorations, the secretly-married couple Lord Weymouth and Daphne Vivian and thirty-year-old Chicago-born writer Henry Channon, known to his friends as 'Chips'. Early in the evening the young Cecil Beaton was frog-marched across the candle-lit lawns and thrown into the river.

In the middle of August, the King was to be found shooting with the Duke of Devonshire at Bolton Abbey in Yorkshire, where lunch was served on the moors on plates bearing the ducal crest, while his son and heir, the Prince of Wales, was at Sandwich with his long-standing friend Mrs. Freda Dudley Ward and her two daughters, Angela and Penelope.

On August 31, wealthy Princess Lowenstein-Wertheim left for America in a tiny Fokker monoplane. Two hat-boxes were among her luggage. It was soon announced from New York that the plane was long overdue and the Princess's sister decided to presume that she was dead.

Early in September, the almost forgotten former Prime Minister Lord Rosebery, who had been living in total seclusion for many years, was to be found staying at Dalmeny House near Edinburgh. Here he created a sensation by driving around the neighbourhood in a coach-and-pair, accompanied by a liveried outrider.

On September 14, holiday-makers on the Riviera were shocked to hear of the violent death of Miss Isadora Duncan, foremost exponent of the ancient Greek dance. After dinner at a hotel in Nice, Miss Duncan's long scarf caught in the front wheel of her car; she was pulled on to the road, dragged under the car and strangled.

During the last week in September, it was announced that Lady Ossulston, wife of the heir to Lord

*Mrs. Dudley Ward, close friend of
the Prince of Wales*

Tankerville, had started a laundry. Lady Ossulston told reporters that she was trying to abolish the use of laundry marks.

At the beginning of October, George Bernard Shaw moved into a new flat, 130 Whitehall Court, near the Houses of Parliament. An American admirer attempted to purchase the fireplace of the playwright's old flat in the Adelphi, but was thwarted by the landlord.

On October 16, an elderly clergyman named G. R. Bullock-Webster stood up in front of a huge congregation at St. Paul's Cathedral and denounced the Bishop of Birmingham, who was about to preach. After accusing the Bishop of attacking the treasured beliefs of Christians and demanding that he should be tried for heresy, Mr. Bullock-Webster marched out accompanied by several thousand supporters. 'I have nothing to say in reference to a brawler like that' said Dean Inge afterwards. 'We could, if we liked, take proceedings against him. I don't suppose we shall.'

On October 21, it was announced that Violet Duchess of Rutland had disposed of the family mansion in Arlington Street to a syndicate, though she herself was continuing to live in the lodge, which she had now done up in oriental fashion.

On October 27, Lord Weymouth and Daphne Vivian were publicly married at St. Martin-in-the-Fields, while still keeping their marriage of the previous year a secret. The King's sister, Princess Victoria, gave the bride a ruby-and-diamond brooch and Mrs. Corrigan gave the bridegroom a pair of white elastic braces with gold fittings engraved with his initials. A reception was held at Dorchester House, Park Lane, now under threat of demolition.

On November 7, it was announced that financial pressures had forced the Earl of Lonsdale to sell Barleythorpe, his famous hunting-lodge in the heart of the Cottesmore country. It was said that the famous sporting Earl's life had become a permanent battle with his Trustees.

On November 22, it was announced that young Lord Alington, a close friend of Tallulah Bankhead, had let

Crichel, his exquisite Adam house in Dorset in the midst of an 18,000-acre estate, to Sir Hugo Cunliffe-Owen, chairman of the British American Tobacco Company. Thirty-two-year-old Lord Alington was now busy standing as Conservative County Council candidate for Shoreditch.

Meanwhile, Lord and Lady Weymouth were back from their official honeymoon on the Riviera. Shortly after their return, Lady Weymouth created a sensation when she appeared at a dance at Wimborne House in honour of the Queen of Spain wearing her wedding-dress.

On December 6, twenty-one-year-old Lady Furness gave a dance in honour of the Duke of Spoleto. Shortly before midnight, the gathering was enriched by the arrival of the Prince of Wales, who had recently made close friends with the young hostess.

On December 16, Stoke Edith, near Hereford, one of the finest sixteenth-century houses in the country, was destroyed by fire. The seventy-year-old owner, Mr. Paul Foley, summoned his private fire-brigade who managed to save some of the works of art in the house, including a fine Flemish tapestry, but the house was ruined. Next morning, Mr. Foley was found resting in a gardener's cottage.

On December 21, the Earl of Lonsdale, Winston Churchill, Lady Diana Cooper and Labour leader Ramsay MacDonald, were present at the opening of the circus at Olympia. At the end of the performance, Lord Lonsdale, puffing at a huge cigar, presented each female artiste with a bouquet.

Over in Paris, on December 23, the Chicago-born Countess de Janzé came up for trial charged with attempted murder of Mr. Raymond de Trafford at the Gare du Nord. At the trial, Mr. de Trafford gave evidence on her behalf and she was sentenced to six months imprisonment and a fine amounting in English money to just 16s.6d. Under the First Offenders Act she was released immediately.

On Christmas Day, Mrs. Meyrick's luxurious new club, the Silver Slipper in Regent Street, was raided by police. Scores of officers charged onto the glass dance-floor just as a Cossack dance was being performed and innumerable arrests were made.

Stoke Edith burning

The newly wed Lord and Lady Weymouth

1928

On January 1, it was revealed that little Princess Elizabeth had already learnt to curtsy and would demonstrate her newly acquired skill to visitors to her nursery at 145 Piccadilly.

On January 6, the Thames burst its banks and many houses near the river were flooded out. Night-clubbers hurried to the scene at daybreak while overhead the sixty-two-year-old Duchess of Bedford inspected the damage in her Gypsy Moth biplane. Lord Desborough, chairman of the Thames Conservancy Board, followed developments from Chatsworth, where he was staying with the Duke of Devonshire. 'The catastrophe was purely the result of a tidal wave' he said. 'It was not caused by conditions in the river itself.'

On January 9, Chancellor of the Exchequer Winston Churchill and his sixteen-year-old son Randolph left for two days boar-hunting with the Duke of Westminster in his forests in Dieppe. A pack of 200 hounds and twenty horses had been shipped from England for the hunt.

On January 24, news came from New York that Mr. James Corrigan, Chairman of the Corrigan-McKinney Steel Corporation, had died leaving the bulk of his sixty million dollar fortune to his wife, Laura – already well-established in London as a most resourceful party-giver. It was soon announced that Mrs. Corrigan, who was rumoured to be totally bald under her wig, would not be entertaining in England this year but instead going on a long cultural tour of Europe.

American hostess Laura Corrigan at a garden party in London

Early in February, it was revealed that the Hon. Henry Lygon, brother of the powerful Liberal leader, Earl Beauchamp, was running a 500-year-old inn near Smithfield Market, the Hand and Shears. 'The ordinary type of public house is nothing less than a drink den' said Mr. Lygon. 'I shall make this historic tavern a place where a man can take his wife.'

Meanwhile, the former Prime Minister, Lord Oxford and Asquith, was dying at his Thames-side home, the Wharf, Sutton Courtenay, with his wife Margot at his side. On February 15, at seven in the morning, the butler appeared at the door and announced that it was all over. Lord Oxford was succeeded by his eleven-year-old grandson, Julian.

On February 16, historic Dorchester House in Park Lane was sold to developers for £500,000. It was announced that a hotel, the most luxurious in the British Isles, would be erected on the site. It would have 600 bedrooms and a dining room overlooking Hyde Park. 'The work of demolishing Dorchester House will begin almost at once' said a spokesman.

On February 20, attention turned to the Old Bailey where a seventy-year-old clergyman, the Rev. Francis Bacon, was on trial accused of supplying poisonous drugs to women. 'Your conduct during the last ten years has been despicable and deplorable. You have concealed your illicit trade beneath a cloak of hypocrisy' said the judge, sending Bacon to prison for fifteen months.

On February 28, the Duchess of Marlborough gave a fancy-dress party at 7 Carlton House Terrace. Winston Churchill came as Emperor Nero, the Prince of Wales was thinly disguised by a red domino mask and the Earl of Birkenhead appeared as Cardinal Wolsey. Powdered footmen in crimson livery were in attendance.

The same night, police were called to deal with riots at the Globe Theatre where Miss Tallulah Bankhead was appearing in a play called *Blackmail*. People who could not get tickets had rushed the doors and forced their way into the auditorium, where there were ugly scenes.

On March 13, King Amanullah and Queen Souriya of Afghanistan arrived in London accompanied by 100 pieces of luggage. A banquet was held for them that night at Buckingham Palace at which the Afghan Queen wore her diamond and sapphire bracelets and her husband glittered in a blue and scarlet uniform, with gold fixtures and fittings. Queen Mary wore the priceless Koh-i-Noor diamond.

Another visitor to London this month was blind American millionaire, Mr. A. J. Wright. It was announced that he had rented Lady Curzon's house, 1 Carlton House Terrace, for the Season. Rumours circulated that Mr. Wright had made his entire fortune on the rubber market since going blind.

On March 16, news flashed round the world that there had been a mutiny on board the battleship *Royal Oak* stationed at Gibraltar. Two officers had decided that their commanding officer, Rear-Admiral Collard, was unfit to run the ship. They were court martialled and found guilty of mutiny but later the sentences were squashed and the Rear-Admiral was put on the retired list. On April 8, the participants in this strange affair all shook hands.

On April 9, it was announced that another daughter of the famous Mrs. Meyrick was to marry into the peerage. Miss May Meyrick, currently managing the Riviera Hotel, Maidenhead, was to marry the young Earl of Kinnoull. 'Please say that I am now a simple country girl' she begged reporters.

On April 13, Royal Academician Charles Sims leapt from a railway viaduct above the River Tweed and fell 150 feet into the swirling waters. Sims, whose controversial portrait of the King had been withdrawn from the Royal Academy Exhibition in 1925, had been staying nearby at Ravenswood, the Roxburghshire mansion of a certain Mrs. Younger, and was said to be suffering from insomnia.

On April 16, self-made businessman Solly Joel celebrated the long run of his show *Desert Song* with a party at the Theatre Royal Drury Lane. Sparing no expense, the stage of the theatre was transformed into an exact replica of the deck of Mr. Joel's yacht, *Eileen*. Among the guests was one-armed General Trotter, close friend and Equerry to the Prince of Wales.

On April 28, Millicent Duchess of Sutherland announced that she was organising a fund for Adolphe, a famous old waiter at the Buffet Terminus at Calais. It was said that Adolphe, who had frequently served the late King Edward VII and had been one of the first recipients of the Royal Victorian Order, had recently lost a leg and fallen on hard times.

On May 2, distinguished economist Sir Leo Money and twenty-two-year-old Miss Irene Savidge appeared in court accused of misbehaving on a bench in Hyde Park. Halfway through hearing the evidence, the magistrate stopped the case and ordered the dismissal of the defendants. 'We sat down for a while to discuss matters of industrial economics' said Miss Savidge afterwards. The subsequent Home Office enquiry into the case took the form of two police officers calling on Miss Savidge at her place of work, whisking her to Scotland Yard and interrogating her for five and a half hours.

Meanwhile, an Indian Army officer named Major Graham Bell Murray had sued the police for wrongful arrest on a drunk and disorderly charge. On May 30, he was offered £500 compensation, much to the indignation of his wife. 'The offer which the Home Office has made my husband is nothing but an insult' she said.

On June 10, the sixty-two-year-old Duchess of Bedford left Lympne Aerodrome in a bid to fly to India and back in eight days, flatly refusing to admit that it was a thrilling venture. 'Interesting, yes, but not thrilling' she snapped. 'I am never thrilled.' Unfortunately, the little plane ran into difficulties en route and the Duchess did not return to England until the end of the summer.

Nightclub Queen Mrs. Kate Meyrick

On June 22, Mrs. Meyrick was again in court accused of selling alcohol without a licence at the 43 Club in Gerrard Street. She pleaded guilty to all the charges and begged for mercy. 'I submit that she is the most inveterate lawbreaker with regard to licensing matters that the police have ever dealt with in the metropolis' said prosecuting counsel, Mr. Muskett. Mrs. Meyrick heard herself sentenced to another term of six months imprisonment and was led away from the court in tears.

On June 26, 10,000 people packed into Olympia to see the Prince of Wales present a gold casket to Lord and Lady Lonsdale on the occasion of their golden wedding. 'Besides this casket' declared the Prince, 'there is a considerable sum which will be handed to Lord Lonsdale for him to distribute to charity in whatever way he thinks fit.' The veteran sporting peer was then given a cheque believed to be for £300,000. In his reply to the Prince, he said 'Anything we have done in the interests of sport has been done because we love it.'

The following night, Lord Lonsdale gave a dinner-party at his town house, 14 Carlton House Terrace, two houses knocked together, at which almost the whole Royal Family were present. After dinner, Jack Buchanan and Cicely Courtneidge presented a cabaret, supported by dancers from the Embassy Club.

On July 9, Lady Ellesmere in an emerald and diamond tiara presided over a ball at Bridgwater House overlooking Green Park. Dancing took place in a vast gallery hung with paintings by Titian, Raphael and Tintoretto, said to be Britain's largest private art collection, and the gathering was honoured by the presence of the much-fêted Earl of Lonsdale, wearing the Garter ribbon and other decorations.

Unfortunately this party had disagreeable repercussions. The following day, Lady Ellesmere announced that several hundred people had gate-crashed the function and identified Cecil Beaton's sister, Baba, as one of the offenders. Lady Catherine Willoughby, daughter of the Earl of Ancaster, was also publicly accused of bringing two uninvited guests. These remarks caused much resentment and for a while, a war was waged in Mayfair between opposing families. Lady Ellesmere stuck to her guns. 'The problem of the uninvited guest will have to be dealt with most severely' she said.

On July 13, Old Etonian Brian Howard threw a party at St. George's Swimming Bath. Guests were asked to bring a bathing-suit and a bottle. A negro orchestra played and a special 'Bathwater Cocktail' was served.

On July 21, former Grenadier Guards officer Ernest Simpson married thirty-two-year-old Baltimore-born Mrs. Wallis Spencer at Chelsea Registry Office. A wedding breakfast was held in a sitting-room at the Grosvenor Hotel, Victoria Station, after which the couple left in a chauffeur-driven yellow Lagonda for their honeymoon in France.

Meanwhile, a number of Indian princes gathered in London for an India Office conference. On July 26, a banquet was held in their honour at Buckingham Palace. Among those present was the Maharajah of Kashmir, the central figure in the 'Mr. A' case of 1924, who was said to own 84,000 square miles and the Maharajah of Patiala, who was rumoured to spend £31,000 a year on his underwear.

At the beginning of August, it was announced that Sir Henri Deterding, powerful chairman of the Royal Dutch Shell Oil Company, had rented Achnacarry Castle, Inverness-shire, historic seat of the Camerons of Lochiel. Sir Henri's guest at the castle was Walter Teagle, president of Standard Oil. 'They are both here for a little fishing and a little shooting. Their meeting has no commercial significance' said a spokesman. The public's credulity was further stretched on August 13 when Sir J. Cadman, chairman of the Anglo-Persian Oil Company joined the party. It was later revealed that the three tycoons faced a glut in oil and were plotting to keep prices up by depressing production.

On August 21, Tallulah Bankhead opened at the Lyric Theatre in *Her Cardboard Lover*. Large crowds gathered outside the theatre and Miss Bankhead's new pale-cream Bentley was practically overturned by her fans.

Meanwhile, a storm had broken over a newly-published novel *The Well of Loneliness* said to describe a lesbian love affair. 'I would rather give a healthy boy or girl a phial of prussic acid than this book' wrote Mr. James Douglas in the *Sunday Express*. A copy had been sent to the Director of Public Prosecutions and on August 23 the Home Secretary ordered that it should be banned. 'Two years of incessant work following many years of deep study have suffered at the hands of wilful ignorance' said the author Miss Radclyffe Hall, a striking figure often to be seen in starched shirt, monocle and dinner jacket, who had shared the last few years of her life with Lady Troubridge, former wife of Admiral Sir Ernest Troubridge.

The following month Mr. Winston Churchill was found staying at Balmoral Castle for a few days fishing and stalking. Also there was the serious-looking two-year-old Princess Elizabeth. Mr. Churchill was the only person present who was not a member of the Royal Family.

Radclyffe Hall, author of the controversial novel The Well of Loneliness

On September 27, the infant daughter of Lord and Lady Weymouth was christened at St. Martin-in-the-Fields. The baby wore a pink satin bonnet and her grandfather, the Marquess of Bath, was resplendent in a frock-coat.

At the beginning of October, the Prince of Wales left for a semi-private tour of East Africa. On reaching Nairobi, he was joined by his new friend, Lady Furness, who nursed him through the bad attack of malaria with which he was struck down a few weeks later. Also on the trip was General Trotter and the twenty-eight-year-old Prince Henry.

On October 22, the remains of eight members of the Royal Family were removed from the crypt of St. George's Chapel, Windsor and re-interred at Frogmore. To avoid publicity, this queer operation took place late at night and in pitch darkness. It was explained that, in future, only sovereigns would be buried at Windsor.

On October 27, the Duke of Manchester applied for a discharge from bankruptcy. He claimed that his debts of £129,656 had arisen partly as a result of the money he had invested in a new cure for consumption. 'I regard this case as one of unjustifiable and reckless extravagance' said the Registrar suspending the Duke's discharge for another three years.

Early in November, twenty-six-year-old boxing baronet Sir John Milbanke announced his engagement to Australian-born Sheila Lady Loughborough. The marriage took place a few days later at the Chapel Royal at the Savoy. Lady Diana Cooper forgot to bring her invitation card and had a few moments difficulty persuading the verger that she was a bona fide guest.

Meanwhile, the controversial novel *The Well of Loneliness* had been republished in Paris and a large consignment of copies destined for the English market had been seized by the police at Dover. On November 17, the author, Radclyffe Hall, was present in the crowded Bow Street courtroom to hear the magistrate decree that 287 copies of the book should be thrown into the Scotland Yard furnace. 'This is not the end' she told reporters as she left the building.

On November 27, Tallulah Bankhead announced her engagement to Count Anthony de Bosdari, man-about-town who was said to be a relation of the King of Italy as well as having an interest in a gramophone company.

Two days later, Mrs. Meyrick was released from Holloway Prison, being met at the gates by her daughter May, now the Countess of Kinnoull. That night there was a supper-party at the Silver Slipper, Mrs. Meyrick's luxury establishment in Regent Street. A rumour circulated that the Queen of the London Nightclubs was going to take up chicken farming.

On December 1, only ten days after her release from Holloway, a new warrant was issued for the arrest of Mrs. Meyrick. This time she faced grave charges under the Prevention of Corruption Act. For some time, rumours had been circulating about large bribes paid to members of the police force by nightclub proprietors, and recently more than £12,000 in cash had been found in a West End safe deposit in the name of a policeman named Goddard. Hearing of the warrant, Mrs. Meyrick returned at once from Paris where she had been enjoying a brief holiday and surrendered to the police at Folkestone. The following day she was released on £1,000 bail. 'The police are always so kind to me' she remarked.

Meanwhile, the King had fallen desperately ill at Buckingham Palace. Alarming bulletins were issued about his feverish condition and anxious crowds of several thousand drifted around the palace gates. At one moment, a rumour circulated that the King was dead.

On December 11, the Prince of Wales arrived back from East Africa having hurried across two continents in a record six days after receiving an urgent summons from the Prime Minister, Stanley Baldwin. On seeing his son and heir again that evening, it was rumoured that the semi-conscious King immediately perked up and said: 'Damn you, what the devil are you doing here?'

Two days later, the Prince of Wales and the Duke of York played a leisurely game of squash at the Royal Automobile Club in Pall Mall and the public attention was diverted away from the national crisis to other matters.

On December 16, actress Hermione Baddeley reported that she had heard strange noises in the old Wiltshire manor-house recently acquired by her husband, David Tennant. The house had been the home of the late Viscountess Grey, a famous spiritualist, and Miss Baddeley had had a disturbing night in her ladyship's old bedroom. 'Without a doubt I formed the impression that there was someone walking in my room' she said.

On December 18, Almina, Countess of Carnarvon threw a party in her large house in Seamore Place, in honour of the ex-King and Queen of Greece. Among the guests was young Lady Ashley, former starlet Sylvia Hawkes, whose sensational marriage to the heir to the Earl of Shaftesbury the previous year had made headline news.

At Christmas, the Royal Family congregated at Buckingham Palace instead of Sandringham for the first time for ten years. The King's health had now greatly improved and, on Christmas morning, he gave Queen Mary a beautiful pink topaz and diamond pendant.

On New Year's Eve, Lady Ednam gave a sedate dance in the ballroom of the new Grosvenor House. Among her guests was Sir Philip Sassoon, owner of one of the last great houses left in Park Lane.

On January 3, the Lord Chancellor, Lord Hailsham, was secretly married to thirty-five-year-old Mrs. Mildred Lawrence. A car whisked him from the House of Lords to Westminster Abbey where the service was performed by the Dean of Westminster, Dr. Foxley-Norris, with the Lord Chancellor's son, twenty-one-year-old Quintin Hogg, acting as best man.

On January 14, a spectacular double suicide took place in a service flat in St. James's. Two eminent Harley Street specialists, twin brothers Arthur and Sidney Smith, were found with their throats cut. A few hours earlier, they had given their services free at an operation and had also contributed £2,000 worth of radium needles. 'I cannot imagine what led to their ghastly resolution' said a shocked colleague.

All three of Queen Victoria's surviving children were meanwhile to be found on the Riviera. Princess Beatrice was at San Remo, silver-haired Princess Louise was at Cap Ferrat, and the Duke of Connaught was at Beaulieu sitting for his portrait by Sir John Lavery, who was staying nearby at the Villa d'Enchantement on Mrs. Benjamin Guinness's estate.

On January 21, Mrs. Meyrick appeared at the Old Bailey facing charges of bribery and corruption. The fifty-two-year-old nightclub proprietor sobbed in the dock as great wads of £10 notes with which it was alleged she had bribed Detective-Sergeant Goddard of the Vice Squad were handed to the jury for their perusal. 'I swear on my soul that I never paid Goddard one penny piece' said Mrs. Meyrick later in the witness-box. But the jury was unconvinced and on January 29, Mr. Justice Avory sentenced her to fifteen months hard labour.

On January 30, beautiful Diana Mitford, third daughter of Lord and Lady Redesdale, married Bryan Guinness, son of the Minister of Agriculture. Randolph Churchill came down from Oxford to join his father at the ceremony at St. Margaret's Westminster. A reception was held at the large Guinness house in Grosvenor Place as the bride's home in Rutland Gate had already been let and the Redesdales were living in its mews cottage, known in the family as 'The Garage'.

Meanwhile, an announcement had come from Buckingham Palace that the King would go to Bognor to continue his convalescence. Industrialist Sir Arthur du Cros had offered the monarch the use of a large green-and-white villa facing the sea, breaking the news to his servants by saying: 'A very rich man who has been ill is coming to stay here.'

On February 8, the King left Buckingham Palace in an ambulance driven by his chauffeur Mr. Humphreys. His silver-plated bed from the Royal Yacht had already been transferred to the villa, along with a retinue of no less than fifty servants. The Queen travelled separately in her own car. Soon after his arrival on the coast, there was more good news. 'The King has begun to smoke again' said a spokesman, 'and he is now able to cut up his own food.'

On February 23, a storm blew up in the village of Sutton Courtenay over plans to move the grave of Lord Oxford and Asquith fifteen yards in order to make room for a larger memorial. Although the move had been sanctioned by the Home Office and the church authorities, villagers feared that their ancestors' graves would be disturbed. 'Why should their bones be dug up to make room for Lord Oxford?' demanded a prominent member of the local community.

On March 5, a certain Colonel Barker, said to be a prominent figure in the British Fascist movement, was arrested for failing to attend a bankruptcy examination. Much public interest was excited when it was revealed that the tall, portly Colonel was, in fact, a woman. Interest rose to fever pitch when it was discovered that on 14 November 1923 the 'Colonel' had married a young woman in a church in Brighton. The marriage had not been a success and the couple had lived apart for several years. 'This is terrible' said the mother of the girl involved. 'My daughter nearly fainted when she read the news.'

On March 7, 'Colonel Barker', whose real name was Lillias Arkell-Smith, was admitted to Holloway Prison.

*The remarkable Colonel
Barker, who turned out to be a
woman*

Mounted Police were called to control a crowd of over 1,000 people who quickly assembled outside the prison-gates in the hopes of catching a glimpse of this astonishing woman. The following day, the Colonel's lawyer, Mr. Freke Palmer, made a successful application for bail.

On March 21, crowds gathered outside St. Columba's Church, Pont Street, following the marriage of Lord Inverclyde, who had inherited £2,000,000 on the death of his father, and the popular musical comedy star, known simply as June.

On March 23, Lord Lansdowne sold his vast family house on the south-west corner of Berkeley Square for £750,000. The last tenant of the house before it was gutted and transformed was Mr. Gordon Selfridge, who had recently become infatuated by one of the Dolly Sisters and was spending his fortune on her.

At the end of the month, Lady Furness, new friend of the Prince of Wales, gave birth to a baby boy at her country home, Burrough Court near Melton Mowbray. Lord and Lady Furness were already drifting apart and the birth of a son did not bring them together.

On April 2, the convalescent King emerged to greet holiday crowds at Bognor and listen to the band. The same day, the Queen visited a local jumble sale and presented the organisers with a bunch of primroses she had picked in the garden of their rented villa. These were put up for auction and raised £6.10.0.

On April 21, Princess Elizabeth's third birthday was celebrated at Naseby Hall in the heart of the Pytchley country. The Queen sent her grand-daughter a clockwork monkey. The Prince of Wales sent his niece a live Cairn terrier pup.

The King and Queen at Bognor

On April 25, Lillias Arkell-Smith, better known as Colonel Barker, pleaded guilty at the Old Bailey to making a false statement in a marriage register. Sir Henry Curtis-Bennett in a plea for mercy suggested that the defendant had already suffered enough, but the judge was unmoved. 'You are an unprincipled, mendacious and unscrupulous adventuress' he told the woman before him. 'You have profaned the house of God, outraged the decencies of nature and broken the laws of man.' On being sentenced to nine months imprisonment, Colonel Barker, who wore a man's mackintosh in court, bowed low and marched out of the dock.

On May 1, Tallulah Bankhead confirmed reports that her engagement to Count Anthony de Bosdari was over. 'Tony and I are still devoted to each other' she said. 'He is a perfect darling and I adore him. We have just agreed that things have become impossible because he has his work to do and I have mine.' It was rumoured that Tallulah had also discovered that the vast diamond necklace her fiancé had given her had not been paid for.

On May 3, Winston Churchill received a £10,000 advance from publisher George Harrap for a biography of his ancestor, the 1st Duke of Marlborough. It was said that Churchill had been longing to write this book since the turn of the century.

On May 21, former Prime Minister Lord Rosebery died at Durdans, his house near Epsom. The eighty-two-year-old peer, who had succeeded Gladstone as Premier in 1894, had spent the last twenty years of his life in total seclusion. For some time, he had been confined to a wheelchair; to accommodate it a special car with double back doors had been constructed. Rosebery left Durdans to his daughter Lady Sybil Grant. It was noted that Mentmore Towers, his famous treasure house near Leighton Buzzard, had been made over to his son and heir Lord Dalmeny some years earlier.

On May 30, Ramsay MacDonald's Labour Party was returned to power in the General Election. Defeated Conservative leader, Stanley Baldwin moved to 10 Upper Brook Street, where yellow net curtains were soon seen in all the windows – an attempt on the part of Mrs. Baldwin to create an atmosphere of permanent sunshine in the house.

The Labour victory immediately revived socialist hostess Lady Warwick's interest in the political scene and the Prime Minister, Ramsay MacDonald, and other Labour leaders were soon to be found staying again at Easton Lodge, Lady Warwick's large stately home in Essex.

On June 18, the King and Queen did not attend the opening of Ascot week. On this occasion they were represented by the King's uncle, the grand old Duke of Connaught, who arrived at the racecourse in a motor-car with the Royal Standard fluttering from its bonnet.

At the end of the month, the public's attention was diverted to the new automatic equipment at the Sloane telephone exchange. It was stated that the equipment was suffering from a new telephone disease called 'permanent busy-back', causing hourly confusion for the area's wealthy subscribers. 'I have two lines and three extensions in this house' said author Arnold Bennett of 73 Cadogan Square, 'and I have had the most fantastic trouble.'

On July 1, there was a rather joyless reception at Londonderry House for the defeated Conservative Party. Many of the guests were glad to go on afterwards to a party given by young couturier Norman Hartnell at 17 Bruton Street, former home of the Strathmore family and the birthplace of Princess Elizabeth. It was described as a 'circus' party. Performing bears and Siberian wolf-cubs were in evidence and Lady Eleanor Smith, daughter of Lord Birkenhead, led a white pony up the staircase. Nancy Mitford, Lady Sibell Lygon and other bright young people were entertained by a circus orchestra, a jazz band and an Italian accordion quartet.

On July 10, many of the same people were present at a much stranger gathering at Mrs. Rosemary Sandars' house in Rutland Gate. Everyone was asked to come as a baby. Dolls, bottles and comforters were provided, a bar was set up in a baby's pen and activities took place which were later described in the Press as 'the type of behaviour which leads to Communism'.

By this time, the Café de Paris, an oval-shaped underground room approached by a double curving staircase beneath the Rialto Cinema in Coventry Street, had emerged as a fashionable new meeting-place. On July 31, the Prince of Wales was seen there with his friend Lady Furness and his faithful Equerry, General Trotter.

On August 4, thirty-six-year-old Lord Loughborough, whose wife Sheila had married Sir John Milbanke the previous year, was found dying in the garden of a house in Holland Road. He had fallen from a fourth-floor window onto some crazy paving. Earlier in the evening he had been in a cheerful mood; one report said he had been in high spirits at the 43 Club, and his unexpected suicide shocked London.

On August 10, it was announced that the Prince of Wales had acquired a permanent residence on the edge of Windsor Great Park. It was a curious, castellated eighteenth-century building known as Fort Belvedere and later described by Lady Diana Cooper as 'a child's idea of a fort'.

On August 13, the Thames was dragged following the sudden disappearance of Eton's Vice Provost, sixty-seven-year-old Mr. Hugh Macnaghten. This much-loved figure, said to be a student of auto-suggestion, had last been seen on August 10 at a country club on the river. 'The circumstance of his disappearance naturally gives rise to considerable anxiety and one cannot rule out the possibility of a mishap' said the Vice Provost's brother.

On August 14, young Lord Howard of Effingham appeared in the dock at Bow Street following a fight outside Mrs. Meyrick's 43 Club in which seventy or eighty people had been involved. He pleaded guilty to insulting behaviour and was bound over to keep the peace.

On August 26, three men appeared at Marlborough Street Police Court charged with stealing Lady Diana Cooper's motor-car valued at £500. In the car at the time were a peacock brooch, a gold pencil-case and a golfing-suit. One of the defendants was wearing the golfing-suit when he was arrested.

In the middle of the next month, Lady Diana was in the news again when she gave birth to a baby boy in Lady Carnarvon's newly-opened nursing home in Portland Place. The child was later given the name John Julius and the Aga Khan, Lady Oxford, Lord Beaverbrook and several other illustrious figures were appointed godparents.

On September 19, the City was shocked to hear that brilliant young financier Clarence Hatry was struggling to save his group of companies. The group, of which the sixty-six-year-old Marquess of Winchester was chairman, had once been valued at £10,000,000. Hatry's house in Great Stanhope Street had a heated swimming-pool in its basement and was said to be 'like something out of Arabian Nights'.

On September 20, Hatry was arrested and charged with conspiring to obtain £209,141 by false pretences. He was removed to Brixton Prison where a woman in his employment was later seen arriving with a large wicker hamper said to be filled with luxury provisions.

Meanwhile, Prime Minister Ramsay MacDonald was preparing for a trip to America, currently engulfed in its Great Depression. He departed on September 28 on board the former German vessel *Berengaria* occupying a suite with his daughter Ishbel that had originally been designed for the Kaiser.

On October 6, the Aga Khan, spiritual head of seventy million people, announced his engagement to Mlle. Andrée Carron, whose name had been linked with his throughout the decade. 'I refused to discuss my intentions till now because I had not made any definite decision' said the oriental potentate, who until now had dismissed rumours of his impending marriage as 'nothing but a cock and bull story'.

Meanwhile, the Aga Khan's handsome eighteen-year-old son, Prince Aly, had rented a vast house in Carlton House Terrace where he hoped to study in peace for his bar exams. 'My ambition is to hunt a pack of hounds in Ireland before I settle down in India in three or four years time' said the wealthy young Prince.

On October 18, Sir John and Lady Lavery gave a lunch-party at their house in Cromwell Place at which young John Julius Cooper made his debut. For the first few months of his life, Lady Diana Cooper carried her baby everywhere wrapped in a monogrammed cashmere shawl.

A few days later, Mary Pickford, who had recently been booed after her first appearance in a 'talkie', arrived in London with her husband Douglas Fairbanks. They had been invited to stay at Brook House, the Park Lane mansion of their friend Lady Louis Mountbatten, where on a previous visit they had signed a photograph of themselves with the inscription: 'To duckie Edwina, from Mary and Doug'.

On November 1, Ramsay MacDonald returned from America in high spirits and went to visit his new friend Lady Londonderry. It was whispered that the Prime Minister's friendship with this most distinguished of hostesses saved Britain from the more extreme forms of Socialism in the years ahead.

On November 15, the mysterious death of the Hon. Richard Bethell, archaeologist son of Lord Westbury, caused much interest and gossip. Superstitious people pointed out that Bethell had been involved in the Tutankhamen excavation and recalled the grim prophecy: 'Death shall come on swift wings to him that toucheth the pharoes tomb.' Bethell was said to be the thirteenth person to die who had been involved in the expedition.

Meanwhile, Queen Mary had completed her Christmas shopping. Her purchases included strange brocade-covered 'cupboards' in which her friends could hide their telephones.

At the beginning of December, Augustus John began work on a portrait of Tallulah Bankhead. The fashionable painter caught a baleful look in the beautiful actress which annoyed many of her friends but seemed to delight the sitter. Sessions took place in the artist's studio in Mallord Street, Chelsea.

On December 15, the release of 'Colonel Barker' from Holloway Prison went more or less unnoticed by the Press. Remaining at the gaol was Mrs. Meyrick, serving a fifteen-month sentence for bribery and corruption. The nightclub owner's weak condition prompted her son, Old Harrovian Lester Meyrick, to petition the Home Secretary for an early release.

On December 20, the Earl of Lonsdale once again attended the opening of Bertram Mills Circus at Olympia. On this occasion, his party included Lord Wavertree, artist Dame Laura Knight and Lady Alexandra Metcalfe, who wore a dress of deep sapphire blue. As was his habit, at the end of the show, Lord Lonsdale presented each female artiste with a bouquet.

The decade ended with Clarence Hatry on remand at Brixton Prison, awaiting trial on charges involving millions of pounds. On Christmas morning, he was offered a choice of tea or coffee and with his Christmas dinner, he was permitted half a pint of wine. The famous financier had now declared himself to be 'irretrievably and irreparably ruined'.

THE THIRTIES
1930–1939

The Thirties began with England, along with the rest of the world, in the grips of an economic depression. Unemployment was soon jumping between two and three million, many more of the great town houses were disbanded and Prince Aly Khan was found running for a bus in Piccadilly. When a contingent of unemployed men invaded the Savoy Hotel and lay down in the lobby, many people feared the Capitalist system itself was doomed. These upheavals at last forced the upper classes to become politically conscious. Many were converted to Socialism, a few to Communism while others appeared to adopt the Fascist cause, rallying around the German Ambassador Herr von Ribbentrop and gathering at Cliveden where Lady Astor's house-parties were said to have a distinctly pro-Hitler flavour. Few went as far as Miss Unity Mitford, who set off for Germany and made intimate friends with the Führer himself. Though social life was somewhat simplified and wealthy women deliberately dressed in a slightly plainer style, the parties and pageantry continued until the outbreak of war. These years saw the debut of Miss Margaret Whigham, beautiful daughter of a Scottish industrialist, and the emergence of the Baltimore-born Mrs. Ernest Simpson, whose friendship with the heir to the throne caused deep distress to the elderly King George V.

1930

The new decade opened with banner headlines proclaiming the engagement of the twice-married Duke of Westminster and Miss Loelia Ponsonby, twenty years his junior. It was reported that the couple were currently cruising down the Dalmatian Coast on board the Duke's 1,000-ton yacht *Flying Cloud*.

This excitement was quickly followed by rumours of a romance between the wealthy Countess of Seafield, peeress in her own right, and Mr. Derek Studley-Herbert. On January 10 it was revealed that the couple had thwarted the Countess's trustees by taking out a special licence and marrying in secret. The *Banffshire Journal* immediately voiced its fury, claiming that local inhabitants had been cheated out of a spectacular occasion.

On January 14, a new novel called *Vile Bodies* was published launching its twenty-six-year-old author, Evelyn Waugh, into high society. It was stated in a gossip column that Waugh had recently been staying with the Longford family at Pakenham Hall in Ireland where he had won a £2 bet by scaling an iron staircase up a tower.

Meanwhile, imposing, white-haired Mrs. George Keppel, a former mistress of Edward VII, had arrived in London for a brief visit. Mrs. Keppel had now established herself as the reigning Queen of the British community in Florence and the treasures that once adorned her house in Grosvenor Street were now displayed at the Villa dell'Ombrellino.

On January 24, ex-millionaire Clarence Hatry was sentenced to fourteen years imprisonment after a trial which had lasted for four days and was said to have cost £25,000. 'Fourteen years' repeated the dazed defendant. 'Well, that's that.'

On January 30, the short and stocky Duke of Portland gave a ball at Welbeck Abbey to celebrate the fiftieth anniversary of his succession to the title. The Duke's threats to close down his vast home, with its famous underground ballroom and library, had not been carried out but his son and heir, Lord Titchfield, was building a smaller house on the estate.

On February 13, ex-Archdeacon Wakeford, central figure in the major ecclesiastical scandal of the Twenties, died at Barmingham Heath Lunatic Asylum, to which he had recently been admitted suffering from depression. His wife had stood by him throughout his troubles and he had maintained his innocence on charges of immorality to the end.

Meanwhile, gifts poured in for the Duke of Westminster and his fiancée Miss Loelia Ponsonby and it was announced that the Duke's 1,000 tenants in London, Flintshire and Cheshire would pay no rent during the week of the wedding and all arrears would be cancelled. It was revealed that the Duke's gift to his bride would be the famous Arcot diamonds, originally given to Queen Charlotte by the Nawab of Arcot.

On February 20, the marriage took place in a London registry office, with Winston Churchill acting as best man. A reception was held afterwards on board the Duke's second yacht the 828-ton *Cutty Sark*, anchored in the Thames, during which the new Duchess, one of the 'Bright Young Things' of the previous decade, accidentally wandered into the gentlemen's lavatory.

The following day, seventy-seven-year-old Lord Westbury committed suicide by throwing himself out of his flat in St. James's Court. His body fell more than sixty feet before crashing through a glass verandah. It was only three months since Lord Westbury's son, archaeologist Richard Bethell, had died in mysterious circumstances and the superstitious were quick to point out that here was yet another violent death of someone connected with the Tutankhamen expedition.

At the end of February, it was announced that Lansdowne House, sold by Lord Lansdowne the previous year, would become a club. The new proprietor, Mr. Benson Grenall, announced plans for a swimming-bath, squash-courts and an 800-seat theatre. The fine Adam house was soon severely mutilated.

On March 7, Society beauty Mrs. Ronald Armstrong-Jones gave birth to a baby boy at her home in Eaton Terrace, Belgravia. He was later christened Antony at the Temple Church. The godparents included twenty-two-year-old baronet Sir Michael Duff and the newly-married Countess of Seafield.

In the middle of the month, Augustus John entered a private nursing-home named Preston Deanery Hall, near Northampton, run by a certain Dr. Cameron, physician to literary hostess Lady Ottoline Morrell. The famous portrait painter required treatment for alcoholism but it is doubtful whether Dr. Cameron, who was soon to be imprisoned for running over a child while drunk, was the right person to help him.

On March 27, the new Duchess of Westminster presided over a vast house-party for the Grand National. Among the forty-five guests at Eaton Hall, Cheshire, were Winston Churchill, the Earl of Birkenhead, Lord and Lady Beatty and the vivacious Duchess of Marlborough. A special train, with a chef on board, conveyed the party to and from the Aintree race course. At dinner that night, the Duchess of Marlborough created a sensation by climbing up some housemaid's steps and taking a photograph.

At the end of the month, Mr. Grant, former butler at Clarence Hatry's house in Great Stanhope Street, appeared in court accused of stealing a vanity case and some diamond and onyx cuff-links from his new employer, a certain Captain Calvert-Jones.

On April 1, the Duchess of Leinster was found unconscious in the gas-filled kitchen of her Brixton flat. The Leinsters had now been separated for many years and the Duchess, former actress May Etheridge, had returned to her old habitat and taken the name, Mrs. Williams. 'Shopkeepers round here knew she was a Duchess' her landlady told reporters after the Duchess had been remanded in custody on a charge of attempted suicide.

A few days later, Evelyn Waugh and eighteen-year-old Randolph Churchill met for the first time. Both were godparents at the christening of Mrs. Bryan Guinness's baby boy, Jonathan. It was rumoured that Mrs. Guinness had wanted her baby to wear black lace trousers at the ceremony but had been persuaded in favour of more orthodox apparel.

On April 10, the Duchess of Bedford, now sixty-four-years-old, left Lympne aerodrome for Capetown in her new Spider aeroplane. At the end of the month, she was back in England having covered the 18,500 miles in twenty days. She was greeted with bouquets of flowers, a telegram from the King and her dog, Tu Fu, who had been specially brought from Woburn Abbey for the homecoming.

In the meantime, it had been reported that Professor Julian Huxley had slipped and fallen on Scafell in the Lake District, dislocating his left shoulder and spraining two fingers.

On May 1, seventeen-year-old Margaret Whigham made her debut at a dance in a house in Audley Square, rented by her father, wealthy Scottish industrialist, George Whigham. Miss Whigham, later named 'Deb of the Year', wore a turquoise embroidered tulle dress created by Norman Hartnell.

On May 6, the eighty-year-old Duke of Connaught arrived from his home in the South of France and a few days later was seen at St. James's Palace watching a march past of Yeomen of the Guard with his great-great-niece, four-year-old Princess Elizabeth.

Meanwhile, Augustus John's portrait of Tallulah Bankhead had created a sensation at the Royal Academy. It was hung alongside an unflattering portrait by the same artist of Sir Gerald du Maurier which was rumoured to have caused the actor great distress on account of its lack of sex appeal. Missing from the same exhibition was a portrait of the Italian dictator, Mussolini. The portrait, for which Mussolini had sat five times, was rejected by the committee, perhaps recalling the sitter's well-publicised observation that there was something even more beautiful than books and paintings and that was guns and aeroplanes.

Tallulah Bankhead and Augustus John

On May 13, bumptious, over-weight American Elsa Maxwell threw a 'murder party' at Lady Ribblesdale's house in St. James's. Two actors were hired to impersonate detectives and a trail of carefully-laid clues led to the 'arrest' of the fifty-eight-year-old Duke of Marlborough.

A few days later, the Aga Khan and his new wife arrived in London. 'All these stories about my jewellery are really much exaggerated' said the new Begum Aga Khan shyly. On May 27, this dazzling couple were present at Buckingham Palace along with the Aga's son, Aly, who wore a knee-length white tunic and white turban. Also being presented that day was the beautiful Margaret Whigham, in a white tulle dress covered with silver and pearls.

On June 3, the Aga Khan and his wife, Miss Whigham, the Duke and Duchess of Westminster and thousands of others were present at the Derby. This year, the famous race was won by the Aga Khan's Blenheim, an 18–1 outsider, and the proud owner was summoned to the Royal Box. 'How much did you have on it?' asked the King. 'Not a penny, Your Majesty' confessed the bulky Indian potentate.

Meanwhile, a romance had blossomed between seventeen-year-old Margaret Whigham and eighteen-year-old Aly Khan. The handsome young prince had recently moved into a maisonette in Aldford Street with his oriental valet, only a few yards away from the Whigham house in Audley Square.

In the middle of June, attention turned to an auction at Hornby Castle in Yorkshire. It was reported that the coronet and coronation robes worn by the Duke of Leeds at King George V's Coronation had been sold for very small sums. The purchaser said that these garments would be used for amateur theatricals.

On June 30, the audience at the Paris Opera House were startled by cries coming from the box containing famous Irish writer James Joyce. 'Thank God for this miracle!' exclaimed the author of *Ulysses*. 'After twenty years I can really see again!' Joyce's eyesight had recently been getting so poor that doctors had resorted to placing leeches on his eyeballs to suck off the excess blood.

On July 3, high society gathered at St. Margaret's Westminster for the marriage of vivacious Maureen Guinness, grand-daughter of Lord Iveagh, and Lord Ava, son and heir to the Marquess of Dufferin and Ava. Best man at the ceremony was curly-headed Frank Pakenham, brother of the Earl of Longford. It was stated that Mr. Pakenham's wedding clothes had been delayed en route from Ireland so he had hired a costume which had to be back in the shop by 5.00 pm.

On July 7, Sir Arthur Conan Doyle, creator of Sherlock Holmes, died at Crowborough in Sussex. Six days later, 10,000 people crowded into the Albert Hall, believing that they were about to receive a message from Sir Arthur's spirit. 'He's here!' announced medium Mrs. Estelle Roberts in a dramatic whisper and all eyes turned to the empty chair beside Lady Conan Doyle – but nothing further occurred.

On July 21, an air-taxi carrying the Marquess of Dufferin and Ava, Society hostess Lady Ednam and three others home from Le Touquet suddenly fell to pieces in the air above Kent. Bits of the plane were strewn over a five-mile radius and the bodies of the passengers fell into an orchard, crashing through heavily laden cherry trees. Over £65,000 worth of jewellery was said to be scattered over the countryside.

On August 4, Sir Francis Laking, twenty-six-year-old Baronet, died in St. George's Hospital after drinking too much yellow Chartreuse. In his will, he left all his motor-cars to his friend Tallulah Bankhead. It was soon discovered that he did not own a single motor-car.

On August 21, attention turned to the picturesque Glamis Castle, following the birth of a second daughter to the Duchess of York. The baby, later christened Margaret Rose, was said to be the first Royal child born in Scotland for more than 300 years. Among those staying at the Castle was the Socialist Home Secretary Mr. Clynes – his presence dictated by an ancient custom that a minister of state should attend each royal birth.

Meanwhile, it was rumoured that famous American gangster, Jack Diamond, was sailing towards England on board the Red Star liner *Belgenland*. It was said that he had had a fight with fellow gangster Al Capone and wished to lie low in Europe for a while. On August 30 the ship arrived at Liverpool but Diamond, who was travelling in a First Class suite and under his own name, was refused permission to land. A fellow passenger described him as 'a perfectly harmless young man'.

On September 7, thieves broke into a house in Abercorn Place, St. John's Wood belonging to Mrs. Dudley

Sir Francis Laking Bart. who
died after drinking too much
yellow Chartreuse

Ward, old friend of the Prince of Wales. Four antique chairs and two electric candelabra were reported missing. Mrs. Dudley Ward was out of London at the time and most of the furniture in the house was under dust-sheets.

In the middle of September, it was announced that the Queen had had a special warning hooter fitted to her car which made a very distinctive sound. Confusion was created when a number of other motorists decided to have the same horn fitted to their vehicles.

On September 25, a new production of Somerset Maugham's play *Home and Beauty* opened bringing the playwright's daughter Liza into the public eye. One gossip columnist regaled his readers with the information that Liza, a sophisticated fifteen-year-old, had neither seen, nor heard of, brown sugar.

On October 5, the giant R101 airship built the previous year crashed in France. Lord Thomson, Minister for Air, and forty-five other passengers were burnt alive. At Chequers later that day, the white-haired Prime Minister Ramsay MacDonald was distraught. In addition to the many political problems he faced, he was not sleeping well. 'Two hours a night is all I get' he remarked.

Meanwhile, work on Mr. Jimmy de Rothschild's new house, 23 St. James's Place, was nearly completed. The crowning touch was to be the installation of a burglar alarm so powerful that it could call police from as far away as Hyde Park Corner or Admiralty Arch.

On October 27, Albert Einstein arrived in London and was surrounded by reporters at Victoria Station. 'The professor will say absolutely nothing about science and he is in a hurry' said his bodyguard, Mr. Samuel Wallrock. The following day, Einstein dined with Bernard Shaw and H. G. Wells.

At the beginning of November, the public cast a curious glance in the direction of the sixty-eight-year-old Marquess of Winchester, former chairman of the Hatry Group who was now facing bankruptcy proceedings. Callers at the peer's sixteenth-century château near Quesnoy-le-Montant in France noticed a Hispano Suiza and a Lancia in the garage but got little satisfaction when they tried the front door. 'What d'you want? Why have you come to disturb me? Why on earth should I make a statement?' said Britain's premier marquess.

On November 4, the Queen wore the Cullinan diamond, said to be the world's largest, at a dinner at Buckingham Palace in honour of the wealthy delegates to the India Round Table Conference.

In the middle of November, the Prince of Wales met Mrs. Ernest Simpson for the first time. The meeting took place at Burrough Court, Melton Mowbray, country home of Lord and Lady Furness. Mr. and Mrs. Simpson, friends of Lady Furness's sister Connie, had been invited to stay at the last moment. It was revealed afterwards that the elegant but somewhat severe-looking Mrs. Simpson practised her curtsies on the train.

On November 27, there was a sensation at the Savoy Grill when a woman rushed up and slapped Tallulah Bankhead across the face. Tallulah ignored the interruption, turned to her companion, Sir Gerald du Maurier and said: 'What were you sayin', dahlin'?' She was soon to sign a lucrative contract with Columbia Pictures and leave England for good.

Early in December, a new art gallery was mentioned in the gossip columns. The place was Queensberry Mews West, SW7, and the proprietor was twenty-one-year-old Dublin-born Francis Bacon. As well as designing furniture in glass, nickel and enamelled wood, it was said that Mr. Bacon painted pictures in the Surrealist school.

On December 15, gaoled financier Clarence Hatry appeared in the Law Courts in connexion with the affairs of his companies. During a break in the proceedings, Hatry had tea with his wife in the court's canteen. It was noticed that the former financier wore an immaculate brown tweed suit, perfectly knotted tie and 'spotless linen'.

At Christmas, photographer Cecil Beaton entertained his family at his newly-acquired William-and-Mary house at Ashcombe in Wiltshire. Beaton's father was perplexed by the extravagant decor of the house, tripped over a bed and sprained his ankle. Meanwhile, Beaton's *Book of Beauty* had been published, displeasing his friend Lady Cunard. 'He calls me a *hostess*. That shows he's a low fellow!' she said, throwing her complimentary copy into the fire.

On New Year's Day, former solicitor's typist Amy Johnson set off on a solo flight to Peking. Two days later she landed at Cologne airport having lost her way. 'She seems to fly more by instinct than by her head' commented a leading Lufthansa pilot.

On January 4, Princess Louise, Duchess of Fife, died in her sleep at her lovely Adam house in Portman Square. Shy and retiring, Princess Louise was one of the first members of the Royal Family to marry out of royalty. In her day, she was said to have been an accomplished salmon-fisher.

On January 5, the Deputy Commissioner of Scotland Yard, Sir Charles Royds, attended the rehearsals of the Strauss Ball at the Savoy Hotel. Waltzing energetically with the beautiful young Lady Furness, Sir Charles suddenly collapsed, frothing at the mouth. He died afterwards in Charing Cross Hospital.

On January 15, the Prince of Wales and Prince George left England for an 18,000-mile tour of South America. Among their luggage on board the liner *Oropesa* were golf-clubs, tennis rackets, guns and a small aeroplane.

Meanwhile, the incorrigible Mrs. Meyrick had been released from yet another prison sentence for contravening the licensing laws. On January 21, she arrived in Monte Carlo where she had been offered a stake in a new nightclub. 'Monte Carlo is chiefly inhabited by older people and therefore you must cater for them' she said. 'I know all my good old British clients will stand by me if I start up here.' Further along the coast at Cannes was Mrs. Meyrick's arch-enemy Lord Byng, Commissioner of the Metropolitan Police, who was currently on sick leave.

On January 31, forty-nine-year-old Old Etonian Horace de Vere Cole married twenty-two-year-old bohemian Mavis Wright, whom he had met at the Café Royal in Regent Street. Mr. de Vere Cole was widely known as the World's Greatest Practical Joker. One of his pranks had been to run through the streets of London with a cow's udder hanging out of his fly-buttons.

On February 4, brilliant Viennese dancer Tilly Losch, who had starred in Cochran's revue *Year of Grace* three years earlier, was married to Edward James, wealthy godson of the late King Edward VII. James had pursued Miss Losch to New York, denying rumours of the romance until the last moment.

On February 13, beautiful baronet's daughter Brenda Dean Paul made the first of many court appearances. Miss Dean Paul, who had recently announced that she was weary of the distractions of modern social life and was going to go and live on a South Sea island, was accused of bouncing a cheque.

That evening, Earl Beauchamp, leader of the Liberal Party, gave a party at his huge house in Belgrave Square to celebrate the twenty-first birthday of his daughter, Lady Mary Lygon. Lady Mary received the guests with her father, a spray of orchids attached to her shoulder. It was revealed that Countess Beauchamp, sister of the Duke of Westminster, had given her daughter a small, blue opal pig.

A day or two later, it was announced that eighty-one-year-old veteran judge Lord Darling was coming out of retirement to help with the backlog of work that had accumulated at the High Court as a result of the illness of seven judges. Lord Darling was himself soon taken ill and ordered by his doctors to cancel all engagements.

Meanwhile, Charlie Chaplin, already white-haired, had arrived in England, staying in a suite at the Carlton Hotel in the Haymarket and being fêted by everybody from Lady Astor to the Duke and Duchess of York. On February 21, the famous film star spent the day at Chequers with Prime Minister Ramsay MacDonald where both men fell asleep after lunch.

On February 28, the première of Chaplin's film *City Lights* was attended by a host of celebrities, including George Bernard Shaw, Lady Astor, Winston Churchill, Elinor Glyn and Somerset Maugham. The last-named was noticed smoking a de-nicotinised cigarette.

On March 10, the Marquess of Winchester, premier marquess of England and hereditary bearer of the Cap of Maintenance, appeared at the London bankruptcy court disclosing liabilities of £462,182. He blamed this state of affairs on his connexion with the Hatry group of companies – an accusation against which Hatry vigorously defended himself from his prison cell.

On March 31, millionaire aviator Glen Kidston set off on a solo flight to Capetown. Before he left, he had a farewell dinner with eighteen-year-old Margaret Whigham, his constant companion of the last few months, and gave her a diamond-encrusted Cartier watch. Six days later, he arrived at his destination having completed the 6,000-mile journey in record time.

On April 9, Charlie Chaplin was over an hour late for a showing of *City Lights* in Nice, keeping the Duke of Connaught and others waiting. The film star explained that he had got held up over dinner with the Prince of Monaco. As a result of the delay, the eighty-year-old uncle to the King faced a long journey back to his villa at Cap Ferrat in the small hours.

On April 14, King Alfonso of Spain fled his country in dramatic circumstances and the news flashed round the world that he would come to England and make a temporary home with his mother-in-law, Princess Beatrice, in Kensington Palace. It was rumoured that the King had a £2,000,000 fortune salted away in England. He arrived at Victoria Station on April 21 and was met by the Marchioness of Londonderry. Observers noticed that he was wearing the same close-fitting brown overcoat and curiously shaped green felt hat that he had worn when he left Spain. Meanwhile, the gallant Duchess of Bedford had flown herself to Madrid for a jaunt, where she visited museums and saw little sign of the recent revolution.

On April 26, the Prince of Wales and Prince George returned from their tour of South America and were greeted with kisses from the little Princess Elizabeth when they clambered out of their aircraft at a landing strip near Windsor Castle. A day or two after his return, the Prince of Wales attended a reception at Lady Furness's house in Grosvenor Square, at which he met Mr. and Mrs. Ernest Simpson for the second time.

On April 30, a scandal engulfed the Royal Academy. Three paintings by world-famous artist Reginald Eves were suddenly withdrawn from the exhibition and returned to him. It had been discovered that the paintings were photographs lightly painted over. 'I was pressed for time' explained a much embarrassed Mr. Eves. 'I did it purely to save time. It has now been brought home to me that I did a very foolish thing.' In the same exhibition, a painting by Dod Proctor was hung upside-down. Mrs. Proctor said she did not wish to discuss the matter.

On May 5, it was announced that millionaire aviator Glen Kidston had been killed in an aeroplane crash in South Africa. Margaret Whigham learned of the death of her friend from a newspaper placard as she emerged from a charity matinée at the Hippodrome Theatre and collapsed into the arms of friends. The next day's papers incorrectly stated that she had slipped on a staircase.

A few days later, a memorial service was held at St. Mark's Church. Before leaving England, Kidston had told his mother that in the event of his death, he did not want 'any weeping or sob stuff of that sort' but the Vicar at St. Mark's refused to comply with his request that 'Rule, Britannia!' should be played at his funeral.

On May 19, phenomenally wealthy Woolworth heiress Barbara Hutton was presented to the King and Queen at the first Court of the Season. A cruel rumour circulated that the heavily-chaperoned eighteen-year-old multi-millionairess had been rejected by New York's most eligible bachelors.

Meanwhile, the aged and venerable Duke of Connaught, recently snubbed by Charlie Chaplin, had arrived at Clarence House where an operation to remove a polypus from his nose was performed.

At the end of May, Mrs. Jimmy White, widow of the millionaire racehorse-owner who had committed suicide in 1927, was found in a one-room flat in Victoria. For many years she had lived in the lap of luxury. Now her only assets were a sable coat and fourteen gold and silver racing trophies. 'I have kept the cups to the last because they meant so much to Jimmy' she said.

Early in June, high society was mystified by an announcement that Earl Beauchamp, Knight of the Garter and Lord Warden of the Cinque Ports, had suddenly left the country and resigned all his positions. The official story was that the fifty-nine-year-old peer had gone abroad for health reasons. Only a few people knew that the real reason for his sudden departure was that his powerful brother-in-law, the Duke of Westminster, had accused him of homosexual practices and he faced a gigantic scandal if he remained in England.

On June 5, eighty-one-year-old Lord Kimberley was sued for breach of promise by an ex-actress named

Earl Beauchamp, Knight of the Garter, Lord Warden of the Cinque Ports and leader of the Liberal Party

Mrs Ernest Simpson on the occasion of her presentation at Court

Queenie Gerald, who claimed £10,000 damages. Lord Kimberley, a colourful figure who had once challenged a fellow member of the Norfolk County Council to a duel, made a generous out-of-court settlement.

On June 10, Mrs. Ernest Simpson was presented at Court. Her friend, Lady Furness, lent her a train, feathers and fan and afterwards gave a small party at which Mr. and Mrs. Simpson met the Prince of Wales for the third time. On this occasion, the Prince gave his new acquaintances a lift back to their flat in Bryanston Court, near Marble Arch, before driving on to Fort Belvedere with his Equerry General Trotter.

On June 25, the King and Queen dined with the Marquess of Crewe at Crewe House in Curzon Street. It was the first time that the King, who wore an opera cloak over his evening clothes, had dined out for many months. The Queen wore a gold lamé coat and a diamond and pearl tiara.

Meanwhile, American tobacco heiress Doris Duke, said to be even richer than Miss Barbara Hutton, had arrived in England. On July 5, she was found dining in the open air beside the Thames with Prince Bismarck, Counsellor at the German Embassy, and Mr. Edward Marjoribanks, a former President of the Oxford Union.

On July 8, Lord Weymouth, heir to Longleat, was found hobbling about with one of his feet in a red bedroom-slipper at a party given by the wealthy composer Lord Berners. It was explained that his foot had been damaged by a rocket incompetently discharged by young Lord Brownlow.

On July 16, there was a stately royal ball at Buckingham Palace, the first function of its kind for many years. The King was in the full-dress uniform of a Colonel-in-Chief of the Black Watch and the Queen was in an ivory chiffon gown embroidered with pearl and diamanté trimmings. Dancing took place in the white and gold ballroom to the music of the Royal Artillery String Band. It was said that the Queen had indulged in one waltz.

On July 20, Lord Kylsant, chairman of the mighty Royal Mail Steam Company, appeared at the Old Bailey charged with publishing and circulating a false prospectus. Throughout the trial, the sixty-eight-year-old peer, who stood six foot seven inches tall and wore a frock coat in the dock, dominated the proceedings. Finally, the judge had to steel himself to sentence a man of his own class to a year's imprisonment. The peer was taken to Wormwood Scrubs where a special suit of prison clothes had to be made to accommodate his great height.

Meanwhile, Lord and Lady Astor, their son David and white-bearded Bernard Shaw had departed for Moscow. A rumour circulated that Lady Astor, having heard grim reports of austere conditions in Russia, took enough tinned food with her to last the party for a fortnight. During their visit, they were received by the Russian dictator, Stalin. 'When will you stop killing people?' asked Nancy Astor boldly.

At the beginning of August, multi-millionairess Mrs. Laura Corrigan was to be found in Venice – where she had rented the Palazzo Mocenigo for the season. On the Lido she created a mild stir by wearing short trousers.

On August 13, it was learned that the Marchioness Curzon, widow of the former Foreign Secretary, was heavily in debt and had decided to pacify her creditors by disposing of her family mansion, 1 Carlton House Terrace, and her famous racing-stable.

A few days later, the country's serious financial situation forced the Prince of Wales to postpone his holiday as Lord Ednam's guest at his château near Bayonne. It was noted that the Prince's new motor-car and speed-boat had already been sent ahead.

On August 22, the King broke off his holiday at Balmoral and travelled to London for crisis talks with his Ministers. On arrival at Euston, he was met by his devoted courtier Sir Frederick Ponsonby and driven to Buckingham Palace. The Queen remained in Scotland, where it was said she was extremely upset to play no role in the drama. 'I will not be left sitting on a mountain' she remarked to a Lady-in-Waiting.

On September 5, the King told Prime Minister Ramsay MacDonald, now running his first coalition government, that he wished to give up £50,000 a year. The rest of the Royal Family soon followed suit, the Prince of Wales making a sacrifice of £10,000. Rumours that the salaries of royal servants were being cut in order to incorporate these cuts were firmly denied.

On September 9, Lord Fitzwilliam had a large party at Wentworth Woodhouse for the St. Leger. Among the forty-five guests at the house, said to be the largest in England, was the beautiful Margaret Whigham,

Wentworth Woodhouse, Yorkshire seat of Earl Fitzwilliam, said to be the largest private house in England

who was said to wear luminous nail-varnish.

Meanwhile, Hindu leader Mahatma Gandhi was sailing for England to play his part at the Round Table conference at St. James's Palace. He arrived on September 12, bare-legged and dressed in a curious loin-cloth affair and full of apologies that an illness made it impossible to stand for any length of time. Among his luggage were eighteen bottles of pasteurised goat's milk.

On September 22, the grave financial situation had no visible effect on a gathering of celebrities at the Embassy Club in Bond Street. Among those present were Lady Louis Mountbatten, in a dress embroidered with sprays of gold flowers, Miss Margaret Whigham and General Trotter, Equerry to the Prince of Wales. Sitting by himself over a bottle of champagne was twenty-year-old Aly Khan.

The quaint, smiling figure of Mahatma Gandhi remained in the news. On September 23, he visited the Aga Khan at his suite in the Ritz. 'We discussed our differences and it was a most friendly meeting' he said afterwards. A few days later, still in his loin-cloth, he attended a garden party at Buckingham Palace – where the Queen inspected him through her lorgnettes.

On September 30, a certain Major Christopher Draper flew under Tower Bridge in a tiny aeroplane and was immediately branded by the Press 'the Mad Major'.

On October 2, it was revealed that heavy taxation had forced Lady Louis Mountbatten to put Brook House on the market. This fabulous Victorian mansion in Park Lane had a dining-room capable of seating 100 people and a huge marble hall known in high society as 'the Giant's lavatory'. It was rumoured that Lady Louis' grandfather, Sir Ernest Cassel, had expressed a wish in his will that the house should never be sold.

On October 8, rapidly rising photographer Cecil Beaton threw a party for platinum-blonde film star Lilyan Tashman. Guests included the new Marchioness of Dufferin and Ava, formerly Maureen Guinness, and Miss Margaret Whigham, a close friend of Beaton's sisters.

On October 27, Randolph Churchill lost a £600 bet when the National Government were returned in the General Election with a majority of 489 seats. Winston Churchill helped his son settle the debt.

The following day, the King and Queen attended Noel Coward's patriotic new musical *Cavalcade* at the Theatre Royal, Drury Lane. During the second interval, the author was presented to the King and a rumour flashed round the auditorium that he had been knighted, there and then, in the Royal Box.

On November 3, there was a big gathering at St. Margaret's Westminster for the wedding of the Hon. Frank Pakenham and Miss Elizabeth Harman, daughter of a leading Harley Street ophthalmic surgeon. Among those present were Evelyn Waugh, John Betjeman, Lord David Cecil and Miss Nancy Mitford. In a speech at the reception, the best man, young Lord Birkenhead, predicted a brilliant future for the curly-headed bridegroom but added that he had never regarded him as a marriageable man.

On November 11, there was a farewell party at the Ritz in honour of Lady Louis Mountbatten, whose husband was to be stationed in Malta for the next two years. Most of the guests were invited by telephone at the last moment.

A week later, men were in medals and decorations at an ice carnival in the ballroom at the new Grosvenor House. The Duchess of Sutherland brought a party which included the Prince of Wales and Mr. Charles Chaplin, who had recently met and made friends in Biarritz.

On December 5, beautiful Brenda Dean Paul, twenty-three-year-old daughter of Sir Aubrey Dean Paul of Westward Ho, Devon, pleaded guilty to seven charges under the Dangerous Drugs Act. She was bound over in the sum of £50 and the court was told that she was to receive treatment for drug-addiction.

On December 9, Mrs. Fred Cripps, the former Duchess of Westminster, organised a Punch and Judy show for her son, Milo. Among the young guests were Lady Weymouth's daughter Caroline, Mrs. Euan Wallace's son Billy, Lord Beaverbrook's grand-daughter Jeanne Campbell, and Lady Diana Cooper's boy John Julius.

On December 11, Winston Churchill arrived in America to give a lecture-tour to offset his heavy losses on the New York stock exchange. Two days later, the news flashed round the world that he had been knocked down by a car on Fifth Avenue. Though badly injured, he had remained conscious and insisted that the accident was entirely his fault. A few days later, while still seriously ill in hospital, he sold his account of the accident to the *Daily Mail* for £600.

Also in New York was the pleasure-seeking Duke of Manchester. On December 18, he attempted to impose some order on his life by marrying an English actress named Kathleen Davis.

Meanwhile, nineteen-year-old Margaret Whigham had left England for a holiday in Egypt with her parents. Here, on Christmas Eve she met the handsome twenty-year-old Earl of Warwick, grandson of the formidable Socialist hostess, the Countess of Warwick, who was in Cairo serving with his regiment. Before the year was out, the young peer had proposed to her.

Mr. and Mrs. Ernest Simpson saw in the New Year at a fancy-dress party given by Lord Sackville and his American wife at Knole. Guests were asked to wear Tudor costume and the gold dinner-service was brought up from the strong-room for the occasion.

Far away in Rome, on January 7, Sir Oswald Mosley had his first meeting with Mussolini, now in his tenth year as Italian dictator. Mosley, who had recently inherited his father's baronetcy along with a landed estate valued at £247,111, was soon to embrace the Fascist cause.

On January 21, writer and critic Lytton Strachey died at Ham Spray House near Reading. His friend, Dora Carrington, with whom he had shared his life for the past fifteen years, was left bereft and suicidal. Soon afterwards, she borrowed a gun from the nearby estate of Mr. and Mrs. Bryan Guinness and terminated her own life.

On January 30, Mr. and Mrs. Ernest Simpson were found weekending at Fort Belvedere for the first time. Lady Furness acted as hostess and the Prince of Wales armed the men in the house-party with bill-hooks and got them to attack the laurel which was encroaching on his garden. In the evening, he astonished Mrs. Simpson by taking out his needlework. 'This is my secret vice', he said, explaining that he was making the cover for a backgammon table.

On February 2, eighty-two-year-old Lord Darling, one of the most famous high court judges, was knocked down by a lorry in Trevor Square, Knightsbridge.

Meanwhile, intense public interest was shown in the activities of a Norfolk rector named Harold Davidson, who had recently been accused in the Press of immoral practices involving up to 1,000 girls and was now threatened with consistory court proceedings. It promised to be the ecclesiastical scandal of the century.

On Sunday February 7, thousands converged on the ancient parish church of St. John and St. Mary at Stiffkey in Norfolk to hear the infamous rector preach. One busload of sightseers came from as far away as Bournemouth. With his war medals clinking on his surplice, the silver-haired rector received rousing cheers from his flock.

In the middle of February, the news broke that Miss Margaret Whigham, Deb of the Year in 1930, was engaged to the young Earl of Warwick. The couple were now on their way back from Egypt by ship and train. They arrived at Victoria Station on March 9 and were met by a battery of Press and friends.

That night, there was a party at the Embassy Club in their honour where guests tucked into Salmon Welcome Back, Petite Pois Prosperity and other dishes renamed to suit the occasion. The following day the young Earl travelled alone to Warwick Castle and Miss Whigham attended another party at the Embassy Club, where she encountered a glamorous young Irish-American named Charles Sweeny.

On March 17, Winston Churchill arrived in England. Waiting for him at Southampton was a brand-new Daimler, which his friends, organised by Brendan Bracken, had clubbed together to buy for him to celebrate his recovery from his unfortunate accident in New York.

On March 21, beautiful baronet's daughter, Brenda Dean Paul, was pronounced cured of drug-addiction. 'Miss Dean Paul's one idea now is to forget the past and occupy her mind with hard work' said a friend. 'She hopes to earn her living in the films.'

On March 29, the trial of the Rev. Harold Davidson opened in the Great Hall at Church House. The fifty-six-year-old rector made a sensational entrance rushing to his place a few minutes after the hearing had begun. The trial was to go on for four months, during which Mr. Davidson's relationship with scores of London waitresses and other girls would come under the scrutiny of the court. Throughout the proceedings, the rector made no secret of his many friendships but claimed that he was entirely innocent of any wrong-doing.

On March 31, Miss Margaret Whigham broke off her engagement to the Earl of Warwick. It was explained that she did not love the Earl enough to marry him. 'They are both so young' said Margaret's mother, 'and it is one of the misfortunes of youth that it is liable to make mistakes.' The young Earl remained silent.

April 7 saw the arrival of the new American Ambassador, Mr. Andrew Mellon. Gentle, unassuming and fabulously rich, he said he had not yet decided whether or not to wear knee-breeches at court.

A week later, musical-comedy actress June was back in England after a year in Hollywood, anxious that her marriage to Lord Inverclyde should be sorted out. It was revealed she had signed a contract to appear in a new revue called *Fanfare*.

On April 28, the Prince of Wales was the principal figure in an audience of 2,000 at a charity film performance at the Plaza Theatre, Lower Regent Street, organised by the untiring Lady Furness. After this event, which was said to mark the beginning of the Season, many of those present went on to the Hungaria Restaurant for breakfast and dancing.

One of the most remarkable of this year's crop of débutantes was Lord Redesdale's fourth daughter, the Hon. Unity Mitford. She was to attend many dances this season with her pet grass-snake, Enid, slung round her neck.

On May 9, the marriage of Fred Astaire's sister, Adele, and Lord Charles Cavendish, younger son of the Duke of Devonshire, took place in a private chapel at Chatsworth and was conducted by the Duke's chaplain, the Rev. W. H. Foster-Pegg. Among those present was the bridegroom's sister, Lady Dorothy Macmillan.

On the same day, Mrs. Meyrick was fined £50 for selling intoxicating liquor without a licence and the magistrate ordered that the 43 Club should be struck off the register and the premises be disqualified for future use as a nightclub. The following day, headlines blazed the news that Mrs. Meyrick had at last abdicated as Queen of the London nightclub scene and was retiring to live in the country. 'She has felt the recent strain very keenly' said a friend. 'She is in far from good health.'

Just one week later, Mrs. Meyrick was back at her 'receipt of custom' at the 43 Club, to the jubilation of her many customers and the astonishment of the police.

On May 23, seventy-nine-year-old Lord Inchcape, described as the world's greatest shipping-magnate, died in his valet's arms on board his yacht at Monte Carlo. His body was brought back to Britain for burial at his estate in Ayrshire, in the midst of gossip to the effect that he had left two wills, one of which he had neglected to sign.

At the end of May, a gruesome murder case rocked Society. A young out-of-work dress designer named Michael Scott Stephen had been found shot dead in a mews house in Belgravia and three days later, his girlfriend, Mrs. Elvira Barney, twenty-six-year-old daughter of chief government stockbroker Sir John Mullens, had been arrested at her parents' house in Belgrave Square and charged with murder.

In the midst of this commotion, the Derby took place. The recently jilted Earl of Warwick, Fred Astaire, the Earl of Lonsdale and Miss Unity Mitford were among the many spectators.

On June 15, Sir Donald Maclean, President of the Board of Education and a former leader of the Liberal Party, died suddenly leaving his wife and five children very little money. His second son, Donald, was twenty years old at the time and was studying modern languages at Cambridge, where his contemporaries included Old Etonian Guy Burgess and Kim Philby, son of the famous explorer St. John Philby.

On June 16, Winston Churchill gave a large dinner-party at Claridge's to celebrate the coming-of-age of his son, Randolph. Guests included the Duke of Marlborough, Admiral of the Fleet Lord Beatty, Sir Oswald Mosley and twenty-four-year-old Quintin Hogg.

On June 30, Major Jack Coats, millionaire sportsman and gambler, was found dead in his flat in Gloucester House, Park Lane. Major Coats, a larger-than-life figure who thought nothing of ordering 1,000 oysters in a restaurant, had been a familiar figure in the gambling clubs of Europe for many years.

On July 4, the trial of Mrs. Elvira Barney opened at the Old Bailey, exciting immense public interest. There were scuffles outside the court and anonymous threats to the trial judge. Many people attempted to queue all night for seats in the public gallery but were sent home by the police. Leading the defence, Sir Patrick Hastings declared that there was no evidence of any kind to convict Mrs. Barney. The shooting had been a tragic accident.

Society girl Elvira Barney following her aquittal at the Old Bailey on a murder charge

*The controversial Harold
Davidson, Rector of Stiffkey,
at a Foyle's Literary Luncheon*

Two days later, Mrs. Barney was acquitted and the crowds massed outside the court sang 'For she's a jolly good fellow'. Loads of flowers and telegrams arrived at the Mullens' house in Belgrave Square and Lady Mullens described her daughter as 'a poor white lamb'. The following day, Mrs. Barney was photographed smiling as she set off on a wild drive round London in her powerful Delage sports-car. 'I am glad the ordeal is over' she said. 'My plans are not settled yet. Everybody had been most kind to me.'

Her flamboyant behaviour continued, however. Shortly afterwards, she stood up at the Café de Paris and shouted: 'I am the one who shot her lover – so take a good look!'

On July 7, Mrs. Bryan Guinness gave a ball at 96 Cheyne Walk in honour of her young sister Unity Mitford. Augustus John was there but passed out fairly soon and was carried out by liveried footmen. Also there was Sir Oswald Mosley.

On July 8, the long, drawn-out trial of the Rev. Harold Davidson, which had fascinated and delighted the public for the past four months, at last reached its conclusion. He was found guilty on all the charges and ordered to be de-frocked. After listening impatiently to the verdict, Mr. Davidson grabbed his silk hat and ran full-tilt out of the Great Hall of Church House.

On July 16, Brenda Dean Paul, recently said to have been cured of morphine addiction, appeared at Marlborough Street Court, again accused of possessing dangerous drugs. This time, the famous magistrate, Mr. Mead, now eighty-five-years-old, discharged her. A month later, on August 15, she was found in Paris where she had gone to seek film-work, penniless and distressed.

On August 18, shipping-magnate Lord Kylsant was released from Wormwood Scrubs where he had spent the last ten months, and driven to his home in Wales. The gateway to his house had been transformed into a triumphal arch and fifty lusty farmers hauled his car on the last stage of its journey. The peer's three daughters, Mrs. Gavin Henderson, Lady Coventry and Lady Suffield, joined in the welcome-home celebrations.

On August 27, the Hon. Mrs. Frank Pakenham gave birth to a baby girl. She was later given the name Antonia and the young Marchioness of Dufferin and Ava was appointed a godmother.

Early in September, the Rev. Harold Davidson was to be found sitting in a barrel on the promenade at Blackpool attempting to raise money for an appeal against his conviction for immoral conduct. Over 3,000 people paid to see him and he was fined for causing an obstruction.

Also turning to the entertainment business to make ends meet was seventy-two-year-old Horatio Bottomley, once the highest paid journalist in the country and now a sadly shrunken shadow of his former self. On September 12, he appeared in a non-stop variety show at the Windmill Theatre. Dressed in a tail-coat, he told a few old anecdotes to a very puzzled audience. After a few nights, he collapsed on stage and was rushed to Middlesex Hospital suffering from a heart-attack.

On September 27, Winston Churchill collapsed in his garden at Chartwell, suffering from a severe haemorrhage owing to a paratyphoid ulcer. An ambulance rushed him to a London nursing-home.

Two days later, the Aga Khan's mother, eighty-six-year-old Princess Ali Shah, arrived in London. It was the old lady's first visit to Europe. During her time in London, she stayed in her grandson's house in Aldford Street, off Park Lane, and was received by the King and Queen at Buckingham Palace. 'My grandmother has a mind as brilliant and astute as my father's' said Prince Aly. 'I cannot tell you how wonderful she is.'

On October 14, the death of the Hon. Katherine Plunket made headline news. Miss Plunket, born in 1820, was 111 years old. It was reported that up to the age of 105, this amazing spinster used to drive herself to church in a coach-and-four.

On October 21, the public's attention turned to Norwich Cathedral where the Rev. Harold Davidson, Rector of Stiffkey, was to be formally de-frocked by the Bishop of Norwich. Cheering crowds greeted the rector as he arrived several minutes late in a small, mud-spattered car. During the grim service that followed, Davidson constantly heckled the Bishop and finally supplanted him in the procession leading to the High Altar.

Early in November, nineteen-year-old Woolworth heiress Barbara Hutton paid another visit to London and was found dining in the illustrious company of Prince George, Lady Portarlington and Major the Hon. Piers Legh. An enormous blood-red ruby ring was noticed on her finger and gossip columnists predicted an engagement announcement soon.

On November 9, a train pulled into Farnham Station with the dead body of a man sprawled across the roof of a carriage. He was identified as Old Etonian Richard Kindersley, son of the famous banker Sir Robert Kindersley, and it was revealed that he was adept at the dangerous art of 'train jumping', a stunt he had first seen on the cinema and later practised in America. Twenty-seven-year-old 'daring Dick' Kindersley had been caught by a bridge and killed.

On November 17, it was announced that Miss Margaret Whigham was to marry handsome young Irish-American Charles Sweeny, the former captain of the Oxford golf team, currently working in the City for his father's Investment Trust.

Three days later, sixteen-year-old violinist Yehudi Menuhin held the Albert Hall audience spellbound. It was noted that the brilliant young musician was having a new concert suit made by the Prince of Wales's tailor.

On November 29, the vivacious Madame Ritz, widow of the world's most famous hotelier, arrived in England and moved into a suite at the Carlton Hotel, the lavish Edwardian establishment at the bottom of the Haymarket created by her husband at the turn of the century.

On December 2, some potatoes grown by the former Prime Minister Lloyd George won first prize at the Chiddingfold Agricultural Association's annual show. The white-haired elder statesman was presented with a cheque for twenty-five shillings.

On December 12, Society flocked to the marriage of Winston Churchill's daughter Diana and Mr. John Bailey at St. Margaret's, Westminster. Among those present were famous hostess Mrs. Ronnie Greville, Mrs. Bryan Guinness and her baby boy, and the Duke of Marlborough in a brown overcoat with a velvet collar.

Meanwhile, former solicitor's typist Amy Johnson had flown her Puss Moth to Capetown and back in record time. On December 18, tens of thousands of Londoners turned out to welcome her home. 'Well here I am again!' she cried, before setting off along the crowded route from Croydon to the Grosvenor House Hotel.

At Christmas, it was announced that the chicly-dressed Lady Furness, intimate friend of the Prince of Wales and one of London's leading charity organisers, was suing her wealthy husband for divorce.

In the New Year's Honours list, art-dealer and benefactor Sir Joseph Duveen was raised to the peerage. He took the title Lord Duveen of Millbank to commemorate his long association with the Tate Gallery.

On January 12, writer Compton Mackenzie popped up in the dock at the Old Bailey charged with contravening the Official Secrets Act with certain revelations in his book *Greek Memories*. 'I think I can do justice without sending you to prison' said the judge, fining Mackenzie £100.

That night, 8,000 people packed into the Albert Hall to hear a concert by famous Polish pianist Paderewski. It was said that the seventy-two-year-old musician dipped his hands in hot water for ten minutes before each recital to make them even more sensitive.

On January 19, the death of Mrs. Kate Meyrick marked the end of an era in London nightclub life. The news was broken to the staff at the 43 Club by Mrs. Meyrick's son-in-law, Lord Kinnoull, and that night a doorman was posted outside the club to pass on the news to would-be customers. It was said that Mrs. Meyrick had died of a mixture of world-weariness and pneumonia. A funeral service was held later at St. Martin-in-the-Fields, a few minutes' walk from Mrs. Meyrick's famous Gerrard Street club.

On January 22, baronet's daughter Brenda Dean Paul, her beauty now marred by a haunted look, appeared in court again charged with possessing drugs. On this occasion, Lord Dawson of Penn, a leading doctor of the day, explained that she was an absolutely incurable case and would need increasing doses of morphia to stay alive. Miss Dean Paul had 'lost the fight against the fiend'.

At the end of January there was much surprise expressed over the engagement of the mysterious and elusive Mr. Montagu Norman, Governor of the Bank of England, to thirty-three-year-old redhead Mrs. Priscilla Worsthorne. It was noted that Mrs. Worsthorne already had two sons, the younger, Peregrine, aged nine.

On February 8, attention was suddenly focused on the Tower of London where it was reported that an officer of a crack regiment of the British Army was under close arrest, suspected of leaking information to a foreign power. Crowds gathered to watch the officer taking exercise. He was soon identified as Norman Baillie-Stewart, twenty-four-year-old Lieutenant in the Seaforth Highlanders and the grandson of a general.

On February 9, the Oxford Union carried by 122 votes the motion 'This House will in no circumstances fight for King and Country.' Young Quintin Hogg, who had voted against this controversial motion, led the subsequent outcry and later attempted to get the resolution expunged.

On February 14, sixty-nine-year-old shipping magnate Lord Kylsant, recently released from Wormwood Scrubs, took his seat again in the House of Lords. He chose a seat immediately behind the Archbishop of Canterbury. Several peers shook his hand and he exchanged a particularly hearty greeting with the Lord Chancellor.

Meanwhile, thousands of gifts poured in for engaged couple Margaret Whigham and Charles Sweeny. Among them was a cocktail cabinet from Miss Whigham's ex-fiancé, the Earl of Warwick, and a red and gold cushion from the Ranee of Sarawak embroidered 'For the loveliest head in London to lean against'. The Prince of Wales sent the bridegroom a pair of cufflinks.

The wedding took place at the Brompton Oratory on February 21; 2,000 people had been invited and a further 1,000 people gate-crashed the ceremony, making life very difficult for the ushers, who included Randolph Churchill, Max Aitken, and the Marquess of Dufferin and Ava. The train of the bride's Norman Hartnell dress was twenty-eight feet long and nine feet wide.

On March 6, the Chancery Court ordered the Duke of Manchester to pay off his debts at the rate of £50 a week. Smoking fat Turkish cigarettes in his suite at the Savoy Hotel, the overweight Duke explained that his new wife had made him much more responsible.

On March 8, it was announced that Mrs. Meyrick had left only £58. Friends estimated that she must have made and lost over half a million pounds in her life, ending up where she had started. Shortly afterwards, her son-in-law Lord Kinnoull announced that he would relinquish his nightclub interests and concentrate on his

Mr Charles Sweeny and Miss Margaret Whigham following their marriage at the Brompton Oratory

'The Officer in the Tower' Lieutenant Norman Baillie-Stewart with his counsel during an adjournment in his Court Martial at Chelsea Barracks

political work. He had recently become Junior Whip of the Socialist Party in the House of Lords.

On March 21, the court-martial of Lieutenant Norman Baillie-Stewart opened at Chelsea Barracks. The young officer, smartly dressed in kilt, tartan leggings and white spats, was accused of selling military secrets to Germany for £90. It was said that he had been trapped into this treachery by a German master-spy named Mary-Louise. He was subsequently found guilty and sentenced to five years penal servitude. Controversy and mystery continued to surround the case.

On March 29, the news broke that former millionaire Horatio Bottomley, now too ill to do any form of work, had applied for an old-age pension. Hearing of his plight, Mr. Reuban Bigland, who had triggered off the millionaire's downfall in 1922, immediately offered him a cottage and an income of £1 a week for the rest of his life. 'Leave the matter with me' said seventy-three-year-old Bottomley. 'I will consider it. Where exactly will this cottage be and what is it like? I should like to know these points before I decide.'

At the beginning of April, tall, pink-faced Lord Blandford, heir to the Duke of Marlborough, opened a shop in Berkeley Square, selling eggs, butter and poultry from his farm in Leicestershire.

On April 11, high society was shocked to learn that Mrs. Bryan Guinness, one of the famous Mitford sisters, was suing her husband for divorce. It was rumoured that she had fallen head over heels in love with Sir Oswald Mosley, who had now founded the British Union of Fascists.

On April 21, Princess Elizabeth's seventh birthday was celebrated with a party at Windsor Castle. The Queen sent her grand-daughter a set of miniature gardening tools.

On May 1, an air crash cut short the life of vivacious young Viscount Knebworth, heir to Lord Lytton. The news was broken to his mother that night at Covent Garden, where she was attending the opening night of *Der Rosenkavalier*. Lord Lytton subsequently wrote a book about his son, which became a run-away best-seller.

On May 16, Lady Cynthia Mosley, titular head of the women's side of the British Union of Fascists, died suddenly following an operation for appendicitis. Sir Oswald was at her bedside. Later, her body was embalmed and moved to the chapel at Cliveden, which had once been her family's home.

Meanwhile, the once notorious Horatio Bottomley was dying behind a screen in a public ward at the Middlesex Hospital. His devoted old friend, actress Peggy Primrose, was at his side. On May 30, there was a big turnout at his funeral at Golders Green, which was conducted by the Rev. Basil Bourchier, Rector of St. Anne's, Soho, to whom Bottomley was a man who could do no harm.

May 31 was Derby Day. This year the great race was won by Hyperion belonging to Lord Derby himself. 'I am too excited to say much. The horse ran splendidly' said the twenty-two stone peer, celebrating his first Derby win for nine years. It was observed that Lord Derby, whose gross income was said to exceed £300,000 a year, very rarely betted on horses himself.

On June 10, twenty-two-year-old Lady Honor Guinness, wealthy daughter of Lord Iveagh, announced her engagement to American-born author 'Chips' Channon, who was rumoured to have Red Indian blood.

June 19 was Mrs. Ernest Simpson's thirty-seventh birthday. That evening, the Prince of Wales gave a surprise dinner-party for her at Quaglino's Restaurant off Jermyn Street and presented her with an orchid plant, which she later placed in a window of her flat in Bryanston Court, near Marble Arch.

On June 29, the Prince of Wales put on grey plus-fours, check stockings and black-and-white shoes and took part in a golf match with Lady Astor. The Prince was very nervous at first and Lady Astor later confessed that it required great ingenuity on her part to let him win.

On July 4, the Prince dined with Mr. and Mrs. Simpson at Bryanston Court for the first time. Mrs. Simpson served black bean soup, grilled lobster, fried chicken Maryland and a raspberry soufflé. Afterwards, the heir to the throne asked for the recipe for the raspberry soufflé.

The same night, Lady Cunard's rebellious daughter Nancy gave a party in the basement of a London hotel in order to raise money for seven negroes imprisoned in America. All racial prejudices were defied as black and white people danced together. One of the most distinguished Englishmen at this controversial party was Nancy's friend, Augustus John.

In the middle of July, it was announced that the thirteen-year-old marriage of Mary Pickford and Douglas Fairbanks was on the rocks and their famous home 'Pickfair' was to be sold. While the world recovered from the shock, the deeply suntanned Mr. Fairbanks was found hiding in London in a flat overlooking Hyde Park.

On July 27, high society gathered for the marriage of Lady Astor's daughter Phyllis and Lord Willoughby de Eresby, heir to the Earl of Ancaster. At the reception afterwards, drinks were limited to tea and lemonade on the strict instructions of the teetotal hostess. Guests at Lady Astor's parties had now got used to this

The Duke and Duchess of Marlborough arrive at a society wedding at St. George's Hanover Square

situation and several of them carried hip-flasks.

On August 7, strange goings-on at the Duke of Marlborough's stately town-house, 7 Carlton House Terrace, made headline news. It was revealed that three private detectives had entered the mansion and disconnected all essential services – gas, electricity and telephone – rendering life very difficult for the Duchess of Marlborough who was living there on her own. Shortly afterwards she moved out, taking her own personal property with her which included paintings by Degas and other nineteenth-century masters. The detectives, under instructions from the sixty-one-year-old Duke, then moved in again and set about barricading the house so that no one could be admitted.

Following this upheaval, the Duchess of Marlborough took up residence at the Carlton Hotel in the Haymarket while her husband, whom she had married in 1921, remained at the Ritz and continued to entertain lavishly at Blenheim Palace at weekends.

On August 9, the seventy-year-old Marquess of Winchester, former chairman of the Hatry group, returned from exile in a bid to vindicate himself. 'I am the greatest sufferer of all' he said from his suite at the Savoy Hotel, where he and his wife were staying at the expense of a kind friend. Britain's premier marquess wore a bow-tie and monocle.

Later in the month, Lord Redesdale's nineteen-year-old daughter Unity Mitford left for Germany where she received much kindness from Ernst Hanfstaengl, public relations advisor to the newly-elected German Chancellor, Adolf Hitler. Together with her sister, Mrs. Diana Guinness, Unity attended the first Nuremberg rally, which began on August 31 and watched Hitler appear before a parade of 400,000 of his supporters. Unity was said to be desperately keen to meet the charismatic Führer, but a meeting could not be arranged on this occasion. 'The first time I saw him, I knew there was no one I would rather meet' she later told an *Evening Standard* reporter. Also at the rally were Lady Diana Cooper and her husband Duff Cooper, who sneaked out a quarter of the way through an oration by Hitler, risking arrest.

Early in September, the famous Bernard Baruch arrived in London. 'Every rumour about me is a damned lie' said the tall, grey-haired American statesman. While in England, he had several meetings with his great friend Mr. Winston Churchill.

On September 11, economist Sir Leo Money was fined fifty shillings for an offence against a passenger on a train travelling between Dorking and Ewell. According to the prosecution, Sir Leo had 'wilfully interfered with the comfort' of a certain Miss Ivy Ruxton. After some consideration, Sir Leo, who admitted kissing the woman, decided not to appeal against his conviction.

On September 15, the funeral of eighty-five-year-old Viscount Barrington, an ardent cricketer since his Eton days, created considerable interest. It was arranged that four cricketers in white flannels should carry the coffin to its grave.

At the end of September, twenty-three-year-old Nancy Meyrick, daughter of the late Mrs. Meyrick, and like her sisters actively involved for a time in the running of her mother's chain of nightclubs, was married to Mr. Fitzroy St. Aubyn, whose cousin, Lord St. Levan, owned St. Michael's Mount.

On October 4, the 6th Earl Cadogan, whose family trust owned vast tracts of Chelsea and Belgravia, went to his grave an undischarged bankrupt.

On the night of October 16, Cecil Beaton's brother Reggie, an officer in the RAF, was killed by an Underground train at Piccadilly Circus station. The verdict at the subsequent inquest, suicide while of unsound mind, astounded his friends and family.

Meanwhile, troubles had hit the two-year marriage of Mr. and Mrs. Edward James. On October 23, divorce papers were served on Mrs. James, former dancer Tilly Losch. The same day she was injured in a taxi-cab accident in Grosvenor Square.

On November 14, the sixty-one-year-old Duke of Atholl, who had fought in the Battle of Khartoum in 1898, found himself in court in connexion with the affairs of his charitable fund. He was accused of selling sweepstake tickets for ten shillings each without disclosing which charities would benefit, and was fined £25. It was said that in private the Duke had described this enterprise as 'my bit of fun'.

On November 21, a crowd of peers and peeresses in crimson, gold and ermine were present when the King opened Parliament. 'You ought to be ashamed of yourselves!' shouted Labour MP John McGovern, who was standing close to the famous Lady Astor at the bar of the House. The King took no notice of this outburst.

At the end of November, Society was astonished to read of the engagement of eccentric composer Lord Berners and Mrs. Violet Trefusis, daughter of Mrs. Keppel, former mistress to King Edward VII. The announcement soon turned out to be a hoax. 'I did not deny it at once' said Mrs. Trefusis. 'I wished first to speak to Lord Berners about it.'

On December 9, a house named the Heronry near Whitchurch in Hampshire was burnt to the ground and it was announced that the twenty-three-year-old Duc de la Tremoille, France's premier Duke, had perished in the blaze. A fellow guest at the house, the Hon. James Rodney, nephew of Lord Wimborne, had been killed when he jumped from an upstairs window.

On December 14, Bridgwater House, London home of the Earl of Ellesmere, was the scene for a huge charity auction, honoured by the presence of the Queen, in a gown of blue sequins and a diamond tiara, and the Duchess of York, in a pale green gown and diamond bandeau, and many other notabilities. One of the items auctioned was the 'swishing block' taken from Eton in 1881. It was sold for £450 and returned to the college.

On December 28, wealthy young scientist Victor Rothschild, heir to Lord Rothschild, was married to Miss Barbara Hutchinson, daughter of barrister Mr. St. John Hutchinson. The ceremony took place, according to strict Jewish rites, in a drawing-room at Tring Park, Hertfordshire. It was said that this venue was chosen in order that Mr. Rothschild's eighty-nine-year-old grandmother, Lady Rothschild, could be present.

On January 1, it was announced that the Prime Minister, Ramsay MacDonald, currently on holiday at Lossiemouth, would visit Loch Ness in the hope of getting a glimpse of the 'monster' which had been the subject of growing interest in recent months.

A few days later, Ernst Freud, son of the famous psychoanalyst, arrived in England with his wife and sons Clement and Lucian. He was rumoured to be furious about the recent burning of his father's books in Germany. 'We have sent the boys to school in Devon' he said. 'England is a paradise for children.'

On January 20, Thelma Lady Furness, left for a six-week visit to America to see her sister, Mrs. Vanderbilt. On the eve of her departure, she invited her friend Mrs. Simpson for a cocktail over which, it was later reported, she urged Mrs. Simpson to look after the Prince of Wales in her absence.

On February 6, there was great excitement when Lord Ashley petitioned his wife for divorce citing world-famous film star Douglas Fairbanks as co-respondent. It was recalled that Lady Ashley was the former starlet Sylvia Hawkes whose marriage to Lord Shaftesbury's heir had created a sensation seven years earlier.

On February 9, fifteen-year-old Esmond Romilly, nephew of Mrs. Winston Churchill, ran away from Wellington College, where it was said he had been attempting to start a Left Wing magazine. Rumours circulated that he was under the power of a group of London Communists. 'We are not worried about his safety' said his mother Mrs. Romilly. 'I have a good idea where he is staying.'

On February 15, newspaper placards printed in purple, the colour usually reserved for announcements about royalty, appeared in the streets announcing that the newly-married Mrs. Charles Sweeny was gravely ill. Mrs. Sweeny, former débutante Margaret Whigham, was in a Welbeck Street nursing-home suffering from double pneumonia complicated by a kidney infection. It was said later that she had been given extreme unction by Jesuit priest Father Martindale and that every newspaper in Fleet Street was preparing her obituary.

At the end of the month, attention turned to the High Court where Princess Youssoupoff, niece of the murdered Russian Tsar, was suing Metro-Goldwyn-Mayer claiming that she has been foully libelled in the film *Rasputin the Mad Monk*. The tall, regal Princess, whose voice was said to be as deep as a man's, accused the film company of portraying her as Rasputin's lover. On March 5, Mr. Justice Avory, trying the last big case in his long career, awarded the Princess the massive sum of £25,000.

By March 21, Mrs. Charles Sweeny had been nursed back to comparative health by Lord Dawson of Penn and she was allowed to leave her nursing-home by ambulance and travelled to Hove on the Sussex coast accompanied by a trained nurse and her old nanny to continue her recuperation. At the same resort was seventy-six-year-old Princess Beatrice, youngest daughter of Queen Victoria, who was recovering from bronchitis and confined to a bath-chair.

On March 22, Thelma Lady Furness returned to England. That night she dined with the Prince of Wales and found his manner changed. At a dinner-party at Fort Belvedere a few days later, she was astonished to realise that the heir to the throne had transferred his affections to Mrs. Ernest Simpson.

On April 6, Tallulah Bankhead arrived in England after a long illness and a hysterectomy. Though thinner and paler, it was stated that the actress had lost none of her style and 'divine droopiness'. A few days after her arrival, she gate-crashed a party given by impresario Charles Cochran in Ivor Novello's flat on top of the Aldwych Theatre, at which Prince George was one of the guests of honour.

On April 10, a strange case opened in the High Court. Magician Aleister Crowley, who had once been dubbed 'the wickedest man in the world', sued writer Nina Hamnett, who had accused him in her recently published memoirs of practising black magic. For the next three days, Crowley's sensational writings came under the court's scrutiny. On the fourth day, Mr. Justice Swift told the jury that he had heard enough. 'I have never heard such dreadful, horrible, blasphemous and abominable stuff. Are you of the same mind or do you wish the case to proceed?' After a few minutes consultation, the jury returned a verdict for Miss Hamnett.

Former Liberal MP and master spy, Trebitsch Lincoln, in the black skull-cap of a Buddhist monk

On April 16, thirty-four-year-old Eric Hatry, barrister brother of the gaoled financier Clarence Hatry, was charged with urging his dog to worry a cat in Soho.

Meanwhile, the sinister Trebitsch Lincoln, former Liberal MP and self-confessed master spy, had become a Buddhist monk calling himself Abbot Chao Kung. He had recently been disowned by China and was making his way towards England where it was rumoured he wished to establish a religious community.

At the beginning of May, he arrived at Liverpool dressed in a grey kimono and black skull-cap and accompanied by ten 'disciples'. He was immediately placed in custody while his followers, under a vow of silence, paced the streets of Liverpool, looking excitedly into the shop-windows. On May 11, Trebitsch Lincoln was deported on board the *Duchess of York* steamship and sent back to Canada and thence to Japan. His devoted followers swiftly converted his cabin into a temple.

On May 16, a taxi carrying Sir Austen Chamberlain overturned in Belgrave Square. Fortunately, the King's physician, the ubiquitous Lord Dawson of Penn, was passing by at the time and was able to escort Sir Austen home in another cab. A few days later, on May 27, Sir Austen had sufficiently recovered to give away his niece, Miss Teretna Dundas at her marriage to Mr. Edgar Smallwood.

Meanwhile, multi-millionairess Barbara Hutton, now married to Georgian Prince Alexis Mdivani, had arrived in England. On May 30, she was admitted to a West End nursing home. It was revealed that she had been on a starvation diet and had been overdoing it, eating nothing for twenty days.

At the beginning of June, Barbara's parents, Mr. and Mrs. Franklyn Hutton arrived in England. Prince Mdivani met them at Southampton and begged them not to take his wife back to America. 'I really will not know for several days what I am going to do about Barbara' said Mr. Hutton. 'I love her and I shall do everything I can to make her happy.'

On June 7, wealthy composer Lord Berners, who had a piano built into the back of his Rolls Royce, was pressed against the railings at Olympia following a clash between blackshirts and Communists at a meeting conducted by his old friend Sir Oswald Mosley. Another spectator at this meeting was thrown on to the pavement completely naked, all his clothes having been torn off.

On June 12, Mrs. Charles Sweeny, who had now recovered from her serious illness, was presented as a married woman at the third Court of the Season at Buckingham Palace. She wore a dress of coral-pink satin and a train of dark-red velvet.

Meanwhile, Thelma Lady Furness, ousted from the affections of the Prince of Wales by her friend Mrs. Simpson, had found solace in the company of the dashing young Prince Aly Khan and had gone on a jaunt with him across Europe. On June 20 she denied a rumour that she and the young Prince were to marry. 'There is no truth in it whatsoever' she said.

On June 26, wealthy Edward James, a godson of Edward VII, was granted a divorce from his wife, dancer Tilly Losch, on the grounds of her misconduct with Prince Serge Obolensky. 'I have not one penny in the world' said Tilly. 'I shall keep on dancing. It is my life.'

On June 30, the sixty-two-year-old Duke of Marlborough died at his town-house, 7 Carlton House Terrace, from which he had ejected his wife in dramatic circumstances the previous year. His devoted cousin, Winston Churchill, was at his side. The Duke's body was conveyed by a special train to Woodstock, where it was met by the Mayor with black crêpe over his mace and a guard of honour of gardeners from Blenheim Palace. The Duke was survived by both his wives and was succeeded by his son, thirty-six-year-old Lord Blandford, who was a familiar figure around Berkeley Square where he had been running a shop selling dairy produce.

A month later, on July 24, magician Aleister Crowley was back in court, this time at the Old Bailey. He was charged with stealing letters which he had used as evidence at this controversial law-suit three months earlier. He was found guilty and bound over for two years to keep the peace. Crowley was said to be the last defendant to wear a black silk top-hat in the dock at the Old Bailey.

On August 1, the Prince of Wales left for a holiday in Biarritz where he had rented a large villa overlooking the ocean. He was accompanied by a small group of friends, who included Mrs. Ernest Simpson and her aunt, Mrs. Bessie Merryman. Mrs. Simpson's husband declined an invitation to join the party as he had business to attend to in New York.

On August 3, it was announced that twenty-eight-year-old Lord Edward Montagu, second son of the Duke of Manchester, was off to join the Foreign Legion. 'I know the life will be very hard indeed but there is no going back' he said.

The same day, Major Charles St. John Rowlandson shot himself in a taxi, just as it was passing St. James's Palace. The driver thought his cab had backfired and drove on taking no notice. On arrival at Albemarle Street, he found his passenger lying dead, shot through the head. Major Rowlandson, who was said to have lost money in a recent business venture, was a familiar figure in the West End. 'He almost lived in taxis' said a friend.

Meanwhile, the recently-widowed Gladys Duchess of Marlborough, ejected from her London home the previous year, had taken up residence in a tiny cottage in an Oxfordshire village. With her, were a companion named Mrs. Grylls and about eighty of the famous Blenheim spaniels. On August 25, the American-born Duchess, who was living under the name Mrs. Spencer, threw a jug of water over an inquisitive journalist. 'It serves you right' said Mrs. Grylls. 'Mrs Spencer wants to be left in peace and quiet.'

On August 26, it was announced that Lord Edward Montagu, a godson of the late King Edward VII, had opened a coffee-stall in Maidenhead. He had built it himself and mounted it on the chassis of a motor-car. 'This is just the beginning' he said. 'I hope to get a chain of stalls going. A couple of weeks ago I was going to join the Foreign Legion but I think this is much better.'

At the end of the month, it was announced that Prince George, now Duke of Kent, was to marry twenty-seven-year-old Princess Marina of Greece. The couple were currently on holiday in Europe where one of the first people to offer congratulations was the Kaiser's son, ex-Crown Prince Wilhelm of Germany. 'The announcement came as a complete surprise to me' said the Duke's Comptroller, Major Ulick Alexander.

At the beginning of September, seventy-four-year-old Dean Inge of St. Paul's, famous for his pessimistic view of humanity, told the world that he was retiring after twenty-three years at the Cathedral. 'I would hate to stay here until I became a bore' he explained. His last sermon, however, did not contain a single reference to the fact that he was leaving.

On September 4, the famous female transvestite 'Colonel Barker', who had caused a sensation five years earlier, plunged into the news again, accused of stealing a woman's handbag from a telephone kiosk. Nine magistrates turned up to hear the case. 'Colonel Barker', a burly figure in horn-rimmed spectacles, brown sports jacket and grey flannel trousers, who now called herself John Hill and said she was working as a kennel-man, denied the charge and was subsequently found not guilty at West Sussex Quarter Sessions.

On September 9, the famous critic and artist Roger Fry died following a fall on a polished floor.

On September 26, the Prince of Wales hurried back from his long holiday with Mrs. Simpson and others to accompany the King and Queen at the launching of the new 81,000-ton Cunard liner *Queen Mary*. The Queen said a few words before christening 'the world's stateliest ship' with a bottle of Australian wine. It was one of the very few occasions on which she had spoken in public and many people were shocked to hear how Germanic she sounded.

Early in October, Thelma Lady Furness left for New York where her twin sister, Mrs. Vanderbilt, was involved in a much-publicised battle over the custody of her daughter Gloria, aged eleven, which had made headline news throughout the world.

On October 9, King Alexander of Yugoslavia was assassinated in Marseilles. The crown immediately passed to his son Peter, an eleven-year-old pupil at a Surrey preparatory school. The boy set off at once by ship and train to his troubled kingdom.

On October 31, the Marquess of Londonderry denied rumours of an engagement between his daughter Lady Helen Stewart and ex-King Alfonso's third son, Prince Juan. 'The Prince has stayed with us in Ireland. We have all been friends for many years. But I have heard nothing about any engagement.' A few days later rumours also circulated that Lord Londonderry's daughter Margaret was on the point of marrying pioneer civil aviator, Alan Muntz, which were again denied by the Londonderry parents.

On November 14, London bandleader Jack Harris and his orchestra arrived in Paris to provide the music for a spectacular party at the Ritz Hotel given by Miss Barbara Hutton and her husband, Prince Alexis Mdivani. The lobby of the hotel was transformed into a Russian nobleman's hall and the ballroom into a Moorish street. 1919 vintage champagne was served. Harris and his orchestra had been recruited for a £2,000 fee.

On November 19, Londonderry House, Park Lane, awash with rumours of romance, was the scene of the traditional eve-of-Parliament reception. As usual, the house was jam-packed and it took guests twenty minutes to scale the great staircase to greet Lady Londonderry and her new friend Prime Minister Ramsay MacDonald.

Two days later, the Londonderrys' daughter Lady Margaret Stewart married aviator Alan Muntz in a London registry office. Neither of the bride's parents, who were said to strongly disapprove of the match, were present.

At the end of November, everyone was heavily preoccupied with the wedding of the Duke of Kent and Princess Marina of Greece. Two days before the marriage, there was a ball at Buckingham Palace. Among the 800 guests were Mr. and Mrs. Ernest Simpson, whose lives were now closely entangled with that of the Prince of Wales. At some stage during the evening, the Prince introduced Mrs. Simpson to his parents. 'It was the briefest of encounters' she wrote afterwards. 'A few words of perfunctory greeting, an exchange of meaningless pleasantries and we moved away.'

On November 29, the Kent marriage took place in Westminster Abbey. Among the guests was thirteen-year-old blond-headed Prince Philip of Greece, currently a pupil at Gordonstoun, a progressive new public school founded by Kurt Hahn, who had been driven out of Germany by the new Chancellor, Adolf Hitler.

On December 5, a gambling-party at Sunderland House, Mayfair, made headline news. Over £80,000 had changed hands and London was soon humming with excitement and rumours that many participants had not settled their accounts. A financier was said to have lost £10,000. 'I have been a first-class fool in the opinion of my City friends' he said.

On December 20, it was announced that Clarence Hatry's former home, 5 Great Stanhope Street, was to become a Bridge club. Almack's were negotiating for the lease of the lavish mansion, which had a heated swimming pool in its basement.

On December 29, the Lord Chief Justice of England, Lord Hewart, married a young New Zealand girl, who was said to have worked as a nurse. 'She has certainly not nursed me in any illness' boomed the burly judge 'because I have not been ill recently. Except in newspaper rumours and according to people who want my job.'

1935

On New Year's Day, there was great excitement over the engagement of wealthy young land owner, Sir Michael Duff, and the Hon. Joan Marjoribanks, youngest daughter of Lord Tweedmouth.

On January 3, Lady Lavery died at her home in South Kensington. Hazel Lavery had been a source of endless gossip over the years – largely on account of her young men. Her husband, Sir John Lavery, painted a last picture of her as she lay dying.

On January 10, Mary Pickford got a divorce from Douglas Fairbanks in a hearing which took just three minutes. Fairbanks was currently reported to be on holiday with former starlet Lady Ashley. They were staying at an Alpine resort and said to be en route to the South Sea Islands where the film star's 750-ton yacht lay anchored.

On January 11, there was an old-fashioned ball at Belvoir Castle in honour of Lady Ursula and Lady Isobel Manners, beautiful young daughters of the Duke and Duchess of Rutland. The frail old Violet Duchess of Rutland, mother of Lady Diana Cooper, was found surrounded by her descendants. Her grandson, fifteen-year-old Marquess of Granby, heir to the dukedom, bounded about in a black suit.

On January 20, Hollywood star Mae West announced that she was coming to London for this year's Silver Jubilee celebrations. She explained that she had been invited by no lesser person than the former Chief of the Metropolitan Police, Lord Byng of Vimy.

Heading the opposite direction was Society drug addict Brenda Dean Paul. At the end of January, she was off to America to lecture on drugs and their effects on young people.

At the beginning of February, the Prince of Wales invited Mr. and Mrs. Ernest Simpson to join him on a winter-sports holiday at Kitzbuhl in Austria. Mr. Simpson tactfully declined the invitation on the grounds that he had business to attend to in New York. His wife joined the party on her own.

On February 9, in Munich, German Chancellor Adolf Hitler invited twenty-year-old Unity Mitford, daughter of Lord Redesdale, to join his table at the Ostaria Bavaria. For several weeks, Miss Mitford had been sitting in the Führer's favourite restaurant hoping to catch his eye.

On February 11, May Etheridge, the music-hall artist who had become Duchess of Leinster, died from a massive overdose of sleeping draught at her Brighton lodgings. The former premier Duchess of Ireland had been living there under the name Miss Murray. One of the great grievances of her life was that she had been forbidden to see her son, the Marquess of Kildare, now twenty-one and a Lieutenant in the Inniskilling Dragoon Guards. She had been obliged to follow his career through the Society columns.

Three days later, it was said that the Duchess's widowed mother spent her savings to pay for the funeral. 'I don't care a damn for the family' said the old lady. 'Society is nothing to me.' The Duke of Leinster was present at the ceremony and the Marquess of Kildare sent a wreath of spring flowers.

A few days later, on February 21, a spectacular double suicide took place. Two sisters, Jane and Elizabeth du Bois, daughters of a United States Consul General, leapt from a Paris-bound airliner 2,000 feet above Essex. It was reported that both their boyfriends had died in a plane crash in Italy a few days earlier. The girls had spent the last two nights in London at the Ritz Hotel and on their last night alive had seemed cheerful enough when they attended a revue at the Savoy Theatre called *Hi-Diddle-Diddle*.

On March 5, Society flocked to St. Margaret's Westminster for the marriage of twenty-seven-year-old Sir Michael Duff and the Hon. Joan Marjoribanks. Among the congregation were sixty workmen from the bridegroom's estate in Anglesey, many of whom had never before left their Welsh villages and were unable to speak even a word of English. Lady Ponsonby, mother of the new Duchess of Westminster, arrived twenty minutes late at the ceremony in a stately, horse-drawn brougham. That night, the summit of Snowdon was floodlit, as a gift to Sir Michael from the North Wales Power Company.

A few days later, attention turned to a hotel in Park Lane where twenty-two-year-old Princess Mdivani, better known as Barbara Hutton, was in complete seclusion surrounded by rumours that her two-year marriage was at an end. On March 23, the multi-millionairess sailed for America to obtain a divorce. 'Alexis and I are still the greatest of friends, always have been and always will be' she said before departure.

On April 5, the uncrowned King of Lancashire, Lord Derby, celebrated his seventieth birthday; 80,000 people each contributed a shilling to buy him a present and special trains were run to carry 5,000 people to a celebration at Preston Town Hall, during which Lord Derby broke down and wept. 'Nobody knows better than I that if I have succeeded in deserving praise it is entirely due to the incidence of my birth, which gave me opportunities given to few' he told the vast audience.

Meanwhile in Munich, Sir Oswald Mosley met Adolf Hitler for the first time. The Führer gave a lunch-party at his flat in Sir Oswald's honour at which the Führer's new friend Unity Mitford was present. Also there were English-born Frau Winifred Wagner and the Duchess of Brunswick, the ex-Kaiser's only daughter. Sir Oswald wrote afterwards that on this occasion he found Hitler charming and gentle and not at all insane.

On April 14, the Duke and Duchess of Kent returned from their honeymoon and moved into 3 Belgrave Square. The house had been sumptuously decorated. It was said that the Duchess's bathroom had been done up in black and silver with the bath itself in a silver alcove surrounded by silver curtains.

Among the innumerable foreign dignitaries now converging on London for the Silver Jubilee celebrations was the Maharajah of Kashmir, who was reputed to have an income of £2,000,000 a year. He arrived at Victoria Station carrying both an umbrella and a mackintosh. He and his party were whisked away in a fleet of limousines driven by chauffeurs in new dove-grey uniforms.

On May 10, the fifty-eight-year-old Duke of Manchester popped up in court charged with pawning some jewellery which belonged to his Trustees. He was sentenced to nine months imprisonment for obtaining money by false pretences and taken to Wormwood Scrubs.

On May 14, the Silver Jubilee was celebrated with a Court Ball at Buckingham Palace, at which the most gossip-worthy guests were Mr. and Mrs. Ernest Simpson. During the course of the evening, Mrs. Simpson, now much bejewelled, danced with the Prince of Wales while the King and Queen looked on frostily. It was said afterwards that throughout the Jubilee celebrations, the Prince was torn between official functions and Mrs. Simpson's company.

The following day, the world was shocked to hear that the legendary Lawrence of Arabia had had a motorcycle accident and was unconscious in a military hospital with a severely fractured skull. While crowds of sightseers gathered round Lawrence's empty cottage, wild rumours circulated. The most far-fetched of these was that the man in hospital was a 'cover' and that Lawrence himself was in the Middle East on a secret mission. Speculation continued after Lawrence's death on May 20. A mysterious black saloon car, seen on the road at the time of the accident, was mentioned at the Inquest but never traced by the police.

At the end of May, Herr Joachim von Ribbentrop arrived in England to lead the German team at the Naval Treaty Talks. On previous visits he had been selling Pommery champagne. He was soon to be seen at the Opera with Lady Cunard.

On June 5, the Duke of Manchester's nine-month prison sentence was quashed by the Court of Appeal. He was collected by his son, Viscount Mandeville, from Wormwood Scrubs and a family friend remarked: 'The Duke actually seems in better health than when he went in.'

That afternoon, thousands of people flocked to Epsom for the Derby. On this occasion, the great race was won by the Aga Khan's horse Bahram. The Aga Khan and his new wife had arrived in England at the last moment, crossing the Channel by night-ferry and disembarking at Newhaven, so that the Aga Khan could enjoy a game of golf before setting off for Epsom. That night, they were guests of honour at a banquet at Buckingham Palace. At the Queen's suggestion, the tables were decorated with the Aga Khan's racing colours, green and chocolate.

On June 11, the Prince of Wales caused an outcry when he suggested at the Annual Conference of the British Legion that its members should 'stretch forth the hand of friendship' to Germany. The speech caused immediate discussion about the Prince's supposed Nazi sympathies. In high society, it was rumoured that he had been influenced by Mrs. Simpson and Lady Cunard.

Two days later, there was another court ball at Buckingham Palace, which was enriched by the presence of Lady Cunard, the young Marchioness of Dufferin and Ava, the Aga Khan and his new wife, interior decorator Lady Colefax and Lord Beaverbrook. The Prince of Wales was said to be looking bad-tempered and complaining about the hostile reactions to his recent speech.

On June 18, wealthy Tory MP Loel Guinness sued his wife Joan for divorce naming Prince Aly Khan as co-respondent. In answer to his friends' enquiries Aly said that he and Mrs. Guinness planned to marry as soon as possible. Soon afterwards, the couple left for the Bahamas to lie low until the divorce became final.

Over in Germany, twenty-year-old Miss Unity Mitford was attending the summer festival at Hesselberg. On June 23 before an audience which some estimates put at 200,000, she made a short speech in which she expressed her solidarity with German people and pledged her support for Julius Streicher, the notorious Jew-baiter.

Meanwhile, Augustus John's son Henry had vanished while bathing off the Cornish coast. The famous artist travelled to the scene and assisted police and coast guards in their search. It was said that he also managed to do a little sketching in the vicinity. A fortnight later, on July 5, his son's decomposed and faceless body was washed ashore.

On July 16, an aeroplane carrying oil millionaire's son Nubar Gulbenkian and half a dozen others to the Silver Jubilee Naval Review at Spithead crashed soon after take-off. With astonishing efficiency, Mr. Gulbenkian's chauffeur, Hewitt, raced to the burnt-out wreck, extracted his master and rushed him to hospital. Gulbenkian later confessed somewhat guiltily that he was in the operating theatre at the London Clinic while his fellow passengers – two of them died – were still waiting for ambulances.

The same day, Douglas Fairbanks and Lady Ashley arrived in England after an extended world cruise. 'Ask me what you like' said Fairbanks to attendant Pressmen. 'But I refuse to discuss my personal affairs.'

On July 19, Mrs. Diana Guinness was on her way to Sir Oswald Mosley's house at Denham in Buckinghamshire when her car collided with a Rolls-Royce in West Halkin Street. Sixteen stitches were required and socialites wondered if her beautiful face would be ruined. Fortunately, the famous plastic-surgeon Sir Harold Gillies took charge of the case and Mrs. Guinness emerged from the accident almost unscathed.

On August 6, the Prince of Wales arrived in Cannes on the first step of a two-month holiday. His pet terrier was under his arm and Mrs. Ernest Simpson was in the party. Once again, Mr. Simpson had declined an invitation to join the expedition. The first few days of the holiday were spent at Lord Cholmondeley's Villa le Roc at Golfe Juan.

Meanwhile at Blackpool, the former Rector of Stiffkey, Harold Davidson, and his daughter Pamela had entered adjoining 'fasting cabinets' to amuse the crowds on the Central Beach. On August 10, both were arrested and charged with attempted suicide. On being found not guilty, the famous ex-clergyman sued Blackpool Corporation for damages and was awarded £382.

At the end of August, the heavily-built Prince Henry, now Duke of Gloucester, announced his engagement to Lady Alice Montagu-Douglas-Scott, daughter of the King's old friend, the Duke of Buccleuch. It was revealed in the gossip columns that Lady Alice smoked cigarettes.

During September, while the shadow of the Abyssinia Crisis hung over Europe, the Prince of Wales and Mrs. Simpson extended their holiday by cruising to Corsica on board the Duke of Westminster's yacht *Cutty Sark*, and then transferring to Mrs. Reginald Fellowes's vessel, the *Sister Anne*, for a cruise to the island of Porquerolles.

On October 9, the Duchess of Kent gave birth to a boy at 3 Belgrave Square. Her parents, Prince and Princess Nicholas of Greece, had come over to England for the confinement and were lodging at Claridge's.

The same day, at 21 St. James's Place, Lady Honor Channon also gave birth to a boy, later christened Paul. One of the first people to fondle the Channon baby was Mrs. Laura Corrigan, the former telephone operator from Cleveland, Ohio who had now established herself in the highest possible social circles.

Meanwhile, unabashed by the Abyssinia Crisis, which had now developed into war, the Duke of

Westminster was calmly fishing in the Red Sea off his luxurious yacht, *Cutty Sark*. 'My movements are uncertain' said the Duke. 'I may visit Abyssinia although I would certainly not like to add to the crush of foreigners in Addis Ababa.'

On October 19, the Duke of Buccleuch died in Scotland. His daughter, Lady Alice, betrothed to the Duke of Gloucester, had flown north in the Prince of Wales's private aeroplane to be at his bedside. The Duke, who had seventeen titles and half a million acres, was succeeded by his son, the Earl of Dalkeith, a young man with considerable financial skills.

The following day, Lord Sysonby, one of the greatest Court officials of the day, died at St. James's Palace. Soon afterwards, rumours circulated that the sixty-eight-year-old peer, who had given devoted service to three monarchs, had died completely penniless and his widow had been given three months to clear out of the Palace, which had been her home throughout her married life.

On November 6, owing to the recent death of the bride's father, the Gloucester wedding took place quietly in the Chapel at Buckingham Palace instead of at Westminster Abbey. Princess Elizabeth and Princess Margaret acted as bridesmaids.

On November 13, the Marchioness of Tavistock sued her eccentric husband for restitution of conjugal rights. The couple had been living apart for over a year and Lady Tavistock claimed that she had been deserted. The Marquess's lawyers put forward the case that their son's tutor, the Rev. Cecil Squire, had influenced Lady Tavistock against him and the petition was dismissed. The case was said to have cost the couple some £20,000.

In the middle of November, multi-millionairess Barbara Hutton and her new husband, Danish-born Count Reventlow, arrived in London and rented a large Regency house, 2 Hyde Park Gardens, from a certain Mrs. Carr-Saunders. It was announced that Barbara was now expecting a baby.

On November 24, the traditional eve-of-Parliament reception at Londonderry House was cancelled at the last moment, even though the invitations had been sent out. It was stated that the new Prime Minister Stanley Baldwin, who had taken over in June from the ailing Ramsay MacDonald, was 'too busy'.

On December 3, the State Opening of Parliament was also cancelled, owing to the fact that the King's sister Princess Victoria was dying at Coppins. Said to be the most diffident member of the Royal Family, Princess Victoria had been known in some circles as 'Her Royal Shyness'.

This lack of ceremony was partly made up for on December 12 by the spectacular trial in the House of Lords of twenty-eight-year-old Lord de Clifford. The handsome young peer, whose marriage to one of the daughters of nightclub Queen Mrs. Meyrick had caused a sensation in 1926, was accused of manslaughter of a fellow motorist on the Kingston By-Pass. His fellow peers turned out in robes of scarlet and ermine to give the young peer a unanimous acquittal. Lady de Clifford sat among the other peeresses. One of the few peers not in full regalia was the Earl of Kinnoull, also married to a daughter of Mrs. Meyrick. Among the celebrities in the crowded galleries was A. P. Herbert, in a tweed suit.

A week later on December 19, the Foreign Secretary, Sir Samuel Hoare, resigned following public anger at his secret proposals to divide up Abyssinia and avoid war. After delivering a moving speech, Sir Samuel sat down and burst into tears. Over his nose, which he had broken in a skating accident in Switzerland a few days earlier, was a big piece of sticking plaster. On December 23, he was replaced as Foreign Secretary by the handsome thirty-eight-year-old Anthony Eden.

At Christmas this year, the King was said to be too old and ill to be worried about the Prince of Wales's much talked-about relationship with Mrs. Ernest Simpson. It was reported later that he had already remarked gloomily to the Prime Minister Stanley Baldwin: 'After I am dead, the boy will ruin himself in twelve months.'

On New Year's Day, Lord Lonsdale's famous yellow Daimler left Lowther Castle for the last time. The veteran sporting peer had been under great pressure recently from his Trustees to give up both the castle and his house in Carlton House Terrace and had finally accepted their advice. 'It can't be helped' he said. 'I am only like a great many others.'

On January 12, a spectacular ball at the State Opera House in Berlin sent ripples of excitement round Europe. It was to celebrate the forty-third birthday of Air Minister Goering, who was covered in decorations, and it was described as Berlin's grandest party since the days of the Kaiser. The former Crown Prince Wilhelm was among the 2,000 guests. The only person missing was the Chancellor, Adolf Hitler.

On January 13, seventy-year-old Rudyard Kipling, once the world's highest-paid writer, was taken from Brown's Hotel, Dover Street by ambulance. He was said to be gravely ill with a gastric ulcer perforating his stomach. Five days later he was dead.

The public's grief was quickly eclipsed by anxiety about the health of the King, also seventy years old. He was at Sandringham suffering from an attack of bronchial catarrh aggravated by his distress over the recent death of his sister, Princess Victoria.

On January 17, the Prince of Wales and the Duke of York travelled to Norfolk on an ordinary train. So did the royal physician, Lord Dawson of Penn. Two days later they were joined by Archbishop of Canterbury, Dr. Lang, who passed the four-hour train journey reading Lord Lytton's newly-published book on his son Lord Knebworth, who had died in an air-crash three years back.

At Sandringham, the King lay in a four-poster bed in his red-carpeted bedroom on the first floor. Oxygen equipment was set up to aid his breathing and, as a last resort, the heart specialist Sir Maurice Cassidy recommended that the monarch's heart should be massaged. To no avail. At 9.35 pm on January 20, it was announced that the King's life was moving peacefully towards its close and at five minutes to midnight, he was dead. Among the silent crowds waiting in the rain outside Buckingham Palace for the last, sad bulletin was Mrs. Charles Sweeny.

The public's attention immediately switched to the new monarch, the first bachelor King since George III and those in the know were particularly fascinated by the new position of his friend, Mrs. Ernest Simpson.

On January 22, following the official proclamation by the heralds of the new King, Mrs. Simpson was spotted driving away from St. James's Palace in a huge black car, with its blinds half down. She had watched the ceremony from the window of a disused flat.

The following day, the new King walked for two miles behind the gun-carriage bearing his father's coffin to Westminster Hall. As the procession turned into Palace Yard, the bejewelled Maltese Cross on top of the Royal Crown fell to the gutter. It was quickly scooped up by a sergeant-major and the new King was heard to mutter: 'Christ! What will happen next?'

On January 25, among the thousands who filed past the purple-draped coffin and paid homage to the dead King was young Lord Howland, eighteen-year-old grandson of the Duke of Bedford. He was the first member of his family to have been seen around London for three generations and was currently living on an income of £98 a year.

On January 28, the old King was ceremoniously buried at St. George's Chapel, Windsor while far away in Monte Carlo play was suspended in the casino for one minute as a mark of respect. The Court had meanwhile plunged into heavy mourning and the sparkling Mrs. Simpson remarked to friends that she had not worn black stockings since she gave up the Can Can.

Early in February, it was announced that Queen Mary would move from Buckingham Palace, her home for the last twenty-six years, to Marlborough House in the Mall, originally built by Sir Christopher Wren for the first Duke and Duchess of Marlborough.

Meanwhile Mr. Chips Channon and his wife and child had moved into 5 Belgrave Square, a huge house two doors away from the home of the Duke and Duchess of Kent. The house had been fabulously decorated and still smelled of paint. Mr. Channon had hired a certain Monsieur Boudin from Paris to create a spectacular blue and silver dining-room modelled on a room in the Amalienburg Palace and soon to be described as 'London's loveliest room'.

On February 18, Mr. and Mrs. Franklyn Hutton arrived in England to be with their daughter Barbara, now Countess Reventlow, during the birth of her child. 'My husband and I are awfully happy about the whole thing' said Mrs. Hutton at Waterloo Station, before being driven to Barbara's rented house in Hyde Park Gardens, where four large rooms had been prepared as a spacious nursery. A few days later on February 23, the Countess demanded that her baby should be delivered by Caesarian operation. There was no medical need for this but her doctor knew better than to argue with her.

Following the birth of her multi-million dollar baby, the Countess sank into a coma and doubts were expressed about whether she would survive. Lord Horder and other specialists called frequently at the house, now guarded by six burly security men.

On February 25, the new King walked from Buckingham Palace on foot to attend a meeting at the offices of the Duchy of Cornwall in Buckingham Gate. He returned to the Palace by motor-car.

On February 26, the World's Greatest Practical Joker, Mr. Horace de Vere Cole, brother of Mrs. Neville Chamberlain, died in seriously reduced circumstances in a remote district of France. His young wife Mavis had left him some time ago and thrown in her lot with the wealthy painter Augustus John, by whom she had already produced a child named Tristan.

On March 7, the marriage took place in Paris of film star Douglas Fairbanks and former starlet Sylvia, Lady Ashley, with whom he had shared his life for many months.

Douglas Fairbanks Snr. and Lady Ashley during their wedding service in Paris

On March 11, Admiral of the Fleet Earl Beatty died in London. The great war-hero had been ill since the previous November and had disobeyed his doctor's advice and taken part in King George V's funeral procession, looking ill and old. He was succeeded by his son, thirty-one-year-old Viscount Borodale.

Meanwhile, a Manchester man had attempted to obtain £200 from Countess Reventlow by means of a false kidnap plot. On March 14, Count Reventlow travelled to Manchester armed with a gun and secured the arrest of the man, who later issued a statement saying he hoped he had not caused the Count and Countess 'any worry or anxiety'.

On March 17, former amateur bull-fighter Rupert Bellville, a member of White's Club, was fined £10 for refusing to obey the 'No Smoking' sign on an airliner flying between Paris and London. This was said to be the first case of its kind.

On April 1, it was revealed that Labour peer Lord Faringdon was adding a swimming-pool, squash-court and private cinema to his Berkshire home, Buscot. It was noted that the house already had seventeen bathrooms.

On April 10, the sudden death of the German Ambassador Leopold von Hoesch shocked London. It was said that the tall, wealthy bachelor had collapsed in the bathroom at his Embassy in Carlton House Terrace, holding the hand of his valet. 'For some years past the Ambassador has been having heart trouble' said Prince Bismarck, Counsellor at the Embassy. 'He refused to take it seriously, however, and insisted on working as hard as ever.' This explanation did not satisfy everybody however and a rumour circulated that von Hoesch, who had never seen eye-to-eye with his Nazi bosses, had been liquidated.

In the middle of April, it was announced that the handsome young Earl of Warwick was to become a film star. Negotiations were under way with a wealthy Hollywood producer Mervyn Le Roy. 'I have no definite parts or stories in view yet' said Mr. Le Roy, 'but I would definitely be starting him in pictures, not giving him minor roles.'

Meanwhile, celebrations had begun on board the *Queen Mary*, soon to leave on speed trials and her maiden voyage. On April 17, world-champion hurdler, Lord Burghley, heir to the Marquess of Exeter, was challenged to run round the entire main deck in less than one minute. Watched by H. G. Wells, Lord Camrose and other celebrities, the thirty-one-year-old aristocrat raced round the ship in full evening-dress, completing the course in fifty-eight seconds.

On April 29, a new heir was born to the Rothschild fortunes when Mrs. Victor Rothschild presented her husband with a baby boy. Mrs. Rothschild's father, the eminent barrister, Mr. St. John Hutchinson, was conducting a case at the Old Bailey when his clerk handed him a pencilled note announcing the news. He smiled and carried on with his case.

Early in May, the news broke that Countess Reventlow was in the process of buying the fourteen-acre St. Dunstan's Estate in Regent's Park. She soon decided to pull down the existing mansion and build another in its place, employing Sir John Milbanke as interior designer. One feature of the new house would be a nursery wing with padded pink calf-skin walls.

On May 15, Lady Cunard gave a dinner-party at her house in Grosvenor Square, which was attended by the King, Mr. and Mrs. Simpson, Winston Churchill and others. During the course of the evening, Mr. Simpson used a gadget attached to his key-chain to open a bottle of Vichy water for His Majesty.

Meanwhile, Prince Aly Khan and Mrs. Joan Guinness had returned to Europe from their hideaway in the Bahamas. On May 18, they were married in Paris and it was noted that the Prince had given his bride 'ropes of pearls'.

The following day, the King spent two hours at the Chelsea Flower Show. He arrived wearing a straw boater just after Queen Mary had left and bumped into his brother, the Duke of Kent, in the orchid tent. Before leaving, he ordered some chunks of rock for his garden at Fort Belvedere.

On May 27, Labour Cabinet Minister, J. H. Thomas surrendered his seals of office to the King at Buckingham Palace following a scandalous Budget leak which had shocked the nation. 'Thank God your old dad is not alive to see this' said Mr. Thomas, a great favourite of King George V.

That afternoon, the *Queen Mary* set off on her maiden voyage to New York. Among the celebrities on board were photographer Cecil Beaton, in a bright yellow double-breasted waistcoat, and young harmonica player, Larry Adler. Two and a half million pounds worth of gold bullion was also said to be on board.

In the evening of this action-packed day, the King gave a dinner party at St. James's Palace to which he boldly invited Mr. and Mrs. Simpson and Mr. and Mrs. Stanley Baldwin. 'It's got to be done' he said beforehand. 'Sooner or later my Prime Minister must meet my future wife.' Soon afterwards Mrs. Simpson began divorce proceedings against her husband.

On May 29, millionairess Mrs. Laura Corrigan, who had taken Crewe House for the Season, gave a lunch-party in honour of the sinister Herr von Ribbentrop. That afternoon, Mrs. Corrigan, Ribbentrop and Lord Londonderry left to spend the long Whitsun weekend at the Londonderry stately home in Northern Ireland, Mount Stewart.

On June 11, the three-month-old Reventlow baby was taken under police escort to be christened at Marlborough House Chapel.

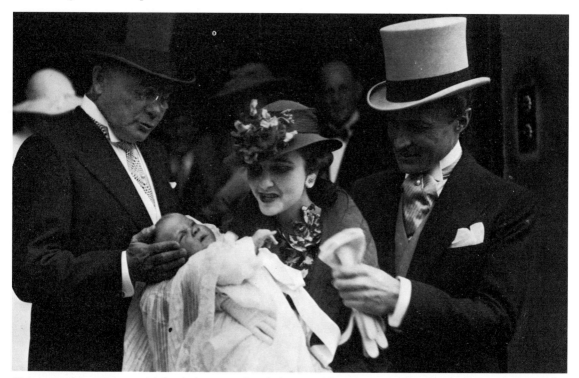

Heiress Barbara Hutton with her baby Lance, her father Franklyn Hutton and her husband Count Reventlow

A few days later, Lord and Lady Louis Mountbatten moved into a thirty-room flat on top of the new building which had been built on the site of Lady Louis's former home, Brook House, in Park Lane. The flat, which was described as 'London's First Penthouse', was approached by an express lift from a private entrance in Upper Brook Street. One of the first people to get stuck in this famous lift was Queen Mary.

At the beginning of July, there was an outcry when it was revealed that the Aga Khan had sold his famous Derby winner, Blenheim, to an American syndicate for £45,000. It was later revealed that the Aga Khan feared that Europe was doomed and wanted to re-establish his stable in America.

On July 10, the King gave another dinner-party at St. James's Palace at which Mrs. Simpson was present but not her husband. The names of the guests were later published in the Court Circular and the absence of Mr. Ernest Simpson did not go unnoticed.

On July 13, Hitler's friend, the Hon. Unity Mitford, was spotted dining at a leading French restaurant in London with **Mr. Duff Cooper**, Secretary of State for War. The couple were said to be engaged in passionate political talk. **Shortly afterwards,** Unity returned to Germany with her sister Mrs. Diana Guinness for the Olympic Games.

On July 20, Somerset Maugham's daughter Liza was married to Mr. Vincent Paravicini at St. Margaret's, Westminster. The famous best-selling author returned from his wanderings to give away the bride. At the reception at the Swiss Legation, a wedding-cake, designed by Mr. Oliver Messel, was cut into and much attention was focused on Lady Mendl's startling bright-blue hair.

The following day, a garden-party at Buckingham Palace for débutantes was ruined by a sudden, heavy downpour of rain. Débutantes sprinted for cover and many costly dresses were wrecked.

Meanwhile, political turmoil in France had forced the King to alter his holiday arrangements. At the end of July, he cancelled his plans to rent the Château de L'Horizon near Cannes, sending an apologetic message to its owner, Miss Maxine Elliott, accompanied by an eighteenth-century silver snuff-box. 'The house will always be available if the King wishes to take it later' said Miss Elliott, former mistress of the King's grandfather Edward VII.

Instead, the King chartered Lady Yule's steam yacht *The Nahlin*, a fabulously luxurious twelve-bathroom vessel, for a cruise along the Dalmatian coast. On August 8, he and Mrs. Simpson left London in a private coach attached to the Orient Express. Everywhere the couple went over the next few weeks, the King and Mrs. Simpson were photographed together. One particular photograph, which showed Mrs. Simpson's hand on the King's arm, excited very special interest.

Meanwhile, on August 19, Hugh Lygon, son of the exiled Lord Beauchamp, had collapsed and died. His funeral was held at the moated family home in Worcestershire and his father, who had now been living abroad for more than five years, received official assurances that he would not be arrested if he returned home to England to attend it. Just to be safe, however, a Tiger Moth aircraft was kept standing by and the white-haired Earl went back into exile after less than a week in England.

On September 2, seventy-three-year-old former Prime Minister Mr. Lloyd George left for a short holiday in Germany. One of the highlights of his trip was tea with Hitler at his chalet high in the Bavarian Alps. 'Mr. Lloyd George is thoroughly enjoying himself' said a spokesman. 'He loves this beautiful spot. It is so akin to his native Wales.'

King Edward VIII at his first garden party at Buckingham Palace

On September 9, the Earl of Lonsdale made headline news when he announced that he could not afford to attend the St. Leger. It was observed that the Earl's family trust still owned 175,000 acres and that the Earl was a steward of the Jockey Club. Soon afterwards, the Earl was found selling champagne from the cellar at Lowther Castle, which was now permanently closed.

On September 5, Winston Churchill's twenty-one-year-old daughter, Sarah, announced her intention of marrying American comedian Vic Oliver and left for America on board the *Bremen*, swiftly pursued on the *Queen Mary* by her brother Randolph, who declared that his sister was too young to know her own mind.

Meanwhile, the King had returned from his holiday. On September 18, a crowd of 10,000 people saw him leave London for Balmoral on board the *Royal Highlander* express.

A few days later, Mrs. Simpson also travelled north. The King met her at Ballater Station and in full public view, placed her in the seat beside him for the drive to the Castle.

Also staying at Balmoral at this time were the Duke and Duchess of Marlborough, the Duke and Duchess of Sutherland, the Earl and Countess of Rosebery and other representatives of the old-fashioned aristocracy. During her short stay at the Castle, Mrs. Simpson introduced the household to the idea of the three-decker toasted sandwich.

Meanwhile, the Marquess of Winchester, former Chairman of the Hatry group and Hereditary Bearer of the Cap of Maintenance had arrived in London. On September 22, he announced that he hoped to serve at the forthcoming Coronation. 'My Coronation robes are ready. I have already been to two Coronations. As for the Hatry affair, what need I say?'

On October 5, Sir Oswald Mosley slipped quietly out of the country. The following day in the drawing-room of Dr. Goebbels's house in Berlin, he was secretly married to his old friend Mrs. Diana Guinness. After the ceremony, attended by the bride's sister Unity, Frau Goebbels gave a luncheon at her lakeside villa, at which the star guest was Adolf Hitler. The newly married couple flew back to England the next day.

On October 14, the Duke of Leinster, who had recently appeared in the Bankruptcy Courts again, this time revealing liabilities of £139,233, set off for Ireland to attend the wedding of his son, the Marquess of Kildare. The Duke travelled Third Class and wore a shabby blue suit. 'This is the only suit I have been able to buy in the last six years' he told reporters.

On October 27, Mrs. Simpson's divorce suit was heard at Ipswich. The proceedings, during which Mr. Simpson was accused of impropriety with a lady named Buttercup Kennedy, took only a few minutes and Mrs. Simpson was whisked away from the court by the King's chauffeur, seventeen-stone George Ladbroke. Police used force to prevent reporters from following her and two cameras were smashed.

German Ambassador Joachim von Ribbentrop leaves his London residence

At the end of October, Herr von Ribbentrop, now the new German Ambassador, arrived in London with his baby son Adolf. It was rumoured that an aircraft was kept standing by so that he could dash back at any moment for consultations with Herr Hitler.

On November 3, the King opened Parliament surrounded by rumours that he wished to marry Mrs. Wallis Simpson. Lady Diana Cooper sat beside Mrs. Stanley Baldwin in the gallery for Ministers' wives and Herr von Ribbentrop was in the Ambassador's box.

Meanwhile, preparations for the Coronation continued. On November 11, the young Earl Marshal, the Duke of Norfolk, organised an exhibition at his stately town house in St. James's Square of correct coronation wear for peers and peeresses. Rumours were circulating simultaneously that the young Duke was to marry twenty-year-old Lavinia Strutt. 'This is the first I've heard of it' said Lavinia's mother, Lady Rosebery, who had recently been staying at Balmoral.

On November 18, the King, who had now told both his mother and the Prime Minister that he wished to abdicate, left for a tour of South Wales. While in this distressed area, he made a number of outspoken remarks about unemployment which led many people to believe that he now had strong Left Wing sympathies.

The following day, he was back in London and he and Mrs. Simpson attended a spectacular dinner at Mr. Chips Channon's glittering new establishment in Belgrave Square. The King was in high spirits throughout the evening and told his host's wife how much he approved of splendour.

Meanwhile, Mrs. Simpson had been seen lunching at Claridge's with Esmond Harmsworth, son of the owner of the *Daily Mail*. It was subsequently revealed that he was proposing and explaining the possibility of a morganatic marriage.

Diners at the Café de Paris read of the King's wish to marry Mrs. Wallis Simpson

On November 27, eighty-six-year-old Sir Basil Zaharoff died in Monte Carlo. Frequently described as the Mystery Man of Europe, it was said that Sir Basil had made £30,000,000 out of arms dealing during the Great War. In recent months, he had been confined to a wheelchair.

On December 1, Mrs. Mavis de Vere Cole arrived at 11 Downing Street to collect the possessions of her husband, who had died in France earlier in the year. His things had been boxed up and sent to his sister, Mrs. Neville Chamberlain. Mavis's silver fox furs created only a mild stir in Downing Street that day where Ministers and spectators had more serious matters on their minds.

On December 3, the world was informed that the King was in love with Mrs. Wallis Simpson and wished to marry her.

The same day, Mrs. Simpson left the country accompanied by Lord Brownlow and driven by the King's chauffeur George Ladbroke. They were pursued by the Press across France to the villa of a certain Mr. and Mrs. Herman Rogers. Here they were soon joined by Mrs. Simpson's solicitor and his doctor. The presence of the latter gave rise to a rumour that Mrs. Simpson was pregnant.

On December 10, a message from the King announcing his Abdication was read to both Houses of Parliament. In the gallery of the House of Lords was Miss Unity Mitford, who had returned from Germany for Christmas with her family. 'Oh, Hitler will be terribly unhappy about this. He wanted Edward to stay King' she whispered to her companion.

The following night, the ex-King, soon to be created Duke of Windsor, left the country on board the destroyer *Fury*. Society swiftly rallied round the new monarch and his family and the public's attention was diverted to other topics.

On December 13, it was announced that Princess Joan Aly Khan had given birth to a son in a private clinic in Geneva. The boy, grandson of the Aga Khan, was later given the name Karim.

Two days later, the Anglo-German Fellowship dinner was held at Grosvenor House. The German Ambassador, von Ribbentrop, in white tie and tails, sat next to the Duchess of Wellington. In a speech he said: 'England and Germany have only had one conflict in their long history of friendly relations and this was a terrible mistake which must never, never be repeated.'

On December 21, seventy-eight-year-old Dr. Winnington-Ingram, Bishop of London since 1901, put on knickerbockers, open-necked shirt and tweed cap and joined in a game of hockey in the grounds of Fulham Palace.

On Christmas Day, Mrs. Elvira Barney, the vivacious Society girl who had been acquitted on a charge of murdering her lover four years earlier, was found dead in her hotel room in Paris, following a high-spirited tour of the cafés of Montmartre and the Latin Quarter. 'We are quite satisfied that it is a case of natural death' said her mother, Lady Mullens.

1937

On January 1, the new Lord Beatty and his beautiful American fiancée were among the large field at the New Year's Day meet of the Quorn at Great Dalby, near Melton Mowbray. It was noted that the Earl had a house nearby, Dingley Hall, Market Harborough.

On January 8, the Duke of Windsor emerged from his Austrian hideaway, Schloss Enzesfeld, to have lunch with King Alfonso of Spain in a suite at the Hotel Bristol, Vienna. The two ex-monarchs ate boiled beef and apple tart.

On January 20, the infamous 'Officer in the Tower', Norman Baillie-Stewart, was released from Maidstone Prison wearing white gloves and a spotted tie. The release came a few days earlier than expected to enable the ex-officer to attend the funeral of his sixty-one-year-old father who had remained blindly loyal to him throughout his incarceration. A fellow inmate at Maidstone, financier Clarence Hatry, was unable to shake Baillie-Stewart's hand because he had been working in the gaol's garden and his hands were dirty.

Meanwhile, London Society was preoccupied with preparations for the marriage of the Duke of Norfolk and Miss Lavinia Strutt. The ceremony took place on January 27 at the Brompton Oratory. Among the 2,000 guests was Mr. Albert Fishpool, the butler at Arundel Castle. Wedding presents included ninety-four ashtrays and a cheese.

On February 4, the German Ambassador Herr von Ribbentrop startled diplomats at Buckingham Palace by greeting King George VI with the Nazi salute. The new King took no notice whatsoever. A few days later, Ribbentrop paid a private visit to Lancashire. On arrival at Liverpool, he was welcomed by the massively built Earl of Derby, now seventy-one years old.

On February 20, the public learned of the death of the Marquess of Huntly, Scotland's premier marquess, whose hereditary nickname was 'Cock o' the North'. At the age of eighty-nine he used to walk from King's Cross Station to the House of Lords. The new 'Cock o' the North' was twenty-nine-year-old Mr. Charles Gordon, who was described as a car salesman.

On March 1, another member of the Mitford family was in the news. It was announced that Jessica, sister of Hitler's friend Unity, had eloped with eighteen-year-old Esmond Romilly, who had recently been fighting with the International Column in Madrid. The couple were said to be in Bilbao and their relatives feared they would contract a Communist marriage. A few days later, from the Spanish frontier town of St. Jean de Luz, Esmond Romilly announced: 'Nothing is decided. I am unable to say what Miss Mitford and I will do.'

Meanwhile, a cockfighting gala in Calais had hit the headlines. It was revealed that the twenty-four-year-old Duke of Northumberland had been among the spectators; 200 cocks were killed and much champagne drunk. 'I was passing through Calais with friends,' explained the young Duke, 'and we went to see a fight. I do not own a fighting cock myself.'

On March 22, it was announced that the seventy-one-year-old Duchess of Bedford had disappeared in her de Havilland Moth aeroplane. 'I am afraid the Duchess may have come down in the flooded fen district' said the Chief Constable of Bedfordshire. 'I have sent out every patrol I can lay my hands on.' After a two-day search over six counties, all hope was abandoned. On April 2, a strut of the missing plane was washed ashore at Great Yarmouth and the Duchess was presumed dead.

Early in April, the Earl of Warwick said he was glad that Metro-Goldwyn-Mayer had released him from his contract. He was now free to take up more ambitious plans. 'They said I was not the type. We will see about that' he said.

Meanwhile, Mrs. Wallis Simpson had moved from Cannes to the ancient Château de Candé, near Tours. Here on April 7, Mrs. Simpson's Cairn terrier, Slipper, died following an adder bite. This melancholy event made headline news in many corners of the globe.

On April 13, the beautiful young Maharanee of Jaipur arrived in London for the Coronation. She was accompanied by her four sons and a retinue of twenty-two servants.

On April 17, novelist Evelyn Waugh married for the second time. His new bride was Miss Laura Herbert, grand-daughter of the late Earl of Carnarvon, and the ceremony took place in a small Catholic Church in Soho. At the reception afterwards, guests were offered olives stuffed with spring onions.

On April 19, the public's attention turned to 148 Piccadilly, huge Victorian mansion of the Rothschild family, famous for its great double staircase. The house and its contents were for sale. Victor Rothschild, heir to Lord Rothschild, was asked afterwards if he was planning to buy another London home. 'I'll think about that when the forthcoming war has come and gone' he replied.

The following day, there was a fifty-minute delay at Covent Garden while prima donna Mme Germaine Lubin coped with a bleeding nose, said to have been brought on by a bad Channel crossing. Sir Milsom Rees, chief laryngologist to the Opera House, attended her.

On April 26, the death of the Dowager Duchess of Roxburghe was announced. It was said that the American-born Duchess, who had brought £8,000,000 into the family, was in the process of refurbishing the dress she had worn at the last Coronation when she died.

Meanwhile, preparations for the Coronation, which were in the capable hands of the young Duke of Norfolk, reached their climax. The great ceremony took place on May 12. Eight hundred peers and MPs travelled from High Street Kensington to Westminster in a special Underground train, while the King and Queen were slowly transported from Buckingham Palace in the golden coach first used by King George III in 1762. Lavatory arrangements at the Abbey were described as 'excellent'.

On May 18, Jessica Mitford and Esmond Romilly were married by the British Consul at Bayonne. The mothers of both bride and groom were present at the ceremony, with funereal expressions on their faces.

That night in London, the newly-crowned King and Queen attended a ball given by the Duke and Duchess of Sutherland at Hampden House, Green Street. It was said to be the first time since before the Great War that the reigning King and Queen had attended a private dance. Vast crowds gathered outside the house to cheer them on their arrival and departure. Lady Cunard, intimate friend of the former monarch, tactfully delayed her arrival until after the Royal Family had left.

Towards the end of the month, interest switched to the forthcoming wedding of the Duke of Windsor and Mrs. Wallis Simpson. Mrs. Simpson had now obtained her decree absolute and the couple had been reunited at the Château de Candé. It was reported that famous London barber Mr. Charles Topper was travelling to France to trim the Duke's hair for the ceremony. On May 28, the couple's happiness was severely marred by an announcement from Buckingham Palace that Mrs. Simpson would not be allowed to use the title HRH after her marriage.

On June 3, the ceremony was conducted by the Rev. R. A. Jardine, rosy-cheeked vicar of an obscure parish in Darlington. Mrs. Simpson wore a long blue satin dress and a superb diamond and sapphire bracelet, her wedding present from the Duke. Mr. Randolph Churchill was among the guests.

Back in London, on June 11, Mr. Ernest Simpson brought a successful slander action against a woman who had declared at a lunch-party that he had been paid not to defend his wife's divorce petition.

On June 17, the beautiful Mrs. Charles Sweeny, who was now eight months pregnant, had a fall outside a Bond Street milliners and was put straight to bed. Two days later, she gave birth to a girl, subsequently christened Frances.

On June 30, the Rev. R. A. Jardine, who had been rewarded with a pair of cuff-links for officiating at the Windsor wedding, left for a lecture tour of America. Mr. Jardine had been severely criticised by the Bishop of Durham, but appeared undistressed. 'I don't mind if it means I have to leave the church' he said. 'I'm getting on now in any case.' Reports soon came from America that Mr. and Mrs. Jardine were in financial difficulties.

On July 7, there was an excitement in the House of Lords when the Earl of Moray began to roll a cigarette during a debate on the Divorce Bill. He was immediately approached by anxious attendants and left the chamber.

Three days later, Cecil Beaton and Sir Michael Duff were co-hosts at a fantastic party at Ashcombe, Beaton's house near Salisbury. The party had a rural theme and guests were asked to come as peasants, milkmaids and shepherdesses. A dozen bleating sheep were penned in front of the house and hired urchins chased a goat with magnesium flares. The only person in ordinary evening dress was Mr. Sacheverell Sitwell. When dawn broke, Jack Harris and his orchestra were still playing and the narrow lanes around the house were blocked by Rolls-Royces, supervised by AA men and police.

On July 24, the Countess of Cardigan plunged to her death from her seventh-floor suite at the Savoy Hotel. It was subsequently revealed that the Countess suffered from bad bouts of pleurisy and bronchitis and her life had become unbearable.

On July 28, Mr. Harold Davidson, the famous defrocked Rector of Stiffkey, was savaged by a lion at Skegness Amusement Park. Mr. Davidson had been addressing holiday-makers from inside a lion's cage when a beast named Freddie suddenly pounced on him. Davidson was rushed to Skegness Cottage Hospital suffering from severe lacerations to the face and neck and two days later he was dead. A funeral was held later at Stiffkey Church which 3,000 people attempted to gate-crash. The Bishop of London sent a wreath of white carnations and members of the British Legion from a neighbouring village formed a guard of honour. It was reported that a local icecream vendor sold out in record time.

Meanwhile, the Duke and Duchess of Windsor, honeymooning in Austria, made a brief excursion to Venice where they were photographed at a beach-party on the Lido with the Countess Reventlow, better known as Barbara Hutton.

In the middle of August, Norman Baillie-Stewart, notorious 'Officer in the Tower', left England telling friends that his sympathies had always lain elsewhere. He later confessed his full guilt to the charges on which he had been imprisoned in a series of articles in the *Daily Express*.

On August 27, sixty-nine-year-old Lord Rothschild died at Tring Park. A bachelor and famous recluse, he was succeeded by his nephew, scientist Victor Rothschild who had recently dismantled the family town-house in Piccadilly.

On September 3, the wealthy Prince Aly Khan, recently back from a tour of the East with his wife, was spotted running for a bus in Piccadilly. He missed it and waited for another, ignoring a nearby taxi-rank.

On September 23, it was reported that Mr. Edward Smith-Wilkinson, whose wife had created a sensation in 1921 by spending £200,000 on clothes and jewellery in a few months, was completely penniless. He was hitchhiking to London with his only presentable suit wrapped in newspaper. Over the years, he had supported himself by working as a farm-labourer and part-time telephone-operator.

The following day, George Ladbroke, chauffeur to the Prince of Wales for eighteen years and the man who had driven Mrs. Simpson across France to Cannes the previous December, was arrested in Charing Cross Road for being drunk and disorderly. It was said that Ladbroke had had a shouting match with a street-corner orator who had attacked his former master. 'I expect the Duke will be annoyed with me' said the seventeen-stone former royal retainer.

Meanwhile, the Windsors' honeymoon was over and there was much speculation about their future plans. On September 26, the couple arrived on board the Orient Express and moved into a nine-room suite at the Hotel Meurice. A few days later, they were surrounded by hysterical crowds at the Paris Exhibition.

On October 11, wigs belonging to three eminent High Court judges vanished from their private rooms at the Law Courts. A man was later found with the missing head-gear on Aldwych Underground station.

On October 14, wealthy Oxford don Derek Jackson was fined £5 for pulling the communication-cord on a train shortly after it had left Paddington. Mr. Jackson, a lecturer in Spectroscopy, explained in court that he had done so as a protest against the fact that the very few First Class carriages on the train all had doors locked.

On October 20, the beautiful Mrs. Dudley Ward, a former constant companion of the Prince of Wales over the years, married the Marquis de Casa Maury. The ceremony was conducted at Marylebone Registry Office and afterwards, a reception was held at the Curzon Cinema, of which the Marquis was a director.

Meanwhile, the Duke and Duchess of Windsor had set off on a tour of Germany, creating much irritation in certain quarters in England. On October 22 they had tea with Adolf Hitler in his drawing-room at Berchtesgaden. Hitler greeted the ex-King with his famous double handshake. After his royal guests had departed, the Führer remarked to his interpreter: 'She would have made a good Queen.'

On November 1, the Duchess's former husband, Mr. Ernest Simpson, arrived in New York on board the *Queen Mary* surrounded by rumours that he was on the point of marrying a certain Mrs. Mary Kirk Raffray. 'It's amazing how you fellows get the news' he told waiting journalists. When pressed for details, he said: 'Oh, please. Let's have a drink.'

On November 4, seventy-one-year-old ex-Prime Minister Ramsay MacDonald left London for a tour of South America with his daughter, Sheila. 'I have no plans' he told reporters. 'I am in search of that most elusive of all forms of happiness – rest.' Five days later, he died at sea.

At the end of November, it was revealed that Willie Hitler, twenty-six-year-old English-born nephew of the Führer, was visiting his mother, who had married Hitler's brother Alois in 1911, at her modest home in Highgate. 'I came back because I felt homesick' said the sturdy, moustached young man, who spoke English without a trace of a German accent.

On December 6, Ernest Simpson and his new wife arrived on the *Queen Mary*. 'We've got to shop for a London house' said Mr. Simpson. On board the same ship was Thelma Lady Furness, now running a dress shop in New York with her twin sister, Mrs. Gloria Vanderbilt.

Mr. Ernest Simpson and his new bride in their state room on board the Queen Mary

Winfield House, Barbara Hutton's new home in Regent's Park

On December 9, the Marquess of Milford Haven, elder brother of Lord Louis Mountbatten, slipped on a marble floor in the sumptuous Park Lane flat of Mrs. Israel Sieff, wife of the chain-store magnate. He was rushed to hospital with a broken thigh.

On December 13, white-haired Earl Beauchamp, now back in England after many years of exile, gave a ball at his palatial house in Belgrave Square in honour of his youngest son, Richard Lygon. The Earl, who wore black, white and pink studs in his shirt-front, spent the night at the Ritz Hotel to save his household staff fuss and bother.

Meanwhile, Barbara Hutton, Countess Reventlow, whose sixty-room new home in Regent's Park, was now nearly completed, had suddenly crossed the Atlantic, signed-away her American citizenship and set off for Europe again. She was only in America two days, but took with her sixteen trunks of clothes. There was no explanation for this astonishing move and Barbara refused to answer ship-to-shore telephone calls. 'It's the first I've heard of it' said her husband Count Reventlow, currently in St. Moritz with their twenty-month-old son.

On December 22, there was great excitement over the arrest of four public-school boys following a robbery with violence at the Hyde Park Hotel. The young men, who were soon to be dubbed the 'Mayfair Men', were charged with attempting to rob Cartier director Mr. Bellenger, now seriously ill in a nursing home, of £13,000 worth of diamond rings.

Shortly after Christmas, rumour flashed round the world that the Duchess of Windsor was expecting 'a happy event'. A statement was promptly issued from Cannes, where the Duke and Duchess had been spending the festive season, that the rumour was 'entirely without foundation'.

In the New Year's Honours List, Mr. George Reeves-Smith, managing director of the Savoy Hotel, was made a knight. Mr. Reeves-Smith, always dressed in silk top-hat and frock-coat, had been a familiar figure in the foyer of the great hotel for many years.

On January 4, Willie Hitler, twenty-six-year-old nephew of the Führer, left England after his short holiday and returned to Germany. 'My uncle is a peaceful man' he assured reporters. 'He thinks war is not worth the candle.'

On January 7, wealthy Maxine Elliott gave a formal dinner-party at her home, the Château de L'Horizon near Cannes, in honour of the Duke and Duchess of Windsor. Winston Churchill and former Prime Minister Lloyd George were present. Speaking of the Abdication to Churchill, Miss Elliott, a former mistress of Edward VII, remarked: 'We did it better in my day.'

Meanwhile, it had been revealed that the Marquess of Milford Haven, in hospital with a broken thigh, had been left wine, books, pictures and £20,000 by Philip Arthur Cohen, a wealthy relative of oil-magnate Sir Robert Waley-Cohen. 'I have no idea what the wine will be like' said the stricken marquess. 'Some of it may be too old. It's ten years since we used to drink together.' In the same nursing-home was Prince Arthur of Connaught, who was being 'investigated' for gastric trouble.

Early in February, the Duke and Duchess of Windsor took a short lease of a house at Versailles. They moved in with fourteen servants and several carloads of luggage. The house was intended to be their base while they set about more serious house-hunting.

On February 17, the trial of the 'Mayfair Men' accused of robbery with violence at the Hyde Park Hotel, opened at the Old Bailey. They were all found guilty and given heavy prison-sentences. The leader of the gang got seven years and twenty-strokes of the 'cat'. 'It's pretty stiff but I can take it' he said.

On February 24, Society was shocked by the death of Lord and Lady Plunket in an aeroplane crash in California. The couple were said to be close friends of both the King and Queen and the Duke and Duchess of Windsor.

Meanwhile, the new American Ambassador, Mr. Joseph Kennedy, was sailing for England. He was accompanied by his daughter Katherine, who would act as hostess at the American Embassy until her mother, currently convalescing in Florida after an operation, arrived. On March 8, the tall, broad-shouldered Ambassador presented his credentials at Buckingham Palace.

On March 10, the retiring German Ambassador Herr von Ribbentrop gave a farewell tea-party at the German Embassy in Carlton House Terrace. Lady Cunard, Lady Diana Cooper and scores of others were present. Tables groaned with sweet and savoury delicacies and there was a choice of orange-juice or china-tea to drink.

Four days later, Adolf Hitler marched into Vienna and was met there by his devoted friend Miss Unity Mitford. Rumours that the couple were now contemplating marriage were vigorously denied by Unity's father Lord Redesdale. 'There is not, nor has there ever been, any question of an engagement between my daughter and Herr Hitler. The Führer lives only for his country and has no time for marriage.' Hitler's sex life, or lack of one, remained a subject of world-wide interest. One authority stated that the only person he had seriously considered marrying was Frau Winifred Wagner, English-born widow of Richard Wagner's son.

On March 26, the new Prime Minister Neville Chamberlain was found weekending at Cliveden, Thames-side home of Lord and Lady Astor. It was reported that, after dinner, the house-party played 'The game', a form of competitive charades recently imported from America by the Duchess of Westminster. Rumours had already begun to circulate of the existence of a 'Cliveden Set' said to favour Hitler. 'The whole thing is a complete mare's nest' said Lord Lothian, whose name had been mentioned as a member of this so-called set.

On April 4, there was an exciting incident in the House of Commons. Labour MP Emanuel Shinwell crossed the Chamber and slapped a Conservative MP hard across the face. He later addressed the Speaker: 'I

Adolf Hitler and mystery female companion

recognise that my action was taken in a fit of temper but I think there was some justification. I beg to apologise to you.' Apparently, the offending MP had shouted at Mr. Shinwell 'go back to Poland'.

That evening, Lady Astor gave a grand and glittering dinner-party at her house in St. James's Square in honour of the Foreign Secretary Lord Halifax. Guests included the Duke of Kent, American Ambassador Joseph Kennedy, the Archbishop of Canterbury and the Italian Ambassador Count Grandi.

On April 8, the forty-five-year-old Marquess of Milford Haven, brother of Lord Louis Mountbatten, died in hospital where he had lain for four months after breaking his thigh at a dinner-party given by Mrs. Israel Sieff. He was succeeded by his eighteen-year-old son, the Earl of Medina.

Meanwhile, Miss Unity Mitford had returned from Vienna by Third Class rail. On April 10, she was attending a Labour Party rally in Hyde Park when an angry crowd suddenly turned on her. Her Swastika badge was torn off and trampled under foot and an attempt was made to duck her in the Serpentine. Unity was shaken but defiant. 'I am looking forward to becoming a German citizen as soon as possible' she said, 'but I can't tell you when that will be.'

On April 20, Hitler celebrated his forty-ninth birthday, receiving greetings from, among others, King George VI.

At the end of the month, there was world-wide interest in Augustus John's sudden resignation from the Royal Academy. His decision followed the rejection of a portrait of T. S. Eliot by Mr. Wyndham Lewis. There were hints that the Prime Minister himself might be brought in to sort out the quarrel. 'My decision is absolutely final' said the bearded artist.

On May 14, German soprano Lotte Lehmann, said to be the highest-paid singer in the world, stumbled off the stage at Covent Garden muttering that she could do no more. Twenty minutes later, she resumed her role and at the end of the performance, took seven curtain-calls. 'I am quite all right' she said later in her suite at the Savoy Hotel. 'I am merely suffering from the effects of my voyage.'

1938

On May 9, Queen Charlotte's Birthday Ball was held in the ballroom at Grosvenor House; 100 nannies were supplied with special tickets so that they could watch the proceedings from the gallery.

In the middle of the month, Mrs. Joseph Kennedy presented her daughters at Court. She said afterwards, 'My girls deliberately went back slowly after their curtsy so as to retain a clearer mental picture of the King and Queen.'

On May 24, tall, pale Lord Howland celebrated his twenty-first birthday with a party in a hotel. Neither his father, Lord Tavistock, nor his grandfather, the Duke of Bedford, were present. Lord Tavistock said he had a cold and the seventy-nine-year-old Duke was preoccupied at Woburn Abbey, surrounded by his vast staff of liveried servants.

A few days later, Sir Adrian and Lady Baillie gave a dance in London at which Barbara Hutton, Countess Reventlow, in a broad diamond head-band, spent most of the evening dancing with the slim young Prince Frederick of Prussia, grandson of the former Kaiser. Over the next few weeks, the Prince was a constant visitor to Winfield House, Barbara's newly-built home in Regent's Park, where footmen in canary yellow and blue livery were in attendance.

Meanwhile, the eighty-two-year-old Austrian psychoanalyst, Dr. Sigmund Freud, had been driven out of Vienna by the Nazis. He arrived at Victoria Station on June 6 and was greeted by members of his family already in England. 'My father has no plans' said his son Martin. 'He is a very old man and what he wants most is peace and quiet for the rest of his days.' Friends hoped that the doctor's financial problems would be resolved by his being awarded the Nobel Prize, worth £8,000.

On June 8, the burly Aga Khan, spiritual head of 20,000,000 people, was present at a performance of *Rigoletto* at Covent Garden. Chatting with friends during an interval, the French-born Begum Aga Khan declared that Hitler was the most attractive man she had ever met.

In the middle of June, a blaze of ugly publicity suddenly surrounded the Reventlow marriage. It was reported that Count Reventlow had threatened to shoot or break the neck of his wife's new friend, Prince Frederick of Prussia, and Barbara had obtained a warrant for his arrest. There were also rumours of an attempt to kidnap the two-year-old Reventlow baby. 'These children have had some misunderstanding and it's too bad' said Barbara's father, Franklyn Hutton in Paris.

On June 22, indefatigable American hostess Mrs. Laura Corrigan gave a party at 11 Kensington Palace Gardens, which she had rented for the Season from the Duke and Duchess of Marlborough. Lady Diana Cooper was in black, Lady Weymouth was in white and silver and Lady Cunard wore a top-knot of roses. The Duke and Duchess of Kent led the dancing and a cabaret was provided by Chinese jugglers and a xylophone player. It was revealed that Mrs. Corrigan was off to stay at Longleat the following weekend.

On July 9, the vivacious Marchioness of Dufferin and Ava, wife of one of the youngest members of government, gave birth to a baby boy.

On July 13, the charges against Count Reventlow were withdrawn and he was mobbed by cheering crowds when he emerged from Bow Street court. A few days later, the Reventlows signed an agreement to part and the Count left England for good, though rumoured to still be in love with his multi-millionairess wife.

Meanwhile, grey-haired Mrs. Ronnie Greville had disobeyed doctor's orders and risen from her bed at Polesden Lacey to attend Ascot. To make things easier for her, the King and Queen, who had spent their honeymoon at Mrs. Greville's house in 1923, permitted her to use the royal entrance to the racecourse.

On July 26, the seventy-seven-year-old Countess of Warwick died at her stately home in Essex. It was revealed that a few weeks before her death, the eccentric Socialist hostess had ordered 100-head of Highland cattle which were now on their way south by train. Another train was later organised to carry mourners from Paddington to the funeral at Warwick Castle.

On August 5, the Duke and Duchess of Windsor, who had now taken a ten-year lease of the Château de la Croe at Antibes, dined with Somerset Maugham at the Villa Mauresque at Cap Ferrat. Also at dinner was Maugham's daughter, Liza Paravicini, who had recently presented the famous writer with his first grandchild.

94

A few days later, Somerset Maugham set off for London with his athletic, heavy-drinking friend Gerald Haxton who had shared his life for the past twenty years.

At the end of August, while Europe's leaders coped with the Czechoslovakia crisis, actress Beatrice Lillie swam in the sea at Eden Roc, Cap d'Antibes with Bobby Kennedy, teenage-son of the new American Ambassador. On the North Wales coast, Labour leader Mr. C. R. Attlee, was found paddling with his family.

On September 7, it was announced that American newspaper proprietor William Randolph Hearst was to sell St. Donat's Castle in Wales which he had acquired some thirteen years earlier and on which he had spent £250,000 installing sixty bathrooms and filling it with treasures.

Three days later, over in Nuremberg, twenty-four-year-old Unity Mitford was present at a tea-party at the Deutscher Hof Hotel in honour of the Führer. Miss Mitford was invited to Hitler's suite after the party. Asked later if there would be war, Unity replied, 'I don't think so. The Führer doesn't want his new buildings bombed.'

On September 15, in a last-minute effort to avert war, Neville Chamberlain flew to see Hitler at his mountain-top retreat. It was the sixty-nine-year-old Prime Minister's first flight in an aeroplane. It was reported that whisky and sandwiches were provided on the out-going journey and chicken and claret on the return flight.

On September 21, Ciro's Club off Leicester Square was reopened after extensive redecoration and the installation of a new lighting system. A new head waiter had been recruited from Le Touquet.

On September 27, the Queen, accompanied by the little Princesses, launched the 85,000-ton liner *Queen Elizabeth* at Clydebank. Officials were somewhat distressed to see the great ship begin to slide down the slipway before the Queen had given her launching speech.

The next day, Queen Mary, recently fitted for a gas-mask, was present in the House of Commons to hear Mr. Chamberlain report on the lack of progress of his negotiations with Herr Hitler. With her in the Ladies Gallery was the beautiful Duchess of Kent.

On September 30, the Prime Minister returned from his third visit to Hitler clutching his umbrella and waving a piece of paper, claiming to have obtained 'peace with honour'. The following day, Duff Cooper, First Lord of the Admiralty, resigned in protest at this agreement, giving up a salary of £5,000 and his official residence.

On October 8, the Marchioness of Dufferin and Ava's baby boy was christened Sheridan at a service in the private chapel at the Marquess's Irish home Clandeboye. The Duke of Devonshire and Lady Honor Channon were among the godparents and the event was celebrated with fireworks.

In the middle of October, it was revealed that Count Leo von Zeppelin, nephew of the famous German airship designer, had exchanged his sixty-room castle in the Austrian Tyrol for a cottage at South Warnborough in Hampshire.

On October 26, celebrated bandleader Jack Hylton ordered a three-and-sixpenny plate of tripe and onions at the Savoy Hotel. 'Too dressy and not enough of the natural tripe' he said after a single mouthful.

On October 28, an eight-foot python belonging to Mr. Adrian Conan Doyle, son of the creator of Sherlock Holmes, was reported missing from its owner's Chelsea flat. A similar snake had been sighted in Hyde Park and experts wondered if it could have made its way through one-and-a-half miles of busy streets. A few days later, the reptile was discovered hiding in the chimney of Mr. Conan Doyle's flat and was charmed down by an expert. This colourful incident reminded many people of the famous Sherlock Holmes story *The Speckled Band*.

On November 11, the Duke of Windsor had his first meeting with one of his brothers since the Abdication. He was visited that day at the Hotel Meurice in Paris by the Duke of Gloucester. The two brothers and their wives were photographed together, the Duchesses kissed and a street violinist played the National Anthem.

On November 14, sixty-six-year-old Earl Beauchamp died in a hotel in New York. The white-haired Earl had led a very unsettled life for the last seven years since being hounded out of the country by his powerful brother-in-law, the thrice-married Duke of Westminster.

The Marchioness of Dufferin and Ava flanked by friends after the State Opening of Parliament

On November 16, Queen Mary wore five diamond necklaces at a party at Buckingham Palace and was seen sharing a joke with the American Ambassador, Mr. Kennedy, who had given an unpopular speech a few weeks earlier at a Trafalgar Day dinner in which he had placed himself firmly on the side of those who wished to appease the dictators.

At the end of the month, following the birth of their son Alexander, Sir Oswald Mosley revealed details of his secret marriage to Mrs. Diana Guinness two years earlier in Germany. It was widely but incorrectly rumoured that Hitler had acted as best man at the ceremony.

On December 7, the King dined with former Prime Minister Lord Baldwin at 69 Eaton Square. Six Socialist MPs were there including the Labour leader Mr. Attlee. After dinner, the King smoked a few cigarettes and then took out his pipe. The object of the dinner-party was for the King to meet some new MPs he did not know.

On December 11, it was revealed that Lady Diana Cooper and Mrs. Euan Wallace had curtsied to the Duchess of Windsor at a cocktail-party in Paris. 'I did it to please the Duke, not for any formal reason' said Mrs. Wallace. Their action had greatly upset the Countess of Pembroke who declared: 'Nothing would induce me to curtsy to the Duchess.'

On December 14, there was a party for 100 children at Buckingham Palace. Among those present were Princess Elizabeth, Princess Margaret, Prince Edward, son of the Duke of Kent, and his sister Princess Alexandra. A long table in one of the State Drawing-Rooms was laden with Christmas crackers, pastries, jellies, ices and lemonade. After tea, there was a puppet-show in the Throne Room staged by Elsa Lanchester's brother, Waldo.

The following day, the Hon. Unity Mitford, her mother Lady Redesdale and a certain Captain FitzRandolph of the German Embassy were found crouching with plates of sausages on their knees at an Anglo-German Fellowship party in Bloomsbury. It had already been widely publicised that Hitler would be giving Miss Mitford an expensive camera for Christmas.

On December 20, the Duke of Kent celebrated his thirty-sixth birthday by taking the King and Queen to see the Cicely Courtneidge and Jack Hulbert Show at the Palace Theatre. Two boxes were taken and the Queen wore a white ermine wrap round her shoulders. 'You've got a grand show here' the Duke told the stars afterwards.

The Duke and Duchess of Windsor saw in the New Year at the Sporting Club in Monte Carlo. Lord and Lady Brownlow, Esmond Harmsworth and the Duchess's aunt, Mrs. Bessie Merryman, were in their party. It was reported that they ate caviar, clear chicken soup, crawfish pilaff, baby lamb, asparagus, foie gras and pear Melba. The Duchess, who had recently been voted the World's Best Dressed Woman, was decked out in diamonds and emeralds and had her hair swept up in the new fashionable style.

On January 2, Neville Chamberlain arrived for a shooting weekend with Lord Iveagh at his luxurious Edwardian house, Elveden. Against the orders of the head keeper, Mr. Turner, a partridge was shot – which, as a joke, was placed in the Prime Minister's bag at the end of the day.

Shortly afterwards, Chamberlain left for a visit to Mussolini in Rome. Here he stayed at the Villa Madama, a recently spruced-up guest-house for distinguished foreign visitors. It was said that many Italians had recently bought umbrellas out of respect for the British Prime Minister.

On January 28, forty-nine-year-old Clarence Hatry was freed after serving nine years of his fourteen-year prison sentence. Three days later, the ex-financier re-visited the City of London, where he was warmly greeted and congratulated on all sides. He then left by chartered plane for a six-week holiday at a villa near Cannes lent him by an old Army friend.

Former financier Clarence Hatry in the lounge of his Paris hotel, before catching the night express to Italy

Meanwhile, the Thames had burst its banks again, flooding into the wine cellar of Dr. Inge, former Dean of St. Paul's, at Wallingford and rendering Eton College an island. Boys fed the swans from the windows of their rooms.

On February 4, oil-magnate Sir Henri Deterding died at his chalet near St. Moritz. Sir Henri, one of the world's most powerful men, left a fortune which some estimates placed at £65,000,000. His ten-year-old daughter Olga was one of the beneficiaries under his will.

On February 6, a contingent of unemployed men entered the Savoy Hotel and lay down in the lounge. Forty others lay down in the street outside. It was noted that the Duke of Kent was dining in the hotel at the time.

On February 22, it was revealed that the Duke of Devonshire had installed a conveyor-belt to transport food from the kitchen to the dining-room at Chatsworth. It was claimed that this gadget could carry a bowl of soup 328 feet in thirty-two seconds without a drop being spilt.

On March 1, it was announced that Ciro's Club off Leicester Square, home of the fashionable Jack Harris and his orchestra, was closing. 'Nobody else can cry' said Harris. 'It's all my money. I put thousands into this place.'

That night, the genial Russian Ambassador, Mr. Maisky, gave a lavish reception at the Russian Embassy in Kensington Palace Gardens. Caviar, vodka and French and Russian champagne were served and there were only three guests not in full evening-dress. The orchestra started to play jazz just as the Prime Minister Neville Chamberlain was leaving.

On March 16, archaeologist R. E. Mortimer Wheeler married beautiful widow Mrs. Mavis de Vere Cole, long-standing girlfriend of Augustus John. The ceremony took place at Caxton Hall and Augustus John and A. P. Herbert were witnesses. One of the guests at the reception was Mrs. Agatha Christie.

On March 18, only a few days after Hitler's armies had marched into Czechoslovakia, the Führer's friend Miss Unity Mitford published a long article in the *Daily Mirror* in which she argued in favour of Anglo-German friendship. A few days afterwards, she returned to Germany and established herself in a flat in Munich from which a Jewish family had recently been ousted.

Meanwhile, London prepared itself for the State Visit of President Lebrun of France. He arrived at Victoria Station on March 21 and was met by the King and Queen and driven in a procession of state landaus to Buckingham Palace. That night, there was a banquet in his honour attended by 196 guests.

The following day, Winston Churchill dropped his handkerchief on arrival at a banquet at the French Embassy and Mrs. Churchill was photographed stooping to pick it up. The banquet was followed by a gala performance at Covent Garden at which everyone was in Court-dress or uniform and the women were covered in jewels and tiaras. Socialites wondered if such splendour would ever be seen again.

On March 24, Queen Mary visited the film studios at Denham, drank three cups of tea and climbed a staircase to inspect the film-processing laboratories. 'I don't mind steps when I am interested' she told officials.

On March 30, Hitler's English-born nephew Willie arrived in America to give a lecture tour. 'I don't see anything I can do at the moment' he had said before departure, 'but in the event of war, I'll join up immediately for England.'

On April 6, twenty-one-year-old Lord Howland, grandson of the wealthy Duke of Bedford, was married to Mrs. Clare Hollway, several years his senior. Neither his father nor his grandfather attended the ceremony at Caxton Hall and, soon afterwards, Lord Howland found himself disinherited. After a night in a friend's suite at the Ritz Hotel, where all the cupboards had been locked against them, the couple left for a honeymoon in the South of France.

On April 20, Hitler's fiftieth birthday was celebrated in Berlin. Among those attending the festivities was Mosleyite Major General J. F. C. Fuller, who wore a grey top-hat and was said to be a fan of black magician Aleister Crowley. From Windsor Castle, King George VI again sent a message of congratulations to the German leader.

On May 3, another of the late Mrs. Meyrick's daughters married into the peerage. In a secret ceremony at St. Peter's, Eaton Square, twenty-three-year-old Irene Meyrick was married to the pipe-smoking Earl of Craven, who had succeeded his one-legged father in 1932.

On May 6, Miss Unity Mitford, sister-in-law of Sir Oswald Mosley, arrived to spend the weekend at Hitler's mountain-top retreat Berchtesgaden in the Bavarian Alps, visited the previous year by Prime Minister Neville Chamberlain. Also at the house that weekend was the Führer's German ladyfriend Miss Eva Braun, who was rumoured to be wildly jealous of Miss Mitford.

Back in England, on May 15, much publicity attended the little Princesses' first ride on an Underground train. It was reported that Princess Margaret, now eight years old, sat next to a certain Mrs. Simmons,

Lord Howland, grandson of the Duke of Bedford, with his first wife Mrs. Clare Hollway

charlady from Muswell Hill.

Meanwhile, a big fuss had blown up over the cleaning of the Elgin Marbles. On May 18, a seventy-three-year-old former employee at the British Museum admitted that he had used a blunt copper tool to remove some of the dirtier spots from the marbles, which were said to be worth well over £1,000,000.

On May 23, Queen Mary was involved in a serious motor accident in Wimbledon. It was reported that her maroon-coloured Daimler had collided with a two-ton lorry carrying steel-tubing. The royal vehicle had overturned and Queen Mary, seventy-two next birthday, had been thrown to the floor, breaking her umbrella. It was stated that she emerged from the car with great dignity and not one curl out of place. 'No fuss' she said. 'I am quite all right.'

The following day, Fred Astaire, Anthony Eden and Lady Oxford were among thousands of spectators at the Derby. That night, the Earl of Rosebery celebrated his first Derby win at a banquet at the Savoy Hotel. A huge jockey cap surrounded by coloured balloons was suspended from the ceiling.

On June 5, shots were fired at the Duchess of Kent as she left her house in Belgrave Square with Lady Portarlington. They were off to see a new film *Wuthering Heights* at the Gaumont Cinema and did not realise about the shooting until they returned later that night and were informed by the police.

The same day, the walrus-like Earl of Harewood called in Scotland Yard when he found a glass-panel broken in the door of his house in Green Street, Mayfair.

In the middle of the month, it was revealed that Lord and Lady Louis Mountbatten were to sub-let their luxurious eighteen-bedroom Park Lane penthouse. It was explained that Lord Louis, who had recently been appointed to the command of the Third Destroyer Flotilla, no longer required a London home.

On June 22, there was a dance at the American Embassy in honour of the Ambassador's seventeen-year-old daughter Eunice. Guests included the Hon. Peter Beatty and Prince Frederick of Prussia. The hostess, Mrs. Kennedy, cut a dazzling figure in diamonds and white lace.

The same night, the Duke and Duchess of Windsor, who had now leased a twenty-bedroom house in the Boulevard Suchet near the Bois de Boulogne in addition to their château at Antibes, dined at the German Embassy in Paris. They were greeted with Nazi salutes.

On June 27, the public's attention turned to the High Court where Mr. Nubar Gulbenkian was involved in a financial dispute with his father, said to be the richest man in the world. In a bid to obtain financial independence, Nubar demanded five percent of his father's profits in the Iraq Oil Company. The action was eventually withdrawn and Gulbenkian senior paid his son's legal costs, which were said to amount to £30,000.

On July 1, seventy-four-year-old Lady Mendl, interior decorator of renown, gave a spectacular party at her house at Versailles. Thirty footmen were in attendance and among the 700 guests were Douglas Fairbanks and his ex-wife Mary Pickford, who had remained on friendly terms since their divorce.

Meanwhile, preparations were going on at Blenheim Palace for Lady Sarah Spencer-Churchill's coming-out ball. On July 7, the house and lakes were floodlit and Tyrolean musicians strolled among the guests. Lady Sarah's wealthy grandmother, Madame Consuelo Vanderbilt Balsan, had come over from France for the party and was seen sitting with Mr. Winston Churchill.

The magnificence of this occasion was slightly marred when it was revealed that Lady Portarlington's sable coat and a silver fox-fur belonging to Lady Long of Wraxall had been stolen from the Duchess of Kent's private cloakroom.

On July 11, the indefatigable Mrs. Laura Corrigan, who had taken Dudley House in Park Lane for two months for a rumoured £5,000, gave a large dinner-party at which Joseph Kennedy and his wife were the principal guests.

The following day, the Kennedys' débutante daughter Eunice was presented at Buckingham Palace. Her young brothers, Bobby and Teddy Kennedy, watched her leave from the balcony of their house in Grosvenor Square.

On July 17, there were wild scenes at Lord's Cricket Ground, after Harrow's first victory over Eton for thirty-one years. The Harrow captain, A. O. L. Lithgow, was carried to the pavilion at shoulder-height.

On July 31, Lady Rachel Howard, sister of the Duke of Norfolk, was married to Mr. Colin Davidson, a former Equerry to the Prince of Wales. At the ceremony at Arundel Castle, the bridegroom wore an eye-patch. It was explained that his eye had been pierced by a cactus thorn in Italy the previous year.

Early in August, while the threat of war hung over Europe, it was announced that Barbara Hutton, Countess Reventlow, had taken a villa in Capri. The multi-millionairess, still only twenty-six years old, had now closed her huge house in Regent's Park and its silver, gold, historic carpets and old masters had been packed away. She was soon joined on Capri by her old friend Lady Milbanke, former wife of the Earl of Loughborough.

On August 18, Winston Churchill arrived for a short holiday at Madame Balsan's château in Normandy, during which he painted several canvases and immersed himself in books about the Victorian era. Packing away his painting materials a few days later, he declared: 'This is the last picture we shall paint in peace for a very long time.'

Back in England, on August 23, the upper classes gathered for York Races. The Hon. Deborah Mitford, youngest of the famous Mitford sisters, and Lord Andrew Cavendish were among the guests at Castle Howard, near York. The Princess Royal was present at the races dressed in a short bolero coat of rose pink crêpe.

On August 29, Mr. Vyvyan Holland, only surviving son of Oscar Wilde, attended a revival of *The Importance of Being Earnest* at the Globe Theatre, starring John Gielgud, Margaret Rutherford and Edith Evans. 'I really found it most amusing' he said afterwards. 'I feel quite proud of the old boy.'

On September 1, while England trembled on the brink of war, the popular Earl of Carnarvon married Miss Tilly Losch, beautiful Viennese dancer who had been divorced by her wealthy husband, Mr. Edward James, some years earlier. After the ceremony at Caxton Hall, the couple drove to Claridge's and thence to the Earl's ancestral home, Highclere Castle in Hampshire.

At 11.15 am on September 3, the seventy-one-year-old Prime Minister Neville Chamberlain announced that the country was at war.

THE WAR
1939–1945

At the outbreak of hostilities, street lighting was extinguished, most of the surviving town-houses were closed and for the next six years many socialites devoted their energies to war-work. Millions of Londoners moved to the country. Queen Mary took up residence with the Duke and Duchess of Beaufort at Badminton, accompanied by a retinue of no less that sixty-three servants. Between assignments abroad with her husband, Lady Diana Cooper ran a farm at Bognor. Eleven thousand women and children from the privileged classes went overseas. Those that remained in London clung together in the big hotels. The Dorchester, Ritz and Savoy were crowded out with celebrities and statesmen. In spite of the war, the Derby was run each year, racing at Ascot resumed in 1943 and representatives of the Aga Khan, safe and well at the Palace Hotel in St. Moritz, continued to pay high prices for bloodstock each year. Many of the upper classes seem to have lived comfortably. Even in the worst days of the Blitz, sixty per cent of Londoners slept at home. Theatres, nightclubs, dance-floors everywhere were packed. While bombs descended on Buckingham Palace, Burlington Arcade, the Carlton Club and the Café de Paris, magnums of champagne were drunk, officers in uniform stuffed themselves with oysters and grouse and Chips Channon continued to entertain stylishly at his house in Belgrave Square. The luxurious lifestyle of Prime Minister Winston Churchill makes particularly interesting reading; during the darkest days of the war he was found having a high-spirited, drunken lunch with Lord Beaverbrook at the Mirabelle restaurant. Nevertheless, this was a time of great social flux. Railings from in front of Brooks's Club and Buckingham Palace were carted off to be turned into tanks, the Archbishop of Canterbury was found waiting at a bus-stop in Victoria Street and in 1944 the great actor/manager Ivor Novello spent a month in Wormwood Scrubs for contravening Defence Regulations by driving around in his Rolls-Royce.

1939

On the day that war was declared, twenty-five-year-old Unity Mitford entered the English Gardens in Munich and shot herself with a small pistol. She was taken to a nearby hospital where her friend Adolf Hitler informed the authorities that he would be responsible for the cost of whatever treatment was possible.

On September 4, Sir George Reeves-Smith, managing director of the Savoy Hotel, shocked his staff by appearing in the front hall of the hotel in a bowler-hat and lounge-suit. It was the first time for over forty years that Sir George had not worn a top-hat and frock-coat.

The same day, seventy-two-year-old Queen Mary set off for Badminton in Gloucestershire where it had been decided that she should remain while the hostilities lasted. She was followed by a cavalcade of motor-cars carrying sixty-three servants, almost the entire staff of Marlborough House. Her niece, the Duchess of Beaufort, watched the arrival of the vast party somewhat apprehensively.

On September 10, officers in uniform were found swaggering about at Buck's Club in Clifford Street and guzzling oysters.

Meanwhile, the Duke and Duchess of Windsor were secretly making their way to England accompanied by Major 'Fruity' Metcalfe and their three Cairn terriers, Pookie, Preezi and Detto. On September 12, the party was met at Cherbourg by the Destroyer HMS *Kelly* with Lord Louis Mountbatten and Randolph Churchill on board. Randolph was in the uniform of a lieutenant in the 4th Hussars and it was noticed that his spurs were strapped on upside down.

On September 18, the valiant old Lady Oxford announced at a lunch-party at Lady Cunard's house in Grosvenor Square that she thought gas-masks were unnecessary and air-raids were not dangerous.

On September 25, Queen Mary, assisted by her Equerry the Hon. Sir John Coke, spent the morning pulling ivy off trees in the grounds of Badminton House and supervising the removal of ivy from the wall of the house near the Duchess of Beaufort's bedroom window.

On September 27, the Duke and Duchess of Windsor lunched with Lady Colefax at 19 Great North Street, Westminster. The Duke, soon to take up his responsibilities as liaison officer with the British Military Mission at Vincennes near Paris, was in khaki with many of his medals. A day or two later, he and the Duchess left for France driven by their old chauffeur George Ladbroke, who had been assessed as too old for military duties.

At the end of the month, royal photographer Cecil Beaton was found working on night-shift at the telephone-exchange near his Wiltshire home. 'I have found this work very interesting' he said. 'Some of the voices I hear strike me as belonging to people who would make excellent and interesting sitters.'

On October 4, Randolph Churchill married the Hon. Pamela Digby at St. John's, Smith Square. The bridegroom was in uniform and his bride was in a dark blue dress trimmed with dyed fox-fur. At the reception afterwards at Admiralty House, one of the most eye-catching guests was the Countess of Limerick, who was in the uniform of the VAD.

The same day, top-hats were temporarily banned at Eton. The headmaster explained that they were a great nuisance in air-raid warnings and took up valuable space in air-raid shelters.

Meanwhile, preparations were going on for the Royal Horticultural Association's show in Vincent Square. 'There will be the usual riot of colour in the autumn flowers and ornamental shrubs' said an official. 'It is our job to impress the world that whatever happens we can carry on.'

On October 13, millionairess Barbara Hutton, whose vast London home had been closed some months earlier, left Naples for New York. On board the same vessel was her former husband, Count Reventlow and their son, Lance, now three and a half years old.

Meanwhile, bearded artist Augustus John had accepted a commission to paint the Queen. A preliminary meeting was arranged to take place on October 30 at which John failed to turn up, sending a weird telegram to Buckingham Palace saying he was suffering from 'the influence'. Sittings began shortly afterwards and bottles of sherry and brandy were placed in a cupboard by the Palace staff to help the great artist with his work.

The London social scene had now been enriched by the presence of Hollywood star David Niven. He had slipped back into the country at the end of October anxious to fight for his homeland. A Press conference was soon convened at the Odeon Cinema, Leicester Square, at which over 100 reporters and photographers turned up to hear the actor express a desire to join the RAF.

On November 2, the Duchess of Sutherland and the Dukes of Marlborough, Northumberland and Leeds were found sipping cocktails at the Ritz Hotel. It was said that the Duke of Marlborough now referred to his wife, Chief Commandant of the ATS, as 'The General'.

On November 16, the Marchioness of Londonderry, who had recently closed her family's palatial town house at the bottom of Park Lane, was found lunching at the Dorchester Hotel with Mr. Harold Macmillan and others. Forty-five-year-old Mr. Macmillan had recently applied to join the Reserve Battalion of his regiment but had been rejected on the grounds that he was too old.

On November 17, at Pixton Park, Somerset, Mrs. Evelyn Waugh gave birth to a baby boy, later named Auberon Alexander. The Hon. Frank Pakenham was named as a godparent but transport difficulties prevented him from attending the christening service.

At the end of the month, the minimum of pageantry attended the Opening of Parliament. Peers were in morning-dress instead of robes and the Duke of Gloucester was in khaki. After the simple eight-minute ceremony, the King and Queen drove back to Buckingham Palace where the American Ambassador, Joseph Kennedy, was due to lunch.

On December 3, the King's great-aunt, Princess Louise, died at Kensington Palace in her ninety-first year. Known in certain circles as 'the Royal Rebel', the Princess had recently shocked officers at a regimental sing-song by refusing a cigarette from a silver box in favour of a cheaper brand which she produced from her handbag. It was noted that the Princess had spent her childhood in the days of the Crimean War.

On December 7, the Queen, in a long black velvet coat trimmed with Persian lamb's wool, visited Chichester and sat down with 264 children evacuated from London to eat a threepenny lunch of stewed steak, potatoes and jam-tart, washed down with water from a bakelite mug. 'This is all very good' she remarked.

A few days later, attention turned to Sussex Assizes where a certain Dr. Parsons-Smith brought an action complaining that his peace had been disturbed by seventy yapping poodles on Mr. Basil Ionides's nearby estate at Buxted Park. On December 19, the judge declared that the dogs must be silenced and counsel for the defence said that this meant they would probably have to be destroyed.

By Christmas, Hatfield House, historic home of the Marquess of Salisbury, had been converted into a military hospital. It was reported that the seventy-eight-year-old peer had also loaned the government his four large limousines and was restricting himself to the use of a small 8-horsepower vehicle belonging to his chauffeur.

At the end of December, the Duchess of Windsor was found in the uniform of the French Red Cross, visiting hospitals and helping to pack-up socks, soap, cigarettes and other luxuries for the French troops. The Windsors' newly-acquired house in the Boulevard Suchet had been re-opened and its tall windows hung with blackout curtains.

On New Year's Day, there was a fashionable gathering at Wilton House, near Salisbury, home of the Earl and Countess of Pembroke, for the first night of a satirical pantomime entitled *Heil Cinderella*. Cecil Beaton and Olga Lynn were the Ugly Sisters and the Hon. David Herbert took the part of Buttons. Costumes had been made up by a firm of West End dressmakers.

Meanwhile, Hitler's friend Unity Mitford, ill and half-paralysed with a bullet in her brain, had been permitted to leave Germany. Rumours circulated that her family had hired a private First Class railway-carriage and guard's van at the cost of £1,600 to transport her across Europe. On January 3, she arrived at Folkestone in a blaze of publicity. The harbour was blocked off and security guards were placed at every entrance. 'My daughter must not be made into one of history's tragic women' insisted Lady Redesdale.

On January 11, the baby son of Mr. and Mrs. Ernest Simpson, born a few weeks earlier at a nursing home in Sutton in Surrey, was christened in the Guards' Chapel, Wellington Barracks. Mother and son were soon to depart for the United States.

On January 21, Lady Howland gave birth to a baby boy in a suite at the Ritz Hotel, all expenses being paid by the baby's great-grandfather, the eighty-one-year-old Duke of Bedford. The baby's father, Lord Howland, was meanwhile residing at the Officers Training Depot at Caterham in Surrey, where his progress was hindered by chronic ill-health.

Also moving into the Ritz was the spritely Emerald Cunard, leading literary hostess of the last few decades. It was reported that her beautiful house in Grosvenor Square was being closed down and she was anxious to part with some of her fine French furniture. She had already sold a spinet to Mr. Alan and Lady Lennox-Boyd.

On February 1, a new list of the World's Best Dressed Women was published in which the Duchess of Windsor and the Duchess of Kent tied for first place.

Meanwhile, seventy-nine-year-old Lord Portsea of 13 Eaton Place had spared himself worries about petrol rationing by travelling around London in a horse-drawn brougham, driven by a top-hatted coachman.

On February 20, a row erupted in Parliament over a plan to move Miss Unity Mitford to Inchkenneth, her family's recently acquired Scottish island. After considering the matter, Secretary for War, Oliver Stanley announced that the move should not be made. 'It is a decision arrived at by those responsible for the safety of our country,' said Lord Redesdale, 'and it would be highly improper for me to question it.'

On February 29, Queen Charlotte's birthday ball was held as usual at the Grosvenor House. Among the hundreds of débutantes present was Miss Mary Churchill, whose father Winston Churchill, now First Lord of the Admiralty, took an hour off from his work to look in on the festivities.

On March 5, news came from the Riviera that Maxine Elliott, actress friend of the late King Edward VII, had died at the Château de l'Horizon near Cannes. The vastly overweight millionairess had clung on to her sumptuous home, arranging for her finest dresses to be cut up and made into clothes for evacuee children. Throughout her life, she had pretended to be much younger than she was and the date of birth on her tombstone was said to be inaccurate by eleven years.

Meanwhile, a mishap had befallen Mrs. John Betjeman as she drove a party of evacuee children to a meet at Lord Berners' Berkshire home. Her four-wheeled buggy had overturned and the evacuees had been thrown into a ditch.

On March 6, it was announced that Royal Academician Reginald Eves had been appointed the first official war artist. 'I shall have to wear uniform but I do not know what my rank is to be' he said. 'I expect I shall be engaged mainly on portrait painting.'

On March 7, American Ambassador Joseph Kennedy returned from the United States, where it was said he had been telling everyone that England was sure to be beaten.

Meanwhile, millionairess Laura Corrigan, one of the leading London hostesses over the past two decades, had moved into the Ritz Hotel in Paris, where her first-floor suite was said to run the entire length of the building. She was now devoting all her energies to war work and was said to have taken a French regiment under her wing.

At the end of March, Duff and Lady Diana Cooper returned from a lecture tour of America and moved into the Savoy Hotel while their house in Chapel Street, Belgravia, was being opened up for them. 'Living in this hotel' declared Lady Diana 'one need never wrestle with the blackout.'

On April 2, it was stated that only six houses in Eaton Square were occupied.

Among those who had taken up permanent residence in the Dorchester Hotel were Mr. and Mrs. Charles Sweeny. It was here that on April 5, Mrs. Sweeny gave birth to a baby boy. He was later christened Brian and multi-millionairess Barbara Hutton, now living in California, was named as godparent.

On April 9, Hitler invaded Denmark and Norway and a cloud descended on the Chamberlain government. On May 10, after a three-day debate in the House of Commons, sixty-five-year-old Winston Churchill took over as Prime Minister. In the Berlin Press, he was described as 'the most brutal representative of the policy of force, whose hateful face is well known to all Germans.'

The same day, German invasions of Holland, Luxembourg and Belgium had begun, causing many Whitsun house parties in England to be cancelled at the last moment.

On May 22, Cecil Beaton, who had now acquired a house in Pelham Place, South Kensington in addition to his country quarters, left for New York where he had been given a six-week assignment taking advertising photographs. He sailed from Liverpool on board the S.S. *Samaria* and was given a cabin the size of a cupboard.

On May 23, Sir Oswald Mosley, who had continued to make anti-war speeches, was arrested outside his flat in Dolphin Square and escorted by courteous Special Branch detectives to Brixton Prison, where he was surprised to find himself placed in a cell next to a negro. Sir Oswald soon sent out for his shabbiest gardening clothes to wear in prison.

Meanwhile, German troops were rapidly overrunning France. On May 28, the Duke of Windsor was driven from Paris to Biarritz by his chauffeur George Ladbroke. In Biarritz, he joined the Duchess and the following day they drove on with their entourage to their house at Antibes, the Château de la Croe.

On May 30, singer Gracie Fields and her Italian-born husband sailed for America. Her departure caused a storm of criticism in the Press and an unfounded rumour circulated that she had taken with her £100,000 worth of jewellery. On arrival in America, Gracie told reporters, 'If I've done anything I shouldn't have done, I will go right back and put it right.'

By June 3, 300,000 British soldiers had been evacuated from Dunkirk. Several of those who had participated in this gigantic operation subsequently gave first-hand accounts of their adventures to the King at Buckingham Palace.

On June 6, Madame Consuelo Balsan, mother of the Duke of Marlborough, fled from her château in Normandy in a small Citroen. She and her husband took only one suitcase each with them. The fountains were still playing in front of the house when they left.

On June 10, Italy entered the war and the Duke and Duchess of Windsor became aware of the dangers of remaining in the South of France. They soon set off for the Spanish frontier, driven by their chauffeur Ladbroke with a few of their belongings in a trailer attached to the car. On meeting barricades in every major town they passed through, the Duke called out: 'Je suis le Prince de Galles. Laissez-moi passer, s'il vous plâit.'

On June 17, General de Gaulle, leader of the Free French, arrived at Croydon airport in a Dragon Rapide aeroplane provided by Mr. Churchill. The following day, the General was found lunching at the Royal Automobile Club in Pall Mall.

On June 19, wealthy Alice Astor, whose father had died on the *Titanic* in 1912, gave a dinner-party at Hanover Lodge, her luxurious Regent's Park home. Guests included Lady Colefax, Lord and Lady Kinross, Harold Nicolson and Chips Channon. Afterwards, Channon drove Harold Nicolson and Sybil Colefax home through the blackout.

Two days later, Paris had fallen and many socialites feared England would be overrun in a matter of weeks.

On June 24, Mr. Channon and his wife, Lady Honor, put their four-year-old son Paul, who was being evacuated to the United States, onto a train for Liverpool. At Euston Station, they found innumerable Rolls-Royces and liveried servants humping vast quantities of luggage.

A few days later, Duff and Lady Diana Cooper, who had now moved into a five-room, top-floor suite at the Dorchester Hotel, despatched their ten-year-old son, John Julius, to Canada on board a neutral ship provided by the American Ambassador, Mr. Kennedy. The little boy was accompanied by his nanny.

On July 1, the arrest of the beautiful Lady Mosley made headline news. She was taken from her house at Denham in Buckinghamshire to Holloway Prison, where conditions were so bleak that she was soon found asking for hotwater bottles at the height of the summer.

On July 10, Mrs. Arthur James gave a lunch-party attended by the King and Queen, the Duchess of Devonshire and Lord Gort. During the meal the Queen revealed that she was being taught how to use a revolver. 'Yes,' she explained, 'I shall not go down like the others.'

Meanwhile, royal economies had extended to the conversion of the Deanery Garden at Windsor into a vegetable-plot. Lettuces also sprouted from the Dean's window boxes. 'Some have already been picked and eaten and more are on the way' said a spokesman.

On July 15, the Rev. Robert Graham, Rector of Bolingbroke-with-Hareby in Lincolnshire was sentenced to four weeks imprisonment for ringing his church bell, contrary to Defence Regulations. He subsequently appealed successfully against this conviction on the grounds that he was ignorant of the order.

On July 19, Lord Redesdale arrived in London fiercely denying that he was a Fascist. 'Why all this interest in me? Why are people so interested in my movements?' he demanded. 'I come to London quite often. I have never been in the slightest way interested in Fascism and never will be. As for Sir Oswald Mosley, who married my daughter, I have only seen him twice.'

On July 28, the public were shocked to hear that Neville Chamberlain had been taken to hospital for a serious operation. Rumours soon circulated that the former Prime Minister had cancer and was not likely to live more than a few months.

On August 1, the Duke and Duchess of Windsor sailed from Lisbon to the Bahamas where the Duke had been appointed Governor. On arrival on August 17, the intense heat caused the khaki-clad Duke to sweat so much that he had great difficulty signing the oaths of allegiance and office.

Meanwhile, Hermann Goering had given orders for the Luftwaffe to begin their air attack on England.

In the middle of the Battle of Britain that followed, the eighty-two-year-old Duke of Bedford died at Woburn Abbey, watched over by six nurses and attended by no less than fifty indoor servants. Many members of his family congregated at the Abbey for the funeral on August 30, including the Duke's tall, pale grandson, Lord Howland, who had recently been discharged from the Coldstream Guards on the grounds of his ill-health and poor physique.

At the same time, Britain's war effort was boosted by a gift of ten ambulances from Woolworth heiress Barbara Hutton, now living in California. It was said that each vehicle would bear the donor's name.

At the beginning of September, mystery surrounded the whereabouts of the seventy-eight-year-old Earl of Newburgh, who had lived in Rome for many years. 'No one could be more pro-British than he has been throughout his life' said his sister, Lady Howard of Penrith. 'Never has he taken part in Italian politics. He is a man of leisure.'

On September 7, German bombers began to attack London every night. One of the first famous institutions to be hit was Burlington Arcade. Six shops were destroyed on September 10 and many valuable trinkets were buried among the rubble. 'Every ounce of this stuff has got to be sifted' said one shopkeeper. 'There are hundreds of pounds worth of small articles in it.'

At lunchtime on September 12, the grouse served at the Reform Club in Pall Mall won high praise.

That evening, high society flocked to the Dorchester Hotel. Among those enjoying the protection of one of London's only concrete built hotels was sixty-six-year-old Somerset Maugham, who had recently been

The concrete-built Dorchester Hotel where many socialites found refuge during the War. Among those to take permanent suites here were Duff and Lady Diana Cooper, Lady Cunard, Mr. and Mrs. Charles Sweeny and Mrs. Ronnie Greville

pronounced missing following the Fall of France. At the end of the evening, many people were observed settling down for the night in the lobby.

The following day, five bombs descended upon Buckingham Palace wrecking the chapel where Princess Elizabeth had been christened in 1926 and smashing 100 windows. Queen Victoria's family Bible, in which all royal births were recorded, was retrieved from the debris. 'A magnificent piece of bombing, Ma'am, if you'll pardon my saying so' a police constable remarked to the Queen immediately after the raid.

On September 22, actor David Niven, now serving as a Captain in the newly formed Commandos, was married to Miss Primula Rollo, grand-daughter of the Marquess of Downshire, whom he had first met a few months earlier at the fashionable Café de Paris in Coventry Street. The ceremony, which took place in a tiny Norman church on the Wiltshire Downs, was enlivened when a small flock of sheep drifted into the building.

At the end of the month, a bomb fell on the London Zoo and a zebra escaped from its cage and raced across Regent's Park towards Camden Town, pursued by the Zoo's secretary, Professor Julian Huxley, and members of the public. Coaxing the beast back into its shed later, Huxley found himself 'wedged into a corner with its hind quarters six feet from my face'.

On October 2, Somerset Maugham forsook the Dorchester Hotel and flew to Lisbon and thence to New York, where he was reunited with his companion of the last twenty years, Gerald Haxton. It was announced that the famous writer was 'on a propaganda job'.

On October 10, a bomb fell on St. Paul's Cathedral making a great, gaping hole above the High Altar but leaving the rest of the building unscarred. Sleeping in a camp bed in the crypt at the time was the aged Canon Sydney Alexander, who hurried up the stone steps of the sanctuary in his pyjamas to inspect the damage. 'The binding of the masonry put in by Wren must have been marvellous' he said.

On October 13, Princess Elizabeth, now fourteen years old, spoke for five minutes on Children's Hour, reading from a prepared script. At the end of the broadcast, ten-year-old Princess Margaret joined her sister in saying 'Goodnight' to the nation's children.

The following day, the Carlton Club, Conservative Party sanctuary in Carlton House Terrace, suffered a direct hit. One hundred and twenty members were in the club at the time, all of whom escaped unhurt. Quintin Hogg was found leading his father, Viscount Hailsham, out of the ruins. Lord Soulbury went round the corner to the Royal Automobile Club for 'the largest whisky and soda I have ever had'.

The same night, a bomb fell fifty yards from 10 Downing Street rendering the upper floors uninhabitable. Mr. and Mrs. Churchill moved into the reinforced basement annexe which was soon prettily decorated with good furniture and good pictures. Shortly after this date, the Prime Minister also began to appear in a bomb-proof armoured car, said to resemble a giant Thermos flask.

On October 23, American Ambassador Joseph Kennedy bade farewell to England. Smiling broadly and waving his black Homburg hat, he said: 'I have been through it all and I have the greatest respect for Londoners.'

The same day, the trial opened at the Old Bailey of a Russian woman named Anna Wolkoff who was charged with attempting to send information to William Joyce, the notorious 'Lord Haw Haw' who had begun propaganda broadcasts from Germany. 'It is difficult to imagine a more serious offence' said the judge sentencing Miss Wolkoff to ten years' imprisonment.

On November 7, a bomb descended upon the palatial home of Mr. Chips Channon in Belgrave Square, smashing the portico and balcony, breaking most of the windows and interrupting a dinner-party attended by Hector Bolitho and Raymond Mortimer. Surrounded by dust and smoke, the suave host rang the bell and asked his butler, Lambert, to bring more drinks.

Two days later, Neville Chamberlain died of cancer at Heckfield Park near Reading, a house said to be screened from German raiders by a row of larch trees. A Berlin newspaper wrote of the former Prime Minister: 'He hypocritically and cynically employed the umbrella symbol, while doing absolutely everything to prepare for and declare war.'

On November 16, Cecil Beaton was found staying with Mrs. Randolph Churchill at her Queen Anne house at Hitchin to photograph her baby son, Winston, who had been born at Chequers under a cloak of secrecy five weeks earlier.

A few days later, Beaton photographed the baby's grandfather in the Cabinet Room at 10 Downing Street. 'Wait till I'm prepared' said the Prime Minister who had been fortified with a glass of port at eleven o'clock in the morning. 'Don't try any cleverness on me.'

By the end of November, Churchill had begun to appear in a strange costume described as his siren suit.

On December 6, Lady Astor made an unintentionally grim jest at a luncheon of Overseas League. 'You've no idea how glad people are to be riding in American ambulances' she declared.

On December 18, the Prime Minister paid a visit to Harrow School where over fifty years earlier he had been a pupil. After joining in the school songs in the school's bomb-damaged Speech Room, he told pupils: 'You have already had the honour of being under fire from the enemy and no doubt you acquitted yourselves with befitting composure and decorum.'

Meanwhile, flamboyant Old Harrovian Nubar Gulbenkian had returned from two semi-secret visits to Europe where, under the code name Orchid, he had helped organize escape routes for British citizens. On Christmas Eve, Mr. Gulbenkian was to be found enjoying a well-earned slap-up champagne dinner at the Mitre Hotel, Oxford.

The year ended with 10,000 incendiary bombs descending on the City of London, destroying the Guildhall and eight Wren churches. The following day, December 31, while a Berlin spokesman gloated over 'London's night of Horror', Cecil Beaton climbed among the ruins taking photographs and then went off to lunch with his publisher.

The Duke and Duchess of Windsor greeted the New Year in Miami, where the Duchess was undergoing a dental operation at St. Francis's Hospital. This was said to be the Duke's first visit to America for sixteen years.

On January 9, American millionairess, Mrs. Laura Corrigan, one of the most lavish London hostesses over the past twenty years, was reported safe and well at the Hotel Majestic in Vichy. It was said that she had taken possession of the only horse-drawn vehicle in the town. 'Life is very sad but very interesting' was her verdict on the contemporary scene.

On January 15, a row erupted over a letter written to *The Times* by Old Etonian Lieutenant-Colonel Ralph Charles Bingham, DSO, a grandson of the fifth Earl of Lucan, condemning the training of secondary-school boys as officers. 'The middle, lower middle and working classes now receiving the King's Commission have very largely fallen down on the job' he wrote. In the storm that followed, Colonel Bingham was described by the Prime Minister as 'a goose' and relieved of his position commanding an officers' training unit. 'I stand by every word I said' he declared. 'The old school tie has much to recommend it.'

Meanwhile in New York, celebrities gathered at the Astor Hotel for the Star Spangled Ball to raise funds for 'The Committee to Defend America by Aiding the Allies'. Among those present was the beautiful English-born Mrs. Douglas Fairbanks, whose husband had died in the first year of the war leaving her several million dollars.

On January 18, it was announced that speculators were buying up the dwindling stocks of champagne. 'In all probability, we shall not be getting any champagne from France until years after the war' said a leading London wine merchant. 'The Germans are in occupation of the Champagne district and are drinking all the stocks.'

In the middle of February, the Prime Minister spent the weekend at Ditchley, Mr. Ronald Tree's beautiful, centrally-heated home in Oxfordshire. He was accompanied by a large team of soldiers, detectives, wireless operators and secretaries. Most of his work was done in bed.

On February 26, the bluff but genial Earl of Rosebery left London for Scotland, where he had recently been appointed Regional Commissioner. Heavy snowdrifts delayed the train and he did not arrive at Glasgow until February 28. The fifty-nine-year-old peer spent the delay pacing the corridors and living off whisky and biscuits.

On March 1, the new American Ambassador, bushy-eyebrowed John Winant, arrived in London. 'I have come here to do a job of work and I want to get to it' he told a Press conference. One of his first appointments was tea at Buckingham Palace with the King.

On Saturday March 8, more than 1,000 people were present at Queen Charlotte's Birthday Ball at Grosvenor House. A birthday cake with 187 candles was wheeled forward. Taking part in the ceremony for the second year running was the Prime Minister's youngest daughter Mary Churchill, who wore a wide-sleeved frock of pale blue.

At 9.50 pm the same night, a bomb fell on the fashionable Café de Paris, killing the owner Mr. Poulsen, bandleader 'Snake Hips' Johnson and eighty-two others. 'I was blown off my feet' said a survivor. 'The sensation was that of being pressed down by a great hand. I could see people lying on the floor all around.' While aeroplanes continued to drone overhead, girls tore their evening-dresses and underslips into strips to make bandages.

Three days later, Prime Minister Winston Churchill and Lord Beaverbrook, Minister of Aircraft Production, were found enjoying a high-spirited lunch at the Mirabelle Restaurant in Curzon Street. It was noted that the Prime Minister drank two whiskies and sodas and two glasses of Kümmel.

Meanwhile, Lady Diana Cooper had left the comparative security of the Dorchester Hotel for her farm near Bognor. Here, her stock soon included two beehives, four goats and a cow named Princess, with whose cream Lady Diana later amused herself making unusual cheeses such as Coulommiers and Pont l'Évêque.

On March 28, the disappearance of fifty-nine-year-old writer Virginia Woolf caused deep distress among her friends and relations. She had left a suicide note and her walking-stick was found floating in the river near her Sussex home. At an inquest held later, the coroner attributed her death to 'the general beastliness of things happening today'.

On April 13, Mrs. Winant, wife of the new American Ambassador arrived in London. 'My husband tells me I must learn to fall flat on my face when I hear a bomb coming. I've been practising' she said. 'I expect I'll do it soon enough when the time comes.'

On April 16, a land-mine fell outside the Savoy Hotel, shattering every window facing the river and putting more than sixty suites out of commission. It was said that more than 5,000 glasses and pieces of china had been smashed. The hotel's immaculately coiffeured head housekeeper, Mrs. Kate Butler, calmly directed the salvage operation.

Meanwhile, it was revealed that *The Nahlin*, the luxurious twelve-bathroom vessel on which King Edward VIII and Mrs. Simpson had made their fateful cruise in 1936, had fallen into the hands of the enemy. The luxurious vessel now flew the Rumanian flag and was staffed by a German crew. The ship's cocktail-shaker, however, was said to be in the possession of the Duke of Windsor in the Bahamas.

On April 19, high society flocked to St. Bartholomew the Great at Smithfield for the wedding of Lord Andrew Cavendish, younger son of the Duke of Devonshire, and Miss Deborah Mitford, youngest of the beautiful Mitford sisters. Guests included Mr. Harold Macmillan, now Parliamentary Secretary at the Ministry of Supply, Margot Asquith and the bride's controversial sister, Miss Unity Mitford. Unity's apparently normal appearance gave rise to more suggestions that she ought to be interned but the Home Secretary, Herbert Morrison, insisted that control was unnecessary.

Unity Mitford, centre, in a happy mood at the wedding of her sister Deborah and Lord Andrew Cavendish

Prime Minister Winston Churchill during a tour of the ruins of Manchester

At the end of April, frizzy-headed Frank Pakenham announced in a letter to the *Tablet* that he had become a Roman Catholic. The conversion was attributed to the influence of his old friend, Evelyn Waugh, who had himself been converted to Catholicism a few years earlier. It was noted that Mr. Pakenham had recently resigned from the Oxford and Bucks Light Infantry owing to a wound in the buttocks.

On May 9, thieves broke into a house in Kinnerton Street, Belgravia, occupied by notorious Old Rugbeian Gerald Hamilton, and made off with the contents of the wine-cellar. Several fine bottles of 1906 Château Mouton Rothschild and some green and yellow Chartreuse, valued at eight guineas a bottle, were stolen.

During the same month, a bomb descended on a wine merchant's cellar in Cannon Street, where Mr. Nubar Gulbenkian was storing 1,000 bottles of rare wine, all of which perished.

On May 11, a bomb fell on the Palace of Westminster. The Chamber of the House of Commons was gutted and the Deanery of Westminster Abbey was destroyed. A clerk explained that the Dean had lost everything – 'including all his clothes'.

The same day, a mysterious German parachutist descended near the Duke of Hamilton's estate in Scotland. He was apprehended by a ploughman and soon after identified himself as Herr Rudolf Hess, the Deputy Führer, and explained that he was on a solo peace mission. In London Prime Minister Winston Churchill was said to be astounded by this bizarre turn of events, but did not alter his plans to go and watch a Marx Brothers film.

Meanwhile, far away in Kenya, the thirty-nine-year-old Earl of Erroll had been found shot through the neck, and wealthy baronet Sir Jock Delves Broughton, owner of Doddington Park, Cheshire, had been arrested and charged with murder. His trial opened in a blaze of world-wide publicity on May 26. Many weeks later, he was to be found not guilty and the crime remained one of the most baffling of all unsolved murder cases.

On May 27, the Minister of Food, Lord Woolton, was found sampling a new pie made of vegetables and fatless pastry created by Latry, the head chef at the Savoy Hotel.

On June 4, the eighty-two-year-old ex-Kaiser died in his bed at his castle at Doorn in Holland, which had been his home since 1918. His death was attributed to intestinal trouble complicated by old age. It was said later that Hitler wished to give the former monarch a State Funeral but this was successfully opposed by the dead man's family.

In the middle of June, reports came from Palm Beach that vivacious Elsa Maxwell had staged a 'Blitz' party to raise money for British war charities. Guests were asked to come in dressing-gowns, siren suits or their oldest clothes and a large tent was scattered with fake debris from which dummy figures were extricated and carried off on stretchers.

On June 18, the Derby was held for the second year running at Newmarket and was won by an outsider, Owen Tudor, owned by Mrs. Macdonald-Buchanan. Enthusiasts came from as far away as Sussex and Lancashire and the 4,000 vehicles in the car park were carefully examined by representatives of the Petroleum Department. 'We can tell almost at once if it is petrol which should be used for flying' said an inspector.

On June 19, Mr. R. A. Butler, Under Secretary for Foreign Affairs, dismissed as 'nonsense' rumours that the Deputy Führer, Rudolf Hess, was staying at Chequers with the Prime Minister.

On July 2, Noel Coward's new play *Blithe Spirit* opened at the bomb-shattered Piccadilly Theatre. In the audience were Bea Lillie, Lord and Lady Louis Mountbatten, Mrs. Randolph Churchill, Lady Juliet Duff and Mr Duff Cooper. From the Dress Circle, an irate woman shouted that the play was unfair to spiritualists and should be taken off immediately.

Five days later, the new Chinese Ambassador, Mr. Wellington Koo, was found dining at a Chinese restaurant in Soho with the Russian Ambassador, Mr. Maisky, whose country was now under attack by Hitler's forces.

On July 8, eighty-three-year-old Colonel Henry Barclay, of Hanworth Hall, Norfolk was fined £6 for obtaining more than three times his meat ration. The Colonel produced a doctor's certificate which said that he required extra meat for health reasons but this carried little weight with the magistrates.

Meanwhile, singer Gracie Fields was on her way home from America to which she had fled a year earlier with her husband, mother and father and other members of her family. 'I am going home to sing' she said on reaching Lisbon. 'I am not coming home to argue with people who have criticised me. I have been doing my bit and it speaks for itself.' A rapturous welcome awaited her at her home town of Rochdale in Lancashire.

On July 16, twenty-eight-year-old Lady Howard of Effingham was released from Holloway Prison, where she had been detained for five months under Defence Regulation 18b. 'I am ready to go into a munitions factory if they can find me work to do' she said from a friend's Mayfair flat. 'I am not one of those women who mind spoiling their hands. We can always scrub them clean after the war is over.'

On July 25, Gerald Hamilton was arrested in the middle of a bid to get to Dublin, crossing the Irish Sea disguised as a nun. It was said that Hamilton's plan was to get the Pope to play a more active part in ending the hostilities. Hamilton's short stay in Brixton Prison was marked by a grim incident when a warder decanted a priceless bottle of 1916 claret into a rusty tin can.

On August 6, Mr. Duff and Lady Diana Cooper set off for Singapore where Mr. Cooper was to report on the chaotic Far East situation. Lady Diana took with her a wardrobe by Molyneux and some blue pills to fortify her against her fear of flying.

Shortly afterwards, under a cloak of secrecy, Churchill crossed the Atlantic for a historic meeting with President Roosevelt in Placentia Bay, Newfoundland. On August 18, he was back in London carrying a gold-topped cane and a cigar. At King's Cross Station, he gave his 'V' sign for the first time during the war.

On August 28, it was announced that Noel Coward, currently living at the Savoy Hotel, having been bombed out of his Belgravia home, had begun work on a film based on the adventures of Lord Louis Mountbatten, who had recently returned to England following the sinking of his ship HMS *Kelly* off the island of Crete. The choice of Coward for the leading role was subsequently criticised on the grounds that he had never been in the Navy.

Duff and Lady Diana Cooper, on their way to Singapore to report on the Middle East situation, pause in New York where they reunited with their son, John Julius

In the middle of September, Mr. Lloyd George was found helping to bring in the harvest of apples at his home at Churt. The ex-premier wore a Welsh cloak and no hat and his long white locks billowed in the wind.

On September 26, it was announced that nineteen-year-old Mary Churchill had joined the ATS. She was training with her cousin, Judy Montagu, grand-daughter of Lord Swaythling, at a depot of the Southern Command. 'It is a wonderful life' she said. 'I sleep in a hut with twenty girls, make my own bed and clean the hut in my turn.'

On October 3, workmen with oxyacetylene torches began removing a section of railings at Buckingham Palace. It was said that these would produce twenty tons of metal, which would later be made up into a tank called *The Buckingham Palace*.

On October 7, it was announced that the Russian Ambassador Mr. Maisky had been made an honorary member of the stately Athenaeum Club in Pall Mall. 'It was a very popular election' said the club's secretary, Mr. Nicholas Udal.

Two days later, Mr. and Mrs. Winston Churchill were in the front row of the stalls at the Piccadilly Theatre to see Noel Coward's *Blithe Spirit*. They tried to sneak into their seats unnoticed but were immediately recognised and greeted with a burst of applause. 'Brilliant' was the Prime Minister's verdict on the play.

The same day, the new Duke of Bedford's refusal to have the railings of his London Squares used for tank metal provoked an MP to ask if the wealthy pacifist should not be interned. 'I am not saying anything about him,' said Home Secretary Herbert Morrison, 'except that I am interested in his activities.' A few days later, the word 'traitor' was daubed over the statue of a former Duke of Bedford in Russell Square. 'I am no Quisling' commented the Duke from his Wigtownshire home. 'I am pro-British and I am acting in what I believe to be the best interests of the country.'

Meanwhile, Lord Teynham, a Lieutenant-Commander in the Royal Navy, had been fined £1 at Campbelltown Sheriff Court for poaching on the Duke of Argyll's Inveraray estate.

In London, Noel Coward's work on his patriotic new film was interrupted by two court appearances. On October 30, he appeared before the Bow Street magistrate accused of breaking currency regulations and was fined £200. A week later, he appeared before the Lord Mayor at the Mansion House accused of failing to register a $5,000 United States Treasury Bond and other securities and was fined a further £1,600. 'The fact that because of your temperament you take no interest in financial matters does not release you from your obligations as a citizen' said the Lord Mayor.

On November 8, a further defeatist pronouncement from the Duke of Bedford caused fresh demands for his internment. 'If this country were invaded and the Germans were surrounding this house, I would not fight to save it' he said from his Scottish home. 'That would be against my principles as a Christian and a pacifist.'

On November 17, ten nine-inch Flor de Allones cigars donated by the Prime Minister were sold at Christies for £502.10.0 to raise money for the Aid to Russia effort. It was explained that the cigars had reached this astronomical price by being sold and handed back for resale several times.

On December 3, representatives of the Aga Khan, safe and well at the Palace Hotel in St. Moritz since the fall of France, acquired a yearling colt at the Newmarket sales for 8,200 guineas, later shipped to the Aga's stud in Ireland.

The same day, the silver collection of the late Lord Rothermere came under the hammer at Christies, raising £30,000. Many friends of the great newspaper proprietor were present and Lord Camrose bid in person for an octagonal Queen Anne teapot with stand and lamp.

On December 4, Lady Astor attacked Geoffrey Lloyd, Minister of Petroleum, in the House of Commons for not being in uniform. 'You ought to be ashamed of yourself' she said.

On December 7, following the bombing of Pearl Harbor by the Japanese, steps were taken to expel the Emperor of Japan from the Order of the Garter and his banner was quietly removed from St. George's Chapel, Windsor. The honour had originally been conferred on the Emperor by the late King George V.

On December 12, Winston Churchill and Lord Beaverbrook left secretly for America, which had now entered the war. They were accompanied by Churchill's doctor, Sir Charles Wilson, who was subsequently criticised for deserting his post as President of the Royal College of Physicians in order to look after the Prime Minister.

That Christmas, Princess Elizabeth and Princess Margaret appeared in a lavish production of *Cinderella* at Windsor Castle. Wigs, gilt shoes and silk costumes were hired and the pantomime was staged in the Castle's stately Waterloo Room. During rehearsals, it was said that the Princesses had disagreed about whether or not the specially invited audience should be charged an admission fee. 'No one will pay to see us' said Princess Elizabeth modestly. 'Nonsense!' exclaimed her sister. 'They'll pay anything to see us.'

Princess Elizabeth and Princess Margaret as they appeared in a private production of Cinderella *at Windsor Castle*

The Prime Minister saw in the New Year on board a train travelling from Ottawa to Washington. As the hour of midnight struck, he proposed a toast to 'a year of toil'. Then his staff, Press men and the train crew joined in singing 'Auld Lang Syne'.

A few days later, Churchill took a break from his discussions with President Roosevelt and flew to Florida where he basked in the sea and lunched with his old friend, Madame Consuelo Vanderbilt Balsan, the former Duchess of Marlborough, who had fled from Europe two years earlier.

Back in England, on January 15, the Earl of Berkeley died in his sleep at Berkeley castle in Gloucestershire. The seventy-six-year-old Earl left no heir and gossip columnists wondered what would become of the Castle which had been in the same family since the reign of Henry II.

The following day, the ninety-one-year-old Duke of Connaught, last surviving son of Queen Victoria and a godson of the great Duke of Wellington, died at Bagshot Park, Surrey. The King immediately ordered two weeks' Court mourning. Fifty of the late Duke's domestic staff, gardeners and farmworkers attended his funeral at St. George's, Windsor.

The Duke of Connaught, last surviving son of Queen Victoria

On January 17, Lord Woolton, Mr. Ernest Bevin and Mrs. Winston Churchill were called away from Wembley Stadium where they had gone to watch the England *v.* Scotland match, in order to welcome home the Prime Minister who had arrived from America by flying-boat.

January 21 saw the resignation of the thin-lipped Dr. Cosmo Gordon Lang, seventy-seven-year-old Archbishop of Canterbury. 'I deem it my duty' he said 'to hand over my charge to someone younger in years, more vigorous in mind and spirit, who will be better able to prepare us for the post-war years.' It was noted that the Archbishop would be relinquishing a salary of £15,000 and would in future have to manage on a tenth of this sum.

At the beginning of February, wine merchants Saccone and Speed received an urgent demand from Badminton House for more hock. It was rumoured that Queen Mary, who had been staying with the Duke and Duchess of Beaufort since the beginning of the war, drank half a bottle every night.

On February 14, a rumpus blew up over the Ministry of Health's plan to pay wealthy Mr. Jimmy de Rothschild £1,700 a year for the use of his stately home in Buckinghamshire in order to house seventy evacuee children from Croydon. 'Under this agreement, Mr. de Rothschild will make a profit of £400 a year and he is already a millionaire' grumbled a Croydon Councillor, Mr. Cork. The public were titillated to learn that the evacuees would eat food prepared by the Rothschild family chef, M. Tissot.

On February 16, Duff and Lady Diana Cooper returned from the Far East, following the fall of Singapore. Lady Diana stepped from the train at Paddington Station wearing a white fur coat and a Royal Yacht Squadron cap.

On February 21, Lady Mosley, whose husband Sir Oswald Mosley had recently joined her in Holloway Prison, appeared in court to give evidence at the trial of a man accused of stealing a white silk bedspread from her flat in Dolphin Square.

At the end of the month, the Duke of Marlborough wrote to the Minister of Food, Lord Woolton, suggesting that the ornamental lake at Woodstock should be fished for tench, perch, pike and eels, which could then be sold in the country's fishmongers. Gossip columnists wondered if the legendary Great Pike of Woodstock would be caught.

On March 17, Londoners flocked to the Royal Horticultural Society's exhibition in Vincent Square. Quantities of snow-drops, crocuses, irises and primroses were on display. It was noted that only one table held vegetables to the production of which most professional gardeners were now devoting their time and energy.

Meanwhile, American troops had begun to appear in London. Among them was Lieutenant Douglas Fairbanks, Jr., whose old flat in Grosvenor Square had now become part of the annexe of the American Embassy. 'I'm afraid, for security reasons, I cannot say why I am here or for how long' he said, 'but I'm going to forget all about films until the war is over.'

April 21 was Princess Elizabeth's sixteenth birthday. That day, she put on an unflattering utility suit, with the minimum of pockets and trimmings, and conducted her first official duty : an inspection of the Grenadier Guards of which she had become Colonel-in-Chief following the death of her great-great-uncle, the Duke of Connaught.

That evening, there was a party at Windsor Castle at which the Princess danced several times with her father. Much publicity was soon to attend her when she signed on at a local Labour Exchange anxious to undertake some form of war-work, though this was rumoured to be against the King's wishes.

On April 22, a group of Commandos led by thirty-year-old Lord Lovat stormed the German defences near Boulogne and caused havoc among the enemy's communications systems. 'How thrilling' said the Dowager Lady Lovat. 'I had no idea that my son was taking part in the raid.'

Two days later, much pageantry surrounded the enthronement of the new Archbishop of Canterbury, Dr. Temple. 'This is not the moment to say much about the war' he said in his address to the congregation, which included forty-five Bishops and his picturesque-looking Dean, Dr. Hewlett Johnson, who had recently been bombed out of his Deanery.

On Saturday April 25, the night the Germans bombed Bath, a dance was held a few miles away at the Wiltshire home of Lady Sybil Phipps, sister of the Duchess of Gloucester. Among those present were Lady Weymouth, Lady Ravensdale, unmarried daughter of the late Lord Curzon, and actor-soldier David Niven. The drone of aircraft overhead and the rattle of the windows was drowned by the band.

On April 30, the wealthy Mrs. Ronnie Greville gave a lunch-party in her suite at the Dorchester Hotel. Guests included Lord Louis Mountbatten, who had now been appointed Chief of Combined Operations, the Duke and Duchess of Kent, the Duchess of Buccleuch and Mr. Chips Channon. Mrs. Greville, a leading hostess since the Edwardian Era, was now confined to a wheelchair but was decked out in her famous, priceless jewels.

On May 1, guests who flocked to the preview of the Royal Academy Summer Exhibition included young Lord Cowdray, who had lost an arm at Dunkirk two years previously, eighty-four-year-old Mr. Gordon Selfridge, Lord Brabazon of Tara, and the elderly Dr. Inge, former Dean of St. Paul's and his wife, who wore an Edwardian hat encircled by an ostrich feather. Among the pictures on show was a composition entitled *My New Teapot* by Royal Academician, R. O. Dunlop.

A month later the public's attention was diverted from the grave Allied losses in Africa and Asia when the King and Queen made a surprise appearance at the Derby which was again run at Newmarket rather than Epsom. The race was won by Lord Derby's Watling Street, ridden by Harry Wragg. Lady Derby received the King's congratulations on behalf of her seventy-seven-year-old husband who was said to be indisposed.

On June 15, a government order limiting meals in hotels and restaurants to three courses and five shillings in price came into force. Partly thanks to the intervention of Mr. Hugh Wontner, young managing director of the Savoy group, catering establishments were permitted to charge extra for oysters and certain other luxuries.

On June 18, thieves broke into American-born Lady Beatty's third-floor suite at the Dorchester Hotel and stole jewellery valued at £40,000. The haul included diamond necklaces, diamond ear-rings, rare black pearls and several gold shoe-horns. Lord Beatty was away on active service at the time.

The following day, it was revealed that Churchill was again in the United States, engaged in further consultations with President Roosevelt at the White House. During the visit, the President broke the grim news to the Prime Minister that Tobruk had fallen. 'What can we do to help?' he asked.

On July 1, Churchill was back in England and facing a Vote of No Confidence in the House of Commons. Leading back bencher John Wardlaw-Milne, a red carnation sprouting from his button-hole, opened the debate and was listened to with respect until he made the suggestion that the Duke of Gloucester should be made Commander-in-Chief of the forces. In the embarrassed laughter that this proposal provoked, Churchill immediately perked up and the following day won the debate by 476 votes, watched by Mrs. Churchill, and his daughters Sarah, now Mrs. Vic Oliver, and Mary in the gallery.

On July 8, news flashed around the world that the twenty-nine-year-old multi-millionairess Barbara Hutton had married British-born actor Cary Grant at a ceremony in Hollywood. It was noted that both bride and groom had contributed generously to the British war effort.

On July 21, the notorious Duke of Bedford annoyed the House of Lords by repeating his plea for a negotiated pcacc, attacking the Prime Minister and 'the selfishness of the great American armaments firms'. Eighty-two-year-old Lord Gainford was so provoked that he moved that 'the noble Lord should no longer be heard', a procedure that had not been used for more than a century.

The 12th Duke of Bedford whose war-time pacifist activities caused much annoyance

On August 4, almost the entire Royal Family gathered at Windsor Castle for the christening of the Duke and Duchess of Kent's new baby boy. Among the godparents was the American President, Mr. Roosevelt, for whom the Duke of Kent stood proxy, and the child was duly named Michael George Charles Franklin.

Meanwhile, the sixty-seven-year-old Prime Minister had set off on a long trip taking in Cairo and Moscow. He travelled in a small, unheated Liberator bomber in which the only sleeping arrangements were a couple of mattresses. On August 24, he was back in England dressed in the uniform of an Air Commodore. Arc lights were set up at Paddington Station to enable photographs to be taken. Pressed to give his famous 'V' sign, he said: 'Not in uniform, it's against regulations.'

The following day, the public were stunned to learn that the Duke of Kent had been killed in an air-crash in Scotland on his way to inspect RAF installations in Iceland. His body was taken to Dunrobin Castle, home of the Duke and Duchess of Sutherland, and thence moved by rail to London. Four days later, the Royal Family gathered at St. George's Chapel, Windsor for the funeral. Queen Mary drove back to Badminton afterwards in a thunderstorm, giving a lift in her limousine to a young American parachutist and an English Air Force Sergeant.

On September 5, it was revealed that the 50,000-acre Balmacaan estate in the Scottish highlands had been acquired by a London concern named Panton Investments Ltd. The company's managing director, thirty-seven-year-old Mr. Charles Clore, stated that he would do everything in his power to preserve the estate's historical associations. It was noted that the fishing rights to Loch Ness were included in the deal.

On September 15, seventy-five-year-old Mrs. Ronnie Greville died in her suite at the Dorchester Hotel. A memorial service took place later at St. Mark's, North Audley Street, amidst much speculation about the future of the famous Greville jewels. It was soon learnt that she had left her famous diamond and emerald necklace, which had once belonged to Marie Antoinette, to the Queen. Her famous stately home near Dorking, Polesden Lacey, went to the National Trust.

On October 1, Lord Woolton presided over the finale of a European chefs potato-cooking contest at the Ministry of Food in Portman Square. Among those competing was the former head chef at the Hotel Imperial in Prague who had invented a potato and carrot dish. The winner, however, was a Greek chef with meatless potato moussaka. 'This competition should convince us that more can be done with the potato than has ever been dreamed of' said Lord Woolton.

Five days later, there was a storm in the House of Lords, following a visit to the home of Sir Lionel Darell, Deputy Lieutenant of Gloucestershire, by two Ministry of Food enforcement officers searching for a secret food horde. 'This deplorable incident is in conflict with the traditional sanctity of the homes of British people' said Viscount Bledisloe. 'Such unwarranted victimisation calls for an explanation and, if not redress, at least an apology.'

Meanwhile, the beautiful Lady Diana Cooper had been accused of wasting bread on her farm animals at Bognor. In a long statement, she explained that she had been supplied with stale bread by her baker and on October 8 the summons was withdrawn and she was awarded one guinea's costs.

On October 23, the formidable Mrs. Eleanor Roosevelt arrived in England with only 44 lb. of luggage. She was greeted at Paddington Station by the King and Queen and driven to the bomb-damaged Buckingham Palace where she was placed in a bedroom with no glass in its windows. That night there was a dinner-party at the Palace in her honour, at which the guests included Lord and Lady Louis Mountbatten, Mr. and Mrs. Churchill and General Smuts, Prime Minister of South Africa. After dinner, there was a showing of Noel Coward's patriotic new film *In Which We Serve*, during which Mr. Churchill went and telephoned for news of the Battle of El Alamein, which had begun at 10.00 pm that night. Hearing that the news was good, he returned to the assembled company singing 'Roll Out the Barrel'.

On November 6, two days after General Montgomery's triumph in Africa, the Prime Minister appeared in his siren suit at a lunch-party in his basement quarters at 10 Downing Street. Sea kale, jugged hare and cherry tart were served and Churchill brandished a hand-written letter from the King congratulating him on the recent victory.

On November 14, writer Evelyn Waugh, now training as a Commando, was found staying in the suite at the Hyde Park Hotel where the notorious 'Mayfair Men' had committed their famous robbery with violence five years earlier.

On November 15, a fire broke out at Lady Weymouth's home near Warminster. While Lady Weymouth and her guests were battling with the blazing drawing-room, the local police rang up to say that too much light was showing from the downstairs rooms.

Meanwhile, Lady Cunard had returned to England after a long spell in America during which her long friendship with Sir Thomas Beecham had finally broken up. After a couple of days lying low at the Great Western Hotel at Paddington, she had moved into the Ritz with her maid Gordon and taken her place again as a leader of London Society.

On November 21, the Earl of Albemarle turned up at a reception of the Anglo-Batavian Society, bringing a box of cigars and a bottle of schnapps as his contribution to the buffet.

On November 26, workmen were found removing a large section of railings, dating from the reign of William IV, from the front of Brooks's Club in St. James's Street.

On December 1, a doll made of pale pink knitted wool, contributed by twelve-year-old Princess Margaret, who had been left £20,000 by the late Mrs. Ronnie Greville, was among gifts on sale at Grosvenor House in aid of the prisoners-of-war. Mrs. Churchill walked round purchasing an item from each stall, accompanied by her daughter Mary, now an officer in the ATS.

On December 5, Sir Jock Delves Broughton, who the previous year had been found not guilty of murdering the Earl of Erroll in Kenya, died in hospital in Liverpool after being found unconscious in his bedroom at the city's luxurious Adelphi Hotel, only two weeks after his return to England.

A week later, Doris Delevigne, former wife of gossip columnist Viscount Castlerosse, was found unconscious in her room at the Dorchester Hotel and taken to St. Mary's Hospital Paddington suffering from a fatal overdose of amytal tablets.

On December 17, there was a dramatic moment in the House of Commons when, following a statement by the Foreign Secretary Anthony Eden about the atrocities inflicted on Jews in Eastern Europe, and an inspiring speech by Liberal MP Jimmy de Rothschild, the entire House, including the Speaker and Press reporters, stood up in silent tribute to those that had suffered.

Meanwhile, Mrs. Laura Corrigan had returned to London from Vichy France, where she had been awarded the Croix de Guerre for her bravery in driving in and out of occupied territory assisting French soldiers earlier in the war. On December 24, she gave a Christmas party in her suite at Claridge's where champagne flowed and everyone was given a present. Lady Cunard upset some of those present by suddenly asking, 'What are the Merchant Navy doing?'

1943

In the New Year's Honours List, Sir Charles Wilson, personal physician to Winston Churchill since May 1940, was raised to the peerage, taking the title Lord Moran.

A few days later, he resumed his duties when he flew off with the Prime Minister to Casablanca for further consultations with President Roosevelt. During the flight, Churchill caused a sensation on the plane by crawling around in his silk nightshirt, presenting his huge bare bottom to anyone who cared to look. While in Africa, the Prime Minister found time to execute an oil-painting of the Atlas mountains – the only picture he did during the whole war.

On January 17, the former Prime Minister Mr. Lloyd George celebrated his eightieth birthday at his Hampshire home. Lunch that day consisted of roast goose and bottled fruits. Among the many gifts he received was a frost-predictor from the workers on his farm. A telegram of good wishes arrived from the elderly Earl Baldwin of Bewdley.

On February 1, news came from New York that the sixty-five-year-old Earl of Gosford, who had been running a Manhattan wine-shop, had now joined the New York City Police. At the Police headquarters, the Earl, son of a former Lady of the Bedchamber to Queen Alexandra, was known as Captain Gosford. 'I am too old to return and fight' he said.

On February 13, motor-car manufacturer Viscount Nuffield caused a sensation by giving £10,000,000 of his private fortune to estabish a charitable trust. 'Lord Nuffield wishes to make it clear' said a spokesman 'that he is not in any way withdrawing from his associations with his companies.'

On February 20, Noel Coward, currently touring England with three plays, was found in a suite at the Grand Hotel, Leicester, basking under an enormous infra-red lamp and wearing only a garment described as a 'triangulo'.

On February 25, there was a champagne reception for 325 people at Mr. Chips Channon's house in Belgrave Square following the marriage of the Earl of Dudley and Viscountess Long. Home Secretary Herbert Morrison was one of the first to arrive and was soon engrossed in conversation with the Duchesses of Buccleuch and Rutland. The gathering was later enriched by the presence of Lord Louis Mountbatten, 'Rab' Butler, the Duke and Duchess of Sutherland and Mr. and Mrs. Ernest Bevin.

The following day, the new Archbishop of Canterbury, Dr. Temple, entered the current controversy raging about venereal disease. At a special conference on the subject at Friends House, Euston Road, the Primate criticised the government for ignoring the moral aspect of the problem. 'There is a great menace and a great evil to be met' he declared. 'What is quite deadly is to give the impression that misconduct should be accepted as normal.'

Meanwhile, Winston Churchill had returned from Africa and had been struck down with pneumonia. For several days he was confined to his room at 10 Downing Street and daily bulletins were issued. From President Roosevelt, there came a telegram urging the Prime Minister to live down his image of being 'the World's Worst Patient'.

On March 1, a dispute between the thirty-one-year-old Earl of Warwick and an interior decorator named Mrs. E. Donald, who had furnished his nineteen-room flat in Lowndes Square, was settled in the High Court. Mrs. Donald had originally sued the Earl for £318 but had to be contented with a smaller sum. 'I see no reason for thinking that she was trying to take advantage of Lord Warwick's wealth and position' said the Official Referee, 'but I think she honestly overestimated the value of her services.'

On March 2, the exiled King of Greece was welcomed at a glittering reception of the Overseas League attended by Mrs. Neville Chamberlain, Princess Arthur of Connaught and other celebrities. A sensation was created when American millionairess Laura Corrigan was presented to the King ahead of many titled women.

Meanwhile, the spritely Lady Cunard had moved into a seventh-floor suite at the Dorchester Hotel and crammed it with a magnificent assortment of fine French furniture which had once graced her house in Grosvenor Square. She was soon entertaining here practically every night.

Literary hostess Lady Cunard who spent the last few years of her life at the Dorchester Hotel

On March 17, details of a new war-time livery for servants at Buckingham Palace and other royal homes were disclosed. In place of the familiar tailcoat, waistcoat, stiff white shirt and white tie, the King's servants would wear a plain battle-dress top buttoned at the neck.

The following day, the ban on transporting flowers by railway was lifted. It was rumoured that the Prime Minister, who had received many flowers during his recent illness, including a big bunch from Mr. Alec Beechman, MP for St. Ives, was the inspiration behind this move.

On March 22, 200 dealers converged on Christie's auction rooms for a sale of wines, spirits and liqueurs from Polesden Lacey and 16 Charles Street, homes of the late Mrs. Ronnie Greville. Among the items of sale were 1,000 bottles of claret and six rare bottles of Grande Champagne 1810 brandy. Altogether the sale raised £6,000.

On April 9, Lady Cunard gave a dinner-party in her suite at the Dorchester which was attended by Mr. Cecil Beaton, Lady Pamela Berry and Old Etonian Mr. James Lees-Milne, who had been invalided out of the Army and was working for the National Trust. Lady Cunard sipped cherry brandy and kissing on the mouth was mentioned.

On April 14, the Duchess of Roxburghe broke her leg when the car taking her from Floors Castle, Kelso, to a war meeting collided with a military vehicle.

On April 26, an era ended with the death of the eighty-five-year-old Duke of Portland at Welbeck Abbey. One of England's greatest landowners, the Duke had succeeded to his title in 1879 and had once numbered Benjamin Disraeli among his friends. He was succeeded by his son, the Marquess of Titchfield, MP, who had recently caused titters in the House of Commons when he suggested there should be a tax on lipstick and face-powder.

At the beginning of May, the bachelor Archbishop of York, Dr. Cyril Garbett, announced that he was giving-up half his £9,000 a year salary but would continue at his 100-room palace in Yorkshire which he shared with his sister. Conservative MP Sir Herbert Williams promptly suggested that this sacrifice was an attempt on the Archbishop's part to avoid tax. 'That was not the case' said Dr. Garbett. 'The measure was fully discussed with the Inland Revenue authority and the Treasury. There had been no kind of evasion.'

On May 15, the King and Queen set off for the first Ascot meeting held since 1939 before the war. 'There will be refreshment marquees' said a Jockey Club representative, 'but it will be beer and sandwiches as long as supplies last.'

Four days later, the Allied victories in Africa were celebrated with a Thanksgiving at St. Paul's Cathedral. At the last moment, the time of the service was changed as it was feared that the enemy had learned of the ceremony, owing to an indiscretion on the part of Lord Londonderry's butler, and might attempt to drop a bomb on the vast crowd of assembled celebrities.

Missing on this occasion was the Prime Minister. He was now in Washington where the previous day he had addressed the Congress, watched by the Duke and Duchess of Windsor in the diplomatic gallery. It was said that the ex-King had been greeted with a burst of applause as loud as that which welcomed the Prime Minister.

On June 3, a letter from Lord Alvingham, former MP for South Dorset, was published in *The Times* protesting against the fact that his title had been omitted from his ration card. He described this innovation as 'an entirely unconstitutional attempt by Ministers to interfere with the rights and privileges of a section of His Majesty's subjects'.

On June 10, there was a sensation in the Divorce Court when a Mr. Harry Newman sued his wife for divorce naming eighty-seven-year-old Lord Grantley, Father of the House of Lords, as co-respondent. The case was not defended but Mr. Justice Pilcher was unconvinced that adultery had taken place and, to the indignation of the ancient peer, adjourned the case for consideration. On July 1, there was much jubilation when he granted Mr. Newman a decree nisi and ordered Old Harrovian Lord Grantley to pay £500 costs.

On July 8, attention turned to the Bahamas where multi-millionaire baronet Sir Harry Oakes, a close friend of the Duke and Duchess of Windsor, had been found brutally murdered in his bed. The following day, the dead man's son-in-law, Count Alfred de Marigny, was arrested on the slenderest evidence and faced a lengthy trial which ended in his acquittal. The murder remained an unsolved mystery.

Meanwhile, a misfortune had befallen the beautiful Mrs. Charles Sweeny, who had been doing useful work for the American Red Cross in London. On her way to an appointment with her Bond Street chiropodist, Mr. Wiberg, she had stepped into an empty lift-shaft and fallen forty feet. She was rushed to St. George's Hospital where thirty stitches were required to sew up the wound in her head.

On July 23, there was a gathering at the National Liberal Club for the unveiling of an early portrait of Mr. Winston Churchill. Since Mr. Churchill had left the Liberal Party some twenty-five years earlier, the portrait had lain in a storeroom where it had recently been damaged by enemy action. It had now been restored and was ceremoniously unveiled by the eighty-five-year-old Marquess of Crewe, a veteran Liberal politician who had served in one of Mr. Gladstone's Cabinets.

On July 26, the day after the resignation of Mussolini as Italian dictator, Churchill visited London Zoo and fed Rota, the lioness which had been presented to him by the Zoological Society.

On August 4, it was disclosed that Sir Oswald Mosley was seriously ill in Holloway Prison with phlebitis and was rapidly losing weight. Accompanied by two prison warders, the former Fascist leader had been taken in a private car to visit specialists in Harley Street and Wimpole Street.

On August 5, the aged Lord Grantley, who had been the source of much interest over the last few weeks, died in a London nursing-home. He was succeeded as Father of the House of Lords by the eighty-six-year-old Earl of Lonsdale, who had now given up all his famous homes and gone to ground at his stud farm at Oakham in Rutland surrounded by his dogs and ponies.

Meanwhile, the inexhaustible Mrs. Laura Corrigan had leased Lord Moyne's house in Grosvenor Place and converted it into a club for young Allied Air Force officers. The opening ceremony was performed on August 9. It was noted that the Duchess of Marlborough, the Dowager Marchioness of Willingdon and Mr. Chips Channon would serve on the club committee.

On August 24, twenty-eight-year-old Captain Patrick Telfer Smollett, a member of the British Military Mission in Cairo, delivered a big box of chocolates at Buckingham Palace. It was a gift from King Farouk's young daughters for Princess Elizabeth and Princess Margaret. A spokesman quickly explained that the chocolates would be passed on to a hospital.

On September 2, seventy-two-year-old Lord Alfred Douglas re-emerged to address the Royal Society of Literature in Bloomsbury Square. During his lecture, he viciously attacked the poetry of Mr. T. S. Eliot. 'It is a frightful reflection on the miserable and abject state to which criticism in England has sunk that this pitiable stuff has for years been accepted without protest as poetry' he declared. Asked for his comments afterwards, Mr. Eliot said calmly, 'Lord Alfred is always having a dig at me.'

The King and Queen followed by the little Princesses inspect a field of barley at Sandringham

Prime Minister Winston Churchill and Russian Ambassador Mr. Maisky drink a toast

On September 8, the Foreign Secretary Anthony Eden gave a luncheon at the Dorchester Hotel in honour of Mr. Maisky, who had been recalled to Moscow after eleven years as Russian Ambassador to the Court of St. James. Before he departed, a portrait of Mr. Maisky by Czechoslovakian artist Oskar Kokoschka was accepted by the Tate Gallery.

The next big event on the social calendar was a big party on October 7 at the Belgrave Square mansion of Mr. Chips Channon in honour of Lord Wavell, recently appointed Viceroy of India. Among those present was Mr. Harold Nicolson, who went on afterwards to the House of Commons where it was his turn to do fire-watching from the platform of the Victoria Tower.

On October 11, novelist Miss Radclyffe Hall died in a furnished flat in Dolphin Square. She had left instructions that her last novel should be destroyed unpublished. 'Miss Hall would not like me to say what it was about' said Lady Troubridge, who had shared her life with the famous novelist for more than twenty years.

On October 23, former Prime Minister Lloyd George married his secretary of the past thirty years, Miss Frances Stevenson. The ceremony at a registry office in Guildford was not attended by any member of Mr. Lloyd George's family and it was reported that many of the former Prime Minister's supporters in Wales broke down and wept when they heard the news.

On November 9, there was an illustrious gathering at the Carlton Cinema, Haymarket, for the première of *For Whom the Bell Tolls*. Among those present were Lady Louis Mountbatten, American millionaire Jock Whitney and Lady Alexandra Metcalfe, whose husband, Major 'Fruity' Metcalfe, a former devoted Equerry of the Duke of Windsor, had now become public relations officer for a film company owned by Mr. J. Arthur Rank.

On November 18, Home Secretary Herbert Morrison's announcement that Sir Oswald and Lady Mosley were to be released from Holloway Prison caused a storm of protest. Cinema companies at once began building scaffolding outside the gates of the gaol and protestors walked the streets of London gathering signatures of people opposing the release. Both efforts were frustrated when at 7.00 am on November 20, the Mosleys were whisked out of the back-door of the prison unseen by the Press and taken to a secret address where they remained under house-arrest.

At the beginning of the next month, Cecil Beaton set off on an assignment for the Ministry of Information to take photographs in India and China. Shortly after take-off from the air-strip at Land's End, the Dakota carrying him caught fire and crash-landed and Beaton retired to bed, suffering from shock. A few days later, he left without incident on another plane.

On December 13, Gladys Duchess of Marlborough, was encountered in a Bond Street jewellers inspecting a ruby ornament. She wore a man's hat, overcoat and trousers and her hair was dyed yellow.

On December 16, Mr. Attlee broke the news to the House of Commons that the sixty-nine-year-old Prime Minister had been struck down with pneumonia again. 'I may say' added the Deputy Premier, 'that highly qualified specialists are in attendance. I can assure the House that every modern facility will be available.' The following day, reports were more cheerful and it was rumoured that Churchill would be treated with the new drug, penicillin.

That Christmas, seventeen-year-old Princess Elizabeth appeared in the title role of a performance of *Aladdin* at Windsor Castle. Princess Margaret, the young Duke of Kent and his sister Princess Alexandra were in supporting roles. In the front row of the audience was the blond-headed Prince Philip of Greece, now twenty-two years old and serving as a Lieutenant in the Royal Navy.

1944

At the beginning of January, the victorious General Sir Bernard Montgomery arrived in London, clad in battledress, beret and British Warm overcoat. On January 4, a big black limousine, driven by an Eighth Army Sergeant, took him to see Jack Hulbert and Cicely Courtneidge in *Something in the Air* at the Palace Theatre. He was cheered as he entered the Royal Box, accompanied by his fifteen-year-old son David, who was said to be half an inch taller than his father.

On January 7, Lady Cunard gave a candlelit dinner-party in her suite at the Dorchester Hotel. The star guest, Lady Oxford, began the evening by accusing the hostess of doing a bunk to America to escape the bombing.

On January 18, Winston Churchill appeared at the House of Commons for the first time since his illness. His appearance was unheralded and MPs gasped with astonishment, jumped to their feet and started cheering.

On February 2, it was reported that Augustus John had begun work on a portrait of General Montgomery, who had now been appointed Commander-in-Chief of the British Group of Armies for the Liberation of Europe. During the sessions at the artist's Chelsea studio, Montgomery remained profoundly suspicious of Augustus. 'Who is this chap?' he declared on one occasion. 'He drinks, he's dirty and I know there are women in the background.' By the end of February, eighty-seven-year-old Bernard Shaw had been summoned to amuse the General during the sittings, part of the deal being that the great playwright should be driven home afterwards in Montgomery's Rolls-Royce.

On March 7, Mr. Chips Channon, one of the most lavish of war-time hosts, celebrated his forty-seventh birthday with a party for some thirty guests. That evening, 5 Belgrave Square was decorated with flowers from Mr. Channon's garden in Essex and salmon, oysters, dressed crab, minced chicken and other delicacies were served. After the brandy had been passed round, the King of Greece proposed the host's health.

The dining-room at 5 Belgrave Square where Mr. 'Chips' Channon continued to entertain throughout the War

On March 20, the young King Peter of Yugoslavia was married to Princess Alexandra of Greece in a specially consecrated room at the Yugoslav Legation in Upper Grosvenor Street. At the reception afterwards, guests included the Duke and Duchess of Gloucester and the Duchess of Kent, who had now come out of mourning and was wearing a pale pink and brown dress and an ostrich feather hat. After a brief honeymoon in a four-room cottage near Ascot, the bride and groom moved into a third-floor suite at Claridge's.

On April 4, thirty-three-year-old Lord Rothschild, who had spent much of the last few years checking that food, drink and cigars which were to be consumed by the Prime Minister had not been tampered with, was awarded the George Medal for bravery.

On April 13, the death of the almost forgotten Earl of Lonsdale at his stud farm in Rutland made headline news. Tributes poured in from many great figures in the sporting world. 'He will be remembered by thousands in every walk of life' said Lord Rosebery. 'He had an uncanny power over animals, particularly dogs.' It was later revealed that a few weeks before his death, Lord Lonsdale had written to his niece saying 'Life has been such lovely fun.'

On April 21, Princess Elizabeth's eighteenth birthday was celebrated with a family lunch-party at Windsor Castle. Among her gifts was a sturgeon, weighing seven and a quarter stone, caught by a Hull fisherman. It was reported that the Princess now had a sitting-room of her own at Windsor Castle and a Lady-in-Waiting, Lady Mary Palmer, daughter of the Earl of Selborne, to help her with her correspondence.

On May 4, the scholarly seventy-two-year-old Duke of Argyll pleaded guilty at Dunoon Sheriff's Court to assaulting the seventy-nine-year-old Inveraray Town Clerk. Accusing him of interfering with matters concerning his estate, the Duke had struck the Town Clerk with a stick, punched him in the chest and then hit him again with the stick. The Sheriff decided that the publicity would be sufficient punishment.

Two days later, the Marquess of Hartington, heir to the Duke of Devonshire, married Miss Kathleen Kennedy, daughter of the former American Ambassador. The ceremony took place at Chelsea Registry Office, with the young Duke of Rutland acting as best man. The couple had become engaged at the beginning of the war but the match had been forbidden by both sets of parents on the grounds of their religious differences.

Actor manager Ivor Novello, left, on his way to court. He was sentenced to a month's imprisonment for conspiring to commit an offence against the Motor Vehicles Act

Meanwhile, actor-manager Ivor Novello, currently starring in *The Dancing Years* at the Adelphi Theatre, had been arrested and charged with committing an offence against the Motor Vehicles Act. It was alleged that on being refused a permit for his Rolls-Royce, he had arranged for the car to be put down in the name of a company engaged in war-work. On May 16, in spite of evidence from Dame Sybil Thorndike to the effect that she had never known him do anything dirty or dishonest, Novello was despatched to Wormwood Scrubs Prison to serve a month's imprisonment.

On May 18, Gertrude Lawrence flew in on a tour of American bases. 'I was given so many charms to protect me against accident that if we hit the water I would have sunk like a stone' she said on arrival at Croydon Airport. On board the same plane was bearded writer Ernest Hemingway, whose suit had been badly soiled during the flight when a dozen eggs carried by Miss Lawrence had smashed.

On Saturday June 3, the traditional Fourth of June celebrations were held at Eton College. Among Etonians found watching the famous 'Boats' ceremony were fifteen-year-old Jeremy Thorpe and seventeen-year-old Lord Montagu of Beaulieu. Among the parents present was Lady de Clifford, daughter of the famous nightclub queen in the Twenties, Mrs. Meyrick.

On June 16, the King paid a one-day visit to France following the Allied landing in Normandy. He was welcomed by Field Marshal Montgomery, who showed him into his famous caravan, carpeted with coconut matting and furnished with canvas chairs. The King was back at Windsor Castle that night.

On June 17, big crowds gathered at Newmarket to see Lord Rosebery's Ocean Swell win the fifth war-time Derby. Lord Rosebery and his wife, who wore a black and white turban, received congratulations afterwards from Lord Willoughby de Broke and Sir Humphrey de Trafford. 'I was merely hopeful about Ocean Swell after his rather disappointing running in the Two Thousand Guineas' said the bowler-hatted peer, who later found no seat on the train back to London and had to travel in the guard's van.

Meanwhile, Hitler had begun a new attack on England with pilotless planes, loaded with explosives. On June 19, one of these robot-like objects descended on the Guards Chapel, Wellington Barracks, killing Lord Edward Hay, Ivan Cobbold and many other friends of the Royal Family.

At the end of the month, news came from Italy that Lord Lascelles, son of the Earl of Harewood and nephew of the King, had been captured in Italy and taken to a special camp for privileged prisoners.

On July 7, the Café de Paris, badly bombed in 1941, reopened. The famous fashionable rendezvous had now been taken over by the Nuffield Centre as a place of entertainment for the troops. On the opening night, young comedian Tommy Trinder, the Dagenham Girl Pipers and others gave their services free of charge. Under its new regime, the restaurant's vast stocks of champagne were no longer required and 675 cases soon came under the auctioneer's hammer.

On July 26, members of the Savile Club in Brook Street gathered to bid farewell to their wine-waiter, Mr. Frank Harris, who had served the club for the past sixty years. It was noted that Mr. Harris, who remembered serving Robert Louis Stevenson, never drank a drop of wine or spirits himself, doing all his tasting by bouquet alone.

The same day, George Bernard Shaw spent his eighty-eighth birthday at his Hertfordshire home. The great playwright was still trying to sort out the financial affairs of his wife who had died the previous year. 'Although she left £150,000, I find I have less to live on than before' he said. 'I am really a poor man. I have paid £100,000 in taxes since the war began.'

On July 29, Home Secretary Herbert Morrison granted permission for semi-invalid Unity Mitford to live on Inchkenneth, the 160-acre Scottish island purchased by her father two years before the war. Soon after her arrival, wild rumours circulated that lights had been seen winking from the island to German ships lurking off the coast.

Meanwhile, the King had set off to see how his Armies were getting on in Italy. In Naples, he was put to stay in the beautiful Villa Emma where Lord Nelson had first met Lady Hamilton. Later, he lunched with General Alexander off caviar, turtle soup, tournedos of beef and peach melba while the BBC put out an announcement that the monarch had 'sat down to his first meal of Army rations'.

On August 15, an Allied invasion landed in the South of France. Among officers present was the thirty-three-year-old Prince Aly Khan who had spent much of the war serving as an intelligence officer in the Middle East. On landing at St. Tropez, Aly commandeered a jeep and drove along the coast to Cannes, where he found his father's sumptuous villa had been untouched by the Germans.

On August 28, Conservative MP Sir Herbert Williams was fined ten guineas for transgressing Defence Regulations by bathing in the sea near Brighton. Lady Williams was fined five shillings for a similar offence. Sir Herbert gave notice of appeal and said he would raise the matter in the House of Commons as a question of privilege.

On September 5, a special train carrying the Prime Minister Winston Churchill to Greenock, on the first step of a journey to a conference at Quebec, suddenly came to a halt. It was explained that the Prime Minister had left his spectacles behind.

On September 10, the death in action of the Duke of Devonshire's heir, Lord Hartington, who had recently married Kathleen Kennedy, daughter of the former American Ambassador, shocked Society. It was reported that Lady Hartington was in America with her parents.

On September 13, Duff and Lady Diana Cooper flew off to the newly-liberated Paris where Mr. Cooper had recently been appointed Ambassador, accompanied by an escort of forty-eight Spitfires. They found the Embassy stuffed with bath-mats, hat-stands and other articles left by the families of fleeing diplomats four years earlier.

At the end of the month, news came from Switzerland that the portly Aga Khan, sixty-eight next birthday, had married for the fourth time. His beautiful new bride, thirty-eight-year-old Mlle Yvette Labrousse, was over six feet tall and rumoured to be the daughter of a bus conductor.

In the middle of October, Churchill spent a week in Moscow where he breakfasted each morning off caviar, smoked salmon and suckling pig and had long discussions in the Kremlin with Mr. Stalin. On October 14, there was a Command Performance at the Bolshoi Theatre which the Prime Minister sat through without interest until some Cossack dancers appeared on the stage.

On October 25, thirty-two-year-old Captain William Douglas-Home was sentenced to be cashiered and imprisoned for one year for disobeying an order during the Allied landing in Normandy earlier in the year.

On October 26, Dr. Temple, Archbishop of Canterbury, died after being struck down with a severe attack of gout while preaching in Canterbury Cathedral. It was said that the Archbishop, who had suffered from gout since the age of four, had recently been spotted standing at a bus-stop in Victoria Street.

The same day, Princess Beatrice, eighty-seven years old and the last surviving child of Queen Victoria, died at Brantridge Park, Sussex, country home of the Earl and Countess of Athlone. She had been evacuated from Kensington Palace to a small house nearby at the beginning of the war.

At the end of the month, Cecil Beaton, already grey-haired, flew to Paris where he stayed at the newly-opened British Embassy and photographed Picasso sitting on the edge of his bath. This controversial painter had remained in his studio in the Rue des Grands Augustins throughout the hostilities and was said to have painted some three or four hundred canvases since the fall of France.

On November 10, Mr. and Mrs. Churchill arrived in Paris for the Armistice Day celebrations. They were housed in a lavishly decorated suite of rooms in the Quai d'Orsay, recently vacated by Hermann Goering. Mrs. Churchill's bedroom was full of white lilac and it was said that her husband's shabby bedroom-slippers and hot water bottle looked out of place amidst such luxury.

On November 20, sixty-three-year-old author P. G. Wodehouse was arrested by the French police and detained pending enquiries into charges of collaborating with the enemy by making broadcasts from Berlin after his release from an internment camp. 'I agreed to give five talks over German radio on my experiences in camp' he said, 'but I refused all offers to do propaganda work.'

On December 1, there was a party at Grosvenor House, Park Lane to celebrate the twenty-fifth anniversary of the entry of women into Parliament. Lady Astor chose this occasion to announce that she would not be standing at the next General Election. 'I believe I have something to give to the House of Lords' she remarked later. 'But I'm not sure they want what I've got.'

Meanwhile, another twenty-five year association had been severed with the death in New York of Gerald Haxton, constant companion of Somerset Maugham since the end of the First World War. The famous writer, who was now living on a plantation in South Carolina, plunged into premature old age. 'I'm a very old party now and no longer care what people think of me' he said. 'On my seventieth birthday, which I passed all alone, I amused myself weighing up the chances of my survival.' It was estimated that the famous novelist had earned at least £90,000 since leaving his villa in the South of France four years earlier.

On December 24, Winston Churchill and Foreign Secretary Anthony Eden flew to Greece where civil war had now broken out. Shortly after their arrival in Athens, they were shot at by a sniper, causing the seventy-year-old Prime Minister to exclaim, 'Cheek!'

1945

At the beginning of January, it was announced that Dr. Geoffrey Fisher, father of six sons, was to be the new Archbishop of Canterbury. It was noted that the central-heating was not working in Canterbury Cathedral and the drawing-room at Lambeth Palace had neither a floor nor a ceiling.

On January 11, it was announced that the Earl of Carnarvon was petitioning his wife, former dancer Tilly Losch, for divorce. The couple had married at Caxton Hall two days before the outbreak of war and Tilly had left for America ten weeks later, refusing frequent requests by her husband to return.

Meanwhile, the Duke and Duchess of Gloucester and their son Prince William were sailing for Australia, where the Duke had been appointed Governor General. They arrived at Sydney on January 28 but their disembarkation was hindered by a Japanese submarine prowling near the harbour.

On February 3, Winston Churchill arrived at Yalta on the Black Sea Coast for high-powered discussions with Stalin and Roosevelt. That night the Prime Minister, his valet, Sawyers, and Foreign Secretary Anthony Eden were badly bitten by bed-bugs. Lord Moran, Churchill's devoted doctor, went round squirting DDT into all the beds. A worse disaster was to strike three days later when a plane carrying fifteen members of the Prime Minister's staff to the conference crashed into the sea near Malta. All the passengers drowned and vital maps and papers sank to the bottom of the Mediterranean.

On February 20, Mr. Chips Channon was granted a decree nisi on the grounds of the desertion of his wife, Lady Honor, daughter of the Earl of Iveagh. Mr. Channon was given custody of his nine-year-old son Paul, who had recently returned from America with his nanny.

On February 28, Princess Elizabeth accompanied the King and Queen to a revue at the Hippodrome Theatre called *Meet the Navy*. A few days later, the Princess joined the ATS, training to become an officer driver, learning how to strip and service an engine, drive in convoy and other skills.

Meanwhile, champagne king, Charles Heidsieck, had arrived in London. 'My visit is of a highly confidential nature' he said on March 1. 'I am here for the French government, although the interests of the champagne industry figure largely on my agenda.' One of the biggest problems now facing champagne producers was the lack of bottles, corks and casks.

On March 16, the Duke of Windsor tendered his resignation as Governor of the Bahamas. It was reported that many of his personal effects and household staff were already on their way to New York for eventual transfer to France.

On March 20, seventy-four-year-old Lord Alfred Douglas, whose life had been haunted by his involvement in the Oscar Wilde scandal of 1895, died at the home of his literary executor at Old Monk's Farm, Lancing. His funeral three days later was attended by, among others, the Marquess of Queensberry, Lord Tredegar and actor Donald Sinden.

On March 25, one of the last rocket-bombs to descend on London fell near Marble Arch. The blast blew out the window of the Hyde Park Hotel suite occupied by Evelyn Waugh, who had recently returned from serving with the British Military Mission in Yugoslavia.

The following day, Lloyd George died at his farm-house in Wales. After announcing the news at Question Time in the House of Commons, Churchill said: 'I do not think we can do any more business today. I feel that should be the feeling of the House.' The former Prime Minister was buried on the banks of the River Dwyvor near his Welsh home.

On April 14, it was revealed that Lord and Lady Astor's stately town-house in St. James's Square, which had been requisitioned earlier in the war for use as a service canteen, had been overrun by rats.

On April 19, it was announced that Hitler had moved his colony of special prisoners-of-war to a more secure place, fearing that their camp would soon be liberated by the advancing Allied Armies. These special, privileged prisoners now included Lord Lascelles, John Winant, son of the American Ambassador, Earl Haig, son of the great Field Marshal, and Michael Alexander, distant cousin of Field Marshal Alexander.

At the end of April, the blackout was abolished and the Savoy Hotel turned on all its lights and left its curtains undrawn.

On May 1, it was announced that Hitler was dead and Winston Churchill was asked in the House of Commons if he had any comment to make on the war situation. 'Yes, it is definitely more satisfactory than it was this time five years ago' he replied.

On May 4, while the world awaited the final Nazi surrender, Londoners flocked to the preview of the Royal Academy Summer Exhibition at Burlington House. Among those present were Dr. Malcolm Sargent, popular new conductor of the Liverpool Philharmonic Orchestra, the Hon. William Astor, eldest son of Lord and Lady Astor, and the Duchess of Westminster, who had been living apart from her wealthy husband for ten years.

That night, Mrs. George Keppel, former mistress of Edward VII, gave a dinner-party at the Ritz Hotel, where she had been living since her flight from Italy in 1940. News of the German capitulation in Holland, Denmark and West Germany came through during the course of the evening and was celebrated with glasses of Kümmel.

On May 8, among peers gathering at the House of Lords to hear the final victory announcement, was eighty-four-year-old Lord Portsea who arrived in an old-fashioned horse-drawn brougham driven by a top-hatted coachman. At 3.00 pm, the Prime Minister, Winston Churchill, declared: 'The German war is at an end. The evildoers now lie prostrate before us.'

THE LATE FORTIES–EARLY FIFTIES 1945–1951

Within months of the end of the war, the upper classes were carrying on as if Hitler had never existed. Lady Londonderry was back at Londonderry House, evening-dress became obligatory again at the Savoy Restaurant and over £1,000,000 in bets were placed on the first post-war Derby. During the years that followed, Princess Elizabeth married Lieutenant Philip Mountbatten, a group of eligible aristocrats formed around her vivacious younger sister and the usual glittering balls were held at the great stately homes. For most people, however, this was a time of unparalleled austerity. Even tighter rationing than that known in the war was introduced and the five-shilling limit on meals continued until 1950. Socialites found side-stepping the rigid currency regulations were thrown into gaol. While splendid dances were taking place at Windsor Castle, Blenheim Palace and Sutton Place, the Attlee government was pushing through a programme of Anti-Upper-Class Legislation which caused many ancestral acres to be sold and proprietors of stately homes to open their doors to the public for the first time. The Savoy Hotel was plagued with a series of strikes and at one stage had its supply of meat cut off by Smithfield Market. No wonder young aristocrats like the Marquess of Tavistock decided to quit England for the more congenial environment of South Africa and Americans such as Elsa Maxwell arrived with hot-water bottles, electric torches, hams, tea and foie gras to make life more bearable for their English friends. People spoke of the country's troubles as the Second Battle of Britain. In the last resort, it would seem that the Attlee government lost the battle when in October 1951, the electorate plumped for the prosperity promised by the Conservatives.

1945

On the afternoon of May 8, the Royal Family made some nine appearances on the balcony of Buckingham Palace. In the evening, Princess Elizabeth and Princess Margaret, now aged nineteen and fourteen respectively, left the Palace and mingled among the crowds, closely escorted by a group of young Army officers.

On May 10, Welbeck Abbey, Nottinghamshire stately home of the Duke of Portland, was taken over by the Army for use as a co-educational college. It was revealed that the Duke had also sold 5,000 acres of his estate for £118,000.

On May 13, a Thanksgiving Service at St. Paul's Cathedral was adorned by the presence of Queen Mary, now seventy-eight years old and unseen by the public at large since before the war. She wore an elaborate pink outfit and many jewels and took attention away from the young Princesses and other members of the Royal Family.

At the end of the month, the publication of Evelyn Waugh's new novel *Brideshead Revisited* sent ripples of excitement through high society. It was widely believed that the story was based on the family of the late Earl Beauchamp and their famous stately home Madresfield, near Malvern.

On June 9, large crowds attended the first post-war Derby and over £1,000,000 in bets was placed. Among the thousands present was Prince Aly Khan, still in battledress and making his first appearance on an English racecourse for five years. This year, the race was won by Dante, owned by wealthy baronet Sir Eric Ohlson.

Meanwhile, Marlborough House, which had been badly bombed during the war, had been made habitable again and, on June 11, Queen Mary moved in with her vast entourage from Badminton. She received her first visitor the following day in the shape of General Eisenhower, who had flown to London to receive the Freedom of the City.

On June 14, high society flocked to St. Martin-in-the-Fields for the marriage of the Hon. William Astor, who had served as a Lieutenant in the RNVR, and the Hon. Sarah Norton, grand-daughter of the late Lord Grantley. The bridegroom's mother, Lady Astor, was in navy-blue and many of the employees from Cliveden attended the ceremony. At the reception afterwards at Admiralty House, Mrs. Randolph Churchill, Mrs. David Niven, Lady Stanley of Alderley and many other beauties were spotted.

By the end of the month, the country had begun preparing itself for the General Election. On June 25, Prime Minister Winston Churchill set off from Chequers for a four-day election tour on a special train in which he slept. Before departure, he remarked to his doctor Lord Moran: 'I feel very lonely without a war.'

Polling took place on July 5, but owing to the complication of gathering Service votes from many corners of the globe, the result could not be immediately announced. It was said that more than one regiment did not vote at all.

In the meantime, Churchill attended the Potsdam Conference where on July 23, he gave a dinner for President Truman and Marshal Stalin, which ended with the Russian leader going round and getting the twenty-eight guests to sign his menu. The others present soon followed suit and the Prime Minister groaned: 'This means signing twenty-eight menus.'

On July 26, the shock defeat of the Conservative Party rendered Churchill without a London home. As a temporary measure, he moved into Mr. Hugh Wontner's private penthouse suite at Claridge's. It was noted that Mr. Wontner remained in the suite, occupying a bedroom next to the former Prime Minister.

On July 28, eighty-one-year-old Lady Oxford, widow of the former Liberal Prime Minister, died at her home in Kensington Square, W.8. Coincidentally, her death followed an electoral disaster for the once-mighty Liberal party, who now had only twelve seats in the House of Commons.

On July 30, there was much excitement over the marriage of the Kaiser's grandson, Prince Frederick of Prussia, one-time friend of heiress Barbara Hutton, to Lady Bridget Guinness, daughter of the Earl of Iveagh. The Prince, who had been interned in Canada for part of the war, was now farming in Hertford and using the name George Mansfield.

Meanwhile, the few remaining great town-houses were beginning to open again. At the beginning of August, Lord and Lady Kemsley moved back into Chandos House, Queen Anne Street. The house, though badly bombed in 1940, had now been restored to its former glory thanks to Sir Kenneth Clark, who had insisted that all the original Adam chimneypieces and carved doorways should be dismantled and stored away during the hostilities.

On August 6, it was announced that 40 Berkeley Square, a newly-built block of flats where the Duchess of Westminster was one of the residents, was to be converted into offices. The ten-floor building had been leased by an American advertising agency, J. Walter Thompson.

On August 15, the beautiful Margaret Sweeny moved into 48 Upper Grosvenor Street, a tall eighteenth-century house acquired by her father ten years earlier and unoccupied for the last six years. Mrs. Sweeny soon set about suing her husband for divorce.

The same day, following the descent of Atom bombs on Hiroshima and Nagasaki, Japan surrendered. At home, a row broke out at St. Albans when the Dean, the Very Rev. C. C. Thicknesse, forbade the use of the Abbey for a Thanksgiving service. 'I cannot honestly give thanks to God for an event brought about by an act of wholesale, indiscriminate massacre' he declared.

On August 21, a new production of *Lady Windermere's Fan* with décor by Cecil Beaton, opened at the Haymarket Theatre. During preparations, Beaton had had discussions with the playwright's only surviving son, Vyvyan Holland, dining in his Sloane Street flat off Château Yquem and marrons glacés. Much ingenuity had been used to make the most of the twenty-four coupons allowed for each costume.

On September 1, the forty-two-year-old Marchioness of Tavistock died of an overdose of sleeping-tablets at a hotel in Sussex. After evidence from the twenty-eight-year-old Marquess, who was said to be the heir to a

£10,000,000 estate, that his wife had frequently taken a lot of pills just to frighten him, an open verdict was returned.

A few days later, there were protests about the lavish redecoration going on at 28 Hyde Park Gate, newly-acquired home of Winston Churchill, now Leader of the Opposition.

On September 14, the Duke and Duchess of Windsor set off from New York for Europe after an absence of five years. En route for Le Havre, their ship called at Plymouth, where Pressmen poured on board. The Duchess was reported to be wearing a coral-red outfit, beige stockings, black snakeskin shoes, sapphire and

The Duke and Duchess of Windsor arrive in Europe on board a United States troopship

emerald earrings and a heavy gold bracelet, incorporating a medallion of her husband's head. Speaking with a slight American accent, the fifty-one-year-old Duke said: 'I've no definite plans for setting up a permanent home in England, but there's no reason why I should not.'

Meanwhile, the Duke's old friend Thelma Lady Furness, and her twin sister Mrs. Gloria Vanderbilt, had already arrived in London. On September 24, they were found walking in Park Lane with Thelma's sixteen-year-old son, Lord Furness, whose father had died during the war leaving £3,661,930.

On September 28, it was announced that the Guards Club had taken over 16 Charles Street, former town-house of the late Mrs. Ronnie Greville, who had installed 18-carat gold scroll work in its drawing-room. Soon afterwards, dry rot was discovered on the premises.

On October 5, the Duke of Windsor flew in, wearing a blue-and-white check overcoat and carrying a green pork-pie hat. He was met at Hendon aerodrome by Group-Captain Sir Louis Greig and driven to Marlborough House, where he was reunited with Queen Mary, whom he had not seen since December 1936. Three days later, he saw the King at Buckingham Palace. The Duchess of Windsor remained in Paris where it was reported that the couple's twenty-bedroom house in the Boulevard Suchet had been untouched during the hostilities.

In the middle of October, Lord Sempill made a speech in the House of Lords in which he defended wholemeal bread. He then produced a loaf he had made himself in the kitchen at Craigievar Castle, Aberdeenshire. 'I have always been interested in cooking' he said afterwards. 'I learned a good deal about it from my mother. In my opinion, we ought to be fed the fresh, pure products of the soil.'

On October 20, ex-officer Norman Baillie-Stewart, who had made headline news twelve years earlier when he was held in the Tower of London, was flown in from Austria where he had been arrested, charged with aiding the enemy during the war. It was disclosed that he had been captured in the Alpine village of Alt Aussee wearing Tyrolean chamois shorts, white stockings, embroidered braces and a forester's green hat.

On November 7, it was revealed that Sir Oswald Mosley, who had now been released from house arrest, had purchased an 1,100-acre estate at Crowood in Wiltshire. The property, which included four farms and a Queen Anne house, was situated a few miles from Faringdon, stately home of Sir Oswald's old friend, Lord Berners.

On November 9, the Lord Mayor gave a luncheon in honour of Mr. Attlee, who was off to America the following day to discuss the dangers of atomic warfare with President Truman. The Archbishop of Canterbury, Dr. Fisher, brought an informal touch to the top table when he took out his old briar pipe.

At the end of the month, the contents of the German Embassy in Carlton House Terrace were auctioned by Messrs. Knight, Frank and Rutley. Theatrical producer Mr. Jay Pomeroy paid £590 for a mahogany desk at which Ribbentrop, now on trial with his colleagues at Nuremberg, was said to have worked. In the same sale a granite bust of Hitler was sold for £500 to Old Etonian Robert Gordon-Canning.

On December 5, an exhibition of paintings by Picasso and Matisse opened at the Victoria and Albert Museum causing a storm of controversy. 'They verge upon the obscene' declared Mrs. Michael Joseph, daughter of the famous Victorian painter William Holman Hunt. 'Surely art should inspire one? How can one be inspired by a grotesque nude or by a figure with three eyes and an arm in the wrong place?' Anguished protests from art-lovers continued to pour in throughout the month.

On December 18, high society gathered at Westminster Abbey for the wedding of Captain the Hon. Robert Cecil, grandson of the Marquess of Salisbury, and the Hon. Mollie Wyndham-Quin. Among the pages, who wore long white trousers and scarlet jackets, were six-year-old Jonathan Cecil and four-year-old Julian Ormsby-Gore. A reception was held afterwards at Lord Salisbury's massive town-house, 21 Arlington Street.

At the end of the year, there was great excitement over the announcement that multi-millionairess Barbara Hutton had presented her huge London home, Winfield House, set in its fourteen-acre estate in Regent's Park, to the American Government as a home for their Ambassador. It was described as 'a Christmas gift'. At the same time, Miss Hutton had given her collection of Canaletto paintings to the National Gallery. It was stated that the heiress was 'not quite sure what she paid for them'.

On New Year's Day, big crowds watched the take-off of the first civil aircraft from the new Heathrow Airport. Lord Winster, Minister of Civil Aviation, wished the passengers 'Bon Voyage' as a Lancastrian Star Light airliner left for Buenos Aires. It was revealed that the plane carried copies of the latest edition of *The Times* for the British Ambassadors at the various re-fuelling stops.

On January 7, Dame Laura Knight was found in the front row of distinguished visitors in the neon-lit courtroom at Nuremberg doing some preliminary sketches of the Nazi leaders. 'I cannot say I have formed any definite impression yet' she said, 'except that they look awfully tragic.'

On January 10, celebrities gathered at Brompton Oratory for the marriage of Lord Ednam and Miss Stella Carcano, daughter of the Argentine Ambassador. The reception at the Argentine Embassy was enriched by the presence of Lady Cunard, Lady Curzon of Kedleston, widow of the former Foreign Secretary and the vivacious Chips Channon. Casting his eye over the crowded room, Mr. Channon declared: 'This is what we have been fighting for.'

The same day, Norman Baillie-Stewart, one time 'Officer in the Tower', pleaded guilty to aiding the enemy during the war. 'You are, I suggest, one of the worst citizens that any country has ever produced' said Mr. Justice Oliver pronouncing a sentence of five years imprisonment. Baillie-Stewart had avoided the death penalty by claiming to have become a German citizen at the beginning of the war.

On January 22, it was announced that the thirty-seven-year-old Duke of Norfolk, now father of four daughters, had taken over from Lord Granard as the King's representative at Ascot. One of his delicate new duties would be to decide who should, or shouldn't, be admitted to the Royal Enclosure.

On February 1, the food quickly ran out at a party at the Soviet Embassy in Kensington Palace Gardens. Sixty-five-year-old Foreign Secretary Ernest Bevin was found going round arm-in-arm with Russia's Deputy Foreign Minister, Mr. Vyshinsky. There were many toasts and the long tables loaded with smoked salmon and caviar were empty within half an hour of the arrival of the first guests.

On February 20, almost the entire Royal Family were present at the re-opening of the Royal Opera House which had been used as a dance hall during the war. The Queen and Queen Mary had turned up in diamond tiaras to watch Margot Fonteyn perform in a production of *Sleeping Beauty* with sumptuous décor by Oliver Messel.

The Royal Family at the re-opening of the Covent Garden opera house

At the beginning of March, it was announced that actress Hermione Baddeley had opened a mussel bar near Victoria Station in partnership with Flight-Lieutenant Francis de Moleyns, heir presumptive to Lord Ventry. It was stated that mussels would be fattened on the premises, kept in brine and fed on oatmeal.

On March 26, nineteen-year-old Princess Elizabeth, who now had her own flag and coat-of-arms, went to Ciro's Club in a party given by twenty-three-year-old wounded Lord St. Just. During the course of the evening, the Princess asked the orchestra, led by Ambrose, to play some of her favourite numbers including 'Sur Le Pont d'Avignon'.

A few days later, Mr. Nubar Gulbenkian, now honorary attaché at the Persian Embassy, returned from a visit to Portugal where he had ordered a rose-velvet smoking-jacket. Lack of an export licence prevented him bringing this garment back to England.

On April 5, twenty privately-chartered planes carried enthusiasts to Aintree for the first Grand National since 1940. Lord and Lady Derby and their twenty-seven-year-old grandson Lord Stanley watched the race from their private box to which a large glass-fronted luncheon-room was attached. The race was won by a nine-year-old outsider called Lovely Cottage.

On April 11, Winston Churchill, slowly recovering from his shock defeat in the General Election nine months earlier, was found dining with his son-in-law Mr. Duncan Sandys at the Savoy Grill, where the evening-dress rule had now returned. On their way out after dinner, they paused in the Savoy Restaurant. The dancing stopped immediately and the former Prime Minister was cheered for ten minutes.

On April 15, the Golden Arrow train left Victoria Station again, though travelling abroad was still restricted to those who could provide a business reason for doing so. Champagne served on this first post-war journey was sold for £3.15.0 a bottle.

Later that day, thirty-five-year-old Earl Fitzwilliam visited Prime Minister Mr. Attlee and Fuel Minister Mr. Shinwell at 10 Downing Street to try to persuade them not to use the gardens of his famous Yorkshire home, Wentworth Woodhouse, for open-cast mining. Said Mr. Alex Third, Head Gardener on the estate: 'Scores of plants and bushes here are rare and have been gathered from all parts of the world. Many could not possibly be replaced.'

On April 21, attention turned to the Astor home in Kent, Hever Castle, which had been burgled in dramatic circumstances the previous night. Driving over the drawbridge in a black Rolls-Royce at four in the morning, a gang of masked men had broken into the house and stolen fourteen precious items including Anne Boleyn's prayerbook and a dagger that had once belonged to Henry VIII. 'The bandits could not have picked more unsaleable items' said Colonel J. J. Astor, who was in Middlesex Hospital at the time convalescing after a bout of flu.

Three days later, an unexploded half-ton bomb was found ticking close to the gates of Buckingham Palace and was immediately nicknamed 'Annie' by the disposal experts. Forty-eight hours later, it was blown up and Queen Mary, Lord Athlone and Princess Alice were surrounded by huge crowds when they went to inspect the crater.

On May 3, Dame Laura Knight's vast canvas of the Nazi leaders was the centre of interest at the preview of the Royal Academy's summer exhibition. Among those present were the elderly Mrs. Neville Chamberlain and nineteen-year-old Lord Montagu of Beaulieu.

On May 9, the Marquess of Tavistock, whose wife had died the previous year, returned from a holiday in India where he had attended the Aga Khan's diamond jubilee celebrations. The young Marquess was soon to take up an appointment as an executive director of an Indian-owned import-export company with offices in Curzon Street, Mayfair.

On May 29, Princess Elizabeth was a bridesmaid at the marriage of her new Lady-in-Waiting, Mrs. Vicary Gibbs, to the Hon. Andrew Elphinstone. At the reception at the Savoy Hotel, the King proposed the health of the bride and groom and Princess Elizabeth was photographed standing beside twenty-four-year-old Prince Philip of Greece, a figure still largely unknown to the British public.

The same day, there was a sad gathering at the Grosvenor Chapel in South Audley Street for a memorial service for Mrs. David Niven, who had died in Hollywood a few days earlier after falling down a flight of cellar steps at a party given by Tyrone Power.

On June 5, the King and his family set off in the Royal train for the first Epsom Derby held since the war. On arrival at the racecourse, the Royal party transferred to motor-car and drove down the middle of the course cheered by a quarter of a million people. The King was in a bowler-hat and grey overcoat.

On June 9, the eighty-three-year-old Marquess of Bath, Master of the Horse in the household of King George V, died at Longleat. He was succeeded by his son, forty-one-year-old Viscount Weymouth, former leader of the 'Bright Young Things' whose secret marriage to the Hon. Daphne Vivian had created a sensation back in the Twenties.

On June 20, it was reported that the Royal Aero Club were negotiating to take over Londonderry House in Park Lane. It was written into the lease that Lord and Lady Londonderry would retain a twenty-two-room flat in the house.

On July 15, the Earl of Warwick's butler appeared in court accused of attempting to sell four waistcoat buttons belonging to his master to pay off some gambling debts. 'I am afraid it is not the first time he has been in racing trouble' said the Earl giving evidence on his butler's behalf. 'I have always stumped up and he has paid me back.'

On July 18, Field Marshal Viscount Montgomery drove through the streets of London in an open carriage to receive the Freedom of the City. At the Mansion House, where he saluted his former colleagues now working in the City, it was noticed that one of his shoe-laces was undone.

July 26 was George Bernard Shaw's ninetieth birthday. He began the day as usual with a bath coloured with green bath-salts and then took a walk through the Hertfordshire village of Ayot St. Lawrence where he lived. 'I've been offered titles' he said later, 'but I think they get one into disreputable company.'

Meanwhile, the world reverberated with rumours of a romance between Cecil Beaton and film star Greta Garbo. The couple had been seen together in Hollywood and Beaton had recently visited the film star in Stockholm where her villa was said to be protected by savage police-dogs. 'Miss Garbo wishes to be left alone' said Mr. Beaton at the end of July. 'We should all respect her wishes.'

On August 5, the new Marquess of Bath opened a flower-show at Horsley in Wiltshire and told villagers that he was obliged to sell off 9,000 acres of the Longleat estate to meet death duties. 'Tradition and inheritance are a thing of the past' he said. 'Today it is the State and only the State that matters.'

On August 14, Winston Churchill was installed as Lord Warden of the Cinque Ports. While he was proudly inspecting a guard of honour at Dover dressed in a magnificent scarlet and gold uniform, it was suddenly noticed that one of his heavy, gold-encrusted epaulettes was missing. A search was organised and it was found in his car.

At the end of the month, interior decorator Lady Colefax slipped and fell as she got out of a London taxi and was taken to University College Hospital with a broken thigh. It was recalled that two years earlier the accident-prone Lady Colefax had broken her back.

On September 10, seventy-two-year-old Somerset Maugham paid his first visit to England since October 1940. He explained that his beautiful villa at Cap Ferrat was still being restored and re-decorated after the ravages of the war. 'My house was occupied by Germans and Italians, bombarded by the British fleet, bombed by the RAF and then looted' he said.

On October 2, Lord Justice Lawrence and Sir Norman Birkett flew in from Nuremberg after doling out death sentences on Goering, Ribbentrop and other Nazi leaders and a life sentence for Rudolf Hess. Both praised the dignity of the defendants. 'Their behaviour in court was a model of dignity and was one of the most impressive things about the trial' said Sir Norman.

A week later, many London hotels were engulfed in a strike. The trouble began at the Savoy Hotel where workers sought official recognition of their union and quickly spread to other luxury catering establishments. On October 8, customers at Simpson's-in-the-Strand had to make do with cold chicken and on October 9, no lunch at all was served at the Ritz Hotel. 'Naturally we are making an exception for very important people' said the Head Waiter, pointing out that Field Marshal Alanbrooke, former Chief of the Imperial General Staff, was lunching at the hotel.

In the midst of these troubles, the Duke and Duchess of Windsor arrived. On October 11, they were met at Dover by their old friend Lord Brownlow and on the journey to Ednam Lodge, Sunningdale, home of the Earl of Dudley, the car was delayed by a puncture. The visit was marked by a worse misfortune when, on October

17, thieves boldly entered the house and £20,000-worth of jewellery belonging to the Duchess was stolen. While fingerprint experts explored the house the following day, the unsmiling Duke and Duchess, who were reported to be very hurt by the incident, went off to see their solicitors at Finch Lane in the City of London.

On October 26, the wedding of Lord Mountbatten's eldest daughter, Patricia, to Lord Brabourne drew crowds of 50,000 at Romsey Abbey. Pullmans were attached to the Bournemouth Belle to carry guests from London to the ceremony. The King, Queen, Princess Elizabeth, Princess Margaret and Prince Philip of Greece were present at the ceremony. 'We wish them long life, every happiness and the best of luck' said the King, proposing the health of the bride and groom.

On November 8, Mary Churchill, youngest daughter of the Leader of the Opposition, announced her engagement to Captain Christopher Soames of the Coldstream Guards. Captain Soames was said to be a skilled dancer and tennis player and a first-rate shot.

On November 30, Winston Churchill celebrated his seventy-second birthday with a party at 28 Hyde Park Gate. After dinner, the company were entertained by American conjurer Harry Green, whose mind-reading skills had recently impressed the former Prime Minister.

On December 3, the Earl of Dudley, at whose house the Duke and Duchess of Windsor had stayed a few weeks earlier, was fined £5 for smashing the window of a motor-car belonging to Lord Graves with a brick. Fifty-two-year-old Lord Dudley said he had done so in order to release the brake of the car and ease it forward, as there was no other means of getting his own car out. The magistrate decided this was a case of irritability, not a real emergency. It was noted that Lord Graves was a well-known figure in the West End and a founder member of Buck's Club.

On December 5, Lady Caroline Spencer-Churchill, daughter of the Duke of Marlborough, married Major Hugo Waterhouse. After the ceremony at St. Mary Magdalene, Woodstock, guests filtered through the Blenheim entrance-hall, adorned by a huge Christmas tree, into the Long Library, where they were received by the Duchess of Marlborough in a wine-red dress.

On December 9, it was announced that the Serjeant-at-Arms at the House of Commons was to investigate the theft of two bottles of liqueur and some cigars from the locker of the Labour MP for Doncaster, Mr. Evelyn Walkden. 'It was more or less my own fault' said Mr. Walkden, 'as I had not locked the door.'

On December 13, the marriage of the Duke and Duchess of Westminster was terminated in the Divorce Court. It was said that the couple, whose fairy-tale wedding had been one of the sensations of 1930, had lived together for only five years. The couple still retained great respect and affection for each other and the Duchess had been given a generous allowance during their separation.

At Christmas, Winston Churchill retired to Chartwell in Kent, to work on his history of the war, for which it was rumoured he had been paid a six-figure sum. As was his usual habit, he did most of his work in bed, dictating the book to his secretary.

Lord Brownlow, the Duke of Rutland and Lord Willoughby de Eresby saw in the New Year at the Belvoir Hunt Ball, which was held this year at Buckminster Park, historic home of ninety-two-year-old Sir Lyonel Tollemache, near Melton Mowbray.

On January 7, Sir Bernard Docker, wealthy chairman of the Daimler company, sailed for South Africa on board his 860-ton yacht *Shemara*, which he had purchased shortly before the war. It was announced in the Court Circular that Sir Bernard could be contacted by radio on board the vessel.

On January 10, Mr. and Mrs. Attlee celebrated their silver wedding. Members of the Parliamentary Labour Party clubbed together to present them with an eighteenth-century silver Dutch porringer.

On January 16, Sir Ben Smith announced that he had paid £45,000 for Himley Hall, historic Staffordshire home of the Earls of Dudley, for use as the headquarters of the West Midlands Division of the Coal Board, of which he was chairman. 'It is a bargain for the nation' he said, adding that he believed there were 2,000,000 tons of coal under the land. Soon afterwards, a fire broke out at the Hall doing £20,000 worth of damage.

On January 23, an exhibition of relics from Hiroshima and Nagasaki opened in Lower Regent Street. Among the celebrities attending the preview was sixty-six-year-old Sir Alexander Fleming, discoverer of penicillin.

On February 1, much publicity attended the departure of the King, Queen and two Princesses to South Africa. They sailed from Portsmouth on board the new battleship *Vanguard* which had been furnished with many of the fittings from the old Royal yacht *Victoria and Albert*. It was revealed that the Royal Family's seven-bedroom, five-bathroom suite was fitted with its own private telephone exchange. Among the Equerries accompanying them was Wing-Commander Peter Townsend, a Battle of Britain hero who had joined the Royal Household during the war. It was noted that Princess Margaret wore a small brown cap adorned with two upward-curling ostrich feathers.

The same day, it was announced that the Duke of Windsor was to write his memoirs. 'I have lots of material and plenty of experience' said the ex-monarch, currently staying at the Palm Beach home of an American railways executive.

On February 11, Winston Churchill's youngest daughter Mary was married to Captain Christopher Soames. Guests at St. Margaret's Westminster included the Prime Minister Mr. Attlee, Lord and Lady Mountbatten, Lord and Lady Redesdale, the Marquess and Marchioness of Londonderry, Lord Rothschild and Mrs. Margaret Sweeny. The only bridesmaid was Miss Judy Montagu, who had served with the bride in the ATS during the war. A reception was afterwards held at the Dorchester Hotel.

The following day, the Marquess of Tavistock was quietly married to Mrs. Lydia Lyle, daughter of the late Lord Churston and sister of Princess Joan Aly Khan.

The next evening, veteran literary hostess Lady Cunard was present at the Boltons Theatre for the first night of *Now Barabbas* a play by the Hon. William Douglas-Home inspired by the author's recent experiences in prison where he had been sent at the end of the war for refusing to obey an order.

On February 19, old English silver from Lowther Castle, home of the late Earl of Lonsdale, came up for sale at Christies. A Queen Anne toilet service of thirty-four pieces was sold to an antique-dealer Thomas Lumley for £7,800 and the magnificent shield of Achilles, which used to stand on the sideboard at Lowther, raised £520.

In the middle of February, great interest surrounded an application by Prince Philip of Greece for British nationality. It was said that the application had cost him £10.2.6.

Meanwhile, Britain had been hit by the bleakest weather known in modern times. On February 24, wealthy Mrs. Howard Dietz arrived from America carrying several dozen hot-water bottles for her stricken friends. On the same ship was actress Adrienne Allen, carrying as many electric torches as she could lay her hands on. The absence of the Royal Family during this grim time was criticised in certain quarters and at the beginning of March, the King cabled Mr. Attlee from South Africa offering to return at once.

On March 14, there were reports of more turbulence at the Savoy Hotel; 850 employees had gone on strike demanding the reinstatement of an Italian waiter named Piazza, who had been sacked for alleged indiscipline. That day, neither the Grill Room nor the Restaurant at the hotel were open.

At the same time, staff problems had hit Hatfield House and the eighty-five-year-old Marquess of Salisbury was found helping with the washing-up. 'I have since been demoted' he told a reporter. 'I broke so much china that Lady Salisbury has taken me off washing and allocated me to drying only.'

On March 15, the new American Ambassador Lewis Douglas arrived, carrying a large supply of vitamin pills. 'I know things are pretty grim' he said. 'As near as we can, we will share the same hardships.' Mr. Douglas's arrival had been delayed for several days as a result of a gold filling falling out of a tooth.

On March 20, Lord and Lady Mountbatten left for India where the Earl had been appointed to succeed Lord Wavell as Viceroy. In spite of an extra coupon allowance, it was stated that Lord Mountbatten would not wear the official gold-braided Viceroy's uniform. Lady Mountbatten would not take a lavish wardrobe either. 'She has not bothered about fashion since I met her' said her husband. 'But she always wears clothes that suit her.' They were accompanied by their seventeen-year-old daughter Pamela and seen off at Northolt by their nephew, now known as Lieutenant Philip Mountbatten.

At the end of the month, Foreign Secretary Ernest Bevin visited Moscow where on March 29 he was found at the Bolshoi Theatre enjoying a performance of *Romeo and Juliet*.

On April 14, the public's attention turned to the Brambles sandbank, eight miles from Southampton harbour, where the world's largest liner, the *Queen Elizabeth* had gone aground. Efforts to dislodge her with tugs had failed, and among the 2,446 passengers trapped on board were actress Beatrice Lillie, the Duke and Duchess of Marlborough and thirty-five-year-old Randolph Churchill. 'It is hoped to re-float her tonight' said a Cunard official.

On April 29, it was announced that Apsley House, London home of the Dukes of Wellington since 1820, would be handed over to the nation. A Bill covering the transaction would be introduced in the House of Lords. It was disclosed that a small flat would be kept on the top floor for the use of the present Duke and his successors, free of rent and rates.

On May 2, Sharman Douglas, beautiful blonde daughter of the American Ambassador, arrived in England. She wore a round 'apple' hat which was soon widely imitated. Her parents had still not decided whether to move into Barbara Hutton's former home in Regent's Park or to remain at their old residence in Princes Gate.

Meanwhile, a fuss had blown-up over the alleged over-cleaning of various paintings in the National Gallery. On May 7, twenty distinguished artists, including Dame Laura Knight, Charles Wheeler and Ruskin Spear, wrote to *The Times* declaring that the famous Velazquez portrait of Philip IV had been rendered 'no longer a great work of art'. In the face of this outcry, gallery director Philip Hendy remained unperturbed.

On May 12, the Royal Family received a tumultuous welcome on their return from their lengthy visit to South Africa. It was subsequently revealed that the King had lost 17 lb. during the tour.

Three days later, the Duke and Duchess of Windsor arrived from America on board the *Queen Elizabeth* and went directly to the newly-built air-conditioned mansion at Ascot of Mrs. Parkinson, widow of a millionaire electrical engineer. It was stated that a night-watchman had been employed and a new burglar-alarm system had been installed for the Windsors' three-week visit.

On May 24, the Earl of Harewood died at his home near Leeds. The sixty-four-year-old husband of Princess Mary had been suffering from cardiac complications and asthma following a severe chill.

Two days later, Queen Mary's eightieth birthday celebrations went ahead as planned. In the morning, she was visited at Marlborough House by the Duke of Windsor and she later set off for a luncheon at Buckingham Palace in her honour. Mounted police were required to clear a way through the vast crowds of well-wishers. At the end of the day, she listened to a special broadcast by the massed bands of the Brigade of Guards.

At the end of the month, it was reported that Boughton House near Kettering, one of several stately homes of the Duke of Buccleuch, had been reopened, the Duke and Duchess were entertaining there again, and the house had been restored to its original magnificence. Fourteen small Van Dycks were to be found hanging in the Duke's lavatory.

On June 11, the Leader of the Opposition, Winston Churchill, was taken to hospital for a hernia operation. He arrived with two fat volumes of Macaulay's *Essays*, from which he read aloud to his doctors before being given an anaesthetic. Thirty-six hours later, he was smoking a cigar and telephoning his secretary in connexion with his war memoirs.

A few days later, the rumbustious Elsa Maxwell arrived, after a seven-year absence. It was said that her suite at Claridge's was full of crates of Scotch whisky, hams, foie gras, tea and other gifts for her English friends. A rumour circulated that she was on her way to Moscow, personally invited by Mr. Molotov, the Russian Foreign Minister whom she had met on board the *Queen Elizabeth*.

On June 17, Miss Maxwell lunched with the Attorney-General, Sir Hartley Shawcross, at the House of Commons, where whale steaks were served. In the afternoon, she was accompanied to Ascot by Lord Sefton where other racegoers included Sharman Douglas and Raine McCorquodale, beautiful débutante daughter of Barbara Cartland.

On July 4, an Independence Day party at the American Ambassador's residence in Princes Gate was attended by over 3,000 people. The mass of the guests were offered gin or Canadian rye whisky while in the Ambassador's private rooms, Scotch whisky and American bourbon were served.

On July 10 came the long-awaited official announcement of the betrothal of Princess Elizabeth and Gordonstoun-educated Lieutenant Philip Mountbatten. That afternoon, the happy couple were present at a garden-party at Buckingham Palace and in the evening, the Princess attended a coming-out dance at Apsley House for Miss Ursula James.

Five days later, the Royal Family boarded the Royal train for Edinburgh. It arrived at the Scottish capital forty-five minutes later than expected owing to a delay while doctors tended some inflammation in the Queen's eye, caused by a speck of grit.

On July 23, the Marquess of Bath launched his eighteen-year-old daughter, Lady Caroline Thynne, at a dance in the premises above Lady Colefax's shop in Brook Street. A crab and lobster bar was provided and among the champagne-drinking guests were the Duchess of Kent and Mr. Evelyn Waugh.

On July 25, Overseas Trade Minister Harold Wilson arrived back in England after five weeks of negotiations in Moscow. His York Airliner made a very bumpy landing at the new Heathrow Airport and the thirty-one-year-old minister asked to see a doctor. On board the same plane was the athletic Lord Burghley, who had been attending a Russian Sports festival.

On August 8, it was revealed that Lance Reventlow, eleven-year-old son of Woolworth heiress Barbara Hutton, was staying at the Dorchester Hotel with his tutor. The tall fair-haired boy, whose life was equally divided between his two parents, was on an educational trip to London.

On August 13, film star Greta Garbo, whose name was still romantically linked with that of Cecil Beaton arrived on board the *Queen Mary*. Her name was not on the passenger list and she was shielded from photographers as she disembarked. 'I just felt I wanted to see England again' she said. 'I don't want anyone to know what I am going to do.' On board the same ship was demure fifteen-year-old film star Elizabeth Taylor.

At the end of the month, a fire at Sunninghill Park, Ascot, recently made over by the King to Princess Elizabeth, made headline news. It was reported that detectives were investigating the possibility that the fire was not an accident. A full report was later sent to the Princess at Balmoral.

Another link with the Edwardian age was broken on September 11 when Mrs. George Keppel, former mistress of King Edward VII, died in Italy. She was buried under the cypress trees in the Protestant Cemetery in Florence and a memorial service was held at St. Mark's, North Audley Street which was attended by the Earl of Rosebery, Lady Colefax, the Marchioness Curzon of Kedleston and other notabilities.

On September 16, Miss Marion Crawford, slim Scottish governess to Princess Elizabeth and Princess Margaret since 1933, was married to a certain Mr. George Buthlay. The event inspired the headline in an American newspaper: 'Governess Beats Liz to the Altar'.

Lord and Lady Mountbatten during India's independence celebrations

On September 17, fifty-seven-year-old Hollywood star Mae West arrived at Southampton on board the *Queen Mary*. She wore two-inch false eyelashes and her platinum coloured hair curled about her shoulders. With her came 150 dresses and sixty pairs of shoes. The purpose of her visit was to tour in *Diamond Lil*, her show which had run for three successful years in America.

On September 26, a sale at Blenheim Palace created great interest. The Duke of Marlborough was anxious to dispose of surplus tapestries and carpets from servants' bedrooms along with excess furnishings from his house in Kensington Palace Gardens, which he had sold earlier in the year to the French government. The Duke had recently acquired a smaller four-storey London house in Shepherd's Place off Brook Street.

On October 15, it was reported that wealthy Mr. Basil Ionides had sold his house in Berkeley Square, unoccupied since being bombed in 1940, to an investment concern. It was noted that there were now only two houses in the Square still in private hands.

On October 18, seventeen-year-old Princess Margaret flew to Belfast on her first solo assignment: the launching of the new liner *Edinburgh Castle*. After she had performed the christening ceremony, she was presented with a bouquet of roses by a young sailor, who was much embarrassed when the Princess suddenly plucked out one of the roses and presented it to him.

At the end of the month, the Savoy Hotel was again afflicted by strike action. Night after night, a growing number of agitators and their supporters gathered outside and on November 6, headlines blazed the news that Smithfield Market had cut off supplies of meat to the hotel. The Savoy Grill that day was operated almost single-handedly by the Head Waiter, Luigi, and it was stated that patrons had to make do with a choice of cold goose or chicken with salad. Among those enrolled as temporary waiters was the Earl of Airlie's nineteen-year-old son, the Hon. Angus Ogilvy.

Meanwhile, news had come from America that John Winant, war-time Ambassador to London, had committed suicide. Friends described the tragedy as 'a casualty of the war'.

On November 12, the Mountbattens arrived from India for Princess Elizabeth's wedding. They moved into a fifteen-room suite at the Dorchester Hotel with their eighteen-year-old daughter Pamela, who was in a bottle-green outfit.

On November 18, thousands of the Royal wedding gifts went on show at St. James's Palace. These included a record-player in a walnut cabinet from the best man, the Marquess of Milford Haven, a de luxe picnic hamper from Princess Margaret, an imitation Fabergé silver box from Chips Channon and a wreath of diamond roses from the Nizam of Hyderabad.

The following day, on the eve of the wedding, the Charles Street, Mayfair, home of one of the royal bridesmaids, Miss Diana Bowes-Lyon, niece of the Queen, was ransacked.

On November 20, Hollywood star Bob Hope, in a brightly-coloured tartan scarf, watched the bridal procession from the terrace of Crockford's Club, Carlton House Terrace. After the ceremony at Westminster Abbey and appearances on the balcony at Buckingham Palace, Princess Elizabeth and her husband left for their honeymoon at Broadlands, Hampshire home of Lord Mountbatten. Hidden under the rugs in the open carriage bearing them to the station were several hot-water bottles and the bride's much-loved corgi, Susan.

Meanwhile, it was disclosed that Lord Wimborne had sold his 200-year-old town house in Arlington Street next to the Ritz for £250,000. The purchaser, Sir Edward Mountain, chairman of the Eagle Star Insurance Company, announced that the twenty-six bedroom house would be turned into offices but its old character would be retained as much as possible.

On December 1, seventy-two-year-old magician Aleister Crowley, who had recently announced that he had discovered an elixir of life which would give him eternal youth, died in Sussex. A storm later erupted over the use of a crematorium in Brighton for the funeral service. 'We shall take all the necessary steps to see that such a thing does not happen again' said the Chairman of the Town Council.

On December 10, Princess Margaret, in a silver-embroidered dress, was present at a dance at the Hyde Park Hotel given by eligible bachelors Lord Wilton, Captain Thomas Egerton and Major Nugent Gerard. Among the other guests was the tall Lord Blandford, twenty-one-year-old heir to the Duke of Marlborough.

On December 17, Home Office pathologist Sir Bernard Spilsbury, who had given evidence at practically every murder trial in Southern England over the past thirty-five years, committed suicide in his laboratory in Gower Street. He had killed himself with carbon-monoxide gas.

On December 23, it was announced that thirty-nine-year-old American industrialist Jack Heinz had sent 1,200,000 tins of much needed food to be distributed to hospitals throughout Britain. This was one of the many acts of kindness perpetrated by Mr. Heinz, who was said to be worth hundreds of millions of dollars.

Shortly after Christmas, it was revealed that Earl Spencer had secretly removed the remains of several of his ancestors from the family vault at Great Brington near Daventry and had them cremated. 'It is a purely private matter and I do not wish to discuss it' said the Earl. 'But at the same time, I would wish to emphasise that the bodies that have been removed are not recent burials.'

1948

The New Year was greeted with the usual tumultuous scenes at the Chelsea Arts Ball at the Albert Hall. This year, the ball was televised and a midnight toast was proposed to viewers by the Petworth gardener Fred Streeter.

On January 14, David Niven was married to beautiful Swedish model Hjordis Tersmeden, whom he had met for the first time ten days earlier. The ceremony took place at Chelsea Registry Office and a wedding-party was held at the home of Mrs. Audrey Pleydell-Bouverie. Niven revealed afterwards that he was suffering from a high fever at the time and running a temperature of 103 degrees.

Over in Morocco, the Leader of the Opposition, tended by his doctor Lord Moran, was recovering from a cold and bronchitis. 'I called Lord Moran out here because at my age everyone has got to be careful' he said. On January 19, he flew home, calmly playing cards as the plane went through two thunderstorms.

On January 22, multi-millionairess Mrs. Laura Corrigan died in New York. Mrs. Corrigan, a former telephone-operator from Cleveland, Ohio, had come to England in 1922 and quickly established herself as one of the most lavish hostesses of all time. Her memorial service at St. Mark's, North Audley Street, was attended by the Duchess of Kent, the Duke and Duchess of Buccleuch, the Duke and Duchess of Marlborough, Princess Joan Aly Khan and her great rival hostess, Lady Cunard.

On January 25, Mae West's controversial show *Diamond Lil* opened at the Prince of Wales Theatre. 'My undulations may be unorthodox, my technique is different but the people understand even if the critics do not.' she declared.

At the end of the month, Earl Lloyd George, fifty-eight-year-old son of the former Prime Minister, left England saying that he would never return. 'The British Government is the most inefficient since the Stuarts' he said on arrival in New York. 'I have come to America to seek life, liberty and happiness, which cannot be found in England today.'

Meanwhile, thirty-five-year-old carrot-haired American comedian Danny Kaye had arrived in England and was given an hysterical greeting. His first night at the Palladium on February 2 was described as the greatest personal success in music-hall life for the past thirty years. 'I would like to stay here for four years' he said. 'Where do you apply for naturalisation papers?'

On February 4, the greatly-loved Earl of Derby died at Knowsley Hall in Lancashire. The eighty-two-year-old peer was succeeded by his twenty-nine-year-old grandson Lord Stanley.

On February 17, Mrs. Sacheverell Sitwell gave a party in honour of Mae West, which went on till nearly 5.00 am. Guests included the Duchess of Kent, the Duchess of Buccleuch, Lady Cunard and Mr. Chips Channon, who wore ruby and diamond buttons.

On February 24, seventy-seven-year-old Lord Horder, the King's doctor, and his wife were involved in a car-crash. Their Humber Snipe left the road at Thames Ditton and mounted the embankment ending up outside the offices of the Milk Marketing Board.

Meanwhile, a new £10,000 Rolls Royce, specially made for millionaire Nubar Gulbenkian, had appeared on the scene. It was painted two shades of bronze and boasted electrically-operated windows. 'Most English cars look a little antediluvian' said Mr. Gulbenkian, who was now living permanently at the Ritz Hotel.

At the end of the month it was announced that Mr. Harold Wilson, now President of the Board of Trade, had moved into a modern cottage-style house in the newly-built Hampstead Garden Suburb. 'It's very pleasant' said Mrs. Wilson, 'but I cannot get any help in the house.' Shortly afterwards, it was revealed that Mrs. Wilson's household linen was almost threadbare. 'It is getting beyond mending' she said. 'I have turned most of the sheets, sides to middle, already.'

On March 1, the thirty-year-old Marquess of Tavistock and his wife flew off to South Africa, where they hoped to start a new life in a warmer climate, running a farm. The Marquess's eight-year-old son, Lord Howland, wore a hunting-cap and carried a hunting-horn.

A few days later, Thelma Lady Furness, now working for an American film company, arrived in England anxious to buy the film rights of one of Daphne du Maurier's books. She was accompanied by her son eighteen-year-old Lord Furness, who had recently been discharged from the Welsh Guards suffering from vertigo.

On March 20, it was revealed that Sir Roderick and Lady Jones were keeping a cow in their back garden at 29 Hyde Park Gate, next door house to the new Churchill home. The cow, a light brown Jersey named Flora Bella, lived on hay and produced two gallons of milk a day, which was said to be enough for the Jones family and left some to spare for their neighbour, sculptor Jacob Epstein.

On April 12, rosy-cheeked Professor C. E. M. Joad, distinguished member of the BBC programme *The Brains Trust* was fined forty shillings for travelling without a ticket from Waterloo to Exeter and lying to the ticket inspector. From his home at Hawkley, near Petersfield, Joad said he had no comment to make.

On April 15, Princess Elizabeth dined with Clement Attlee at 10 Downing Street, her first official visit to the Prime Minister's residence.

At the Royal Academy Summer Exhibition, which opened on April 30, much attention focused on a controversial three-headed portrait of the beautiful Mrs. Daphne Wall, which had taken artist John Merton 1,200 hours to execute. Mrs. Wall could not be present at the preview as she was confined to her Oxfordshire home suffering from measles. It was revealed that the portrait had at first been rejected by the hanging committee and the Academy's sixty-nine-year-old president, Sir Alfred Munnings, had threatened to resign if they did not change their decision. 'It is a remarkable picture, never mind what the highbrows say' he said.

On May 6, artist Augustus John was to be found in the downstairs bar at the House of Commons drinking champagne with Mr. Chips Channon.

On May 13, Society was deeply shocked by the death in an aircrash of the young Marchioness of Hartington, daughter of former American Ambassador, Joseph Kennedy, and her friend Earl Fitzwilliam, owner of the 365-room Wentworth Woodhouse, Britain's largest private house.

On May 20, Mrs. Liza Paravicini, daughter of Somerset Maugham, announced her engagement to Lord John Hope, son of the Marquess of Linlithgow. It was revealed that Mrs. Paravicini was currently staying with her future in-laws at Hopetoun House, West Lothian.

On May 21, Queen Mary's eighty-first birthday was celebrated with a small iced cake being made by M. Gabriel Tschumi, Swiss chef at Buckingham Palace for the past thirty-four years.

A few days later, Lady Cunard declined an invitation to dinner at the American Embassy on the grounds that she was allergic to tobacco smoke. The Ambassador, Lewis Douglas, promptly gave his assurances that no one would smoke and Lady Cunard was persuaded to attend the party after all.

On May 28, Unity Mitford, who had never recovered from her bullet-wound nine years earlier, was admitted to the West Highland Cottage Hospital at Oban, where she died a few hours later. A funeral was held later at Swinbrook in Oxfordshire, which was attended by Sir Oswald and Lady Mosley and other members of her family. On her tombstone was written: 'Say not the struggle nought availeth.'

June 7 saw the arrival of General Smuts in a giant York airliner. The great plane got bogged down in the mud at Northolt and could not taxi to the airport buildings. Lord Tedder's Rolls-Royce was sent out to the stranded aircraft. During his visit, Smuts was sworn in as Chancellor of Cambridge University, lunching afterwards with philosopher Bertrand Russell, who had been a fellow undergraduate with the General fifty years earlier.

On June 23, Princess Margaret, in a pink taffeta confection, attended a party at the Ritz given by Mrs. Herbert Agar on the occasion of the twenty-first birthday of her tall, elegant son, Billy Wallace.

On July 5, American statesman Bernard Baruch arrived in England, refusing to answer questions about the purpose of the visit. 'I ain't gonna do nothing about nothing' he said.

On July 10, there was a spectacular dance at Sutton Place, Elizabethan home of the Duke and Duchess of Sutherland. The house was decorated with the finest blooms from the gardens and hot-houses and the women present wore their finest jewels. The Duchess wore a necklace that had once belonged to Marie Antoinette and Lady Ednam wore a spray of diamond flowers nine inches in length. The only girl who did

The Aga Khan, one of the most colourful figures of the twentieth century, leads in the 1948 Derby Winner, My Love

not wear jewellery was Lord Bath's daughter, Lady Caroline Thynne, who had recently begun working as a receptionist at Rootes in Piccadilly. 'The greatest thrill was my first pay-packet' she said. 'Daddy thinks it is excellent experience for me.'

The same evening, Lady Cunard died in her suite at the Dorchester Hotel. Art connoisseur Sir Robert Abdy and opium-smoking diplomat Tony Gandarillas were at her bedside. The great hostess's ashes were later scattered in Grosvenor Square amidst rumours that her famous emeralds were false and that, in spite of the outward show, she had been on the verge of poverty during the last years of her life.

On July 21, high society gathered for the wedding of Raine McCorquodale, beautiful daughter of novelist Barbara Cartland, and Mr. Gerald Legge, nephew of the Earl of Dartmouth. After the ceremony at St. Margaret's Westminster, a motor-coach transported the sixteen bridesmaids, who included Lady Pamela Mountbatten and Lady Caroline Thynne, to the reception at Londonderry House. Lord Mountbatten arrived towards the end of the celebrations, having come on from the House of Lords where he had been formally introduced along with his nephew, the Duke of Edinburgh.

On July 23, the Duke and Duchess of Marlborough gave a dance at Blenheim in honour of Princess Margaret. Fairy lights twinkled in the Italian Gardens and the seventeen-year-old Princess danced several times with the young Marquess of Blandford. 'They played everything from old world waltzes to the most modern dances' said the hostess, who wore the famous Marlborough pearls.

On August 12, Mr. Ernest Simpson plunged into the news again when he took as his fourth wife Mrs. Avril Leveson-Gower, daughter of the late Sir John Mullens and sister of Elvira Barney, who had been the central figure in a sensational murder case in 1932.

At the end of the month, a large party congregated at Balmoral. Among those present were Lord John Hope and his wife, daughter of Somerset Maugham, twenty-four-year-old Lord Porchester, son of the Earl of Carnarvon, and the twenty-two-year-old Marquess of Blandford, whose name was now closely linked with that of Princess Margaret. Journalists had now begun to write of the existence of a 'Margaret Set'.

At the beginning of September, it was announced that Douglas Fairbanks, Jr. and his wife were in England looking for a house and school for their three children.

Princess Margaret was back in the news on September 5 when she arrived in Holland for the inauguration of Princess Juliana as Queen of the Netherlands. Three days later she attended a dance at the exclusive International Culture Centre in Amsterdam where, adorned in a diamond tiara and silver embroidered dress, she danced with her father's Equerry Wing-Commander Peter Townsend till three in the morning. It was noted that thirty-three-year-old Townsend was married with two children and living in a cottage in Windsor Park.

On September 14, the ten-year-old Marquess of Dufferin and Ava gave away the bride at the marriage of his mother to Major H. A. D. Buchanan. It was afterwards announced that the bride, who had recently made news by carrying around a transparent plastic handbag, would continue to use her title, out of deference to the wishes of her first husband who had been killed in Burma in 1945.

On September 30, Lady Diana Cooper was found at an exhibition at the National Book League wearing a white satin pancake hat, long white gloves and a huge monogrammed white shawl which had once wrapped her baby son John Julius, now nineteen years old and doing his National Service in the Navy.

On October 8, it was announced that famous couturier William Wallace Reville-Terry, who had designed the dress worn by the Queen on her wedding day in 1923, had died in poverty aged seventy-eight. A friend revealed that the great couturier had fallen on hard times and been too proud to ask for help.

In the middle of the month, the Duke of Windsor arrived in London to have his knee massaged by the manipulative surgeon, seventy-year-old Sir Morton Smart. The Duke's knee still suffered from the after-effects of his famous riding accident in 1924 and the great surgeon occupied the same consulting rooms in Grosvenor Square that the Duke had first visited twenty-four years earlier.

On October 26, much grandeur was revived at the State Opening of Parliament. The Marchioness of Londonderry, now sixty-eight years old, wore a vast diamond tiara and two broad diamond bracelets, and Lady Astor, now sixty-seven years old, wore a tiara incorporating a huge diamond said to have been worn by Charles the Bold at the Battle of Nancy in 1477. Observing the glittering parade, Lady Astor announced: 'I hate the peerage – it ought to be abolished.'

The following day, the Motor Show opened at Earl's Court. Wealthy Sir Bernard Docker was found admiring a new two-and-a-half-ton saloon made by the Daimler Company, of which he was chairman. 'This is my baby' he cooed.

On November 1, Danny Kaye's performance in the Royal Variety Show at the Palladium met with a very mixed reception. 'Something was wrong' he said afterwards. 'This has been the toughest audience I've met. Perhaps it was my fault. I should have given them more of the numbers they knew . . .' The red-haired comedian went on later to a party at the American Embassy, also attended by Princess Margaret, where he stayed till three in the morning.

On November 14, attention turned to Buckingham Palace where at 9.14 pm, Princess Elizabeth gave birth to a baby boy. The King and Queen were in evening-dress when they first saw their grandchild and it was reported that the King shook the Duke of Edinburgh warmly by the hand and the Queen embraced him.

On November 25, Miss Margot Fonteyn injured her ankle at Covent Garden while dancing in a new ballet by Mr. Frederick Ashton. It was announced that the prima donna would not be appearing for the next few nights.

The legendary Marchioness of Londonderry waits for her car after attending the first full dress opening of Parliament since before the War

On December 13, Cecil Beaton arrived at Buckingham Palace to take the first photographs of the young Prince Charles. 'Financially it is of little benefit' he said. 'The whole point is that it is a great honour.'

Meanwhile, the relationship between thirty-seven-year-old Prince Aly Khan and Hollywood star Rita Hayworth had been making headline news throughout the world. On December 23, the couple arrived off the coast of Ireland on board the liner *Britannic*. On disembarking, they transferred to a powerful American sedan and made their way to the Aga Khan's stud farm at Gilltown. Soon after Christmas, they crossed to England, flew to London in the Prince's private plane and on December 29, were found rushing through the foyer of the Ritz Hotel. They left by separate exits and flew on together to Paris.

The New Year was greeted at the International Sporting Club in Monte Carlo by an illustrious group, which included the Leader of the Opposition Winston Churchill, the Duke and Duchess of Windsor and the sixty-nine-year-old Duke of Westminster, who had recently got married for the fourth time.

On January 2, Princess Joan Aly Khan hurriedly left Switzerland on hearing that her husband and his new love, Rita Hayworth, were on their way there. Back at her home in Wilton Street, Belgravia, she said: 'I have no idea what my husband's plans are. If he wants to return here, well the house is his.'

A few days later, Aly and Rita arrived at the Château de L'Horizon, the famous villa near Cannes which the Prince had recently purchased from the executors of the late Maxine Elliott, and where Winston Churchill had often stayed before the war. On January 17, journalists were summoned here for a Press conference. An English butler served whisky and aperitifs from a silver tray and a statement was issued that Prince Aly Khan and Miss Rita Hayworth planned to marry as soon as possible. Later, the Aga Khan and his wife, Aly and Rita posed for photographs. 'There are 150,000 divorces in Britain annually' remarked the seventy-one-year-old Aga Khan. 'Why criticise my son?'

Back in England, a more mundane matter had obsessed the public. On January 25, Mr. Justice Lynskey published his findings after his lengthy enquiry into alleged bribery and corruption in the government. Parliamentary Secretary to the Board of Trade John Belcher was found guilty of accepting gifts from an entrepreneur named Sidney Stanley as an inducement to secure influence. 'I am frankly amazed and very distressed' said Mr. Belcher, who later resigned from the House of Commons and resumed his job as a clerk with British Railways.

On February 3, the marriage took place at Caxton Hall of company director Sir Bernard Docker and forty-two-year-old Norah Collins, wealthy widow of a former chairman of Cerebos Salt. At the ceremony, the bride, one-time dance hostess at the famous Café de Paris, wore a cyclamen pink frock and a full-length mink coat. The couple left afterwards for the South of France where Sir Bernard's 860-ton yacht, *Shemara*, lay anchored, staffed by a crew of thirty-five.

On February 5, it was revealed that genial sixty-five-year-old Earl of Portarlington had had his big toe amputated. The operation had been necessitated by the peer's diabetic condition.

On February 10, beautiful twenty-year-old Sharman Douglas was back in England, carrying a fur-hood and snow-boots and vigorously denying rumours of a romance between her and the tall Marquess of Blandford.

At the end of the month, Sharman's father, the American Ambassador to the Court of St. James was struck down with an attack of non-stop hiccups. 'We have cured him at last' said Mrs. Douglas on March 11, 'but it was distressing while it lasted.'

On March 12, a lumbar sympathectomy was performed on the King to improve the blood supply to his right foot. Professor J. R. Learmonth of Edinburgh University brought his own team to Buckingham Palace where the operation was carried out in a surgical theatre created in rooms overlooking the Mall.

The same day, an elderly woman was found strangled in the grounds of Winfield House, former home of Barbara Hutton, still unoccupied by the American government. Rumours circulated that the murdered woman had been a servant at the mansion and used to wander about the grounds gazing wistfully at its empty windows.

On March 18, it was announced that an £8,000 Rolls-Royce was being built for Prince Philip's use on State occasions. The car would have eight cylinders and be dark green in colour.

On April 5, the American Ambassador Lewis Douglas was injured while salmon-fishing on the Test in Hampshire. A sudden gust of wind blew the hook into his left eye and he was rushed to Southampton Hospital. 'I believe there is every hope that the eye will be saved' said the Ambassador's host, aviation chief Sir Richard Fairey, who had a house at Stockbridge.

On April 8, Sir Bernard and Lady Docker had returned from their honeymoon and were seen shopping in Bond Street. Lady Docker wore a light beige tweed suit and Sir Bernard had a white carnation in his buttonhole. The couple had recently acquired Hays Lodge, Chesterfield Hill, former home of General Eisenhower.

At Easter, Longleat House, ancestral home of the Marquess of Bath, was opened to the public. On Easter Monday, April 18, the forty-four-year-old peer was found directing the carloads of sightseers in his shirtsleeves while his sixteen-year-old son, Viscount Weymouth, helped mend a vehicle that had broken down. Visitors paid two-and-sixpence to view the house, said to be Britain's oldest unfortified home.

Meanwhile, the London social scene had once again been adorned by the presence of the Duke and Duchess of Windsor. On April 22, the fifty-two-year-old Duchess spent four hours in a hairdressing salon in Grafton Street, Mayfair, owned by a certain Mr. Raymond. 'The Duchess is quiet and easy to please' said a girl assistant afterwards.

On May 3, comedian Danny Kaye, now in his second season at the London Palladium, was taken in a chauffeur-driven Rolls-Royce to have tea at the Hertfordshire home of ninety-two-year-old playwright Bernard Shaw, who received his guest wearing tweed knickerbockers and sandals. On the journey home, the Rolls-Royce collided with a smaller car in a narrow street in Ayot St. Lawrence and the thirty-six-year-old star's bruised ribs were treated at the Middlesex Hospital.

On May 19, Norman Baillie-Stewart, the former 'Officer in the Tower', was released from Parkhurst Prison, Isle of Wight, following his second term of imprisonment. To avoid contact with the Press, Baillie-Stewart hired a three-seater plane to fly him to the mainland. To foil the Press further, he had also grown a red beard.

On May 27, the wedding of Prince Aly Khan and Rita Hayworth took place in the South of France. After the ceremony at a local Town Hall conducted by a Communist Mayor, the couple fled in the Prince's white convertible Cadillac to the reception at the Château de L'Horizon, where it was said that 200 gallons of *eau de cologne* had been emptied into the swimming pool. It was rumoured that the Duke and Duchess of Windsor had been on the original invitation list but had let it be known that they could not accept.

Eight days later, the newly-wed couple were present at the Derby, where other racegoers included Mr. and Mrs. Churchill, Princess Elizabeth and Prince Philip, and the redoubtable Queen Mary. The King, still recovering from his recent operation, missed the race.

This year, the Derby ended in a spectacular photo-finish. M. Léon Volterra's Amour Drake was just beaten by an outsider named Nimbus. To avoid disappointing her husband, who was desperately ill with heart trouble, beautiful Madame Volterra told him that his horse had won. He rallied, but died shortly afterwards.

By June 17, the King was well enough to give a ball at Windsor Castle. That night, the stately rooms were filled with flowers and music was provided by Maurice Winnick's band. Sixty-eight-year-old Lady Astor was one of the most vigorous dancers and even the King took to the floor several times, resting his leg between dances on a small footstool. The Queen did not order the band to stop playing until a quarter to five in the morning.

On June 23, it was learned that chronically unpunctual Aly Khan and his new wife had arrived ninety minutes late at the Duke of Windsor's fifty-fifth birthday party at the Plaza Athenee hotel in New York. The charismatic couple turned up just as the Duke and Duchess, Elsa Maxwell and Mrs. Randolph Hearst were settling into the dessert.

Meanwhile, Sir Oswald and Lady Mosley and their two children Alexander and Max, aged ten and nine, had left Southampton for a cruise on board their newly-purchased 60-ton ketch accompanied by two seamen and a butler. They eventually made their way to the South of France where they anchored alongside the *Sister Anne*, magnificent yacht of millionairess Mrs. Reginald Fellowes.

On July 11, £52,000-worth of jewellery was stolen from the Mayfair home of Sir Bernard and Lady Docker. The haul included a pearl necklace, valued at £11,500 which Lady Docker had worn at her wedding six months earlier. After giving the police full details of their loss, the Dockers left for the country in their Daimler. This was said to be the biggest jewel robbery since the theft of Lady Ludlow's historic gems in 1924.

On July 19, there was great excitement over the engagement of the twenty-six-year-old Earl of Harewood,

Prince Aly Khan and Miss Rita Hayworth shortly before their marriage

eleventh in line of succession to the throne and twenty-two-year-old concert pianist Miss Marion Stein, whose family had fled from Vienna in 1937. That afternoon, Miss Stein had tea with the Princess Royal at St. James's Palace.

The drama of the recent Docker jewel robbery was forgotten when on August 4, the Aga Khan and his wife were victims of an armed attack near their villa in the South of France. Bandits with tommy-guns stopped the potentate's car on its way to the airport and snatched the Begum Aga Khan's jewel case containing gems worth £200,000. 'My wife has lost every jewel of any value that she possessed' said the seventy-two-year-old Aga Khan. Rumours that the robbery was the work of American gunmen drew an angry response from the detective in charge of the case. 'There were no foreigners on this job, no Americans, no Italians, no nothing. This was a job conceived, planned and executed entirely by Frenchmen.'

On August 15, it was revealed that the Prime Minister Mr. Attlee had purchased a small property, Cherry Cottage, near Great Missenden, on which to fall back if he ever lost his official residence. In the meantime, he wished to let the house furnished to a suitable tenant.

On August 20, the untidy bachelor Duke of Argyll died at Inveraray Castle aged seventy-seven. He was succeeded by his elegantly-dressed second cousin, Ian Campbell, once married to Lord Beaverbrook's daughter and a familiar figure in London's clubland.

On September 6, Mrs. Christopher Soames gave birth to a girl at her farm near Chartwell in Kent. The baby, later christened Emma, was Winston Churchill's sixth grandchild.

The following day, the thirty-three-year-old President of the Board of Trade, Mr. Harold Wilson, was among guests at a party at the Empress Club given by dress-designer, Mr. Digby Morton. It was noticed that he had shaved off his moustache. 'He told me that he first grew the moustache to make him look older' said Mrs. Wilson. 'Now he thinks he is quite old enough and the moustache makes him look too old.'

Meanwhile, there was much interest in the relationship between the thirty-year-old Marquess of Milford Haven, best man at Princess Elizabeth's wedding, and American-born Mrs. Romaine Simpson. It was noted that this was not the first time a Mrs. Simpson had been romantically involved with a member of the Royal Family.

By September 29, the couple had officially announced their engagement but Mrs. Simpson did not accompany the Marquess that day to the marriage of the Earl of Harewood at St. Mark's, North Audley Street. 'As Mrs. Simpson has not been presented at Court, it was thought her presence might be a source of embarrassment both to her and to any member of the Royal Family whom she would meet' explained Lord Milford Haven's publicity-agent.

At the end of the month, the Duke and Duchess of Windsor came to the end of their lease of the Château de la Croe, near Cannes. Eighteen lorryloads were needed to transport their furniture to 85 Rue de la Faisanderie, the new Paris home they had acquired earlier in the year.

On October 13, it was announced that sixty-four-year-old Mr. Reginald D. Parker, special Scotland Yard chauffeur attached to 10 Downing Street, was retiring after twenty-three years service. It was noted that Mr. Parker had driven for every Prime Minister since Ramsay MacDonald.

On October 26, racehorse owner Peter Beatty, younger son of the late Admiral Beatty, threw himself from the sixth floor of the Ritz Hotel. It was revealed that thirty-nine-year-old Mr. Beatty suffered from a serious eye affliction and faced total blindness. For the last few months, he had been accompanied everywhere by his valet. His death came as a particular shock for his old friend, Prince Aly Khan, who flew to England in his private plane for the funeral.

On October 31, Princess Margaret was accompanied by the Marquess of Blandford to the Halloween Ball at the Dorchester. The Princess wore a blue and pink tulle gown and a five strand pearl choker held with a diamond clasp. It was reported that neither the Princess or her friend Sharman Douglas had any success at the Hoop-la stall.

On November 9, the dignity of the Lord Mayor's Show was upset when the horses drawing the State Coach of the retiring Lord Mayor, Sir George Aylwen, took fright in Queen Victoria Street and plunged into the crowd. Twenty-three people were injured and Sir George had to abandon his coach and ride for the rest of the journey with the new Lord Mayor, Sir Frederick Rowland.

On November 22, it was announced that Maureen Marchioness of Dufferin and Ava had become a director of the Guinness Brewery. 'It's hard to say what my duties will be, but I think I shall go to the office every week' said the Marchioness, who was said to be a teetotaller.

Meanwhile, two portraits of Italian noblewomen by Florentine artist Pietro Annigoni had created a stir at the Royal Society of Portrait Painters exhibition. On November 28, there was a dinner at Prunier's in his honour. Guests, who were offered lobster cooked in champagne, included Sir Alfred Munnings and the artist's only English pupil, ex-Irish Guards officer, Timothy Whidborne.

On December 10, headlines blazed the news that the infant Prince Charles had been struck down with an acute attack of tonsilitis, known in certain circles as quinsy. His nurse Helen Lightbody was looking after him at Clarence House and a bulletin was soon issued, signed by four doctors, to the effect that the one-year-old Prince had recovered.

On December 20, the King wore black suede shoes with his dinner-jacket at a staff party at Buckingham Palace. The Queen was in a lime-coloured silk dress and a tiara. Following a cabaret by Jimmy Edwards, Florence Desmond and Frankie Howerd, the Queen danced with senior footman Mr. R. J. Evitts. Princess Margaret's partner was Mr. Freddie Mayes, who looked after all the Ormulu clocks in the Palace.

After Christmas, attention turned to luxurious Montchoisi Clinic in Lausanne where on December 28, Rita Hayworth, wife of Aly Khan, gave birth to a baby girl. 'Let's all have a drink' said Aly to the attendant pressmen. 'My wife had a tough time of it, but everything went off well.'

In the New Year's Honours List, Mr. Hugh Wontner, managing director of the Savoy Group, was made a member of the Royal Victorian Order. It was revealed that the previous year, he had advised Buckingham Palace how to put its catering arrangements on an economical basis.

On January 13, Mrs. Margaret Sweeny gave a lunch-party at her house in Upper Grosvenor Street for the wealthy Baron Alexis Rede. Among others present was the handsome new Duke of Argyll, whom Mrs. Sweeny had first met two years earlier on the Golden Arrow train from Paris.

On January 17, it was announced that Stanley Spencer had been reinstated as an Associate Member of the Royal Academy. Some years ago this controversial artist had resigned from the Academy following the rejection of two of his paintings. 'It is now clear that it was a misunderstanding, mostly on my side' said the fifty-nine-year-old painter, interviewed sitting on his bed at his home at Cookham in Berkshire.

On January 26, details were disclosed of a carpet created by Queen Mary. It measured ten foot by seven foot and had taken the King's mother eight years to make. Before being sold for charity, the carpet, said to contain over a million stitches, went on show at the Victoria and Albert Museum where 90,000 people paid sixpence to inspect it. 'It is the Queen's view' said her Lady-in-Waiting, Lady Cynthia Colville 'that it is the duty of every individual to contribute something directly to help the country in its need for dollars.'

Meanwhile, the Royal Commission on Capital Punishment had begun sitting. On February 3, wealthy abolitionist Mrs. Van der Elst interrupted the Archbishop of Canterbury, Dr. Fisher, while he was giving evidence. 'You dare to call yourself a Christian after what you have said?' she shouted. 'You are a wicked man!' The Commission's chairman and the Archbishop promptly withdrew and Mrs. Van der Elst, dressed as usual in black, stormed out of the hall and was whisked away in her Rolls-Royce.

Sharman Douglas, daughter of the American Ambassador, dining with the Marquess of Blandford at the Café de Paris in Coventry Street

On February 4, the absence of the Marchioness of Milford Haven at the wedding of her son and wealthy Mrs. Romaine Simpson was a great talking point. It was revealed that she had left Washington shortly before the ceremony took place. Arriving in London a few days later, the Marquess said tersely: 'I have no comment to make on reports that my mother did not approve of my wedding.'

On February 23, it leaked out that the King had taken delivery of two tartan dinner-jackets. 'I shall not make any comment on the new costume' said the editor of the *Tailor and Cutter*, Mr. John Taylor. 'Presumably it is intended for wear in private only.'

On March 1, one of Britain's top atomic scientists, thirty-eight-year-old Dr. Klaus Fuchs, appeared in the dock at the Old Bailey. The pale young boffin, who had been arrested at his pre-fab at Harwell, pleaded guilty to passing information to the Russians since 1942. Describing the defendant as 'one of the most dangerous men the country could have on its shores', Lord Chief Justice Goddard pronounced a sentence of fourteen years. 'I have had a fair trial. I thank you, my Lord' said Fuchs. Among spectators in court was the Duchess of Kent in a veil.

Meanwhile, Royal photographer Cecil Beaton had arrived back in England following a holiday in Tangier, where he had struck a new fashion-note by wearing his shirt unbuttoned, with its tails tied in a knot around his waist.

On March 31, Lord Furness celebrated his twenty-first birthday by taking young Mrs. Gerald Legge and other friends to Paris on the Golden Arrow. That night there was a sumptuous dinner of oysters, caviar, foie gras, truffles and steaks at Maxim's given by the young peer's mother Thelma Lady Furness and his aunt Mrs. Gloria Vanderbilt. 'It's just like old times' said Albert the head waiter. 'We dreamed of the days when the English milords would be back with us again.'

On April 4, the Hon. Peter Ward, twenty-four-year-old son of the Earl of Dudley, vigorously denied rumours that he was unofficially engaged to Princess Margaret. 'I am a close friend of the Royal Family' he said. 'I greatly resent the report of any engagement announcement.'

Meanwhile, off the coast of Scotland, divers under the instructions of the Duke of Argyll were searching Tobermory Bay for the wreck of a Spanish Armada treasure ship said to have sunk there 360 years earlier. 'So far, I have heard little of the progress' said the forty-six-year-old Duke. 'But I did not expect to hear anything as early as this.'

The Duke had other things on his mind. On April 12, he took his new friend, Mrs. Margaret Sweeny, to *Ring Round the Moon* at the Globe Theatre. At the end of the play, they got up to leave and found the door of their box had jammed. During the twenty minutes it took to free it, the couple had become engaged.

On April 13, the Marquess of Blandford celebrated his twenty-fourth birthday with a party at Ciro's Club. Among those present were Lady Caroline Thynne and her handsome young fiancé Mr. David Somerset, heir presumptive to the Duke of Beaufort. Missing was Lord Blandford's father, the Duke of Marlborough, who was suffering from laryngitis as a result of opening Blenheim Palace to the public. 'I've been standing in the north-west door for three days and the winds are pretty cold' he explained.

On April 27, both Mr. Attlee and Mr. Churchill were present at the Royal Academy dinner, where they sampled lobster patties, cold roast beef and Stilton. After dinner, the Prime Minister and the Leader of the Opposition clinked glasses in the friendliest possible manner.

Early in May, it was announced that seventeen-year-old débutante Antonia Pakenham, oldest of the eight children of Lord Pakenham, now Minister of Civil Aviation, had given up her temporary job in order to devote more time to her social life. In the autumn she would be going to Oxford to study politics. 'I have not joined a party yet' she said, 'but I expect it will be the Socialists.'

On May 12, the public's attention turned to a private beach on the Devon coast where forty-one-year-old amateur jockey Lord Mildmay of Flete had disappeared after an early-morning swim. An intensive search for the bachelor peer was organised, involving estate staff, coast-guards, police and an aeroplane, without success.

On May 22, Princess Margaret was found dining with Captain Tom Egerton and others in a small restaurant in Jermyn Street. After dinner, the nineteen-year-old Princess created a stir by smoking a cigarette through a long ivory holder.

The following day, Aly Khan arrived for the Derby. He was found hobbling through the foyer of the Ritz on crutches, following a ski-ing accident. Already, rumours circulated that his marriage to Rita Hayworth was in trouble. 'My wife will follow' he said. 'She won't miss the Derby.'

On May 25, there was a dance at Londonderry House in honour of seventeen-year-old Lady Jane Vane-Tempest-Stewart, grand-daughter of the famous hostess Lady Londonderry. The great mansion had been leased to the Royal Aero Club since 1946 but the Londonderry family still had the use of its great ballroom on special occasions. 'We can't afford to have the sort of party my father would have given' said Lady Jane's father, the new Marquess. 'Nor would it be right in these days.' It was noted that the seventy-year-old Dowager Lady Londonderry did not travel from her home in Northern Ireland for the party.

On May 27, Rita Hayworth, hidden behind a fashionable bee-catcher veil, joined her husband at the Derby. Also present at Epsom that day was the rumbustious Elsa Maxwell who had introduced the couple two years earlier in the South of France.

Two weeks later, there was another fashionable gathering at Ascot. Among those present were the glamorous Lady Docker, in a two-tier lace dress, eighteen-year-old actress Elizabeth Taylor, now married to American hotelier Conrad Hilton, and beautiful widow Madame Susy Volterra. Mr. and Mrs. Winston Churchill's arrival at the racecourse was delayed when their car collided in Chiswick High Road with the police car escorting it.

On June 19, a party given by heiress Barbara Hutton in a floodlit garden adjoining the British Embassy in Paris sent ripples of excitement across Europe. Miss Hutton, now thirty-seven years old and married to Prince Igor Troubetzkoy, wore sapphire earrings and necklace and an orange sari embroidered in gold. Among her guests were the Duke and Duchess of Windsor, who were currently the object of renewed interest on account of the publication of the Duke's memoirs, for which it was said he had been paid over £300,000.

On June 21, it was reported that the Duke of Bedford had sold a bison from Woburn Abbey, weighing over 400 lb., to a London restaurant. Some of the animal would be served as steaks; other bits would be stewed.

On the night of June 24, a man broke into Marlborough House, home of Queen Mary, and attacked both the housekeeper, Mrs. Alice Knight, and the assistant housekeeper, Mrs. Winifred Ralph. Queen Mary's Comptroller, sixty-year-old Lord Claud Hamilton was woken up and organised a room-by-room search. On being arrested in the cellar, the intruder, a Ministry of Works gardener, asked if he would be hung for the offence. Eighty-three-year-old Queen Mary slept through the incident undisturbed.

On June 26, many Londoners were present at a party given by Lady Diana Cooper in Paris. Rustic decorations were provided by Cecil Beaton and the hostess, with a sprig of lilac round her head, received her guests in front of a vast red velvet curtain, surrounded by lilies.

On July 4, there was a huge charity dance at Blenheim Palace. 1,800 guests danced in the Long Library and women powdered their noses in the room in which Winston Churchill was born. The splendour of the occasion was tarnished when it was discovered that many guests had stubbed out their cigarettes on the valuable carpets. 'I consider what has happened is disgraceful' said the Duke of Marlborough.

On July 13, Princess Margaret was present at a dance given by Lady Baillie at her house in Chesterfield Street. The ballroom was banked with herbacious flowers and thirty-four-year-old Frank Sinatra, now appearing at the Palladium, gave a cabaret.

On July 25, Lord Brougham and Vaux, who had gambled away a fortune of £500,000 and was now in debt to the tune of £18,000, faced his creditors at Bristol. Among his assets, a few dozen poultry were mentioned. Rumours circulated that the peer had once bet £10,000 on the turn of a single card in Monte Carlo.

The following day was Bernard Shaw's ninety-fourth birthday. Ignoring a statement that all gifts would be rejected, actress Ellen Pollock sent the famous playwright a bison's foot converted into an ink-stand. Shaw wrote back saying that he had given this wobbly object to the local vicar for his bring-and-buy sale.

Early in August, attention turned to Clarence House, residence of Princess Elizabeth. On August 9, Sister Helen Rowe moved in and, on the 15th, in a room overlooking the Mall, the Princess gave birth to a baby girl, later christened Anne Elizabeth Alice Louise. A few minutes after the birth, a forty-one-gun salute was fired in Hyde Park and play was interrupted at the Oval by a loudspeaker announcement: 'Ladies and Gentlemen – we have a new baby Princess.'

The same day, a green and red parrot was found fluttering in the grounds of Marlborough House. A gardener who tried to catch it was bitten on the finger and the RSPCA and police were summoned. 'It is a friendly bird' said an RSPCA official, 'but so far it has not said a word.'

Six days later, Princess Margaret celebrated her twentieth birthday with a party out on the moors above Balmoral. The chef at the castle had prepared a cake covered in pink icing and adorned with twenty candles. Continental newspapers now predicted the imminent engagement of the Princess to the Earl of Dalkeith, son and heir to the wealthy Duke of Buccleuch.

At the end of August, a report came from Korea that Randolph Churchill, now working as a correspondent for the *Daily Telegraph*, had been wounded in an ambush. On being asked by the authorities if he was the son of Winston Churchill, he had replied: 'Well, I'm certainly not the son of Clement Attlee.'

On September 12, attention turned to the Luton and Dunstable Hospital where ninety-four-year-old Bernard Shaw was recovering from an operation for a fractured thigh. The great playwright, who had a fall in his garden, was described as a model patient but insisted on keeping to his vegetarian diet. Special cereal was brought in for him by his secretary.

On September 14, Osbert and Edith Sitwell left for a lucrative lecture tour of America. 'Oh yes, my goodness, the fees are high' said sixty-three-year-old Edith while packing at her London club. 'For one reading I will give on Lady Macbeth, I will be paid five hundred dollars.'

On September 18 it was revealed that the American government had purchased a 999-year lease of the West Side of Grosvenor Square. The buildings there would soon be demolished and in due course, a new Embassy erected. The Duke of Westminster had made a million pounds out of the deal.

At the same time, it was announced that the popular American Ambassador Lewis Douglas was retiring. 'Most of all, it is my friends I am going to miss' said his twenty-one-year-old daughter Sharman, a close friend of Princess Margaret. 'It is going to be strange leaving London. After all, I have been here four years.'

On October 4, much publicity surrounded Bernard Shaw's departure from hospital by ambulance. The dust-sheet normally used to cover Shaw's Rolls-Royce was made into a huge screen to prevent sightseers getting a glimpse of the aged writer as he was carried into his home on a stretcher. 'I don't think I shall ever write again' he told a reporter soon afterwards.

A dust sheet hides 94-year-old Bernard Shaw as he is carried into his home at Ayot St. Lawrence

On October 19, Lord Adam Gordon, secretary of Brooks's Club in St. James's Street, was fined £15 for an offence under the 1949 Eggs Order. It was stated that over 3,000 eggs had been sent to the club earlier in the year. Lord Adam had not realised that they were still a restricted product.

The following day, Lewis Douglas, retiring American Ambassador whose eye was still covered by a black patch following his fishing accident the previous year, was guest of honour at the Flyfishers' Club dinner at the Savoy Hotel where he was presented with a new collection of salmon flies. Fellow guests included the famous plastic surgeon Sir Harold Gillies, Admiral of the Fleet Lord Cunningham and the new Bishop of Willesden, Dr. Gerald Ellison. The only non-fisherman present was the Lord Chief Justice, Lord Goddard, who begged that the fact should be kept a secret.

Fourteen-year-old jockey Lester Piggott (right) with a colleague on the day he won his first race as a senior

On October 25, fourteen-year-old jockey Lester Piggott was hauled before the Jockey Club Stewards at Newmarket accused of injudicious riding and was suspended for the rest of the season. 'He is well-behaved and as as quiet as a mouse in the changing-room' said a fellow jockey. 'In the saddle he's a different lad.'

On October 26, the King opened the new air-conditioned chamber of the House of Commons. He was accompanied by Queen Mary, who leaned on the arm of twenty-year-old Princess Margaret. Mr. Ernest Marples, young Conservative MP for Wallasey, arrived for the ceremony on a bicycle.

At the end of the month, the Lord Lieutenant of Lancashire, Earl Peel, appeared in the dock at Liverpool Assizes accused of overspending on building work at his stately home, near Carnforth. 'It is a sad thing for a man in your position to stand where you stand' said Mr. Justice Lynskey, fining him £25,000.

Meanwhile, Bernard Shaw had sunk into a coma and a bulletin had been issued that his strength was slowly ebbing away. In the early hours of the morning on November 2, his grey-haired Scottish housekeeper put up a notice on the gates of his Hertfordshire home announcing his death. The playwright's old friend, Lady Astor, immediately took charge of the funeral and cremation arrangements and invited reporters into the house to view the body. Shaw's ashes were later mingled with those of his wife and scattered in a flowerbed where, it was said, they took on the appearance of slug poison.

On November 11, sixty-nine-year-old Pablo Picasso stepped off the boat-train at Victoria Station. The controversial artist, who was dressed in a thick herringbone tweed suit and pale-blue tie, had come to attend the World Peace Conference at Sheffield and to stay with his old friend, Mr. Roland Penrose.

On November 14, beautiful Sharman Douglas gave a going-away party in the candle-lit ballroom at the American Embassy. Princess Margaret, in a short blue taffeta dress, arrived after attending an official function in the East End and stayed till 4.00 am dancing the foxtrot, samba and Charleston with Lord Ogilvy, Lord Blandford, the Earl of Westmorland and the Hon. Peter Ward.

On November 26, the fifty-five-year-old Duke of Devonshire died suddenly at his house near Eastbourne. The new Duke flew back at once from Australia, where he had been studying farming methods, and was met at London Airport by his wife, youngest of the famous Mitford sisters. The couple drove off in a Rolls-Royce.

Meanwhile, Sir Laurence Olivier and his wife Vivien Leigh were slowly sailing home from California on a French cargo vessel. During the five-week voyage, the couple played shuffleboard and canasta and both read the complete works of Scott Fitzgerald. On December 18, they arrived in England and Miss Leigh stepped off the ship wearing a full-length mink coat.

The day before, Winston Churchill had departed for Morocco. On December 21, he was found dining with the Pasha of Marrakesh off whole roasted sheep and chickens stuffed with almonds, honey and lemons.

On Christmas Day, there was great excitement over the theft of the Stone of Scone from Westminster Abbey. This historic slab of granite had been taken from Scone Palace in Scotland some 600 years earlier and since then had lain beneath the Coronation Chair. A gigantic police operation was immediately mounted and for the first time in four centuries, the border between Scotland and England was closed. 'This senseless crime has clearly been carefully planned and carried out' said Dr. Don, the Dean of Westminster in a special broadcast on December 27. 'You can imagine my feelings when early on Christmas morning the Clerk of Works rushed into my bedroom and told me that the Coronation Stone was missing.' In Scotland, the Earl of Mansfield, owner of Scone Palace, expressed quite different sentiments. 'If the Scottish Stone of Destiny is ever brought to Scone Palace,' he said, 'I should be extremely reluctant to hand it over to the English authorities.'

1951

At the New Year's Eve dance at Broadmoor Prison, one of the institution's most distinguished inmates, Mr. Ronald True, collapsed and died. This wealthy ex-Air Force officer had been found guilty of murder in 1922 and been detained at the prison ever since. Rumours had often circulated that he was the son of a famous peeress by her first marriage.

On January 4, eighty-four-year-old millionaire meat king, Sir Edmund Vestey, asked for a cut in rates on a large, Italian-style home near Broadstairs. It was stated that the house, Thanet Court, required an indoor staff of six and at least five gardeners. Hearing that his application had been refused by the East Kent Valuation Panel, Sir Edmund sighed: 'The day of riches has gone.'

On January 28, oyster bar owner Captain Cunningham was attacked by armed robbers at his Mayfair home. After attempting to defend himself with a brass pestle, he was blindfolded, bound and gagged. It was reported that the Captain's dogs treated the incident as 'a bit of fun' and one of them even went as far as to bite his master.

Early in February, attention turned to the High Court where two brothers, Toby and Tom Fitzwilliam, laid rival claims to be heir presumptive to the Fitzwilliam earldom. 'I like them both and wish them both good luck' said the childless present Earl. 'The outcome of the petition does not affect me.' With the title went ownership of 365-room Wentworth Woodhouse, currently let to Yorkshire County Council as a training school for women PT instructors. The case was to drag on for several weeks at an estimated cost of £7 a minute. During the course of the hearing, Mr. Toby Fitzwilliam protected himself against the hard court benches by bringing armfuls of cushions into the court.

On February 15, Winston Churchill was found fidgeting on the front Opposition Bench at the House of Commons and searching for something in his pockets and elsewhere. Asked by Chancellor of the Exchequer, Hugh Gaitskell, what the matter was, he stood up and explained in a solemn voice that he was only looking for a jujube.

Meanwhile, the Foreign Secretary sixty-nine-year-old Mr. Bevin had been incapacitated by pneumonia. On February 18, he left his official residence in Carlton Gardens to convalesce in Eastbourne where it was stated he would pay out-of-season rates for his hotel suite.

On March 6, the great Ivor Novello died suddenly in the flat high above the Aldwych, which he had shared for several years with a close friend. 'He was a very wonderful bloke' said Miss Cicely Courtneidge, who was currently appearing in *Gay's the Word* at the Saville Theatre. Following his death, it was revealed that for many years the famous actor-manager had carefully dyed his hair black.

The next day, came reports from the South of France that Lady Diana Cooper's car had rolled into the sea while she was attending a cocktail party on board Mrs. Reginald Fellowes' yacht *Sister Anne*. 'I am certain that my car was pushed into the sea by Communists' she said. 'They hate my husband.'

On March 14, Judge Pilcher decreed that Mr. Toby Fitzwilliam had failed in his claim to be nominated heir presumptive to the Fitzwilliam Earldom. 'I am very glad it is all over' said his victorious brother Tom. 'I realise it is very bad luck on my brother, but the question had to be decided.'

On March 15, the late Bernard Shaw's Rolls-Royce Silver Wraith was sold by auction for £3,400. The purchaser was an elderly bearded stockbroker named Mr. Charles Goff. 'I have bought it because I want to use it' he said. It was recalled that on acquiring the car at the beginning of the war, Shaw had usually travelled in the front beside his chauffeur.

On March 22, the Duke of Argyll married Mrs. Margaret Sweeny, recently voted one of the best-dressed women in the world. The Earl of Carlisle acted as best man at Caxton Hall and a reception was held afterwards at the bride's home, 48 Upper Grosvenor Street, which was attended by the wealthy Lady Baillie, banker Henry Tiarks and other close friends. The following day, the new Duchess was piped into Iveraray Castle to the strains of 'The Campbells are coming'.

On April 11, the historic stone of Scone was found lying on the high altar of the ruined Abbey at Arbroath on the east coast of Scotland. A letter addressed to the King lay nearby. Mr. William Bishop, Custodian of the Fabric of Westminster Abbey, immediately hurried north to identify the ancient relic, which was soon on its way back to London in a shooting-brake escorted by no less than four police cars. 'I am very much relieved that the Stone of Scone is safe. More than that would be improper for me to say' said the gaunt Dean of Westminster, Dr. Don. Attorney-General Sir Hartley Shawcross later announced that no prosecutions would be brought in connexion with the theft of the famous stone.

On April 24, Lady Oakes, whose husband Sir Harry Oakes had been brutally murdered eight years earlier, arrived in England for a short holiday. It was noted that Australian-born Lady Oakes had been left £3,671,724 in her husband's will and been appointed sole executrix.

On May 3, eighty-four-year-old Queen Mary, who had now begun to make public appearances in a wheelchair, was present at the opening of the Festival of Britain.

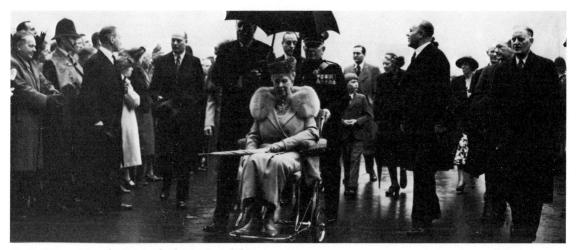

Queen Mary tours the Festival of Britain exhibition

On May 16, eighteen-year-old Edwina Wills, daughter of the tobacco millionaire Colonel Edward Wills, made her debut at a ball at the Hyde Park Hotel dressed in red satin shoes and a white dress. Music was provided by ex-Scots Guards Pipe Major James Robertson, who commented afterwards: 'They don't dress as well as they did before the war, they don't drink as much – but they dance better.' It was observed that no cigarettes were laid on at the party.

On May 30, the Derby was won by Arctic Prince owned by seventeen-stone Joe McGrath, a former IRA gunman, who had spent two years in British prisons at the end of the First World War. 'I was an officer in the revolutionary movement and I carried a gun. I'm proud of it but I saw the light' said Mr. McGrath, who after the race was summoned to the Queen's box.

On June 4, the Duke of Windsor arrived in London, this time staying with his friend Mrs. Margaret Biddle in Upper Brook Street. During the visit, he was visited by his sixty-seven-year-old barber, Mr. Charles Topper. 'The Duke looks wonderfully well. I have never seen him look better' said Mr. Topper, who fourteen years earlier had travelled to France to cut the ex-monarch's hair before his wedding at the Château de Candé.

Meanwhile, a colossal rumpus had erupted over the disappearance of two Foreign Office officials who were believed to have fled the country and be on their way to Moscow 'for idealistic purposes'. On June 7 they were identified as Mr. Donald Maclean, son of the former leader of the Liberal Party, and Old Etonian Mr. Guy Burgess. 'Everything is being done to find the missing men by the police forces of Western Europe' said a Foreign Office spokesman. 'Enquiries are also being made in America.' In the middle of the commotion, Maclean's wife, Melinda, gave birth to a baby girl at the London Hospital, Whitechapel. 'I'm told she is a fine baby' said her mother-in-law, Lady Maclean.

A few days later, the London social scene was enriched by the presence of multi-millionairess Barbara Hutton, who had not been seen in England since before the war. On June 25, the heiress, noted for her expressive dark eyebrows, was found among spectators at Wimbledon where her old friend German tennis star Baron Gottfried von Cramm was playing. She dined with him that night and was at Wimbledon again the next day. It was revealed that the previous week, Barbara had sold £6,000,000-worth of shares in the British Woolworth company.

On July 2, high society flocked to Syon, Thames-side home of the Duke of Northumberland, for a coming-out dance for seventeen-year-old Lady Mary Baillie-Hamilton, daughter of the Earl of Haddington. 'This is all terribly exciting' said Lady Mary, 'but really, it's the house that makes it seem grander than it actually is.' Among the 600 people present were the Queen, Princess Elizabeth and Princess Margaret along with the Dukes of Northumberland, Marlborough, Somerset and Buccleuch. Actor David Niven was found dancing with the Duchess of Kent. Scotland Yard detectives moved among the guests.

By the middle of July, 30,000 flowers and shrubs had been planted in the newly-planned gardens of Eaton Square. Gravel paths had been relaid and benches made of timber from the Duke of Westminster's Cheshire estate had been installed. It was noted that many of the houses in the Square had now been converted into flats.

On August 2, there was a dance at Broadlands, Hampshire in honour of twenty-two-year-old Lady Pamela Mountbatten. Blue-and-white road-signs guided guests to the house and footmen in dark-blue livery were in attendance in the white-and-gold ballroom. Among those present were Princess Elizabeth, Noel Coward, now casting his new play *Relative Values*, nineteen-year-old Elizabeth Taylor and Sir Malcolm Sargent. Princess Margaret arrived late after Goodwood Races, in a party which included the Hon. Peter Ward and Billy Wallace.

The next big event on the social calendar was Princess Margaret's own coming-of-age party on August 21. It was held at Balmoral and most of her regular escorts were present. Twenty-four-year-old Billy Wallace, in a brown check suit, arrived from London on the same train as the Princess's birthday cake, an eighteen-inch high creation inscribed with her coat-of-arms. After a formal dinner at the Castle that night, the Princess left by grey shooting-brake for an impromptu dance at Birkhall, a nearby castle also owned by the Royal Family. Group-Captain Peter Townsend remained behind at Balmoral with the King.

These festivities were eclipsed a few days later, on September 3, by a spectacular masked ball given by Old Etonian Charles de Beistegui at the Palazzo Labia in Venice. 'As you know, I have been to many parties starting in Queen Victoria's days' said the seventy-four-year-old Aga Khan, 'but I am certain that this was the best one of them all.' Mrs. Winston Churchill was in a black lace gown and a three-cornered hat, Barbara Hutton in a black domino mask and white wig, and Oliver Messel in a red velvet uniform. Two incidents occurred during the party. As she arrived, Lady Diana Cooper, in a pearl-festooned silver concoction, had some water thrown at her. Later, a long red ostrich-feather head-dress worn by Mr. John Russell, First Secretary at the British Embassy in Rome, caught fire as he helped himself to foie gras.

On September 6, forty-nine-year-old Tallulah Bankhead arrived after an absence of sixteen years. 'I suppose most of my old friends will be in wheelchairs or on crutches' she declared. Moving into a three-room suite at the Ritz Hotel, she added: 'I'm afraid I may put on weight in England. I am told most of the foods you have available are starchy.'

On September 11, it was revealed that the Dowager Marchioness of Headfort, former Gaiety Girl Rosie Boote, had started serving 'TV dinners' at her home in St. John's Wood, to enable her friends to watch television while dining.

Meanwhile, deep concern had been expressed about the health of the King, who was now suffering from a respiratory disease. On September 22, five doctors spent the entire day at Buckingham Palace and it was noted that six cylinders of oxygen had been delivered. One of the King's last actions before being operated upon the following day was to instruct the Master of the Household to send three brace of grouse to his brother, the Duke of Windsor, who was currently in London.

On September 25, the surgeon in charge of the operation, Mr. C. Price Thomas, was involved in a car-crash. Just ten yards outside the gates of Buckingham Palace, his Rolls-Royce collided with a baby blue Austin.

On October 2, seventy-six-year-old Conservative Leader Winston Churchill left Euston Station for Liverpool to begin his election campaign. He carried a cigar, gloves and a walking-stick.

On October 5, forty-seven-year-old bachelor Cecil Beaton, dressed in a green beret, drove to Southampton to collect his friend Greta Garbo off an incoming French liner, the *Liberté*. The couple drove back to Beaton's new Wiltshire home, Reddish House, Broadchalke, where the Hollywood star settled in for a short stay.

On October 17, the centrepiece at the opening of the Motor Show at Earl's Court was a gold Daimler bearing the initials of Lady Docker. The upholstery was made of handwoven gold brocade and every fitting, inside and outside, was gold plated. 'The car is without price,' said the designer Mr. Rivers. 'Sir Bernard wanted the British public and overseas visitors to see something really choice.' Lady Docker was soon to be seen sailing round London in this motor-car with her chauffeur, Prattley, at the wheel.

On October 19, Winston Churchill interrupted his electioneering to attend the wedding of twenty-five-year-old Marquess of Blandford and twenty-one-year-old Miss Susan Hornby. Billy Wallace was best man at the ceremony at St. Margaret's Westminster and over 1,000 guests, including Princess Margaret and Queen Mary, attended the reception at the Goldsmiths' Hall. It was disclosed that the bridegroom had now received a share of his father's fortune. 'I am fifty-five' said the Duke of Marlborough. 'This is the time when one should begin to hand over one's property to one's sons.'

Polling took place on October 25. That night, Lord Camrose gave a great election night party at the Savoy Hotel which was attended by Cecil Beaton and Greta Garbo, Noel Coward, Somerset Maugham, Sharman Douglas and other celebrities. During the course of the evening, the news began to filter through that the electorate had voted for the prosperity promised by the Conservatives.

THE FIFTIES–EARLY SIXTIES
1951–1964

Although rationing continued until 1954, this era has an unmistakable air of affluence. Backed by expense accounts and an increasingly buoyant money market, stockbrokers, bankers and advertising men flourished. Clubland came back into its own and scores of new restaurants opened. The fabulous Lady Docker flaunted her newly-acquired wealth. At long last, men became conscious of the fashion world. In the new social fluidity, property developers and oil magnates like Charles Clore and Paul Getty emerged as leading socialites, purchased country estates and entertained Royalty at their much-publicised parties. Model girls like Bronwen Pugh and Fiona Campbell-Walter married aristocrats and Old Etonians like Jimmy Goldsmith and Dominic Elwes eloped with heiresses. Sir Winston Churchill showed his approval of the new regime by making friends, in the winter of his life, with the phenomenally wealthy shipping magnate Aristotle Socrates Onassis. In the course of these thirteen years, the largely aristocratic Margaret Set was replaced as the leading social group by the more bohemian Chelsea Set and in 1960, Princess Margaret, the leading social figure of the era, confirmed the transition of power when she married photographer Antony Armstrong-Jones. All classes shared an illusion of prosperity. Soon after becoming Prime Minister, Harold Macmillan removed hire purchase restrictions and assured the working classes that they had 'never had it so good'. Aristocrats like the new Duke of Bedford cashed in on the new wealth. Woburn Abbey, which clocked up 181,000 visitors during its first season, was one of many stately homes opened for the first time during this period. Not until the scandal-packed early Sixties and the exposure of pin-striped figures such as Mr. Kim Philby, did confidence begin to wane and it became no longer possible for the Englishman to maintain his Stiff Upper Lip.

1951

A few days after the General Election, seventy-six-year-old Winston Churchill returned to 10 Downing Street after an absence of six years. He arrived with the flag of the Cinque Ports fluttering from the bonnet of his motor-car and was cheered by a crowd of 500. His bed from 28 Hyde Park Gate moved in with him.

On October 29, Noel Coward made his cabaret début at the Café de Paris before a glittering audience, which included Princess Margaret, the Duchess of Kent and Lucian Freud, artist grandson of the famous Austrian psychoanalyst. It was said that Coward performed without a hint of nervousness.

On November 3, Princess Margaret was to be found weekending at Cliveden with twenty-three-year-old Angus Ogilvy, thirty-nine-year-old William Douglas-Home and other friends. This was said to be the first house-party for young people that Lady Astor had given since the war.

A week later, Cliveden was in the news again when thieves broke in while Lord and Lady Astor were having dinner and stole the silver tops from five toilet bottles on Lady Astor's dressing-table.

On November 19, film star Greta Garbo flew from Northolt to Paris, accompanied by her friend Cecil Beaton, who wore drainpipe trousers and spats. In Paris, the couple stayed at the Crillon Hotel and visited shops, restaurants, theatres and museums. One of the highlights of their visit was a party given by Duff and Lady Diana Cooper at their house at Chantilly. It was reported that Lady Diana provided a hot supper of curry, hardboiled eggs and rice and John Julius Cooper, now an undergraduate, entertained the guests on his guitar.

On November 30, the King left Buckingham Palace for the first time since his operation ten weeks earlier. Accompanied by the Queen, he was driven to the Royal Lodge, Windsor Park where a suite of downstairs rooms had been prepared for his use.

On December 1, Surrealist painter Salvador Dali arrived in England for an exhibition of his works at the Lefevre Gallery. At a Press conference, the forty-seven-year-old artist wore a blue pin-striped suit and carried a thin walking-stick made of rhinoceros horn. 'I have a passion about rhinoceroses' he said. 'They are symbols of evil.'

On December 6, the Earl of Rosebery issued a dramatic statement from his Scottish seat, Dalmeny House, near Edinburgh, to the effect that one of his horses had been doped. He offered £1,000 reward for information leading to the identification of the culprit. 'There are several reasons why I cannot disclose the name of the horse' he said.

The following day, the Prime Minister Winston Churchill paid one of his annual visits to Harrow School. After listening to a rendering of his favourite school songs, he told the assembled pupils, 'The term has begun again. The arithmetic and also the subtraction are very hard indeed'.

On December 19, the 83,000-ton liner *Queen Elizabeth* arrived at Southampton after passing through the worst Atlantic storms known since the war. Passengers had been thrown out of their bunks and many wrists had been sprained and ankles twisted. 'Surprisingly, there was very little sea sickness' said a ship's medical officer.

On December 29, Winston Churchill's departure for America on board the *Queen Mary* was delayed by thirty-six hours owing to an anchor being jammed in the bows of the vessel. The Prime Minister remained on board during the delay, giving a dinner party in his suite to which Lord Mountbatten and the new Foreign Secretary Anthony Eden were invited. After dinner, sixteen choirboys from Winchester Cathedral came on the ship to sing carols and a three-minute film showing Churchill feeding robins at Chartwell was screened.

Greta Garbo at the Wiltshire home of her friend Cecil Beaton

1952

At the New Year's Eve party given by Princess Elizabeth's Private Secretary, Lieutenant-Colonel Martin Charteris, eleven fur-coats were stolen, altogether worth an estimated £4,000 or £5,000. Among guests who had been robbed were Miss Clarissa Churchill, niece of the Prime Minister, and Mrs. G. Bonsack, wife of an interior-decorator. 'We were all dancing to Scottish reels and I suppose a terrible din was going on' said Mrs. Charteris. 'We didn't hear a thing.'

On January 4, Princess Margaret was the centre of interest at the Berwickshire Hunt Ball. During the evening, her dance-partners included the Earl of Dalkeith, son of the Duke of Buccleuch, and the Rev. Simon Phipps, an ex-Guards officer who had become a curate in the Church of England. Also there, were the Earl and Countess of Home, who had travelled along snowy roads to join in the fun.

On January 15, it was announced that the pacifist Duke of Bedford had purchased the Great Maytham estate in Kent for more than £200,000. The acquisition, which suggested that the Russell family's financial resources were unlimited, created a great thrill.

On January 28, the Prime Minister Winston Churchill returned to England on board the *Queen Elizabeth*. Before disembarking, he lunched in his suite off oysters, entrecôte steak, asparagus in Hollandaise sauce, ice-cream and meringues.

On January 31, the King appeared on the roof of London Airport to wave goodbye to Princess Elizabeth and Prince Philip, who were off on a Commonwealth tour. The King was hatless and scarfless and rumoured to be going duck-shooting in the next few days.

One week later, the nation was deeply shocked by the King's sudden death. At 7.15 am on February 6, he was found dead in his bed at Sandringham by an under-valet named MacDonald. Also staying at the house were the Queen, Princess Margaret, Prince Charles and Princess Anne. On his last day on earth, the King had shot nine hares and a pigeon.

Later that day, the Duke of Norfolk drove from Arundel Castle to London to take charge of the funeral arrangements and the new twenty-five-year-old Queen began her flight home from Africa. It was said that at the moment of her father's death, she had been sitting in a tree watching rhinoceroses gather at a water-hole.

At the funeral on February 15, the Duke of Windsor wore the same uniform he had worn at King George V's funeral in 1936. The outfit, that of an Admiral of the Fleet, had been stored in London for the past fifteen years. The young Duke of Kent wore his father's morning suit, which was several sizes too large for him.

Returning from the service at St. George's Chapel, Windsor, the Marchioness of Dufferin and Ava and her daughter, Lady Caroline Blackwood, were involved in a car accident. Lady Dufferin had to go into the London Clinic for treatment while her daughter escaped with a black eye.

On February 19, nineteen-year-old film star Elizabeth Taylor flew into London to get married to actor Michael Wilding, twenty years her senior. A thousand stampeding, screaming fans gathered outside Caxton Hall to wish her well. 'This wedding was supposed to be entirely private' said an MGM publicity man.

On February 29, Nubar Gulbenkian, resplendent in a full-length purple overcoat, left London to visit his multi-millionaire father in Lisbon. Gulbenkian and his valet were the only passengers on a specially chartered forty-seat BOAC aircraft. Asked to explain the purpose of the trip, Gulbenkian produced a lemon from his pocket and said 'There is your answer.'

Meanwhile, it was rumoured that nineteen-year-old tobacco heiress Edwina Wills and twenty-five-year-old Lord Savernake, currently on holiday in the South of France, were on the point of marrying. It was said that Edwina's father, Colonel Edward Wills, disapproved of the match and the couple were seeking special permission from the French authorities to go ahead with their wedding. On March 16, the Colonel withdrew his objections after a talk with Lord Savernake's father, the Earl of Cardigan, and the marriage took place the next day in Menton.

On March 24, forty-three-year-old Commander Ian Fleming married Lady Rothermere in Jamaica, with Noel Coward and his secretary Cole Lesley acting as witnesses. After the ceremony, Commander Fleming flew

Lord Noel-Buxton attempts to ford the River Thames near Westminster Bridge

to New York and then to London carrying the rough manuscript of his first book, provisionally entitled *Casino Royale* whose hero was named James Bond.

On March 25, thirty-five-year-old Lord Noel-Buxton attempted to walk across the Thames at Westminster. Dressed in corduroy trousers and armed with a rough ash rod, the young peer wanted to prove that a ford had existed on this spot in Roman times. Watched by police boats, a Port of London Authority launch and the Speaker of the House of Commons, he waded into the river but was soon out of his depth and the walk turned into a swim. 'I am afraid there was much more water than I expected' he said. 'It must be all that rain up in the Cotswolds.'

At the beginning of April, fashionable playwright Terence Rattigan moved into a centrally heated, penthouse flat at 29 Eaton Square and gossip columnists declared that Belgravia had now become a more exclusive place to live than Mayfair. Other noteworthy residents of Eaton Square included Robert Boothby MP, Princess Joan Aly Khan and Noel Coward's mother.

On April 23, the Queen, Prince Philip and Princess Margaret travelled to Badminton in Gloucestershire for the Olympic Horse Trials. For the next three days, the Royal party, dressed in headscarves, cloth-caps and berets, bumped around the Duke of Beaufort's estate in farm-cars, watching events from specially refurbished wagons.

On May 7, 245 débutantes in white dresses attended Queen Charlotte's Birthday Ball at Grosvenor House. During the course of the evening, three firework crackers were found underneath the ceremonial cake, with a twelve-minute fuse attached, designed to explode as the Duchess of Roxburghe cut the cake. Fortunately, the fireworks were discovered before the cake was wheeled forward.

On May 15, the buoyant General Eisenhower, soon to stand for the American Presidency, flew into London in battle-dress uniform. That day, he lunched at Buckingham Palace, spent thirty-five minutes with Queen Mary and dined at 10 Downing Street, where the meal ended with Pudding Diplomatique.

On May 28, the Derby was won by the Aga Khan's Tulyar. The Aga Khan learned of his fifth Derby win on the wireless at his villa near Cannes. In the House of Commons that afternoon, Winston Churchill finished a statement on the war in Korea to quickly turn back from the Front Bench and ask: 'Who won?'

On June 6, a dance at Mereworth Castle in Kent, given by Mrs. Leo d'Erlanger for her daughter Tess, was pronounced to be the Party of the Year. Millionaire Charles de Beistegui, who had given a spectacular ball in Venice the previous year, whispered to Lady Diana Cooper, 'This is the best party since mine.' The dome and marble terraces of the Palladian-style house were floodlit and guests included such figures as Cecil Beaton, the Marchioness of Dufferin and Ava and twenty-six-year-old Vere Harmsworth, only son of Lord Rothermere.

Four days later, a ball at the Spanish Embassy in honour of eighteen-year-old Lady Caroline Child-Villiers, daughter of the Earl of Jersey, also claimed attention. Princess Margaret, in a black tulle stole, came on from a dinner at the Embassy Club to dance with Billy Wallace and Mark Bonham Carter. Another late arrival was twenty-year-old film star Elizabeth Taylor, accompanied by her new husband Michael Wilding.

On June 17, the young Queen was warmly welcomed when she drove down the course at Ascot for the first time in her reign. The twenty-six-year-old monarch, who wore a dress of lilac-coloured silk, was accompanied in her open landau by the Prince Philip and the Duke of Beaufort, Master of the Horse. A few days later, Prince Philip was struck down by jaundice and confined to his room at Buckingham Palace.

On June 24, the Kensington home of designer Oliver Messel was filled with wild roses and ivy for another remarkable party. Margot Fonteyn, Noel Coward, Terence Rattigan and others ate food specially flown from Denmark off tablecloths sewn out of ivy leaves.

On July 1, Nubar Gulbenkian's seventy-seven-year-old mother died in Paris. For the next twelve months, Nubar and his wife wore black and refrained from eating in any public place. To complete the picture, Gulbenkian had his dark bronze car, the bonnet of which was modelled on the Parthenon, painted black and its light fawn upholstery changed to a more sombre colour.

On July 2, there was great excitement over the marriage at Caxton Hall of the eighty-nine-year-old Marquess of Winchester and Miss Bapsy Pavry, forty-nine-year-old daughter of a Parsee high priest. It was recalled that twenty-five years earlier, the Marquess had been the chairman of Clarence Hatry's ill-fated group of companies.

On July 5, news broke of the engagement of twenty-two-year-old John Julius Cooper and Anne Clifford, daughter of a former Governor of Trinidad. The couple were currently cruising about the Mediterranean on Mr. Loel Guinness's yacht, with John Julius's parents. On the same day Duff Cooper's peerage was gazetted with the title Viscount Norwich.

Meanwhile, a storm had blown up over the unpatriotic speeches that Dr. Hewlett Johnson, Dean of

The 89-year-old Marquess of Winchester, former chairman of the Hatry group of companies, and his beautiful Parsee bride Miss Bapsy Pavry

Canterbury, was making during his tour of Communist countries. In the House of Commons on July 14, Conservative MP Miss Irene Ward asked the Attorney-General if 'this wicked and irresponsible old man' would be prosecuted for treason. Labour MP Mr. Emrys Hughes jumped to his feet and asked: 'In the event of this witch hunt being successful, will the Dean be hung at Tynemouth or Canterbury?'

On July 28, there was a gathering at 28 The Boltons, newly acquired home of Mr. and Mrs. Douglas Fairbanks, Jr., to celebrate the engagement of Princess Margaret's friend, Lord Ogilvy, and American heiress Miss Virginia Ryan. The Duchess of Kent, in a fashionable black eye-veil, and other guests were fed with cold salmon, curried chicken and Boston baked-beans.

On August 4, attention turned to the South of France where Sir Jack Drummond and his wife and daughter had been found murdered. Sir Jack, war-time adviser to the Ministry of Food, had been taking his family on a camping holiday in their grey Hillman Minx. Later, a powerfully built farmer named Gaston Dominici confessed to this mysterious and apparently motiveless crime, which caused many people to cancel their holidays in France.

Back in England, another friend of Princess Margaret, the Earl of Dalkeith, announced his engagement. His fiancée was Miss Jane McNeill, who had worked for a time as a fashion model. 'I first met Miss McNeill four years ago at a friend's house on the Border' said the Earl, heir to the wealthy Duke of Buccleuch.

On August 14, Foreign Secretary Anthony Eden married thirty-two-year-old Clarissa Churchill, niece of the Prime Minister. As the cheers died away and the couple left for a honeymoon in Portugal, the twice-married Mr. Eden, who had divorced his first wife two years earlier, was savagely criticised in the *Church Times*. 'It is now apparently to be accepted as a matter of course that those who occupy the highest positions in political and public life may break the Church's law without embarrassment or reproach.'

At the end of August, the Duke and Duchess of Leinster returned home after a caravan trip to the music festival at Bayreuth. 'With only £25 each in foreign currency, it seemed the only way' said the sixty-year-old Duke.

On September 3, a glamorous and glittering audience greeted the opening of the Sadlers Wells ballet season at Covent Garden. The newly married Mrs. Anthony Eden was in the Royal Box in a party given by Lord Waverley. In an adjoining box were Mr. Harold Macmillan, Minister of Housing, and Mr. R. A. Butler, Chancellor of the Exchequer. Mr. Anthony Eden was absent, as he was giving an all-male dinner-party that night in honour of the Egyptian Ambassador.

On September 12, Elizabeth Forbes-Sempill of Brux Lodge, Aberdeenshire, daughter of the 18th Baron Sempill, issued a formal statement to the effect that she had changed her sex. 'The facts are as stated' she told a reporter. 'I am not prepared to say anything further.' As a result of this move, said to be the first case of its kind, Miss Forbes-Sempill had become heir presumptive to the Forbes of Craigievar baronetcy.

On September 23, Charlie Chaplin arrived in England with his twenty-seven-year-old wife Oona and their large family. It was the film star's first visit to England for twenty-one years. Reaching the Savoy Hotel, where three suites had been booked for his party, Chaplin told reporters, 'For the next few days, I want to soak myself in London.'

Two days later, Harrow School reassembled for the autumn term. Among new boys was thirteen-year-old Ernest Henry Child Simpson, whose much-married father, Ernest Simpson, was now living quietly in a three-storey house in Upper Phillimore Gardens and still working for his family's shipping firm.

On September 30, seventy-three-year-old Lord Astor died at Cliveden. His widow, Nancy, soon handed over the Thames-side mansion to her son Bill and moved into a new house of her own, 35 Hill Street, Mayfair.

Early in October, a new figure was noticed in Fleet Street circles. He was a fifty-eight-year-old Canadian named Roy Thomson, who wore pebble-glass spectacles, drank only in moderation, and was rumoured to be interested in purchasing a British daily newspaper.

On October 9, the thirty-one-year-old Countess of Derby was watching television in the smoking-room at Knowsley Hall, Lancashire, when a young footman plunged into the room and shot at her with a sten gun. She was only wounded but the butler and under-butler who attempted to grapple with the footman were both shot dead. In court later, the footman stressed that Lord and Lady Derby had always shown him every kindness and he was found to be suffering from 'gross hysteria'.

On October 17, celebrities gathered at the Odeon Cinema, Leicester Square for the première of Charlie Chaplin's film *Limelight*. A rumour circulated that Chaplin had wept during the Press showing of the film earlier in the day. After the show, Princess Margaret gave an informal supper-party at Buckingham Palace, where her guests included the Earl of Westmoreland, the Master of Elphinstone and Lord Plunket.

At the end of the month, it was revealed that the Duke and Duchess of Windsor had acquired an old mill known as the Moulin de la Tuilerie, within easy reach of Paris. This was the couple's first home of their own. With the assistance of a well-known gardener named Mr. Russell Page, the Duke set about creating an English garden with herbaceous borders and a rockery.

On November 4, the radiant young Queen opened Parliament for the first time in her reign. Princess Margaret attended the ceremony with her aunt, the Princess Royal, who was said to be wearing no make-up of any kind. Among those attending the Queen was the Duke of Beaufort, in tightly fitting kid trousers and shiny black boots.

A few days later, forty-nine-year-old Earl Beauchamp announced that he was selling 13 Belgrave Square, at which his parents had given many spectacular parties before the war. The mansion had been occupied until recently by the North Atlantic Treaty Organisation and Lord Beauchamp had been living in converted stables at the back of the house.

On the night of November 28, thieves broke into Mereworth Castle, Kent by means of an underground tunnel and made off with snuff boxes, wristwatches and eight bottles of whisky. 'They spent some time roaming through the Castle' said the present inhabitant, Mr. Michael Tree. 'They made themselves at home and had a meal.'

On November 29, seventy-three-year-old Sir Thomas Beecham struck his head on the roof of his taxi on arrival at Broadcasting House. He felt no immediate ill effects, but a few days later he was suddenly overcome by delayed concussion and had to go to bed.

On December 9, it was announced that the Marquess of Bath was preparing his family's state coach for use at the next year's Coronation. A Birmingham brewery had offered the loan of some horses and ex-jockey Michael Beary had offered his services as an outrider or postilion. 'I often rode with a coach as a boy in Ireland' he explained.

On December 15, two veteran peers were married in London. Eighty-year-old philosopher Earl Russell married Miss Edith Finch and eighty-two-year-old Marquess of Bristol married Señora de Zulueta. It was Russell's fourth marriage and Bristol's second.

On December 19, thirty-eight-year-old Group-Captain Peter Townsend, the former Battle of Britain pilot who had served the Royal Family since the early years of the war, was granted a decree nisi in the Divorce Court.

Mr. and Mrs. Winston Churchill spent Christmas quietly at Chequers. The Prime Minister's pet poodle, Rufus, and his tropical fish were moved to his official country residence from Chartwell, which had been closed for the winter. On December 30, the Churchills sailed for America to see the new President, General Eisenhower. Among the couple's luggage on board the *Queen Mary* were four cases of champagne.

1953

Six thousand people celebrated the arrival of the New Elizabethan Age at the Chelsea Arts New Year's Eve Ball at the Royal Albert Hall. Among those waltzing together around a mock medieval tower were the thirty-three-year-old Duke of Rutland and the beautiful young model Fiona Campbell-Walter.

Over in New York on January 5, socialites gathered for The Duchess of Windsor Ball organised by Miss Elsa Maxwell at the Waldorf Astoria. The Duke and Duchess of Windsor gave a demonstration of the polka and the Duchess, with little velvet bows in her hair, took part in a fashion tableau arranged by Mr. Cecil Beaton. During the evening, a rift took place between Miss Maxwell and the Duchess, which was to obsess gossip columnists for many months.

On January 10, the Earl of Dalkeith, whose name had frequently been romantically linked with that of Princess Margaret, was married to Miss Jane McNeill at St. Giles Cathedral, Edinburgh. Princess Margaret, accompanied by the Queen and Prince Philip, arrived by overnight train from Sandringham for the service.

The same day, Lord Hawke, father of six daughters, announced that he had banned television from his Sussex home. After a fortnight's trial, he had returned his set to the local dealer. 'Television is a dreadful habit' he said. 'It amuses people when they should amuse themselves. I could not get my daughters away from that set. It was corrupting their education.'

On January 29, the Prime Minister Winston Churchill arrived at Southampton after a month in America. Carrying a nine-inch Jamaican cigar, he walked to a special Pullman car attached to the boat-train. 'I have had a change rather than a rest but I think I have come back better for it' he said.

On January 31, Sir Bernard Docker was charged with conspiring with the crew of his yacht *Shemara* to defeat the currency regulations. 'I will take the rap for anything my husband is supposed to have done' announced Lady Docker. 'He is the most perfect husband any woman could possibly have and I think I am the luckiest woman in the world.'

On February 2, it was announced that fifteen-year-old Lord Elveden, heir to many of the Guinness millions, had sustained an eye injury on the playing fields at Eton and would spend the next few weeks in a nursing home. It was noted that the young Lord had recently received a life-interest in Elveden Hall, where the bathrooms were said to have solid silver fittings.

On February 9, Queen Mary, now tired and ill and in her eighty-sixth year, was driven from Marlborough House to inspect the Coronation stands being erected in the Mall.

Two days later, the new American Ambassador Winthrop Aldrich, former chairman of the Chase Manhattan bank and reputed to be the world's richest Ambassador, arrived in England and declared that he was looking forward to the Coronation. 'I have all the right clothes in my baggage' he said, 'but there are no knee breeches.'

On February 14, fifty-seven-year-old Nubar Gulbenkian appeared in a new hat made of Canadian otter skin with big ear-flaps and a silk lining. 'I feel the cold especially about the ears' the millionaire explained. 'And this hat is excellent for driving.'

On February 25, Sir Bernard Docker faced the magistrate at Bow Street and was charged with conspiring to infringe currency regulations during three trips to the Mediterranean on board his 860-ton yacht *Shemara*. Sir Bernard vigorously denied the charge and gave evidence of big gambling wins in the Casino at Cannes. Two days later, he was fined £50 for a trivial infringement of the law. 'I am very happy' said Lady Docker who had sat with her husband throughout the hearing. 'I feel we have been virtually vindicated.'

On March 5, the coming-of-age of Mr. Jocelyn Stevens was celebrated with a dance at the home of his uncle, Mr. Edward Hulton, 42 Hyde Park Gate. Mr. Stevens was in white tie and tails and one of the reception rooms was rigged up like a saloon bar with posters advertising beer, brewers' ash-trays and dart-boards.

On March 9, attention turned to the Ritz Hotel where a certain Baron Pierre de Laitre had been found hanged in his room. Nearby lay the body of the Baron's English girlfriend with her throat cut. It was said that this ghastly occurrence did not disturb the peace and elegance of the hotel.

Lady Docker drives away from Bow Street magistrates' court after hearing evidence against her husband under the Exchange Control Act

Meanwhile, Marshal Tito of Yugoslavia was steaming towards England on board a Yugoslavian ship named *The Caleb*. He arrived on March 16 and was greeted at Westminster Pier by Prince Philip, Winston Churchill and Anthony Eden. During his brief stay in England, the Communist leader acquired two English setters priced at over £50 each from a Mayfair dog-kennel. 'He wants them for shooting' said the kennel's owner. 'He may also use them for breeding.'

On March 24, it was announced that Queen Mary's strength was ebbing away. She died later that day after visits from the Archbishop of Canterbury, Dr. Fisher, and many members of the Royal Family. A week later, a special train from Paddington took mourners to her funeral at Windsor. The Minister of Education, Miss Florence Horsbrugh, travelled by car and was injured in a collision, breaking her nose and hurting her thumb.

On April 3, Lady Docker's new metallic blue Daimler, upholstered in lizard skin, was flown to the South of France in a specially chartered Bristol freighter. Sir Bernard and Lady Docker followed the next day and that night were found installed at the casino in Cannes.

On April 15, Aly Khan and a new friend, actress Gene Tierney, were found in the audience at the Ambassadors Theatre where Agatha Christie's play *The Mousetrap*, starring Richard Attenborough, was now in its second year. The couple left the theatre a few minutes before the final curtain. Miss Tierney dashed to a waiting Rolls-Royce while Aly lingered to talk to reporters about his Derby hopes.

On April 24, the Queen hurried away from the Badminton Horse Trials to invest Winston Churchill as a Knight of the Garter. After the ceremony in the Green Drawing-Room at Windsor Castle, Sir Winston and Lady Churchill stayed on to watch television with the twenty-seven-year-old monarch.

On May 1, a Bachelors' Ball, held at the Hyde Park Hotel, was attended by eighty-four of London's most eligible bachelors. Twenty-nine-year-old Lord Foley explained his bachelor state by asserting that he was in love with the eighty-eight notes of the piano while twenty-three-year-old Lord Carnegie declared: 'I prefer cars to women. You don't get caught on the sequins.'

On May 5, sixty-one-year-old Major Christopher Draper created a sensation by flying a light Auster aeroplane under ten London bridges. Twenty-two years earlier, Draper had flown a plane under Tower Bridge, earning himself the nickname 'the Mad Major'.

On May 12, Mr. Norman Hartnell, who had been working overtime on Coronation clothes, was ordered to take a few days rest by his doctors. At first, a duodenal ulcer was feared; now it was decided that the Queen's dressmaker was simply run down.

In the middle of May, it was announced that the Cambridge undergraduate magazine *Granta* had been temporarily banned by the university authorities following the publication of a mildly blasphemous poem. The magazine's twenty-two-year-old editor, Mark Boxer, had been rusticated until the end of the year.

On May 20, the Queen, Princess Margaret and the Queen Mother were present at a coming-out dance for Miss Elizabeth Ward at Hutchinson House in St. James's. Soon after the Queen had left, the Duchess of Kent removed her tiara and handed it to the band-leader Tommy Kinsman, complaining that it was far too heavy. Kinsman placed the tiara on the piano while the Duchess danced with her old friend Chips Channon.

On May 30, the Queen's Coronation gown was delivered to Buckingham Palace. 'We delivered the gown in our own van' said Norman Hartnell. 'I followed in a taxicab just to keep an eye on it.'

On June 1, on the eve of the Coronation, £30,000 worth of jewellery was stolen from the Duke and Duchess of Sutherland's house in Wilton Crescent. Detectives were still making enquiries the following morning when the Duke and Duchess left for the Abbey.

As in 1937, a special Coronation Day Underground train transported assorted peers and MPs to Westminster from High Street Kensington. In the annexe to the Abbey, Viscount Montgomery, in the heavy robes of the Garter, was found reading *The Times*'s account of the conquest of Everest.

Among the hundreds of beautiful peeresses present was the Duchess of Argyll, in robes of red velvet and ermine, specially made by Victor Stiebel. Like many others, the Duchess sustained herself by chewing malted milk tablets during the long ceremony.

That night, the Savoy Hotel staged an elaborate ball with decorations by Cecil Beaton at which 3,000 bottles of champagne were drunk. The Prime Minister Sir Winston Churchill arrived on the arm of his friend, the Pasha of Marrakesh, and was greeted with a roar of applause.

Three days later, Foreign Secretary Anthony Eden flew to the United States for a third bladder operation. Sir Winston and Lady Churchill saw him off in a Royal Canadian Air Force plane.

On June 22, fashionable playwright Terence Rattigan and other socialites were among spectators at the Old Bailey trial of John Halliday Christie, who was thought to have been responsible for the deaths of at least six women. Also interested in this grim case was sixty-five-year-old poet Edith Sitwell, who was to pay several visits to the house in Rillington Place, North Kensington, where the ghastly crimes had been committed.

On July 2, Group-Captain Peter Townsend, whose name had been romantically linked with Princess Margaret, was appointed Air Attaché at the British Embassy in Brussels. He had already left to take up this appointment before Princess Margaret had returned from official duties in Rhodesia.

On July 8, wealthy financier Charles Clore threw a spectacular party at his Mayfair home, which was attended by such illustrious figures as the Duchess of Kent, the Duke of Buccleuch and the Maharajah and Maharanee of Jaipur. On the stroke of midnight, silk scarves, printed with the date of the party, were distributed to each female guest. At a later stage, five fire-engines drew up at the house, summoned by a hoaxer.

On July 19, the mighty Duke of Westminster died aged seventy-four at his Scottish home. He was outlived by his four wives and succeeded by his cousin, a mysterious figure who lived in a small house on the outskirts of Whitstable and was said to have been an invalid since childhood.

Towards the end of July, Sir Bernard and Lady Docker were to be found living on grapefruit at a private health-centre at Tring in Hertfordshire. 'It is an internal spring-clean' explained fifty-seven-year-old Sir Bernard. On July 25, this wealthy couple left for Monte Carlo.

Along the same coast, at Rapallo, the Duke and Duchess of Windsor were found beside the swimming-pool at the Hotel Excelsior. The fifty-seven-year-old Duchess was in brief white shorts and the Duke was in a baggy tartan swimming-suit and underwater goggles.

On August 24, there was much interest in a new production of *Hamlet* at the Edinburgh Festival. Twenty-seven-year-old Welsh actor Richard Burton, who was said to earn £2,000 a week in Hollywood, had accepted the title-role for a salary of £45 a week. His performance was praised for its vigour and freshness.

On August 27, Lord Noel-Buxton, whose attempt to wade across the Thames the previous year had proved unsuccessful, now tackled the Humber Estuary. This time, the walk was a success and the services of a helicopter hovering above him bearing the legend 'Pest Control', were not required.

On September 1, a mammoth fancy-dress party in Biarritz, given by the Marquis de Cuevas, made headline news. Among those present were Charles Clore, the Duchess of Kent, the Duke and Duchess of Marlborough, Prince Aly Khan, who was in a costume designed by Schiaparelli, and Salvador Dali, who brought a troop of gypsy dancers. Also there, dressed as a Dresden china figure, was twenty-four-year-old Olga Deterding, vivacious daughter of the late Sir Henri Deterding, founder of the Royal Dutch Shell Oil Company.

In the middle of September, the news broke that Mrs. Melinda Maclean, wife of missing diplomat Donald Maclean, had vanished with her three children. Two British security officers were making investigations in Geneva where Mrs. Maclean had spent the last year. When asked if Mrs. Maclean had gone to join her husband behind the Iron Curtain, a Foreign Office spokesman said, 'It is entirely a matter of speculation.' He added that Mrs. Maclean was 'an entirely free agent'.

On September 17, the Prime Minister Sir Winston Churchill flew off for a holiday at Lord Beaverbrook's villa at Cap d'Ail in the South of France. He was accompanied by 800 lb. of luggage, which included his painting equipment.

On September 22, the German Ambassador, Dr. Hans Schlange-Schoeningen, gave a party at the Savoy Hotel following the opening of the Bavarian State Opera Season at Covent Garden. Among the 300 guests were the Earl and Countess of Harewood and Prince and Princess Frederick of Prussia. Prince Frederick, grandson of the late Kaiser, told fellow guests that he had learned to do all his household repairs at his farm in Hertfordshire.

Meanwhile, the relationship between the thirty-four-year-old Marquess of Milford Haven and Hungarian actress Eva Bartok had become a subject of growing interest. On October 1, the Marquess flew in from Munich and took Miss Bartok out to dinner at a club in Grosvenor Street. Deluged with questions about his private life, Lord Milford Haven snapped, 'I don't wish to discuss it any more.'

Eva Bartok and the Marquess of Milford Haven

On October 6, controversial broadcaster Gilbert Harding caused a storm with his speech at a dinner of the Hounslow Magistrates. 'I have been dragged along to this third-rate place for a third-rate dinner for third-rate people' he began. In the uproar that followed, he was asked to leave. The following day he apologised profusely. 'I behaved abominably' he said. Two days later, he fell asleep at the première of *The King and I* starring Miss Valerie Hobson at the Theatre Royal, Drury Lane. 'I'm sorry' he said. 'I've had a tiring day.'

On October 9, the sixty-four-year-old pacifist Duke of Bedford was reported missing from his Devonshire home; 200 soldiers, policemen and estate workers searched the thickly wooded estate and the river Tamar was dragged. The Duke's ill and elderly head gamekeeper, Mr. Buckingham, directed the search from his bed.

Two days later, the Duke was found shot dead in deep undergrowth a few hundred yards from the house and his son and heir, the thirty-six-year-old Marquess of Tavistock, flew home from South Africa to take up his responsibilities as 13th Duke of Bedford. After a brief trip to Devon, he revisited Woburn Abbey which had been unoccupied since the death of his grandfather thirteen years earlier and had fallen into considerable disarray.

On October 20, Lady Docker unveiled her two-seater Silver Flash Daimler at the Earl's Court Motor Show. Lady Docker was carrying a handbag to match the car's red crocodile leather upholstery. Among those who stopped to gape at the vehicle was Sir Edmund Hillary, conqueror of Everest.

On October 28, sixty-four-year-old financier Clarence Hatry was hit by a taxi in Knightsbridge and taken to St. George's Hospital with a fractured pelvis. It was noted that Mr. Hatry, whose companies had crashed in dramatic circumstances twenty-four years earlier, had now re-established himself in the world of high finance and was living with his wife in a flat in Onslow Square.

On November 5, seventy-nine-year-old Somerset Maugham attended a party in Terence Rattigan's Eaton Square penthouse following the première of *The Sleeping Prince*. Maugham was suffering from writer's cramp and being treated by the orthopaedic surgeon, W. E. Tucker, who had told the aged writer to hold his pen in a different way.

On November 23, the Queen flew off on a tour of the Empire accompanied by twenty-nine officials and household staff. 'I shall look forward to receiving your letters' she told Sir Winston Churchill before setting off along fifty yards of red carpet to her plane.

No sooner had the Queen departed than the Duke and Duchess of Windsor arrived, accompanied by thirty-five pieces of luggage. It was the Duchess's first visit to England since Easter 1949. A secretary explained that Her Grace had brought 'just an ordinary wardrobe for a week's stay'. During their visit, the Duke and Duchess went to see the Agatha Christie thriller *Witness for the Prosecution* at the Winter Garden Theatre, Drury Lane, where they were cheered as they entered the Royal Box. Afterwards, they dined at Quaglino's, where they had first dined together in 1933, three years before the Abdication.

On December 9, Lady Caroline Blackwood, twenty-two-year-old daughter of Maureen Marchioness of Dufferin and Ava, was married to thirty-one-year-old Lucian Freud, grandson of the great psychoanalyst. After the ceremony at Chelsea Registry Office, there was a party on the top floor of Wheeler's Restaurant in Old Compton Street, where the guests included painter Francis Bacon, Cecil Beaton, Cyril Connolly and the Marquess of Bath and his new wife.

On December 18, ash from Sir Winston Churchill's cigar ignited a box of matches at a Trinity House luncheon. The matches flared up, badly blistering the Prime Minister's left hand. Two days later, he left to spend Christmas at Chequers with his arm still in a sling.

On December 24, it was revealed that missing diplomat Guy Burgess had written to his mother at her home in Arlington House, Mayfair. Burgess's stepfather, Lieutenant-Colonel J. R. Basset, described the letter as 'a wonderful Christmas present'. The letter was 'a purely personal message from a son to his mother'.

On New Year's Day, sixty-three-year-old Viscount Norwich, better known as Duff Cooper, died on board the French liner *Colombie* on his way to a holiday in the West Indies. His grief-stricken wife chartered a plane and flew the body home in a mock-antique Spanish coffin. Burial took place at Belvoir Castle, ancestral home of Viscountess Norwich, who was soon to resume her old name, Lady Diana Cooper.

Meanwhile, a fuss had blown up over the runaway romance of seventeen-year-old heiress Isabel Patino and twenty-year-old Old Etonian James Goldsmith. The couple had fled to Scotland, pursued by Isabel's father, Bolivian multi-millionaire Señor Antenor Patino. 'The reason why Isabel's parents oppose the marriage is that her mother wanted her to marry royalty' commented Mr. Goldsmith's brother, Edward.

Jimmy Goldsmith and his heiress bride Isabel Patino

On January 7, it was announced that Señor Patino had withdrawn his objections to the marriage. A few hours later, the couple were married at the Scottish border town of Kelso and went off to celebrate at the George Hotel, Edinburgh. 'I'm tired' said Mr. Goldsmith. 'I'm sorry about the fuss and I'm very, very happy.'

A few days later, fifty limousines carried the chairmen of Britain's five big banks and numerous other celebrities to a party on board a vast new oil-tanker, the *Tina Onassis*, which was anchored at Purfleet following its maiden voyage. The ship's owner, forty-seven-year-old Aristotle Onassis, received his guests in the captain's quarters which were adorned with mimosa, specially flown from the South of France. Guests were offered champagne and retsina, caviar, foie gras, fresh salmon and stuffed vine-leaves.

At the end of the month, it was announced that the Marchioness of Blandford, who had been doing all her own catering at her home at Charlbury near Blenheim, was advertising for a cook. It was noted that her fourteen-month-old son had been boarded out with his nanny and grandparents at Blenheim Palace.

Meanwhile, the Dowager Marchioness of Townshend had started giving sherry parties and dances at her house in Chester Street, Belgravia, for local trades people. 'I am making new friends' she declared, as she whirled around her drawing-room in the arms of the man who served behind the cold-meat counter at her local grocers.

On February 2, a cat burglar broke into the Upper Grosvenor Street home of the Duchess of Argyll and stole £8,000 worth of uninsured jewellery. The Duchess was dining at the time with Mr. David Rose, head of Paramount Pictures, and was leaving the following day for a holiday in South Carolina.

On February 10, Princess Alice and the Earl of Athlone celebrated their golden wedding quietly at Kensington Palace. The couple's Canadian secretary, Miss Goldie, explained that the seventy-nine-year-old Earl had 'flu and their party had to be postponed.

On February 26, the famous Dr. Inge, former Dean of St. Paul's, died aged ninety-three at his Thames-side home at Wallingford. 'If I could live my life again, I don't think I would be a clergyman' he had declared in a

Dean Inge with his twin grand-children Nicholas and Caroline

recent interview. 'I know as much about the after-life as you do. I don't even know if there is one – in the sense the Church teaches.'

On March 6, headlines blazed the news that thirty-five-year-old wartime fighter pilot Robert Cowell, son of Major-General Sir Ernest Cowell, had changed his sex and would be known in future as Roberta. 'All this has been a shock' said Lady Cowell. 'I was having eye operations while Roberta's transformation was going on and I had no idea how far it had progressed until I saw her as a woman.'

The following day, Herr Alfred Krupp, son of the man who had armed Hitler, flew into London after an absence of seventeen years. That night, he dined at the Savoy Grill with his beautiful American wife and was given the same suite at the hotel which he had occupied in 1937. It was noted that the Krupp family had recently vacated their 800-room palace in Germany and were building a new house nearby.

On March 10, Lady Annabel Vane-Tempest-Stewart, grand-daughter of the famous Lady Londonderry, was married at Caxton Hall, to twenty-three-year-old Mark Birley, son of the late Sir Oswald Birley. After the ceremony at Caxton Hall, a reception was held at Lady Annabel's father's home, 101 Park Street, Mayfair.

Later in the month, it was announced that the Albany Club, luxurious haunt of rich showmen and sportsmen, was closing down. 'This is the last thing I wanted to happen' said Mr. Frank Little who had been running the club for the last few months. The premises were soon acquired by showman Jack Hylton and re-named Hylton House.

On April 7, an exhibition of recent paintings by Italian artist Pietro Annigoni opened at Wildenstein's in Bond Street. At a party afterwards, given by the famous photographer Baron, Annigoni spoke of the young Duchess of Devonshire, whose portrait he had recently executed for £2,000 at his studio in Florence. It was noted that his next commission was a portrait of the Rector of Exeter College, Oxford. 'The portrait will take its place in a long row of predecessors' said Annigoni. 'There it will remain for centuries to come, unless an H bomb finishes us all off.'

On April 8, the seventy-six-year-old Aga Khan, winner of five Derbys, announced from his villa near Cannes that he was selling many of his race-horses. 'Of course I shall still race but on a smaller scale.' He added, 'I am taking other and new responsibilities on my hands.'

In the middle of April, the English social scene was enriched by the presence of Thelma Lady Furness, and her sister Mrs. Gloria Vanderbilt. Stepping off the liner *United States* at Southampton, Thelma explained that it was her first visit to England for three years. 'It looks so beautiful and it's such a lovely day' she remarked.

On May 7, former Labour Minister Aneurin Bevan, of Cliveden Place, Belgravia, was fined £20 for dangerous driving and £5 for failing to stop after his Humber Hawk had crashed into a bus at Gerrard's Cross. 'I was anxious to avoid the sort of publicity which is inevitably attendant upon such an incident' he explained.

On May 14, there came the tragic announcement that Mrs. James Goldsmith had died of a brain tumour while expecting a child. 'There is a good chance that the child will live' said her young husband. 'It is not yet certain, but there is a good chance.'

Meanwhile, Princess Margaret had been enrolled as associate director of an amateur production of an Edgar Wallace thriller called *The Frog*, organised by her friend Billy Wallace in aid of charity. After several weeks of rehearsals, the play opened on June 1 at the Scala Theatre, with a dazzling cast of celebrities. Young Viscount Norwich, whose father had died five months earlier, had a walk-on part. Maureen Marchioness of Dufferin and Ava played a ladies' lavatory attendant. The Duke of Devonshire was a prison governor and Sir Michael Duff a prison chaplain. Mrs. Gerald Legge was the heroine and the Frog itself was played by the Hon. Colin Tennant, wealthy young heir to Lord Glenconner.

In the star-studded audience that night were Prince Aly Khan, Noel Coward, the Duke and Duchess of Argyll and Sir Bernard and Lady Docker, whose gold-plated Daimler had been parked in a side street, guarded by a policeman. Afterwards Princess Margaret went to the 400 Club, Leicester Square where she sat up waiting to see how the following day's newspapers had reacted to the show.

On June 2, eighteen-year-old Lester Piggott had his first Derby win, on an outsider called Never Say Die, watched by the Queen, who had recently returned from a lengthy tour of the Empire. 'It was not until the last 200 yards that I thought I was going to win' said the soft-spoken jockey after the race.

On June 21, Marlene Dietrich floated down the staircase at the Café de Paris to begin a six-week cabaret season. In the illustrious audience that night were the Earl and Countess of Harewood, Lord and Lady Norwich, the Nivens, the Oliviers and the Duchess of Argyll who was at a table with actress Deborah Kerr. It was noted that Miss Dietrich wore a white fur coat and a close-fitting flesh-coloured chiffon dress.

On June 30, it was revealed that a Buckingham Palace sentry was receiving treatment for a septic leg wound after being bitten by one of the Royal corgis. It was thought that Susan, eldest of the Queen's three dogs, was the culprit.

On July 9, the Eton and Harrow cricket match at Lord's was honoured by the presence of the Queen Mother in a cool pink outfit and large hat, and Lady Docker in white. It was noticed that Lady Docker, whose son by an earlier marriage, Lance Callingham, was at Harrow, carried a dark-blue stole. 'It's white fox dyed blue' she explained. 'I have to wear Harrow colours of course.'

On July 31, headlines blazed the news that forty-eight-year-old Lord Vivian, brother of the former Marchioness of Bath, had been taken to Devizes Hospital suffering from three bullet wounds. The same day, his friend Mavis Wheeler, former mistress of Augustus John, was arrested and charged with malicious wounding. On being remanded in custody, the beautiful Mrs. Wheeler asked, 'Can't it be bail or something?'

Meanwhile, the popular Press was full of rumours of the imminent engagement of Princess Margaret and twenty-seven-year-old Colin Tennant, who had taken the title role in the production of *The Frog* months earlier. On August 7, the couple were found staying at Mr. Tennant's father's home near Innerleithen in Peeblesshire and a few days later they were together again at Balmoral for the Princess's birthday. 'There is no romance at all' said a mutual acquaintance. 'They are just friends.'

On September 15, the eccentric Lord Noel-Buxton waded across the River Severn, dressed in golfing-jacket and shorts and armed with an eight-foot pole to probe for unexpected pot-holes. Fighting a 10-mph current and cheered by a crowd of 200, the thirty-seven-year-old peer took almost three hours to cross the estuary. 'I want to prove that our big rivers can be forded' he declared.

The following day, news came from Paris that the four-month-old Goldsmith baby had been kidnapped by her wealthy Bolivian grandparents. 'I have filed a complaint of abduction of a minor against a person or persons unknown' said the baby's twenty-one-year-old father, Mr. Jimmy Goldsmith. 'I will fight the case in every court in the world if necessary.' In the tussle that followed, Mr. Goldsmith was to emerge victorious and the baby was returned to his flat near the Eiffel Tower, accompanied by an English nanny, Miss Deborah Cockbill.

On October 5, the trial of Mrs. Mavis Wheeler, now charged with attempting to murder her friend Lord Vivian, opened at Salisbury Assizes. Among those who packed into the crowded courtroom was journalist Godfrey Winn, on an assignment from the *Sunday Dispatch*. During the trial, Lord Vivian, now partly recovered from his wounds, gave evidence on Mrs. Wheeler's behalf. 'I cannot believe she tried to murder me' he said. 'I know it is untrue. I know it must be an accident.' On October 5, Mrs. Wheeler was found not guilty of shooting with intent to murder but guilty of malicious wounding and sentenced to six months imprisonment. After the verdict, Lord Vivian struggled through thick crowds to spend ten minutes with Mrs. Wheeler before she was driven away to the accompaniment of cries of 'Good luck!' from women in the crowd.

On October 19, it was announced that actress Valerie Hobson, currently starring in *The King and I* at the Theatre Royal, Drury Lane, was to quit the stage and marry thirty-nine-year-old bachelor MP John Profumo. 'Miss Hobson will abandon her acting career' said Mr. Profumo. 'That is her own idea as well as mine.'

At the end of the month, there was great excitement at a private view of the Diaghilev Exhibition at the Tate Gallery when fifty-three-year-old Sir John Rothenstein suddenly punched art critic Douglas Cooper, whom he claimed afterwards had been following him from room to room making offensive remarks. In the presence of Dame Edith Evans, the Countess of Harewood and other celebrities, Mr. Cooper, an intimate friend of Picasso, fell to the floor groping for his spectacles.

On November 3, Lord Vivian visited Mrs. Wheeler at her open prison, Hill Hall in Essex. Her fellow prisoners stood on tip-toe to try and catch a glimpse of the aristocratic visitor.

On November 15, twenty-five-year-old Mrs. Gerald Legge, who had recently been elected a Westminster City Councillor, created a sensation at London Airport by protesting at the cigarette ash and half-empty coffee cups in the departure lounge. Waiting for a flight to Paris with her friend the Vicomtesse de Ribes, Mrs. Legge suddenly exclaimed in a loud voice, 'Is there no one to clear up this disgraceful mess?'

A week later, the beautiful Maharanee of Jaipur set off for London Airport en route to India when she suddenly remembered she had left her jewellery behind in the safe at the Dorchester Hotel. While the jewels were collected, a Bombay-bound Super Constellation was kept waiting with twenty-five passengers on board.

On November 30, members of both Houses of Parliament gathered in Westminster Hall to see Sir Winston Churchill presented with a portrait of himself by Graham Sutherland on the occasion of his eightieth birthday. Churchill described the picture ambiguously as 'a remarkable example of Modern Art'. Many other people had stronger views to express. 'It's disgusting, ill-mannered and terrible' declared a leading young Conservative peer, Lord Hailsham. A few days later, Somerset Maugham, who had been painted by Sutherland three years earlier, entered the controversy. 'Now I've got used to mine, I like it immensely. I

Westminster City Councillor Mrs Gerald Legge

imagine Sir Winston will feel the same.'

On December 5, Lady Docker threw a champagne party at Claridge's for 200 show-business friends. 'I want to thank all those people who have amused and entertained me so much during the past year' she said. Among those who turned up to drink magnums of champagne and eat sole in champagne were Norman Wisdom, Frankie Howerd, Jimmy Edwards, Michael Redgrave and Margaret Leighton. Lady Docker received her guests wearing a dress of flame-pleated tulle. A few hours later, she retired to bed with a severe cold.

Shortly before Christmas, eighty-year-old Sir Winston Churchill acquired a budgerigar named Toby which was soon hopping about and sitting on his shoulder. A friend urged that he should teach the bird his telephone number in case it ever got lost, to which the Prime Minister replied: 'I don't know my telephone number.'

On December 31, Conservative MP John Profumo and actress Valerie Hobson flew off on honeymoon following their marriage at St. Columba's Church in Pont Street. At London Airport, they received VIP treatment and the Royal Lounge was thrown open to them. 'Normally I am only allowed in here when I am seeing someone off' said Profumo.

The New Year was greeted with chaotic scenes at the Chelsea Arts Ball at the Albert Hall. Soda-water was squirted at dancers from the balconies and thirty-six casualties were reported, four of which required hospital treatment.

On January 5, reports came from Egypt that the seventy-seven-year-old Aga Khan had been struck down with bronchial pneumonia. It was noted that the great potentate had already chosen his tomb, of rose-red granite, and was said to be in the process of choosing his successor. It was by no means certain that this would be his son, Prince Aly Khan.

Meanwhile, the romance between former Home Secretary Herbert Morrison and a Lancashire lady named Miss Edith Meadowcroft had excited great interest. On January 6, the couple were married in Rochdale, receiving a present of a silver cigarette-box from the Prime Minister and Lady Churchill. 'We knock each other about in the House of Commons' remarked Mr. Morrison, 'but there are times when controversies are put aside.'

On January 18, American Ambassador Winthrop Aldrich at last moved into Winfield House, the huge mansion in Regent's Park which Woolworth heiress Barbara Hutton had built during the Thirties and presented to the American Government in December 1945. Many alterations had been carried out at the house, including the moving of its fine staircase, which had been imported by Miss Hutton from a French château.

On January 27, former prisoners at Colditz Castle held a reunion ball at Claridge's, following the première of the film *Colditz Story*. A huge picture of the castle loomed over the dance floor. 'Every time I look at it I feel depressed' remarked ex-prisoner, Earl Haig.

At the end of the month, twenty-four-year-old Princess Margaret flew off to the West Indies on her first solo royal tour. A staff of thirteen travelled with her on board a white-and-blue Stratocruiser Canopus, including her personal maid, Ruby, and her detective, Inspector Fred Crocker of Scotland Yard. It was rumoured that the real purpose of the trip was to put further distance between the Princess and her close friend, Group-Captain Peter Townsend, now in his second year at the British Embassy in Brussels.

On February 2, much publicity attended the release of Mrs. Mavis Wheeler from Hill Hall open prison. At Epping Station, she was reunited with Lord Vivian and they drove together to her Belgravia home. 'Lord Vivian and I are going away for a short rest in some quiet spot' said Mrs. Wheeler. 'Then we shall come back and live here.' That evening, the much-publicised couple wandered along King's Road to a coffee bar run by a certain Roy Alderson.

On February 12, the Marquess of Milford Haven and Miss Eva Bartok were spotted sipping soft drinks in the Stork Room night-club in Swallow Street. 'Oh look, there's David and Eva!' cried a fellow socialite – and they left immediately.

Meanwhile, Pietro Annigoni's work on a portrait of the Queen for the Worshipful Company of Fishmongers had been temporarily disreputed by a dispute over the ownership of the reproduction rights. 'If they are not granted to him' said a friend of the artist on February 15, 'I think he will regard the contract as null and void.'

On February 18, a committee of six peers refused permission for twenty-nine-year-old Socialist MP Anthony Wedgwood Benn to renounce his peerage in the event of the death of his father, Lord Stansgate. The hearing took place in the historic Moses Room at the House of Lords and Mr. Wedgwood Benn's wealthy American wife sat beside him as he cited legal precedents dating back to the fourteenth century.

On February 21, the Shah of Persia and his twenty-one-year-old wife Queen Soraya gave a party at the Savoy Hotel at which over £1,000,000 worth of jewellery was worn. Guests ranged from the Duke and Duchess of Gloucester to the Marquess and Marchioness of Salisbury. Caviar and vodka were served and the young hostess wore a diamond and emerald tiara and emerald earrings fashioned like bunches of grapes.

The following night, the American Ambassador, Mr. Aldrich, gave a house-warming party at Winfield

House, attended by the Queen and Prince Philip and more than fifty policemen. Prince Philip danced first with the Queen and then with Mrs. Douglas Fairbanks. The eighty-year-old Prime Minister Sir Winston Churchill appeared for just half an hour and sat by the door.

On March 3, Lady Docker arrived in a gold-plated Daimler at the Festival Hall, Castleford, Yorkshire, to take part in a marbles championship. Dressed in a £350 peacock-blue gown and watched by an audience of 800, she played marbles against some factory girls, won the contest and was nominated World Women's Marble Champion. This result caused deep distress to Mr. George Burbridge, secretary of the British Marble Board of Control. 'Lady Docker knows nothing about marbles and never will' he said, accusing her of trying to mock an ancient sport.

The following day, Princess Margaret arrived back from the Caribbean, wrapped in mink. She found her first Rolls-Royce of her own waiting for her, and a Welcome Home luncheon laid on at the Mansion House, at which she was observed in earnest conversation with Dr. Fisher, Archbishop of Canterbury.

On March 8, Prince Philip flew off to the South of France to stay with his aunt, the Dowager Marchioness of Milford Haven, at her house at Golfe Juan. A few days later, he was stopped for speeding along the coast in a grey Rolls-Royce to a lunch appointment in Monte Carlo.

On March 11, poet Stephen Spender walked out of a literary luncheon after eighty-four-year-old Lord Samuel had attacked modern poetry. 'Oh dear, I hope he is not upset' said the organiser Miss Christina Foyle. 'Poetry lunches are always difficult.'

On March 22, Sir Winston Churchill spent eighty minutes at Buckingham Palace while rumours circulated that his resignation as Prime Minister was imminent.

Meanwhile, a series of goodbye parties were being held at 10 Downing Street. On April 1, there was an informal gathering for friends and family, including the Leader of the Opposition and Mrs. Attlee, at which Sir Winston expressed his distaste for his recent portrait by Graham Sutherland. 'I wouldn't be surprised if no one got the opportunity of looking at it after my day. It's a horrible portrait.'

On April 4, Sir Winston welcomed the Queen and Prince Philip to a formal dinner-party. This was the first time in history that the reigning monarch had visited 10 Downing Street and there was a moving moment when the twenty-eight-year-old Queen proposed the Prime Minister's health.

The following day, the Old Warrior, in silk-fronted frock-coat, surrendered his Seals of Office to the Queen at Buckingham Palace. The handsome but delicate Sir Anthony Eden took over as Premier and Sir Winston and Lady Churchill left for a holiday in Sicily.

On April 8, faced with death duties of over £4,500,000, the young Duke of Bedford threw open Woburn Abbey to the public. On the opening day, Good Friday, a visitor was found snipping a piece out of the curtains as a souvenir and a small dog, which the Duke had brought with him from South Africa, vanished and was never seen again.

Meanwhile, a new chapter also opened in the life of Fort Belvedere, former home of the Duke of Windsor, which had lain empty since December 1936. On April 21, it was announced that thirty-year-old Gerald Lascelles, younger son of the Princess Royal, had taken a long lease of the house and would be restoring its overgrown gardens and demolishing its Victorian additions. 'We do not want the additions to the original eighteenth-century structure' said Mr. Lascelles, whose only home to date had been a mews-house in Belgravia.

On April 26, Sir Winston and Lady Churchill returned from their holiday and moved into a seventh-floor suite in the Hyde Park Hotel. Sir Winston's house in Hyde Park Gate was not yet ready to be reoccupied, though his cats, Gabriel and Whisky, had already moved there from 10 Downing Street.

On April 29, socialites flocked to Burlington House for the preview of the Royal Academy Summer Exhibition. Crowds, sometimes ten deep, gathered round the Annigoni portrait of the Queen. 'I tried to show her not simply with the regal dignity of a Queen, but as she appeared to me – a beautiful young woman' explained the painter. Guests at the preview ranged from Mary Duchess of Devonshire, Mistress of the

Robes, to flamboyant Italian sculptress Fiore de Henriques, in Black Watch tartan trousers and a heavy gold necklace.

The deb season opened on May 10 with Queen Charlotte's Birthday Ball at the Grosvenor House. This year, the cake which had recently become an object of sabotage, was guarded by a detective. 'Just to be safe, I decided a detective was a wise precaution' said the Ball's president, Margerita Lady Howard de Walden. 'You never know what these young men will get up to next.'

The following day, seventy-two-year-old Elsa Maxwell arrived on board the Golden Arrow from Paris, and went off to lunch with the beautiful Duchess of Argyll. It was announced that Miss Maxwell would be organising a cultural cruise later in the summer on board a ship loaned by Greek shipping magnate, Stavros Niarchos.

Elsa Maxwell, the world's most famous party-giver, above with Stavros Niarchos and, below, with the Duke and Duchess of Windsor

On May 12, Oscar Wilde's son, Vyvyan Holland, whose financial affairs had got into a muddle when the copyright on his father's plays had run out in 1950, faced examination in the London Bankruptcy Court. It was noted that Mr. Holland's wife Thelma advised the Queen on make-up and beauty preparations.

On May 24, many débutantes were present at the first night of William Douglas-Home's new play *The Reluctant Débutante* starring seventeen-year-old Anna Massey, herself one of this year's débutantes. Twenty-three-year-old Jocelyn Stevens said afterwards, 'The caricature of a deb's delight was terrifyingly accurate.' Said Viscountess Tarbat, 'Frankly, in my day there weren't such things as reluctant débutantes.'

On May 25, the Derby Day crowds were enriched by the presence of ninety-three-year-old Alice Countess of Derby, who had driven to Epsom in a new Jaguar sports saloon. This year, the race was won by Mme. Susy Volterra's Phil Drake. 'I am gloriously glad I won because it is the most wonderful race in the world' said Mme. Volterra, who later that day gave a dinner-party at the Savoy Hotel at which the Derby Cup, brimming with champagne, was passed around her guests.

On May 26, the General Election showed a further swing to the right and re-affirmed the appointment of Anthony Eden as Prime Minister. Sir Winston and Lady Churchill celebrated the victory the following day by lunching quietly at the Savoy Grill. They entered the hotel by a side door and lunched at a quiet table out of sight of the main crowd. The former Prime Minister ate dressed crab, Irish Stew, ice-cream and Stilton, while Lady Churchill tackled cold lobster and strawberries.

On June 7, Marlene Dietrich began in a new cabaret season at the Café de Paris. Her act was introduced on the opening night by TV personality Nancy Spain, to whom Miss Dietrich presented a white carnation. It was noted that the German-born singer was staying in the Oliver Messel penthouse suite at the Dorchester Hotel, obligingly vacated by Mr. Danny Kaye who was again appearing at the Palladium. 'My love,' Marlene had purred down the house telephone to the American comedian, 'it is so sweet of you. I thought I would have to go to another hotel.'

Notorious bon viveur
Gerald Hamilton

On June 21, the unveiling of a vast bronze statue of Sir Winston Churchill by sculptor Oscar Nemon at the Guildhall was followed by the revelation that the sinister Gerald Hamilton, twice interned by Churchill for his pro-German sympathies, had modelled the figure. 'It so happens I have exactly the same measurements as Sir Winston' explained sixty-seven-year-old Hamilton. 'I was only the body, you understand. The statue is only me from the head down.'

On June 23, eighteen-year-old Frances Sweeny made her debut at a ball at Claridge's given by her mother, the Duchess of Argyll. This spectacular occasion was enriched by the presence of the Duchess's ex-fiancé the Earl of Warwick, and ex-husband Charles Sweeny. Inevitable comparisons were made with the Duchess's own coming-out dance in 1930. 'Mine was a much smaller affair' she declared. 'I'm sure this is much more fun.'

On June 30, a coming-out dance at the Savoy Hotel for Miss Primrose McKenna, grand-daughter of the Earl of Albemarle, was enlivened when one of the guests, the Honourable Richard Bigham, Master of Nairne, stripped down to his underpants and swam across the Thames to win a magnum of champagne.

A week later, there were more high-jinks on the Thames when the Duke and Duchess of Devonshire gave a fancy-dress party on two boats. Among the 230 guests were Princess Margaret, in a white calypso number, Princess Alexandra in a purple neckerchief and Mrs. Xan Fielding, the former Marchioness of Bath, in ballet tights.

On July 20, Calouste Gulbenkian, reputedly the world's richest man, died alone in his hotel bedroom in Lisbon. Attention immediately turned to his son Nubar, a permanent resident at the Ritz Hotel in London. 'Nobody has an inkling what my father's oil interests were worth' he said. 'I personally have been royally provided for. I have certainly got more money than I can ever want.'

On July 27, interior decorator Syrie Maugham died in London. Her former husband Somerset Maugham heard the news at his villa in the South of France in the middle of a game of Patience. It was said that the world's richest writer put down his pack of cards and burst into song. 'Tra-la-la-la. No more alimony. Tra-la, tra-la.'

August 5 was the Queen Mother's fifty-fifth birthday. The Duke of Edinburgh paid his respects to his mother-in-law that day by dipping low over Clarence House in his helicopter.

On August 13, a glittering gathering at the Sporting Club in Monte Carlo made headline news in British newspapers. Sir Bernard and Lady Docker and Lady Docker's Harrovian son Lance, mingled with ex-Ambassador Joseph Kennedy and Mr. and Mrs. Aristotle Onassis, whose newly-delivered yacht *Christina*, already dubbed 'the world's most luxurious vessel', lay anchored in the harbour.

On August 21, Princess Margaret celebrated her twenty-fifth birthday in an atmosphere of mounting tension; 300 reporters hovered around Balmoral Castle anticipating the announcement of the Princess's engagement to Group-Captain Peter Townsend. No such announcement came and the Press had to content themselves with photographs of the Princess assisting at a charity fête with her old friend Dominic Elliot, son of the Earl of Minto.

At the end of the month, 128 people carefully selected by Miss Elsa Maxwell left Venice on a cultural cruise to the Greek Islands on board a ship loaned by multi-millionaire Stavros Niarchos. Among those present were the Duchess of Argyll and her children Frances and Brian Sweeny, and Lady Diana Cooper and her twenty-six-year-old son, Viscount Norwich. Mr. Niarchos followed on board his own sumptuous 697-ton yacht the *Creole*, which was loaded with caviar and champagne.

On September 11, Foreign Secretary Harold Macmillan took part in a show-biz cricket match at East Grinstead in Sussex. Incorrectly dressed in brown shoes and pin-striped trousers, he was bowled out by Mr. Pastry after scoring only two runs.

On September 18, Prince Aly Khan's eighteen-year-old son Karim left London for America to continue his studies at Harvard University.

On September 21, it was announced that an intruder had entered the wine cellar of the Junior Carlton Club in Pall Mall and helped himself to twenty-nine bottles of vintage port. 'The wine was not only valuable but irreplaceable' said the chairman of the club's wine committee.

On October 5, attention turned to Le Tremblay racecourse near Paris where Prince Aly Khan and Group-Captain Peter Townsend were competing in the annual Grand Prix for Amateur Riders. On this occasion, Aly came in second and Townsend was not placed. 'This is the fifth time we have raced against each other' said Townsend afterwards. 'I think the score so far is about evens.'

Five days later, young Viscount Weymouth, eldest son of the Marquess of Bath, plunged into the limelight when he was bitten by a great dane at a party at Oxford given by Sir Kenneth Clark's son, Colin. 'I hope I don't go mad' he said as he was rushed to the Radcliffe Infirmary for an anti-rabies injection. 'You must all run if you see me biting the carpet or frothing at the mouth.'

Two days later, on October 12, the much talked-about Peter Townsend at last flew into England and drove to London in a green Renault which had been air-freighted over on the same plane. 'I shall be here for two to three weeks. I have no particular plans' he said. Shortly after 6.00 pm the following day, he and Princess Margaret were reunited at Clarence House. Huge crowds of Press and public gathered outside and headlines blazed the news that the couple were 'together at last'.

On October 18, Lady Docker unveiled a new cream-and-gold Daimler at the Motor Show, upholstered with the skins of six zebras. 'Mink is too hot to sit on' she explained.

Meanwhile, the White Paper on the disappearance of Burgess and Maclean had been published amidst much speculation about the identity of a Third Man. On October 25, Labour MP Colonel Marcus Lipton asked the Prime Minister Anthony Eden if the activities of a former Foreign Official, Mr. Philby, would be investigated. The Prime Minister gave a non-committal reply and attention turned to the five-bedroom house near Crowborough in Sussex where Mr. Philby was living. 'My husband is staying in town' said Mrs. Eleanor Philby. 'I'm not sure exactly where he is.'

On October 27, much publicity surrounded Princess Margaret's visit to the Archbishop of Canterbury at Lambeth Palace. In reply to Press enquiries, Dr. Fisher's chaplain declared, 'No statement will be made. No information will be given out.'

That evening, the twenty-five-year-old Princess joined the Queen, the Duke of Edinburgh and the Prime Minister Anthony Eden in the Royal Box at Covent Garden for a gala performance of Smetana's *The Bartered Bride*. It was noticed that not a single word was exchanged between Princess Margaret and the Duke of Edinburgh, who sat beside her resplendent in knee-breeches.

Four days later, a formal statement was issued from Clarence House that Princess Margaret would not be going ahead with her marriage to Group-Captain Peter Townsend. 'Mindful of the Church's teaching that Christian marriage is indissoluble and conscious of my duty to the Commonwealth, I have decided to put these considerations before any other' she announced.

On November 7, the Foreign Secretary Harold Macmillan made a formal statement in the House of Commons concerning Mr. Harold Philby. 'I have no reason to conclude that Mr. Philby has at any time betrayed the interests of this country or to identify him with the so-called "Third Man", if indeed there was one.'

On November 8, Philby broke his silence and, attired in a well-cut pin-striped suit, gave a Press conference at his mother's flat in Drayton Gardens, South Kensington. 'I say! Mind the furniture' he said as journalists, including the bespectacled Alan Whicker, squeezed into the tightly-packed drawing-room.

The same day, millionairess Barbara Hutton embarked on her fifth marriage. This time, the bridegroom was an old friend, German tennis champion Baron Gottfried von Cramm. 'It should have happened eighteen years ago when I first met him' said Barbara at the reception at the Paris Ritz, which was attended by among others, the Duchess of Argyll to whose son Brian Barbara was godmother.

Meanwhile, Princess Margaret had plunged back into the social whirl with a certain zest. On November 15, she attended a dance at Winfield House, where she was found smoking American cigarettes through a long holder and laughing and joking with her old friend, Mark Bonham Carter, step-grandson of the late Lady Oxford. A week later, she accompanied her friend Sharman Douglas to a performance of *The Pajama Game* returning afterwards to a party in Miss Douglas's flat in South Audley Street, where she remained until 3.00 am.

On December 3, it was announced that thirty-eight-year-old Viscount St. Davids had disappeared from his London home, dressed in duffle-coat and jeans and telling his wife that he had gone to buy newspapers. A rumour circulated that he had gone to sea.

On December 16, there was an aristocratic gathering at the Royal College of Art fancy-dress ball. The theme was 'A Roman Holiday' and the Marquess of Bath and Lord Melchett turned up in togas and the Duke of Devonshire wore a garland of leaves. Towards the end of the evening, the news broke that Princess Margaret's friend Colin Tennant was engaged to Lady Anne Coke, daughter of the Earl of Leicester. 'Oh dear,' said Tennant. 'I hoped to keep this secret until later today.'

On December 22, Harold Macmillan, now Chancellor of the Exchequer, was unnoticed when he made his way through the snack bar at Lyons Corner House in Coventry Street. He was on his way to an upper room where a Christmas party was being held by his family publishing house.

Barbara Hutton, the world's richest woman, with her sixth husband, Baron von Cramm

1956

In the New Year's Honours List, thirty-six-year-old ballerina Margot Fonteyn became a Dame. At a party at Covent Garden to celebrate the event, Dame Margot gave a very brief speech explaining: 'My dancing teacher told me that I should always be seen and never be heard.'

On January 15, Viscount St. Davids, missing for over a month from his London home, re-surfaced explaining that he had been working as a seaman on a cargo ship, at a salary of threepence a week. 'I am one of those peers who cannot afford to loll about' he explained.

Meanwhile, the English social scene had been enriched by the presence of Princess Beatrix of Hohenlohe-Langenburg and Princess Christina of Hesse, German nieces of the Duke of Edinburgh. On January 16, they were found at a charity dance at the Dorchester Hotel dancing with twenty-year-old Paul Channon, son of Mr. Chips Channon and twenty-six-year-old David Hicks.

Another visitor to England was fifty-six-year-old King Frederik of Denmark who on January 20 was found in the third row of the stalls at the Folies Bergères revue at the Prince of Wales Theatre, accompanied by two men friends.

On January 26, Sir Bernard Docker held a Press conference at the Savoy Hotel at which he defended his extravagant life-style and attacked the punitive new rates of taxation. 'What seems important to me,' said the Old Harrovian industrialist, 'is that it is our money we are spending.'

At the beginning of February, Mrs. Xan Fielding, the former Marchioness of Bath, revealed that she and her husband were going to live in Tangier. 'We shall stay away from England for a year to establish our residence abroad for tax purposes' she explained.

On February 11, missing diplomats Guy Burgess and Donald Maclean popped up at a Press conference in the National Hotel in Moscow looking fit and well. After issuing a prepared statement defending their departure from Britain five years earlier, they donned astrakhan-collared overcoats and disappeared into the Moscow fog.

On February 19, fifty-seven-year-old Noel Coward announced that owing to tax problems, he was selling his studio home in Belgravia, where he had lived since 1925, and his farm in Kent and would be living in future in Jamaica and Bermuda. 'I am a writer and like writing in the sun' he added.

The following day, the Duchess of Windsor's autobiography *The Heart Has Its Reasons* was launched at a publishing party in New York. The Duchess appeared serene in a plain black velvet gown with a white fur collar while the Duke fidgetted and fingered the large knot of his tie.

On February 25, attention turned to a cellar in Liverpool where eighty-one-year-old Lord Muskerry had been living since the end of the war cooking on a paraffin stove and doing all his own washing. 'It is just that he is Irish and terribly independent' said his daughter Mrs. Anthony Deane from her flat in Lowndes Square, Belgravia.

On March 2, it was announced that the Duke of Argyll had been left £40,000 by a female member of the Campbell Clan, whom he had never met. The Duchess telephoned the Duke at White's Club to tell him the good news. 'I feel deeply hurt' said the husband of the dead woman. 'If I had enough money, I would contest the will.'

On March 13, there was an all-night party at the stately Londonderry House to celebrate the engagement of writer Quentin Crewe, twenty-eight-year-old grandson of the late Marquess of Crewe, to American-born Martha Sharp. Four bands played and most of the guests were in jeans and polo-neck sweaters. Into this informal gathering walked the Chancellor of the Exchequer Harold Macmillan in a pin-striped suit. 'I feel slightly overdressed' he said. 'I should have come along in my ski-ing outfit.'

On March 22, far away in Sydney, Australia, sixty-two-year-old British conductor Sir Eugene Goossens was fined £80 for attempting to import into Australia indecent articles, books, prints, photographs and films. Sir Eugene, who had recently been appointed conductor of the Sydney Symphony Orchestra, was described in court as a timid and nervous man.

On March 24, spectators at the Grand National were horrified to see the Queen Mother's horse, Devon Loch, collapse with an attack of cramp within inches of the winning post. With remarkable presence of mind, the Queen Mother left her box to go and comfort the jockey, trainer and stable lads. 'It was the most perfect display of dignity I have ever witnessed' said the Duke of Devonshire afterwards.

In the middle of April, some 600 photographers converged on Monte Carlo for the marriage of Prince Rainier and Hollywood star Grace Kelly. On April 18 on the eve of the wedding, there was a gala performance at the Monaco Opera House at which Dame Margot Fonteyn danced a scene from *Sleeping Beauty*. The following day, the wedding took place in the Monaco Cathedral with the women in sumptuous gowns and most of the men in white tie and tails and decorations. Among the English guests at the ceremony were Sir Bernard and Lady Docker, whose gift to the bride was a clover-engraved powder compact.

Three days later, attention turned to the small, flintstone church at Holkham in Norfolk where the Hon. Colin Tennant, heir to Lord Glenconner, was married to Lady Anne Coke, daughter of the Earl of Leicester. Princess Margaret and the Queen Mother flew to the ceremony in a private aeroplane. Among photographers covering the event was twenty-six-year-old Antony Armstrong-Jones.

Meanwhile, Soviet leaders Mr. Bulganin and Mr. Kruschev had arrived in England on board a Russian cruiser. The Prime Minister Anthony Eden greeted them at Victoria Station and escorted them to Claridge's where the entire first floor had been taken over for their use. On April 24, the Soviet Embassy gave a reception at the hotel which was attended by the famous Dr. Hewlett Johnson, Dean of Canterbury, and Mr. Charlie Chaplin.

The departure of Bulganin and Kruschev three days later was swiftly followed by an announcement from the Admiralty that frogman Commander Lionel Crabb had disappeared during a diving operation in Portsmouth Harbour where the Russian cruiser had lain anchored. 'It would not be in the public interest to disclose the circumstances in which Commander Crabb is presumed to have met his death' said a spokesman. It was noted that the forty-six-year-old Commander was an extremely eccentric man who was fond of wearing his diving-gear in bed.

On May 2, it was announced that Pietro Annigoni had been invited to attend the Royal Academy dinner at Burlington House. 'The trouble is I have not got a tail-coat. The way I have lived I have never needed one before' said the artist, whose picture of Dame Margot Fonteyn had already been heralded as the portrait of the year.

A few days later, it was announced from Rapallo in Northern Italy that Sir Max Beerbohm had sunk into a coma from which he was not expected to recover. When he died on May 20, his widow said wistfully, 'Sir Max has always been as fragile as a Chinese cup.'

On May 31, headlines blazed the news that Sir Bernard Docker had been sacked from his job as chairman of the £24,000,000 BSA Group. 'I could hardly have got more publicity if I had cut someone's throat' he said as he went off to dine with his wife at the Caprice that night. It was said that one of the things Sir Bernard's fellow directors had objected to was an £8,000 bill for dresses and furs worn by Lady Docker at the opening of the Daimler showrooms in Paris.

On June 4, the 400 Club in Leicester Square celebrated its twenty-first birthday with a party attended by the Duchess of Argyll, Lord and Lady Derby, the Duke of Devonshire and Herr Sigismund von Braun, counsellor at the German Embassy. 'This is the biggest week for us since the Coronation' said the proprietor Mr. Rossi. 'We will be stiff with titles every day for a week.'

On June 14, wealthy young Jocelyn Stevens was married to Miss Jane Sheffield at the Holy Trinity, Brompton Road. A £2,000 reception was held afterwards at the home of the bridegroom's uncle Sir Edward Hulton in Hyde Park Gate. Rolls-Royces and Bentleys blocked the street.

Later that day, Emma Tennant and Mrs. Jonathan Guinness gave a Persian fancy-dress party at a house in Cheyne Walk. Among the men present were the young Duke of Kent, the Marquess of Milford Haven and Lord Montagu of Beaulieu. Guests in oriental costume danced to 'Rock Around the Clock'.

On June 15, Sir Bernard Docker purchased a three-minute spot on commercial television in which he made a nationwide appeal to BSA shareholders for their support in his battle with his fellow directors. Sir Bernard was reported to have appeared somewhat nervous.

Three days later, Irish playwright Brendan Behan, whose play *The Quare Fellow* had been receiving much critical acclaim, established himself as a national figure by appearing blind drunk and completely unintelligible in a television interview with Malcolm Muggeridge on the *Panorama* programme.

On June 22, there was a ball at the Savoy Hotel in honour of the Aga Khan, now seventy-eight years old and confined to a wheelchair. 'I'm so sorry to be late' he said. 'The traffic was so thick we could not get through.' In the course of the evening, the Savoy's Blue Room orchestra played the Aga's personal anthem which he had specially annotated for the occasion.

On July 11, almost the entire Royal Family were present at a coming-out dance at St. James's Palace in honour of eighteen-year-old Lady Anne Fitzalan-Howard, eldest daughter of the Duke and Duchess of Norfolk. Staff from Arundel Castle sat and watched the guests arriving from the top of a staircase.

In the middle of July, it was disclosed that Mrs. J. R. Bassett was on her way to Moscow to visit her son, missing diplomat Guy Burgess. It was noted that the two had been corresponding regularly for some time, and Mrs. Bassett had remained totally loyal to her son since his disappearance five years earlier.

On August 1, there was a huge meeting of BSA shareholders at the Grosvenor House, at which Sir Bernard Docker lost his fight to remain chairman of the company. Leaving the meeting in a Bentley, the tearful Lady Docker declared, 'If I have done anything to harm the company, I am very sorry. But I did it to help my husband.'

Meanwhile, President Nasser had seized the Suez Canal, precipitating a grave international crisis. On August 8, Lucian Freud, James Pope-Hennessy and others gathered in Sir Harold Nicolson's Albany chambers to listen to a broadcast by the Prime Minister Anthony Eden.

On August 15, twenty-three-year-old Antonia Pakenham, daughter of Labour peer Lord Pakenham, announced her engagement to Tory MP Hugh Fraser, brother of the Commando leader Lord Lovat. 'In politics, I shall support my husband, as a good wife should' said Antonia, who was currently working for a publishing house.

On August 22, the Duke of Marlborough presented the millionth visitor to Blenheim Palace with a valuable eighteenth-century silver salver engraved with the family crest. It was noted that the millionth visitor to Arundel Castle had only been given a box of chocolates.

On August 28, eighty-one-year-old Sir Winston Churchill lunched at 10 Downing Street to discuss the Suez Crisis with the Prime Minister.

On August 29, a Soviet discus champion named Nina Ponomareva was charged with stealing five hats from C & A Modes in Oxford Street. The following day, she failed to turn up in court, claiming sanctuary of the Russian Embassy. In the public outcry that followed, the Bolshoi Ballet Company, due in England at the end of next month, threatened to cancel their trip if the charge were not withdrawn.

Five days later, twenty-four-year-old fashion model Fiona Campbell-Walter was married to Ruhr industrialist Baron Heinrich von Thyssen, whose vast fortune had survived the war more or less intact. The ceremony took place beside Lake Lugano in Switzerland and a reception was held at the Baron's private art gallery, where his £5,000,000-collection of Holbeins, Titians and El Grecos was housed. 'Fiona is the perfect woman' said the happy bridegroom.

On September 25, American pianist Liberace set foot in England for the first time. A special train of Pullman cars, dubbed *The Liberace Special*, carried the entertainer to London where he was met by screaming and weeping women. 'I am deeply touched' said Liberace, whose first concert at the Royal Festival Hall was followed by appearances in the provinces and at the Café de Paris in Coventry Street.

Also heading for England, in spite of their threats to the contrary, were the Bolshoi Ballet Company. Their opening performance at Covent Garden was attended by a star-studded audience including Sir Anthony and Lady Eden, Dame Margot Fonteyn and Gilbert Harding.

On October 12, Russian discus champion Nina Ponomareva popped up unexpectedly in court to answer the charge of stealing hats from an Oxford Street store. 'I realise the fallibility of human nature and perhaps the hats at C & A Modes constitute a considerable temptation to a number of women' said the magistrate, giving the athlete an absolute discharge. Later that day, Nina was whisked away to London Docks, where a Russian ship was waiting to ferry her home to her native land.

On October 17, Greta Garbo, who had not made a film for fourteen years but was still an object of immense curiosity value, was taken to tea at 10 Downing Street by her friend Cecil Beaton. A few hours later, the couple were seen together at Covent Garden. 'I will speak to no one concerning Miss Greta Garbo' said Beaton afterwards. 'I have no comment to make as to whether or not I or she were at the ballet.'

The following day, Bolshoi star Ulanova called at Beaton's home in Pelham Place to meet Miss Garbo and went on to dinner with Oliver Messel, who had designed all the sets for the current season at Covent Garden.

Early in November, Pietro Annigoni began paying frequent visits to Clarence House, where he was working on a portrait of Princess Margaret whom, it was said, he had wished to paint since he first caught a glimpse of her in Italy in 1947. 'It is a private matter' he said.

Millionairess Olga Deterding, who forsook the high life to work as a nurse in Dr Albert Schweitzer's leper colony

On Prince Charles's eighth birthday on November 14, new photographs of the Prince and his six-year-old sister were published taken by young society photographer Antony Armstrong-Jones. 'I do not want to tell you which camera I used or how I took the pictures' he said. 'I think that would spoil it.'

On November 19, it was announced that Cecil Beaton had been struck down by measles. 'I'm much better now' he told a reporter. 'I had the German variety. It takes a week in bed. I have no idea how I caught it.'

Meanwhile, the strain of the Suez Crisis had affected the Prime Minister's health. On November 23, he and Lady Eden left for a three-week holiday in Jamaica where Ian Fleming's house, Goldeneye, had been loaned to them. 'It's no luxury place' said Mr. Fleming in London. 'The Edens will have to rough it.' The house was said to have no telephone but offered a garden running down to the sea. 'He is not ill' said Deputy Leader R. A. Butler as the Prime Minister flew off. 'He has simply had a helluva time . . . He has been submitted to more pressure and more attacks than any statesman in our history.'

On November 30, Sir Winston Churchill celebrated his eighty-second birthday at his house in Hyde Park Gate in the company of his seven-year-old grand-daughter Arabella. In the evening, he left for Chartwell wearing a huge duffle-coat with broad fur collar which had been given him by Lady Churchill.

On December 17, high society flocked to an elaborate fancy-dress party at the Casanova Club. The hostess, Miss Judy Montagu, appeared as a Victorian housemaid. Mrs. Gerald Legge was in a scarlet ballet dress, twenty-two-year-old Princess Margarethe of Sweden came as Little Red Riding Hood and Dominic Elwes, son of the painter Simon Elwes, was an American cowboy.

Missing from the contemporary scene was twenty-seven-year-old heiress Olga Deterding, who until recently had been living in the Ritz Hotel in London and enjoying the fortune which she had inherited from her father, founder of the Royal Dutch Shell Company. On December 21, headlines blazed the news that she had abandoned the high life and begun working in Dr. Albert Schweitzer's leper colony in French Equatorial Africa. 'Having so much money makes it necessary for me to cleanse myself' she said.

Meanwhile, it was announced that photographer Antony Armstrong-Jones would be spending Christmas in London. 'I shall be working' he explained. 'So no parties and festivities for me. I think all my friends will be out of town. I would be if I could. My ideal Christmas is sunning myself in Trinidad.'

New Year celebrations at the Savoy Hotel were enlivened by the presence of the flamboyant Nubar Gulbenkian, with a purple Mexican sombrero on his head and a purple orchid in his buttonhole. Mrs. Gulbenkian, in diamonds and pearls, explained that she was recovering from the 'flu. 'I had to get medicine from the chemist before coming here tonight' she said.

On January 9, the severely over-worked Sir Anthony Eden handed over as Prime Minister to sixty-two-year-old Mr. Harold Macmillan. That night, Macmillan dined off oysters, steak and champagne at the Turf Club with Tory Chief Whip, Edward Heath. Asked afterwards what they had discussed together, Mr. Heath replied, 'Racing'.

The following day, sixty-eight-year-old poet T. S. Eliot astonished the literary world by suddenly marrying his thirty-year-old secretary. The ceremony took place at 6.15 in the morning at St. Barnabas's Church, West Kensington. 'She has worshipped Mr. Eliot since she was fourteen, but the marriage is a complete surprise' said a close friend of the couple.

On January 21, twenty-year-old rock-and-roll star Tommy Steele made his debut at the Café de Paris. In the audience that night were Mr. and Mrs. Douglas Fairbanks, young Lord Montagu of Beaulieu, Oliver Messel and the silver-haired Baroness Ravensdale, spinster daughter of the late Lord Curzon. 'I love the rhythm but I don't think I'll try dancing it myself' said Douglas Fairbanks.

At the end of January, eight-year-old Prince Charles became a pupil at Hill House Preparatory School in Knightsbridge, an exclusive establishment run by an eagle-eyed former artillery officer, Colonel Townend.

On February 6, the Royal Yacht, carrying the Duke of Edinburgh home from the Olympic Games in Melbourne, paused at Gibraltar and disgorged Lieutenant-Commander Michael Parker, who had recently resigned as the Duke's Private Secretary following the break-up of his marriage.

On February 13, fifty-nine-year-old Lord Inverclyde was thrown from his sleeper on board the Glasgow–Euston express and struck his head on an ashtray. Five stitches were required to sew up the wound. Arriving in London later, he said: 'All this fuss is really most embarrassing.' It was recalled that before the war, Lord Inverclyde had been married to the famous music-hall star, June.

Meanwhile, preparations were going on at Winfield House for the arrival of the new Ambassador Jock Whitney. The butler at the house, Charles Epps, who in his earlier days had worked for the Prime Minister Mr. Asquith, explained 'Here we entertain in the English style. I tell all the Ambassadors that if they want to do things the American way they will have to teach me.'

On February 14, Old Etonian writer Jeremy Sandford was married to twenty-year-old Nell Dunn, whose grandfather Sir James Dunn had died the previous year leaving £25,000,000. The reception at the Ritz Hotel was graced by the presence of seventy-nine-year-old Augustus John, who had come up from his home at Fordingbridge in his most casual clothes.

On February 17, the Queen and the Duke of Edinburgh were reunited at Lisbon after 134 days separation. Rumours in the foreign Press that all was not well between husband and wife were quickly dispelled and reporters looked in vain for signs of tension or displeasure on the Queen's face.

On February 28, Sir Winston Churchill, on holiday in Monte Carlo, lunched for the first time on board Aristotle Onassis's luxurious new yacht *Christina*. It was described as the meeting of two great minds. Sir Winston remained on board the vessel until 7.00 pm playing chemin de fer.

Meanwhile, the Queen and Prince Philip had returned to England. On their first night out together after their return, they went to the Fortune Theatre in Covent Garden to see the much-talked about revue *At the Drop of a Hat* starring Michael Flanders and Donald Swann. It was reported that the Queen joined in singing the popular 'Hippopotamus Song'.

On March 11, Lord Vivian, victim of a famous shooting accident three years earlier, began work as a director and manager of Le Pavillon restaurant off Sloane Square. 'I expect to be at work most of the time from lunch till one in the morning' he said.

On March 26, Old Harrovian Cecil Beaton put on conventional morning-dress and drove to Buckingham Palace to receive the CBE. 'I am very grateful to the Royal Family' he said. 'In the tens of thousands of pictures I have taken of them they have shown monumental patience and understanding.'

On April 5, the contents of Lowther Castle, famous seat of the 5th Earl of Lonsdale came under the hammer. A stained-glass window presented to the Earl by the Kaiser in 1895, was bought back for £50 by the Kaiser's grandson, Prince Frederick of Prussia, who had been living in England for many years. Following the sale, the 270-room castle was partly demolished and its stable block was turned into a broiler chicken unit with accommodation for more than 300,000 birds.

On April 8, the Queen's diamond tiara and other jewellery dazzled the audience at the Paris Opera. 'Frankly the Queen is not much interested in fashion' said Royal dress designer Norman Hartnell, who was also present on this occasion. 'She doesn't want to set styles. She wants to be comfortable.'

At the end of April, it was revealed that Sir Winston Churchill's bodyguard, Detective-Sergeant Edmund Murray, had submitted three pictures to this year's Royal Academy, all of which had been rejected. 'It's jolly bad luck' said Royal Academy Secretary Humphrey Brooke. 'But more people than ever are painting. We got 11,000 entries this year.'

When the show opened on May 4, there was much controversy over a portrait of Sir Winston by Ruskin Spear. 'That great big tapioca blob of a head, that's what fascinated me' said the artist. Sir Winston's old opponent, Earl Attlee, described the picture as 'a disgusting caricature'.

On May 7, seventy-eight-year-old Jimmy de Rothschild died in London, leaving £11,000,000. His vast Victorian mansion, Waddesdon Manor in Buckinghamshire, was bequeathed to the National Trust together with its entire contents.

In the meantime, a great fuss had blown up over the unhappy romance between twenty-five-year-old Robin Douglas-Home and twenty-two-year-old Princess Margarethe of Sweden, who had met for the first time the previous September. It was understood that the match had been banned by Margarethe's mother, Princess Sibylla. 'I really cannot say much at this stage' said Robin, who was working as an advertising copywriter at the J. Walter Thompson agency during the day and playing the piano at night at the Berkeley Hotel.

On May 16, Mr. Douglas-Home was present at a lavish coming-out dance at the Dorchester Hotel in honour of twin sisters Marina and Tessa Kennedy, nieces of the wealthy shipowner Mr. Vane Ivanovic. Flunkies in wigs were in attendance and over £4,000 had been spent transforming the hotel's ballroom into a miniature Versailles.

The following day saw the arrival of seventy-nine-year-old great-grandmother Mme. Consuelo Vanderbilt Balsan, former Duchess of Marlborough. It was her first visit to England since 1939. She was met off the night-ferry at Victoria Station and driven to Blenheim Palace to spend the weekend with her son, the Duke of Marlborough.

On May 20, fifty-four-year-old Tallulah Bankhead arrived in England for a cabaret season at the ailing Café de Paris. 'I haven't worked out any details yet' she said at a Press conference at the Ritz. 'My first night will be a kinda dress rehearsal.' Sadly, her act got a very mixed reception and for the next six weeks, she played to a half-empty restaurant.

On June 3, the infant daughter of Mr. and Mrs. Hugh Fraser was christened Rebecca Rose at the Church of the Assumption in Warwick Street. Among the godparents were the wealthy Mrs. Israel Sieff, Viscount Chandos and the Countess of Eldon.

On June 5, the Queen, resplendent in delphinium-blue silk, arrived at the Derby in a special train along with the Queen Mother and Princess Margaret. Also at Epsom that day was the new Prime Minister Harold Macmillan, leaving his Defence Minister Duncan Sandys to explain his absence to the House of Commons. 'My Honourable Friend is at an important meeting' said Sandys wittily.

On June 23, the twenty-one-year-old Duke of Kent, now stationed at Catterick with his regiment, was found playing tennis at nearby Hovingham Hall with beautiful, golden-haired Katharine Worsley. 'The

Duke and my daughter are just good friends' said Katharine's father, Sir William Worsley. 'A romance? Good gracious. I don't think so.'

On June 27, Westminster City Councillor Mrs. Gerald Legge climbed into a tightly-belted sewerman's coat and thigh-length rubber boots and descended into the London sewer system. 'I was surprised' she said afterwards. 'The LCC sewers smelt to high heaven but our Westminster ones didn't smell at all.'

Later that day, Princess Margaret attended a Dockland Settlement ball at the Savoy Hotel with her old friend Billy Wallace. It was noticed that at one moment during the evening the Princess took three matches to light a cigarette. A supply of toothpicks was also spotted on the Royal table.

On July 11, a great era in European life ended with the death of seventy-nine-year-old Aga Khan. Hundreds of pressmen gathered outside his villa in Switzerland anxious to know who would succeed him. The following day, the great potentate's will was flown from London and the world was informed that the title Aga Khan had passed to his twenty-year-old grandson Karim, now in his second year at Harvard. 'My religious responsibilities begin as of today' he told his assembled followers.

That night, there was a ball at Woburn Abbey for the Duke of Bedford's stepdaughter, eighteen-year-old Lorna Lyle. It was said to be the first dance held at the Abbey for eighty or ninety years. The Queen had been invited but had politely declined.

On July 27, the new Aga Khan arrived in London to stay with his mother Princess Joan Aly Khan at her Eaton Square home, amidst rumours that he was about to announce his engagement. 'I think the newspapers have married me to three women already and given me innumerable people as fiancées' he said. 'There is nothing in it.'

On August 3, an attack on the Queen by thirty-three-year-old Lord Altrincham made headline news. Writing in a magazine called the *National and English Review*, the young peer had declared that the Queen sounded like 'a priggish school girl . . . a recent candidate for confirmation.' In the outcry that followed, Altrincham was slapped on the face as he emerged from Television House, Kingsway after an interview with Mr. Robin Day. His attacker was later fined £1 at Bow Street and told by the magistrate that he had 'made a most unsavoury episode even more squalid'.

On August 7, loyal crowds stood twenty-feet deep to cheer the Queen as she left by train for Balmoral, accompanied by enough luggage to fill five station trollies.

On August 11, twenty-seven-year-old John Osborne, whose play *Look Back in Anger* had established him as a national figure the previous year, was married to actress Mary Ure at Chelsea Registry Office. 'We both have the strongest possible objections to marrying in church. We loathe all clergymen' the couple declared on their way to a reception at the Au Père de Nico restaurant.

In the middle of August, the Royal Family was subjected to another attack, this time from nineteen-year-old Lord Londonderry, whose sister Lady Jane Vane-Tempest-Stewart had been a maid of honour at the Coronation. In a letter to the *New Statesman*, the young peer attacked the Royal Family's 'toothpaste smiles' and 'deplorable taste in clothes'. He was immediately rebuked by his seventy-seven-year-old grandmother the Dowager Lady Londonderry, who issued a statement from her Irish home describing her grandson's letter as 'not only vulgar but also silly and childish'. On August 26, Lord Londonderry publicly apologised for his bad manners and left for an Outward Bound course on the Cumberland fells.

On September 4, Sir John Wolfenden's long awaited report on Prostitution and Homosexuality was published. One member of Sir John's team, the former Procurator Fiscal of Scotland, James Adair, disagreed fiercely with the committee's findings. 'I do not know what will happen if these recommendations become law' he said. 'I would have the darkest fears for the future.'

On September 12, the once fashionable Café de Paris reopened as a dance-hall. 'This is the new age' said the Duke of Bedford, who had been recruited to judge a skiffle-group competition. 'We must cater for it.' Gum-chewing teenagers had replaced the dinner-jacketed patrons of the past.

On September 23, Prince Charles joined the new boys at Cheam School, making the long journey from

Princess Margaret and Billy Wallace during a holiday in Scotland

Balmoral by the Royal Train and his father's Lagonda and accompanied by a large leather trunk bearing the legend 'HRH Prince Charles'.

On October 2, eighty-three-year-old Somerset Maugham arrived in London. After a twenty-four-hour train journey from his home in the South of France, he was dismayed to learn there were no crumpets for tea at the Dorchester Hotel. 'When I was young, one could have crumpets and muffins for tea. One cannot any more in this hard life we lead.'

The same day, it was revealed that Prince Charles had been struck down by the wave of Asian flu that was sweeping the country. 'I have patients in hospital and a busy practice' said the doctor in charge of the case. 'Enquiries about Prince Charles are not helping me.'

A few days later, the same epidemic hit Eton College where it was reported on October 8 that 615 boys were in bed, including sixteen-year-old Winston Churchill, grandson of the former Prime Minister. 'The disease hit hard and quick' said the headmaster Dr. Birley. 'But we think we will be back to normal within a week.'

On October 14, it was announced that Malcolm Muggeridge had joined the Queen's critics describing her as 'frumpish and banal' in an American magazine. In the outcry that followed, the white-haired broadcaster was temporarily barred from appearing on the BBC, on the instructions of the Director General, and it was said that his future was 'under consideration'.

On October 16, Princess Margaret's friend Billy Wallace left his home in South Street for a sanatorium in the country. 'I am going away for a complete check-up. I am not fit. But I hope all will be well after a time in the country.'

Four days later, the Duke of Devonshire replied to the Queen's recent attackers in a speech at a London dinner. 'Her Majesty is, in every sense of the word, this nation's crowning glory. Let us dismiss the mouthings of these people as the bleatings – or should I say the bleepings? – of a publicity-seeking sniffle group.'

At the end of the month, attention turned to the Ritz Hotel where one of the residents, a hitherto unknown oil magnate named Paul Getty, had recently been named in an American magazine as one of the world's richest men. 'I can't say that it thrills me' said Getty, whose wealth had been assessed at between $700,000,000 and $1,000,000,000. 'If you can actually count your money you are not really a rich man.'

On November 6, novelist Barbara Cartland and her daughter Mrs. Gerald Legge threw an elaborate party at the Carlton Gardens home of Sir Alfred Bossom. The highlight of the evening was 'A Pageant of Famous Beauties Down the Ages', featuring Mrs. Hugh Fraser as Nell Gwynne, the Duchess of Argyll as Marie Antoinette and Lady Anne Tennant as Helen of Troy.

On November 14, it was announced that the formal presentation of débutantes at Buckingham Palace would cease the following year. 'How horribly disappointing for all the darlings now at school who won't meet the Queen' said Lady Aylwen, wife of a former Lord Mayor of London. 'It is a magnificent decision' said Lord Altrincham, who four months earlier had been one of the Queen's attackers.

Further excitement emanated from the High Court a few days later when Mr. Justice Roxborgh granted an injunction restraining eighteen-year-old heiress Tessa Kennedy from marrying Mr. Dominic Elwes and prohibiting her from leaving the jurisdiction of the courts. Swiftly after the issue of this injunction, the couple disappeared. A further injunction was issued on December 3 ordering Mr. Elwes to return Miss

Runaway lovers nineteen-year-old Tessa Kennedy and twenty-six-year-old Dominic Elwes

Kennedy, whose coming-out dance at the Dorchester Hotel six months earlier had been described as the Ball of the Year.

On December 13, the new Aga Khan celebrated his twenty-first birthday with a party at the Savoy Hotel. Among the 100 guests who sat down to dinner in a room overlooking the Thames were the Duchess of Argyll, Robin Douglas-Home, Lorna Lyle and seventeen-year-old Sylvia Casablancas. Afterwards, there was dancing to the strains of an eight-piece Cuban band brought over from Paris for the occasion. At the end of the evening, Prince Aly Khan escorted his old friend, the Duchess of Argyll, to her car.

Shortly before Christmas, Hungarian actress Eva Bartok flew into England to spend the festive season at a cottage at Kingston-on-Thames, where she was later visited by her old friend the Marquess of Milford Haven. Arriving at the cottage in a cream-coloured Ford Prefect, the Marquess vigorously denied that he was contemplating marriage to the actress. 'These rumours are all made up. I'm saying nothing.'

1958

The New Year was welcomed with a wild party in Felix Topolski's studio under Waterloo Bridge. Mick Mulligan's band played Dixieland music and Eva Bartok danced cheek-to-cheek with the Marquess of Milford Haven. Others present included Lady Jane Vane-Tempest-Stewart, Prince Rupert von Lowenstein and Lord and Lady Kilmarnock. 'We must get all these socialites jiving and having a good time' said the debonair co-host, Michael Alexander, who had been imprisoned in Colditz Castle during the war.

On January 5, the Prime Minister Harold Macmillan had lunch with Sir Winston Churchill at Chartwell. Sir Winston's poodle, Rufus, danced around at the feet of the two great statesmen.

On January 10, wealthy John Aspinall appeared at Marylebone Court charged with keeping a common gaming-house at a flat in Hyde Park Street. Twenty-one other people were charged with him including Lord Willoughby de Eresby, heir to the Earl of Ancaster, and his sister Lady Jane Willoughby. On being released on bail, Aspinall was whisked away from the court in a chauffeur-driven Rolls-Royce.

On January 14, Mrs. Anne Chamberlain, seventy-four-year-old widow of the former Prime Minister Neville Chamberlain, was knocked down by a motorcycle in Victoria Street and taken to hospital with a suspected hip fracture.

On January 23, heiress Tessa Kennedy and her friend Dominic Elwes, who had been forbidden to marry by a High Court judge two months earlier, fled the country and were soon reported to be on their way to the Dutch West Indies. 'I don't suppose I shall go back to England again' said Dominic, who now faced a prison sentence for defying the judge's order.

On January 28, it was revealed that Lady Docker was selling a sapphire and diamond Cartier necklace at Christie's. On board his 860-ton yacht *Shemara*, now anchored at Cannes, Sir Bernard Docker explained 'Norah has never been very fond of sapphires. She prefers rubies and emeralds.' Asked whether he and his wife were suffering financially, Sir Bernard said: 'As far as it is humanly possible to see, I anticipate that we shall have all the money we shall want for our rather expensive life and we shall be able to leave Lance as much as we want to.'

The following day, Princess Margaret drove in a green Rover car to Cambridge to have lunch with the Rev. Simon Phipps, now Chaplain of Trinity College. It was revealed that the couple ate tournedos steaks, with cauliflower Bearnaise and creamed potatoes, washed down with a bottle of Château Calon-Ségur, 1949.

Early in February, Mr. and Mrs. Hugh Fraser returned from the Middle East with two wooden rhinos and an African drum for their nine-month-old daughter, Rebecca.

On February 11, the Duke of Bedford announced that he was to go on a lecture tour of America, talking about Old England, English Castles and Etiquette. Asked if he would appear in cabaret in Las Vegas, he replied: 'Of course I would. I would do anything to attract American visitors to Woburn.'

On February 24, the Queen's Chaplain, the Venerable Kenneth Bickersteth, who had a heart attack in the Canary Islands, was flown home in a specially chartered Viscount airliner, costing his family £4,000.

At the end of the month, it was announced that film star Diana Dors had hired a butler, twenty-four-year-old Patrick O'Connor. Asked to pose for a photograph with Miss Dors, O'Connor replied, 'Such a thing would be unthinkable. Her ladyship has her dignity, you know.'

At the beginning of March, details were released of Mr. Nubar Gulbenkian's new car, covered in wickerwork and somewhat resembling a handsom cab. 'We made it specially' said Rolls-Royce dealer Jack Barclay. 'It took eighteen months and cost £3,000. Mr. Gulbenkian spent many hours planning it with me.'

On March 7, Lord Moran flew home after visiting Sir Winston Churchill in Monte Carlo who had been taken ill there. 'He is a very good patient' he said. 'So many people seem to have the idea that he is a bad one but really it's not true.' A few days later, Sir Winston was found lunching off a roast saddle of lamb with provençal herbs at a hill-top restaurant overlooking Villefranche.

On March 14, twenty-year-old Frances Sweeny, who had recently announced her engagement to the young Duke of Rutland, was dismounted while riding side-saddle in Kensington Road. 'Miss Sweeny has

Millionaire Nubar Gulbenkian takes delivery of his taxi car. Right, close up of rear of vehicle

been riding with me since she was five years old and is very competent' said her instructress, Miss Dickson, who ran a riding-school in Jays Mews.

Four days later, John Aspinall and his friends were cleared of gambling offences. Celebrating over champagne at his home in Eaton Place, Mr. Aspinall declared 'I have been giving parties since the age of ten. I am awfully fond of playing the party host.' Said his mother, Lady Osborne, 'It is a poor thing if you can't have a private party in a private flat without the police coming.'

The following day, it was announced that runaway couple Dominic Elwes and Tessa Kennedy, who had married six weeks earlier in Havana, were now stranded in Florida. 'We're flat broke and need food and money' said Dominic.

On March 26, Group-Captain Peter Townsend called at Clarence House, had tea with Princess Margaret and stayed for three hours. It was the couple's first meeting for two-and-a-half years and caused such excitement that Buckingham Palace was forced to announce that nothing had changed since the Princess's statement in 1955.

Field Marshal Lord Montgomery leaves Chartwell after dining with his old comrade Sir Winston Churchill. Note the forward slanting windscreen of his Rolls-Royce, designed to deflect rain at high speed

At the beginning of April, it was announced that Field Marshal Viscount Montgomery had purchased the 1936 Rolls-Royce which had been borrowed from the Army for the past four years. The car was noted for its strange forward-sloping windscreen, designed to deflect rain at high speed.

Meanwhile, a romance had blossomed between Commander Michael Parker, former secretary to Prince Philip, and Miss Nancy Oakes, whose multi-millionaire father, Sir Harry Oakes, had been murdered in sensational circumstances in the Bahamas during the war. On April 21, Nancy flew into London saying she was coming to see her doctor. On being questioned about Commander Parker, she replied: 'Is he in London? If he is, I should like to see him.'

The same day, the news broke that Prince Rainier of Monaco was asking his Council of State for a decree expelling Sir Bernard and Lady Docker from his principality. The announcement followed an incident at the Casino where Lady Docker had criticised the sovereigns of Monaco and ripped up the country's flag. 'As far as I'm concerned, Prince Rainier can go and jump in the sea' said fifty-one-year-old Lady Docker from her suite at the Majestic Hotel at Cannes. 'The whole thing is too silly and ridiculous. Monte Carlo is a dump. Anyway, I've already banned myself.' From his suite at Claridge's Hotel in London, Sir Bernard commented, 'Ban or no ban, you can take it we're not going back to that dreary little country.'

A few days later, a formal expulsion order banning Lady Docker from not only Monaco, but the entire Riviera, was served on her at her hotel in Cannes. On April 27, she arrived at London Airport in a long white mink coat with a huge emerald ring glittering on her left hand, declaring 'I'm at war with Rainier!'

Meanwhile, Sir Winston Churchill had also returned from the Riviera. His first night out was on April 29 when he attended the annual dinner at Burlington House launching the Royal Academy's Summer show. This year's star exhibit was a startling portrait of the young Countess of Dalkeith which had taken artist John Merton 1,500 hours to complete. At the crowded Private View the following day, the Countess remarked: 'I like it but I think it flatters me.'

At the beginning of May, Robin Douglas-Home was found staying at the Hampshire home of his uncle, William Douglas-Home, after an inconclusive visit to Sweden to see his friend Princess Margarethe. 'Robin is ill and tired' said his aunt. 'He cannot speak to anyone on the telephone.' A few days later, he broke his silence to deny rumours that the romance was over. 'That's inaccurate poppycock of the sort you expect in certain papers' he said.

Sir Bernard and Lady Docker on their return from the Riviera

On May 15, twenty-year-old Frances Sweeny, daughter of the Duchess of Argyll, was married to the Duke of Rutland. At the ceremony at Caxton Hall, the bride wore a pink Hartnell gown adorned with ostrich feathers which onlookers attempted to pluck out as mementoes. At the reception at Claridge's, at which the guests included Charles Clore, Jocelyn Stevens and Douglas Fairbanks, Jr., Tim Clayton's band played Dixieland and rock-music. It was noted that the thirty-eight-year-old Duke had given his bride a Mercedes as a wedding present.

The same day, Sir Winston Churchill cut his hand in the door of the lift at the House of Commons and Dr. J. Dickson Mabon, Labour MP for Greenwich, was summoned from the chamber to dress the wound.

On May 16, the twenty-year-old Marquess of Londonderry married seventeen-year-old Nicolette Harrison, daughter of a Lloyds underwriter. After the service at Wilton Church, near Salisbury, the bridegroom's formidable grandmother, the Dowager Lady Londonderry, now seventy-eight years old, waved a stout stick in the air to summon her motor-car.

On May 20, the coming of age of Guinness heir, Viscount Elveden, now in his second year at Cambridge, was celebrated with a party for 1,500 Guinness employees at Elveden Hall, Suffolk. 'He's a wonderful boy and he'll make a big success of running the estates' declared ninety-year-old gamekeeper, Tom Turner.

The following day, Cecil Beaton arranged a private preview of the film *Gigi* for his old friends Nancy Lady Astor, Oliver Messel, Mrs. Daisy Fellowes and Maureen Marchioness of Dufferin and Ava.

On June 10, it was announced that eighteen-year-old Auberon Waugh, a cornet in the Royal Horse Guards, was seriously ill in the British Military Hospital in Cyprus following an accident with a machine-gun. As his mother flew out to see him in a specially chartered plane, the headmaster at Downside was questioned about his former pupil. 'He is a rather clever boy, brilliant writer, rather like his father, you see, but not much of an athlete.'

On June 11, Oxford undergraduate Viscount Encombe, heir to the Earl of Eldon, was hauled before his Magdalen College proctors and accused of killing college deer with a bow and arrow. A 2.00 am barbecue party given by the young Viscount had been raided and one of the college deer had been found roasting. 'The deer was decidedly off' said one of the guests. 'In fact, it tasted more like kipper.' The Viscount's sending-down party a few days later also ended in trouble and a Black Maria was summoned.

On June 27, Somerset Maugham, now eighty-four years old, returned to his old school, King's College, Canterbury, to open a new science wing. 'I am very, very old and I shall never see you again' he told the assembled pupils. Shortly afterwards, the aged writer began a course of treatment at a clinic in Montreux, run by Professor Paul Niehans who claimed to be able to keep old men young by cellular therapy.

At the beginning of July, the Duke of Marlborough spoke of the hardships of having Blenheim Palace open to the public. 'I shut myself away behind the green railings in the East Wing and on the whole life is liveable' he said. 'People are very good but they will shuffle and wear out my carpets.'

On July 11, the relationship between Mr. Robin Douglas-Home and Princess Margarethe of Sweden took another turn for the worse when it was announced that Mr. Douglas-Home had cancelled his plan to go to the Swedish Royal Family's summer Palace at Oeland. 'For reasons which must remain private, I have decided not to visit Sweden in the foreseeable future' he said.

Meanwhile, Mr. and Mrs. Dominic Elwes, who had run away to get married at the beginning of the year, were sailing home to submit to the jurisdiction of the court. On July 15, the liner the *Liberté* docked at Southampton and the couple were given VIP treatment to get them through the immigration formalities. That evening, Mr.Elwes was deposited in Brixton Prison to purge his contempt of court. A fortnight later, he was released and reunited with his wife after a High Court judge had decided that he had been in prison 'long enough to vindicate the rule of law and deter like-minded youths from imitating his foolish escapades'.

On July 31, sixty-two-year-old Lord Teynham, Deputy Speaker in the House of Lords, spoke of his relationship with an escaped Borstal girl whom he had met in a West End bar. 'All I did was befriend the girl. Yes, we did go swimming in the nude – but if I'd known she was a Borstal escapee, I should have had nothing to do with her.'

In the middle of August, Prime Minister Harold Macmillan was found staying with the Duke and Duchess of Devonshire at Bolton Hall, Yorkshire where he and Lady Dorothy had spent part of their honeymoon thirty-eight years earlier. Mr. Macmillan appeared on the moors dressed in a green tweed suit, knee-breeches, spats and cardigan.

A few days later, veteran politician Earl Winterton was yachting on his lake at Chiddingfold when his boat suddenly capsized and the seventy-five-year-old Earl was thrown into the slimy, weed-choked water. Fortunately, his chauffeur Mr. Thomas Boase was watching from the bank and was able to rescue his master. 'It might have been very nasty' said Lady Winterton afterwards. 'I should be quite terrified to sail on that lake.'

On September 1, fifty-four-year-old Cecil Beaton was fined ten shillings for parking in a prohibited street in Salisbury.

On September 10, celebrities gathered at the Adelphi Theatre in London for the first night of *Auntie Mame* starring sixty-year-old Beatrice Lillie. Among those present were heiress Nancy Oakes and her friend Lieutenant Commander Michael Parker and Mr. and Mrs. Dominic Elwes. 'It is the first time we have appeared together' said Dominic. 'We hide ourselves as much as we can but we do hope to come out sometimes.'

Meanwhile, the Marquess of Tavistock and former débutante Henrietta Tiarks had returned from holiday together vigorously denying rumours of a romance. 'It is so ridiculous. We have been on holiday together before and no one has thought anything about it' said Miss Tiarks. 'After all, I have known Henrietta for fourteen years' said the young Marquess, heir to the showman Duke of Bedford.

On October 1, the fifty-nine-year-old Earl of Carnarvon was reported to be recovering from a serious illness in New York. 'I was as near to death as anyone could be but great faith and a lot of prayers pulled me through' said the famous sporting peer. 'You can say it was a photo-finish for the survival stakes.'

On October 7, the wealthy and popular Chips Channon, who had been knighted the previous year, died in hospital aged sixty-one. A memorial service was held later at St. Margaret's Westminster amidst much speculation about the contents of the diaries which Chips had been keeping for many years and many of which had already been deposited in the British Museum. 'Unfortunately I haven't read them' said his twenty-two-year-old son Paul. 'He made no secret of writing them but he never volunteered to let me have a look.'

On October 21, the first life peers and peeresses were welcomed into the House of Lords. It was noted that the ermine robes worn at the ceremony by the fifty-year-old Earl Marshal the Duke of Norfolk were beginning to go brown, perhaps owing to excessive use over the years or the antiquity of the garments themselves.

Later that day, the Queen and Prince Philip attended a dazzling reception at the German Embassy at 21 Belgrave Square – said to be the first visit to the Embassy by a reigning British sovereign since 1913. Prince Philip was in knee-breeches with the jewelled Order of the Garter strapped below his left knee. It was noted that a German Military Attaché wore the Iron Cross, but without the swastika.

The same night, a few streets away in Egerton Crescent, the Marchioness of Northampton threw a party which was attended by Frank Sinatra and his friend Lady Beatty, Lady Lewisham, film producer Ivan Foxwell and other notabilities. Arriving with Eva Bartok, the Marquess of Milford Haven turned to the attendant Pressmen and said: 'What's the matter with you all? You are a lot of morons. Leave the girl alone.'

On November 4, Earl Lloyd-George, sixty-nine-year-old son of the former Prime Minister, suddenly reappeared after ten years in America. The peer was found living in a labourer's cottage on his brother's estate, where one of the only pieces of furniture was a canvas chair. 'I'm just a nobody' he said. 'I'm a poor man. My brother, Lord Tenby, has been very kind to me.'

On November 8, multi-millionairess Barbara Hutton arrived in London by the boat-train accompanied by twenty-eight-year-old James Douglas, son of America's Air Secretary. From her Claridge's suite, forty-five year-old Miss Hutton rang her old friends and insisted that her recent marriage to Baron Gottfried von Cramm was still going all right.

On November 22, Mr. and Mrs. Aristotle Onassis arrived to spend the weekend with Sir Winston Churchill. After a delay at the airport, when customs officials opened the shipping magnate's cases and spread out his suits, shirts and ties on the counter, the couple drove to Chartwell, where a large crowd had collected. 'It hasn't been like this for years' said a policeman on duty. 'Who is this bloke Onassis anyway?' During the course of the weekend, Sir Winston made his guests play croquet and showed off his goldfish. Handing Onassis a tin of grain, he said 'Have a shot at feeding 'em.'

On November 27, American Vice-President Richard Nixon arrived and was driven to Winfield House where the Queen was due to dine that night. One hour before dinner, it was discovered that the Vice-President had arrived without his dinner-jacket. He later appeared in an outfit borrowed from an aide, several sizes too big.

Three days later, Mr. Ernest Simpson, former husband of the Duchess of Windsor, died in London aged sixty-one. It was noted that Mr. Simpson had shunned publicity all his life and had never given interviews to the Press or attempted to publish his side of the Abdication story. At a memorial service held later at St. Peter's, Eaton Square, one of the mourners was Lord Brownlow who had accompanied Mrs. Simpson on her flight across France in December 1936.

On December 3, more old memories were revived when the Dowager Lady Londonderry, the greatest political hostess of her day, celebrated her seventy-ninth birthday with a party at Londonderry House, Park Lane, where her family still retained a flat. The guest of honour was the Prime Minister, Mr. Harold Macmillan, who was described as 'an old family friend'.

A fortnight later, on December 16, Noel Coward celebrated his fifty-ninth birthday at a party given by his old friend Miss Gladys Calthrop at her home in Cadogan Place. Guests included Vivien Leigh, Beatrice Lillie, sixty-nine-year-old Gladys Cooper and Rex Harrison, who was currently starring in *My Fair Lady* at the Theatre Royal, Drury Lane. At the end of the evening, Coward sat down at a grand piano and gave his latest version of 'Let's Do It'.

At Sandringham at Christmas, it was noted that Prince Charles's leg was in plaster. It was revealed that he had tripped on a staircase at Cheam School. The first to leave the Queen's house party after Christmas was the Duke of Kent. He left to visit his old friend Katharine Worsley at Hovingham Hall near York.

1959

The New Year was welcomed with a party given by the vivacious Mrs. Bunty Kinsman at her home in Milner Street, Chelsea. The theme of the party was the Vie de Bohème. Mrs. Kinsman was attired as a Salvador Dali painting and her Lloyds underwriter husband was dressed as the Eiffel Tower by Moonlight. Duncan Sandys, Minister of Defence, wore a painter's smock.

On January 7, Charlie Chaplin, now sixty-nine years old, white-haired and portly, travelled by Underground from Leicester Square to the Bank. 'It's been one of my favourite rides since I was a boy and I get too few chances of doing it' he said. That evening, Chaplin and his wife went to see Tommy Steele in *Cinderella* at the Coliseum. 'A very versatile young man, Mr. Steele. He will go far in show business' commented Mr. Chaplin.

On January 12, Sir Winston Churchill flew off in an aeroplane provided by his friend Mr. Onassis for a painting holiday in Marrakesh, which he had not visited for eight years. A Moroccan guard of honour greeted him on arrival and Churchill and Onassis dined together that night at the Hotel Mamounia. It was noted that Onassis and his wife Tina had spent Christmas apart for the first time during their married life.

On January 18, twenty-one-year-old Lord Valentine Thynne, younger son of the Marquess of Bath, bicycled through Sloane Square wearing pale-blue pyjamas. He was followed by seventeen-year-old Greville Howard, in gold pyjamas, and a convertible white Rolls-Royce piled with young débutantes. 'We hope to make this an annual event' said one of the revellers.

At the end of the month, twenty-three-year-old Paul Channon was elected MP for Southend West after a By-election caused by the death of his father, Chips Channon, the previous autumn. It was noted that Mr. Channon, now the youngest MP, was the fourth member of his family to hold the seat.

On February 2, Viscount Montgomery was struck down by toothache while on holiday in Gstaad. 'Please find me a suitable dentist at once' he demanded. 'A fellow who can speak decent English. I want to be able to talk to the man and not merely gesticulate.' A suitable man was quickly produced and the Field Marshal's trouble was dealt with. 'Splendid' he said. 'Absolutely splendid.'

On February 10, the Duke of Bedford attended a private showing of the controversial film *Nudist Paradise*, part of which had been shot at Woburn Abbey. 'I don't care as long as it brings money' he said. 'I wouldn't mind going nudist myself. Don't see what all the fuss is about.'

Two days later, Lord Harewood, first cousin to the Queen, appeared at a party at the Dorchester Hotel dressed as a woman. He had hired his costume, that of a nineteenth-century English governess, from Covent Garden Opera House but had to wear his own shoes. 'They didn't have a lady's size for my big feet' he explained.

On February 21, Harold Macmillan arrived in Moscow wearing a Russian-style white fur hat which he had first worn in Finland in 1940. A convoy of cars took the Prime Minister to Mr. Krushchev's dacha fifty miles south-east of Moscow where talks took place over vodka and Caucasian wines. 'The talks went awfully well' said a British spokesman. 'The two got on well and they were very relaxed. They all laughed a lot.' During the visit, Mr. Kruschev presented Macmillan with a mounted elk's head which was soon found hanging in the servants' hall at the Prime Minister's country home, Birch Grove in Sussex.

On March 9, it was announced that a case containing £150,000 worth of jewellery had been stolen from Lady Docker's Rolls-Royce while she was opening a new hairdressing salon in Southampton's town centre. 'I have lost everything' she wept. 'The sapphires were as big as half crown pieces.' During the next few days, the River Itchen was dragged in the search for the gems and Lady Docker was visited at her Mayfair home by Mr. Billy Hill, self-styled former King of the Underworld. 'I promised her I would not leave a stone unturned until I got those jewels back for her. I admire Lady Docker. She's not afraid to mix with people like me.'

On March 19, some 200 young people, described as members of 'the Chelsea set', attended a riotous party on the Inner Circle Underground line. Fights broke out in the course of the evening. Lord Valentine Thynne was pushed off the train at Farringdon Station and other participants were removed by the police. 'There ought to be a bit more of this to waken up life' said one of the revellers.

On March 24, a uniformed chauffeur arrived at the Savoy Theatre with important papers for Defence Minister Duncan Sandys to sign during the interval. 'I've been away all day visiting the Thor Rocket site and didn't get back to the office to sign anything. That's why I'm doing it now' he explained.

On April 1, there was much excitement over the marriage of seventy-seven-year-old bachelor millionaire racehorse owner Sir Victor Sassoon and his thirty-nine-year-old nurse Evelyn Barnes from Dallas, Texas, who had been his constant companion for the past six years. The ceremony took place at Sir Victor's ultra-luxurious villa in the Bahamas.

Four days later, it was announced that Princess Margaret's friend, Colin Tennant, was negotiating to purchase the 1,250-acre island of Mustique in the West Indies. 'My plan is to appoint a resident manager and I would visit the island as often as my interests in the City would allow' he said. It was noted that the island had eight beaches and two harbours.

On April 11, thirty-two-year-old Lord Montagu of Beaulieu married Miss Belinda Crossley, niece of Lord Somerleyton. The bride arrived twelve minutes late for the ceremony at Beaulieu Abbey in a 1906 Renault borrowed from the bridegroom's motor museum. Heavy rain caused many of the guests' cars to sink into the mud and several had to be towed away by tractors.

On April 23, the great Lady Londonderry died at Mount Stewart in Northern Ireland in her eightieth year. The funeral took place in the private chapel at the house and a memorial service was later held at St. Paul's Knightsbridge which was attended by many of Lady Londonderry's contemporaries such as the seventy-one-year-old Duke of Sutherland and seventy-nine-year-old Nancy Lady Astor as well as some younger figures such as twenty-three-year-old Paul Channon, MP.

Meanwhile, it was thought that the romance between the Duke of Kent and twenty-six-year-old Katharine Worsley had petered out. 'He has not visited me and he certainly isn't with me tonight' said Miss Worsley on May 3. 'I have no plans for meeting him at all.'

On May 5, the House of Lords debated the Vice Bill with great gusto. Lord Massereene and Ferrard said he had been frequently accosted by prostitutes and it had never annoyed him while sixty-three-year-old Baroness Ravensdale, daughter of the late Marquess Curzon of Kedleston, demanded that the streets should also be cleared of men. In a maiden speech, the Earl of Arran shocked the house by stating that one in every 540 women in London was a harlot.

That evening, Noel Coward, the Duke of Bedford, the Marquess of Milford Haven, the newly-married Lord and Lady Montagu of Beaulieu and many other illustrious figures were present at the First Night of John Osborne's musical *The World of Paul Slickey*. It was described as the most disastrous First Night the West End had known for many years and the twenty-nine-year-old author was booed as he left the stage door.

The following day, Somerset Maugham, whose books were now said to have sold over 60,000,000 copies, was present at a coming-out dance at the Savoy Hotel for his grand-daughter Camilla Paravicini. The eighty-five-year-old author left the festivities before midnight.

On May 15, it was announced that wealthy shipbuilder Harry Dowsett, who had recently secured a multi-million pound contract to build trawlers for Russia, had hired detectives to track down his twenty-year-old daughter Katherine who had disappeared with her boyfriend Edward Langley. 'Nothing will convince me that Langley is the proper person for my daughter to marry' he declared. A few days later there was a dramatic confrontation between Mr. Dowsett, who wore a spotted bow-tie, and the missing couple beside Loch Lomond, and on May 21, it was announced that the shipbuilder had invited the couple home to Greatford Hall, Lincolnshire, to discuss the matter. 'I hope we will come to an amicable arrangement' said Katherine. 'Whatever happens, I am determined to marry Edward.'

On May 26, Princess Margaret, photographer Antony Armstrong-Jones and a party of six others went to see *West Side Story* at Her Majesty's Theatre. The Princess wore a red satin dress and short fur jacket.

Early in June, the great American entertainer Liberace began a libel action against the *Daily Mirror* whose columnist Cassandra had indirectly branded him as a homosexual. On June 8, Liberace spent a gruelling-

two-and-three-quarter hours in the witness-box during which his elderly counsel, Gilbert Beyfus, asked him whether he was a homosexual. 'I am not, sir' he replied. Asked whether he had ever indulged in homosexual practices, Liberace replied, 'No sir, never in my life.' On June 17, it was decided that he had won his case and he was awarded £8,000 damages. That night, he played to two packed, cheering houses at the Chiswick Empire and celebrated afterwards at the Saddle Room in Mayfair, a new club run by Miss Hélène Cordet.

The same night, Aristotle Onassis gave a supper-party at the Dorchester Hotel for opera singer Maria Callas, following her performance in *Medea* at Covent Garden. Among those present were the deeply suntanned Randolph Churchill, Lady Churchill, her hair dyed pale lilac, Dame Margot Fonteyn, Cecil Beaton and Mr. and Mrs. John Profumo. At three o'clock in the morning, Mr. Onassis was photographed in the foyer of the hotel locked in a triple embrace with Miss Callas and her husband Signor Meneghini.

On June 22, the popular Mr. and Mrs. Jack Heinz threw a party in their house in Hays Mews, Mayfair, which was attended by Antony Armstrong-Jones, actress Jacqui Chan, Henrietta Tiarks, Charles Clore, the Duke and Duchess of Argyll and many other distinguished figures. On the arrival of Mr. Duncan Sandys, somebody quipped, 'Ah, here comes the cabaret.'

At the end of June, the Duke of Bedford was found taking the cure at Enton Hall Health Farm in the company of French film producer Nicole Milinaire. 'We had a sort of house-party' the Duke explained afterwards.

On July 7, writer Brendan Behan flew in from Dublin and made his way singing and shouting to Wyndham's Theatre where his play *The Hostage* was currently playing to packed audiences. From his seat in the fifth row of the stalls he constantly interrupted the actors and finally, he joined them on the stage and danced a jig. He continued shouting after the curtain had been brought down.

On July 9, the Duchess of Windsor was treated by plastic surgeon Sir Archibald McIndoe at the London Clinic for the removal of a facial scar which she had incurred by tripping over a suitcase during an Atlantic crossing earlier in the year. 'The operation was highly successful' said the Duke of Windsor's secretary at Claridge's. 'Everyone is pleased with the result and the Duchess is feeling fine.'

The same day, Robin Douglas-Home was married to model Sandra Paul at St. James's Piccadilly. A reception was held afterwards at the home of Lady Fermoy at Hyde Park Gardens. 'I have never seen anyone so calm and collected as Robin' said his father, Major Henry Douglas-Home.

In the evening of this eventful day, the coming of age of the Marquess of Dufferin and Ava was celebrated with an elaborate party at the Hurlingham Club, which was attended by, among others, the young Aga Khan, who had flown in specially for the occasion, Princess Margaret and Fred Astaire. During the course of the evening, lawn-sprinklers suddenly burst into action drenching several of the guests.

On July 26, forty-nine-year-old Brenda Dean Paul, the famous Society drug addict who had been constantly in the news in the early Thirties, was found dead in her Kensington flat. 'She really was one of the sweetest people you could ever have known' said her friend Miss Jean Baird, who had remained loyal to her to the end.

A few days later, it was revealed that millionairess Barbara Hutton had bought the entire Lanvin winter collection at an estimated cost of £120,000. 'She is so delicately boned, she is a delight to dress' said a spokesman for the famous fashion house.

On August 10, eighty-year-old Sir Thomas Beecham, conductor of the Royal Philharmonic Orchestra, married twenty-seven-year-old Shirley Hudson. After the ceremony at Zurich Town Hall, Sir Thomas admitted that the marriage was 'preposterous, even monstrous.'

On August 25, undergraduate Anthony Haden-Guest gave a pyjama-party at the Whisky-A-Go-Go Club in Wardour Street in Soho which ended in chaotic scenes and bottles being hurled at the guests by frustrated gatecrashers.

At the beginning of September, a blaze of world-wide publicity suddenly engulfed Aristotle Onassis and opera singer Maria Callas. On September 2, the couple flew in a private plane from Nice to Milan and the following day, Maria's husband Signor Meneghini announced, 'The break between Maria and myself is now

Society drug addict Brenda Dean Paul a few years before her death

William Somerset Maugham, the world's richest writer, dives into his private swimming pool at Cap Ferrat

irrevocable.' Asked if there had been a separation between his wife and himself, Onassis replied, 'I don't like to think about it. We have been married thirteen years.'

Rumours of divorce also surrounded the Duke and Duchess of Bedford. On September 10, the Duke flew home after a holiday in Portofino with his friend thirty-eight-year-old Nicole Milinaire. Checking in at Claridges, he said, 'I'm very tired. All I want to do is sleep.' A few days later, Mme. Milinaire announced, 'I know people are talking about me. But I don't care. Let them talk.'

Eight days later, an astonishing application by the Duke of Argyll to have his wife banned from Inveraray Castle was pinned up on the walls of the Edinburgh Law Courts.

On September 22, Maria Callas flew into London to give a concert at the Royal Festival Hall. Questioned about her relationship with Mr. Onassis, she said 'There is no romance. I only wish there were.' The following day, Miss Callas was offered a £250,000 contract by impresario, S. A. Gorlinsky.

On October 5, the seventy-seven-year-old Earl of Rosebery was accused of dangerous driving in a Rolls-Royce near Leighton Buzzard. After explaining that he had known the stretch of road in question for seventy years, he was acquitted of the charge and drove himself back to his home, Mentmore Towers.

Three days later, the Conservative majority was strengthened in the General Election. 'It's all gone off rather well' remarked Harold Macmillan on being voted back to 10 Downing Street. Among the new Tory MPs who had been elected was thirty-three-year-old Mrs. Margaret Thatcher, daughter of a Grantham grocer.

On October 16, it was announced that oil magnate Paul Getty, now dubbed the World's Richest Man, had purchased Sutton Place, Surrey home of the Duke of Sutherland, for a reputed £400,000. Among the many improvements Getty was planning to make at the sixteenth-century mansion was the installation of modern oil central-heating.

Meanwhile, the Duchess of Argyll had been granted one day from dawn till dusk on which to identify her possessions at Inveraray Castle. On October 21, she travelled North on The Aberdonian express accompanied by her solicitors and her maid. After laying claim to Louis XV chairs, paintings by Gainsborough and many other heirlooms, she flew back to London.

On November 1, there was great excitement over the engagement of Lady Pamela Mountbatten, younger daughter of Earl and Countess Mountbatten, and thirty-year-old interior decorator Mr. David Hicks, whose clients including some of the leading Society figures. 'He did my curtains and pelmets' said Mrs. Gerald Legge, now Lady Lewisham. 'They're marvellous. They never move out of place or hang wrongly or do any of the horrible things that curtains usually do.'

On November 8, it was announced that the Duke of Norfolk was moving out of historic Arundel Castle into a newly built Georgian-style house in the park. 'We find it very difficult to carry on in the castle' he explained. 'The move into the new house is purely because the moment has arrived to save some money that at present we see no return on.'

A few days later, it was announced that take-over tycoon Charles Clore, son of an East End clothing manufacturer, had acquired Lord Rootes's 2,000-acre estate at Stype in Berkshire and was planning to start a beef herd.

On November 24, headlines blazed the news that the Duchess of Bedford was suing her husband for divorce. It was revealed that the Duchess had left Woburn Abbey some time ago and was now living in a £20,000 house at Chobham in Surrey.

The following day, it was announced that Mrs. Tina Onassis was seeking a divorce, adding that Miss Maria Callas was not involved in the case and that she did not want any of Mr. Onassis's money. 'He had become one of the world's richest men' ran her statement, 'but his great wealth has not brought me happiness with him, nor, as the world knows, has it brought him happiness with me.'

On November 30, Sir Winston Churchill celebrated his eighty-fifth birthday at his home in Hyde Park Gate. A four-tier birthday cake, weighing 80 lb. was delivered at the house the same day and Sir Winston's doctor, Lord Moran, arrived with half a pound of caviar from Harrods.

On December 3, fifty-four-year-old Earl Beatty embarked on his fourth marriage. His new bride was eighteen-year-old Diane Kirk, who had been one of the previous year's débutantes. After the ceremony at Midhurst Registry Office, at which the bridegroom wore a velvet-collared overcoat, the couple sailed off on board the *Queen Mary* for America, where, it was noted, the Earl's previous three wives were all living.

The following day, Mrs. John Profumo, formerly actress Valerie Hobson, bought an £80 fur-coat at a London auction which had once belonged to Lady Docker.

On December 15, nine-year-old Princess Anne was the hostess at a party for the twenty members of the Buckingham Palace pack of Brownies, which had been formed earlier in the year. Among the girls present were the daughter of a taxi-driver and the daughter of a hotel maintenance engineer. Marzipan toadstools were served.

On December 21, news came from Belgium of the marriage of forty-five-year-old Group-Captain Peter Townsend and twenty-year-old Marie-Luce Jamagne, handsome daughter of a wealthy Belgian tobacco manufacturer.

At Christmas, Noel Coward was found installed in a new tax-free Swiss home, overlooking Lac Leman, which he found advertised in the property columns of the *Daily Telegraph* earlier in the year. Sharing the festive season with him was actress Vivien Leigh, now leading a somewhat separate life from her husband Sir Laurence Olivier. 'Vivien has given me a lovely green and gold cigarette box, a lighter and some ashtrays' said Coward.

The New Year was greeted at the Savoy Hotel by a mixture of revellers, including Lady Docker, Greek shipowner George Livanos, Lord and Lady Mountbatten and their daughter Pamela and her fiancé, interior decorator David Hicks. It was noticed that Lady Pamela won three blocks of toilet soap in a tombola.

On January 5, it was reported that Mr. Duncan Sandys, now Minister of Aviation, was boar-hunting on an estate near Hamburg with Prince Otto von Bismarck, Counsellor at the German Embassy before the war.

On January 8, fifty-four-year-old Lord Beatty and his eighteen-year-old bride flew in after their honeymoon in America. Lady Beatty carried a black poodle in her arms. The couple drove by Bentley to Chicheley Hall, Newport Pagnell where the Earl was soon struck down by bronchitis and transferred to the London Clinic.

Five days later, there was a huge gathering at Romsey Abbey for the marriage of Lady Pamela Mountbatten and Mr. David Hicks, who wore a specially made wedding-suit described by his tailor, Mr. Corbett, as 'divine'. Princess Anne was a bridesmaid and the reception afterwards was enriched by the presence of Noel Coward and Earl Attlee. The 150 lb. wedding-cake was an exact replica of the bride's home, Broadlands, where the reception was held.

On January 28, white-haired Sister Helen Rowe arrived in London to prepare for the birth of the Queen's new baby. 'I have ordered two new overalls for my time at the Palace' she said. 'I always wear kingfisher blue; much nicer than nasty old grey.'

The following day, the forty-six-year-old Duchess of Argyll, now involved in complicated divorce proceedings, flew off for a holiday in America. 'As always, I am delighted to be returning to New York where I spent a very happy childhood' she said on departure.

On February 9, it was announced that heiress Bobo Sigrist had taken over the house in Cheyne Walk, Chelsea, recently vacated by Mr. and Mrs. Jeremy Sandford who were now living in a humble terraced house in Battersea.

A few days later, it was announced that twenty-two-year-old Lord Valentine Thynne, younger son of the Marquess of Bath, had been evicted from his flat in Ashley Gardens, Westminster following complaints from neighbours about a rowdy party. 'I lent my flat so that an American fellow could meet the London equivalent of beatniks' explained Lord Valentine. 'It went like a bomb.'

On February 18, old memories were revived when the famous female transvestite known as 'Colonel Barker' died at Kessingland on the Suffolk coast. This strange woman, whose marriage to a Brighton girl and subsequent imprisonment thirty-one years earlier had made headline news, had put on a lot of weight towards the end of her life and been confined to a bath chair. 'He was very ill towards the end' said a neighbour, 'but he never let the village know his secret.'

The following day, the birth of a baby boy to the Queen caused great rejoicing. The Queen Mother and Princess Margaret called to see the baby who was laid in a cream-coloured cot lined in pink satin. Gynaecologist Mr. John Peel returned to his Harley Street home where his housekeeper, Mrs. Hobbs, later spoke to the Press. 'He looked so tired' she said. 'But he flushed with excitement when I asked him what the baby was like.'

This joyful event was followed two days later by the sudden death of fifty-eight-year-old Lady Mountbatten in the middle of a tour of the Far East. Her husband, Lord Mountbatten of Burma, received over 6,000 letters and telegrams of sympathy and Lady Mountbatten, who had embraced the Socialist cause towards the end of her life, was later buried at sea in the middle of the English Channel after a short service on board the frigate *Wakeful* conducted by the Archbishop of Canterbury, Dr. Fisher, and recorded by Press photographers on an adjoining vessel.

Meanwhile, fifty-six-year-old Cecil Beaton had retired to bed after catching a chill on the train carrying him between London and Salisbury. 'The carriage was like an ice box' he complained. 'I have travelled in much discomfort in many backward countries in the world but never have I suffered from the cold so much as I have on the stretch between London and Salisbury.'

On February 26, the engagement was announced between Princess Margaret and photographer Antony Armstrong-Jones. 'It is the best and most exciting secret I've kept' said Mr. Billy Wallace in the oak-panelled drawing-room of his home in South Street, Mayfair. 'Princess Margaret and I and three friends have pulled off the greatest coup.' In America, Sharman Douglas, old friend of the Princess declared, 'I cried with joy when I got the telegram from London.'

The happy couple made their official début together at Covent Garden on March I. Mr. Armstrong-Jones was in white tie and tails with his hands clasped behind his back and the Princess wore a silver satin dress embroidered in rose sequins. During the evening, the dress got caught on a nail sticking out of the woodwork of a box occupied by Dr. Roberto Arias, husband of Dame Margot Fonteyn, causing Princess Margaret to exclaim, 'Christmas!'

On March 6, attention turned to the fabulous Villa Mauresque at Cap Ferrat where Somerset Maugham, now eighty-six years old, had returned after an 80,000-mile journey round the Far East. 'The first thing I did was to pluck an avocado pear from my tree . . . the only avocado pear tree in Europe' he said.

On March 8, Sir Winston and Lady Churchill's flight to Gibraltar, where they were due to join Aristotle Onassis for a cruise across the Atlantic, was marked by hazards. The plane first landed at Madrid for emergency refuelling, then over-shot Gibraltar and landed at Tangier where the British Consul-General interrupted a dinner in honour of Mr. T. S. Eliot to meet the ex-Premier at the airport. Onassis remained

Sir Winston Churchill is driven through the streets of Istanbul by his new friend Aristotle Socrates Onassis

dutifully at Gibraltar airport where he announced: 'It's dirty weather but we'll be off as soon as they arrive.'

On March 13, Princess Margaret and her fiancé were found staying at Widcombe Manor, Bath, with Mr. Jeremy Fry, a prominent member of the chocolate family who was soon to be named as the couple's best man. During the weekend, Margaret and Tony drove in Mr. Fry's black Citroen to have tea at Broadchalke with fellow photographer Cecil Beaton, who had recently returned from taking the first photographs of the infant Prince Andrew. 'No business matters were discussed during the afternoon' said Beaton. 'The tea-party was a purely social affair.'

On March 18, it was announced that the recently-widowed Earl Mountbatten had dismissed four of the staff at his house at Wilton Crescent. 'It was a great shock' said butler John Collier, 'but we all realise that he had no alternative. I've started looking around for another job already. I went for an interview the other day. But I didn't like the people. Nouveau riche. Pots of money and all that but I couldn't stand them.'

On March 28, Prince Philip, the Duchess of Kent and Princess Alexandra arrived twenty-five minutes late at a Royal Film Performance, explaining that they had got stuck in a lift at Buckingham Palace. Nineteen-year-old pop singer Cliff Richard, in white tie and tails, had been kept waiting in the cinema foyer.

On April 2, the eighty-nine-year-old Dowager Duchess of Devonshire, mother of Lady Dorothy Macmillan, died at her flat in Kensington Church Street. It was noted that the Duchess had begun her married life at Devonshire House, Piccadilly, sold by her husband in 1920 for £1,000,000 and subsequently demolished.

On April 3, Sir Winston and Lady Churchill and Aristotle Onassis flew in after a leisurely Atlantic cruise during which the Greek shipowner had spoon-fed the ex-Premier with caviar. They were greeted by a hostile headline in the *Sunday Express*, owned by Lord Beaverbrook who was rumoured to be jealous of the new friendship, 'Is Onassis losing his millions?'

The following day, Churchill took Onassis to dinner at the Other Club, the exclusive dining-club he had founded with Lord Birkenhead forty-nine years earlier, where that evening, fellow guests included Viscount Montgomery, Prime Minister Harold Macmillan and Captain Christopher Soames. 'This is something that rarely happens to an ordinary fellow like me' said Onassis.

On April 6, there came an announcement that Jeremy Fry had resigned as Mr. Armstrong-Jones's best man 'for health reasons'. He was promptly replaced by neurologist Dr. Roger Gilliatt, whose wife Penelope had just published an article in *Queen* magazine deploring gossip columns.

On April 17, a march from Aldermaston to London organised by supporters of the Campaign for Nuclear Disarmament was enriched by the presence of nineteen-year-old Judith Pakenham, daughter of Lord Pakenham, and some fifteen Eton boys who included Andrew and Richard Collins, sons of Canon John Collins of St. Paul's Cathedral.

On April 27, Mr. Armstrong-Jones's step-aunt Lady Bridget Parsons was charged with drunken driving following a dinner-party at the Hyde Park Hotel. Fellow guests at the dinner, the Duke of Devonshire and Lord Kinross gave evidence about how little she had drunk and she was found not guilty. She was escorted home by Mr. John Betjeman.

On May 4, two watercolours by Adolf Hitler came up for sale at Sotheby's drawing a protest from art dealer Jacques O'Hana. 'I am speaking for many people in this room,' he announced. 'These paintings should not be offered for sale.' The pictures were later sold for £280 and £320 each to the Marquess of Bath, who subsequently described Hitler as 'one helluva man' in an interview with the *Evening Standard*. In the outcry that followed, the Marquess announced that the pictures would not be placed on public view at Longleat. 'Some people feel strongly about them and I do not want any unpleasantness so they will be in my private quarters.'

That night, the Queen gave a reception for 2,000 people at Buckingham Palace in honour of Princess Margaret and her fiancé. Joe Loss's band played music from the popular current show *Fings Ain't What They Used To Be* and Mr. Armstrong-Jones's bohemian friends mingled with staid members of the establishment. At the end of the evening, the Duchess of Buccleuch found that she had lost a brooch valed at £2,700. In the search, furniture and heating units were dismantled and even some floor boards were taken up.

The fairytale wedding took place on May 6. Guests at the Abbey included Sir Winston Churchill, leaning on a stick, Dominic Elwes, Jacqui Chan, Noel Coward, Hugh and Antonia Fraser, the latter in a white shepherdess's bonnet, John Betjeman and a scattering of European Royalty. Later in the day, over-enthusiastic crowds did £200 worth of damage to the Rolls-Royce carrying the Princess and her husband to the Pool of London, where the royal yacht *Britannia* was waiting to take them on their honeymoon. The Princess's hairdresser René admitted afterwards that the Princess's hair had been lightened a shade and that she wore a hairpiece. 'I am so terribly thrilled that it actually stayed on. You know, I was worried.'

Six days later, the world was shocked to learn that veteran playboy Aly Khan had been killed in a car-crash. The accident occurred as the forty-eight-year-old Prince was driving himself in a new Lancia to a dinner-party outside Paris. His body was later buried in the garden of his Riviera home, the Château de L'Horizon, after a ceremony attended by, among others, Jean Cocteau.

On May 20, it was learned that Sir Laurence Olivier was seeking a divorce from his wife Vivien Leigh in order to marry Miss Joan Plowright. A maid at Sir Laurence's Eaton Square flat said, 'He has nothing to say.'

Meanwhile, Princess Margaret and her husband Antony Armstrong-Jones were slowly cruising around the Caribbean on board the royal yacht *Britannia*. On May 26, they landed on Mustique, the 1,250-acre island recently acquired by the Princess's old friend Mr. Colin Tennant. It was later revealed that Mr. Tennant had given his friend a plot of land on the island as a wedding present.

On June 1, Sir Winston Churchill, Lord Attlee and Mr. Harold Macmillan were all present at the Derby. Mr. Macmillan was found having a lively exchange with a barmaid over the price of two glasses of gin and tonic. He had been distressed to find that a ten-shilling note did not cover the price. On this occasion, the race was won by St. Paddy, ridden by Lester Piggott and owned by seventy-eight-year-old Sir Victor Sassoon who watched the race from a wheelchair with his beautiful young wife at his side.

On June 18, Princess Margaret and her husband returned to England and moved into the Princess's old suite of rooms in Clarence House while finishing touches were being put to their new home, 10 Kensington Palace. It was revealed that every room was being painted white and a staff of seven was soon recruited, headed by a plump, white-haired butler named Mr. Thomas Cronin who had previously worked for the American Ambassador, Mr. Jock Whitney, at Winfield House.

On June 24, sixteen-year-old Lord Rudolf Russell, younger son of the Duke of Bedford, ran away from Gordonstoun School. The following day, he turned up at Woburn Abbey and after discussions with his father in his suite at Claridge's, he voluntarily returned to the school. 'He is rather highly-strung and needs careful handling' said his stepmother, Lydia Duchess of Bedford. 'Perhaps Gordonstoun is not the right place for him.'

On June 30, Mr. Paul Getty's vast house-warming party at Sutton Place made headline news. Over £3,500 was spent on champagne and a milk bar was also set up at the house, with a prize Guernsey cow tethered in

Multi-millionaire Paul Getty in the grounds of Sutton Place

front of it. It was said that almost 2,000 people attempted to gate-crash the festivities which went on till seven in the morning. Among the 1,000 bona-fide guests were the Duchess of Argyll, now emeshed in grim legal proceedings prior to her divorce case, David and Lady Pamela Hicks, Jocelyn Stevens, Sir Victor Sassoon, and Lord and Lady Beatty. Soon after the party, it was announced that an eighteenth-century silver sugar sifter was missing from the house. It later turned up in a telephone kiosk in Chelsea.

The next big social event was the coming-of-age of Lord Herbert, heir to the Earl of Pembroke which was celebrated with a spectacular party at Wilton House near Salisbury on July 15. The entrance arch and a Palladian bridge in the grounds were floodlit and dancing took place in the famous 'Double Cube' room designed by Inigo Jones. Among the hundreds of illustrious people present was Mr. Cecil Beaton who, some thirty-three years earlier at the coming of age of Lord Herbert's father, had been thrown into the river.

On the Monday after the Ball, Beaton made his way to Fordingbridge to sit for his portrait by eighty-three-year-old Augustus John. Beaton chose to wear a panama hat and almond-coloured suede coat for the portrait and, at one sitting, brought along a blue-and-white china tea service which he hoped would inspire the aged artist.

At the beginning of August, staff troubles hit the newly formed household of Princess Margaret when her butler, Mr. Cronin, left after a tiff with Mr. Armstrong-Jones. Departing from Kensington Palace with several trunks and an armchair, Mr. Cronin said 'There was a difference of opinion – a clash of personalities. This led to a climax and I have taken the only step open to me.'

On August 29, the thirty-seven-year-old Earl of Lonsdale, nephew of the famous sporting Earl, took delivery of a four-seater aeroplane. It was revealed that both the Earl and his wife held pilots' licences and were members of the Cumberland Flying Club. 'It's a peach' said the Earl, admiring his new acquisition, 'and it's going to be so useful for business and social trips.'

On September 2, fire swept through Polesden Lacey near Dorking, stately home of the late Mrs. Ronnie Greville, now in the hands of the National Trust, badly damaging the suite of rooms occupied by the Queen Mother on her honeymoon with the then Duke of York in 1923. Girls from a nearby riding-school helped to rescue Old Masters and Louis XV furniture from the blaze.

The following day, the great showman Duke of Bedford married forty-year-old French TV producer Nicole Milinaire at Ampthill in Bedfordshire. Mme Milinaire wore a Balmain dress of old gold and declared that she had been stung by a wasp on her way to the registry office. 'We wanted this to be a quiet wedding' said the forty-three-year-old Duke. 'When you've been divorced, it's better that way.'

Four days later, the Duke's son and heir, Lord Tavistock, at last announced his engagement to banker's daughter Henrietta Tiarks. 'I've loved Robin since I was four' said Henrietta, who had frequently denied that there was any romance between them.

On September 13, it was announced that twenty-year-old Auberon Waugh had been rusticated from Christ Church Oxford for failing his examinations. He was currently on holiday in Italy and said to be toying with the idea of a journalistic career. 'Auberon worked as hard as most' said Lord Rowallan's son Robert Corbett, who had also been rusticated.

On September 19, eleven-year-old Prince Charles spent forty minutes at a Harley Street dentist, had his hair cut and had lunch at Buck's Club in Clifford Street, before returning later in the day to Cheam School. He was taken to Buck's Club by an unidentified elderly man.

Meanwhile, the escape of two Himalayan bears from their pit at Mr. John Aspinall's private zoo at his home in Kent had brought anxious protests from the chairman of a local fruit-canning company. 'In the fields around, we had eighty women picking apples and pears and many had their children with them. We feel this is a dangerous situation.' On September 21, Mr. Aspinall gave his assurances in the High Court that he would employ a full-time keeper to look after the animals in his zoo.

On October 8, it was reported that eighty-year-old Lady Redesdale, mother of the famous Mitford sisters, was drawing a thirty shillings a week salary from the Post Office for delivering letters on the private island of Inchkenneth off West Scotland. She collected the letters in her launch from Mull and delivered them on the island, where there were only thirteen inhabitants.

On October 11, the Duchess of Argyll gave a lavish party at Claridge's in honour of her twenty-year-old son Brian Sweeny, who was leaving at the end of the month to study at the Harvard Business School. Guests on this occasion included the Duke of Bedford, Mr. and Mrs. Douglas Fairbanks, Paul Getty, Jocelyn Stevens and Miss Barbara Cartland. Seventy people attended the dinner and 500 came in to dance afterwards.

On October 14, fifty-three-year-old Viscount Astor, one of Britain's richest men, married twenty-nine-year-old top model Bronwen Pugh at a registry office in Hampstead. The bridegroom's famous mother, Nancy Lady Astor now over eighty, was present at the ceremony, remarking to her companion: 'I don't like her hat, my dear.'

On October 20, there was great excitement over the prosecution of the publishers of D. H. Lawrence's novel *Lady Chatterley's Lover* under the recently introduced Obscene Publications Act. At the opening of the Old Bailey trial, prosecuting QC Mervyn Griffith-Jones asked the jury to consider if it was a book they would wish their servants to read, and went on to list the four-letter words he had discovered in the novel. 'The word "fuck" or "fucking" occurs no less than thirty times' he declared. The jury were then sent off to read the novel and the public's attention was diverted to other matters.

On October 25, it was announced that rival property millionaires Charles Clore and Jack Cotton had combined their interests. 'We have been getting in each other's way on big deals both here and in New York, so it was a natural thing that we should merge our interests' said Mr. Clore celebrating over a glass of whisky and soda at his Park Street, Mayfair office.

The same day, a strange incident occurred when the Queen and Duke of Edinburgh were flying back from a private visit to the King and Queen of Denmark. Suddenly two sabre-jet fighters of the German air-force approached the plane. 'They had iron crosses underneath their wings' said the co-pilot. 'They turned in as a pair and passed only fifty feet above us. It was a very nasty moment.'

At the end of the month, the Lady Chatterley trial resumed and Dr. John Robinson, Bishop of Woolwich, led a troop of distinguished witnesses testifying in favour of the novel. On November 2, the jury delivered a Not Guilty verdict and Sir Allen Lane, chairman of Penguin Books announced: 'I have set things in motion for a second print of either 200,000 or 300,000.'

On November 10, Labour MP William Hamilton questioned the appointment of the Prime Minister's nephew, the Duke of Devonshire, as Under-Secretary of State for the Commonwealth. 'Can you tell me what are the qualifications of the Duke of Devonshire for the office he has just been given?' In his reply, Mr. Macmillan said: 'I try to make the best appointments I can.'

On November 17, the Marquess of Milford Haven was married for the second time. His bride was Miss Janet Bryce and the ceremony took place in a Presbyterian Church in Hampstead. An unconventional reception was held afterwards at Claridge's where dancing took place to the music of jazz pianist Cliff Hall, who had been specially flown from America. Among the guests were the newly-married Lord and Lady Astor, Lord Mountbatten, Lord Montagu of Beaulieu and Queen Louise of Sweden, who left early by a side entrance. It was noted that neither the Queen nor Prince Philip, at whose wedding in 1947 Lord Milford Haven had acted as best man, were present.

On November 23, the Earl and Countess of Harewood were present at Sotheby's where the Earl was parting with a lot of his family jewellery in order to pay for improvements on his estate. Among the items on sale was a diamond and sapphire necklace which had once belonged to Grand Duke Michael of Russia, which eventually was bought for £28,000 by dealer Mr. Levi Cohen on behalf of American jeweller, Mr. Harry Winston.

On November 30, it was announced that Viscountess Lewisham, had signed the pledge. 'My daughter found she could get much cheaper car and life insurance if she did so' explained her mother novelist Barbara Cartland.

On December 2, much publicity attended the meeting of Dr. Fisher and Pope John – the first visit to the Vatican by an Archbishop of Canterbury since 1397. The Pope greeted his visitor on the threshold of his private library and led him to a central table, habitually reserved for distinguished guests. Afterwards at the British Embassy, Dr. Fisher said, 'The whole interview was as friendly and natural and sympathetic as possible . . .'

On December 7, the Duke and Duchess of Windsor arrived in London on the night-ferry for ten days shopping. During their visit, they were found in the audience of *Oliver*, a new musical already seen twice by the Queen, and by most of the Royal Family.

On December 22, Miss Edwina Sandys, daughter of Duncan Sandys, was married to thirty-one-year-old Piers Dixon, son of the British Ambassador in Paris, Sir Pierson Dixon. The ceremony took place at the unusual hour of five o'clock at St. Margaret's Westminster and the reception was held at Claridge's. 'It does mean that you don't have to drink at the unreasonable hour of half-past two in the afternoon' explained the bridegroom. Afterwards, the couple visited the bride's grandfather Sir Winston Churchill at 28 Hyde Park Gate.

The following day, four cars were required to ferry Sir Winston and Lady Churchill, two turkeys and their staff, to Chartwell. The ex-Prime Minister's much-loved pet budgerigar, Toby, travelled beside him in a big black Humber.

1961

Princess Margaret and her husband greeted the New Year at Birr Castle, Irish home of Mr. Armstrong-Jones's mother, the Countess of Rosse, where the regular staff of housekeeper, butler, cook, two footmen and two housemaids were reinforced by extra local labour. Flying back to London later, one of the house-party, Billy Wallace, confided to a friend: 'I'm so glad Margaret has Tony. I could not have gone on much longer covering up for her men friends.'

On January 4, Mr. Reginald Maudling, President of the Board of Trade, was present at the opening of the newly-built Carlton Tower Hotel in Cadogan Place. It was revealed that a large portrait of the new Lady Astor, former model Bronwen Pugh, had suddenly been removed from the hotel. 'Lord Astor told me he was very distressed at his wife's portrait being hung in the hotel' said artist Felix Topolski. 'He begged me not to include it with the others.'

On January 16, it was announced that Paul Getty was installing an indoor swimming-pool at Sutton Place. 'Walking and swimming are my big recreations' explained the sixty-eight-year-old multi-millionaire. 'Swimming is a little out of the question in an outdoor pool in the English winter. Hence, the new pool . . .'

Two days later it was announced that Antony Armstrong-Jones would be joining the Council of Industrial Design. He would work at their offices in Panton Street, his main role being to produce ideas.

On January 26, it was reported that the twenty-one-year-old Earl of Lichfield, now serving as a Lieutenant in the Grenadier Guards, had been billeted along with 100 men on his own Staffordshire land, one mile from his family's stately home, Shugborough Hall. 'Although I don't live at Shugborough at the moment, I hope to one day. It is the house where I was brought up and I am very fond of it' said the Earl, a godson of the Queen Mother.

On February 12, much publicity attended the wedding of twenty-eight-year-old tycoon John Bloom, who had built up a vast washing-machine empire in the space of just two years. Four men were required to carry two huge wedding cakes, replicas of a washing-machine and a dishwasher, to the reception at the Savoy Hotel. 'I shall ask my wife's advice about my business' said Bloom. 'She will use my machines in our home and, I suppose, what she says will affect housewives all over the country.'

Two days later, it was announced that Sir Winston Churchill's budgerigar, Toby, had escaped from the ex-Prime Minister's suite at the Hotel de Paris in Monte Carlo. Sir Winston had offered 150 francs for its return – an offer which was immediately doubled by M. Oudibert, manager of the Monte Carlo casino. 'I know how fond Sir Winston is of Toby – and I am fond of him too.'

On February 23, Princess Margaret's black convertible Nash Metropolitan motor-car was stolen from outside 10 Upper Phillimore Gardens where she and her husband were having lunch with Mr. and Mrs. Michael Brand. A fourteen-year-old boy was later arrested after an exciting police chase.

Meanwhile, work on the three million pound production of *Cleopatra* had been delayed by the ill-health of film star Elizabeth Taylor. On Saturday, March 4, a series of minor illnesses culminated in a severe attack of pneumonia and the actress spent the day in an oxygen tent in her penthouse suite at the Dorchester Hotel. At midnight, she was transferred to the London Clinic where it was reported at one stage that she had only an hour left to live. A tracheotomy was performed the following day and she was then put on to an electric lung.

On March 7, Tina Onassis, former wife of the Greek shipping magnate, flew in from St. Moritz for treatment for a broken knee-cap after a ski-ing accident. A National Health ambulance took her from the American air-base at Brize Norton to the Nuffield Orthopaedic Centre at Oxford, where in the course of the next few weeks, she was to receive many visits from the young Marquess of Blandford, whose own marriage had recently been dissolved.

On March 8, it was announced that the Duke of Kent would marry golden-haired Miss Katharine Worsley, the daughter of the Lord Lieutenant of the North Riding and a descendant of Oliver Cromwell. Said Katharine's local postmaster, 'Many people in the village thought the whole thing had fizzled out some time ago. Of course, we at the Post Office knew otherwise, but we didn't say a word.'

On March 22, the marriage of the fun-loving twenty-four-year-old Lord Valentine Thynne to the daughter of an Indian Army Colonel was noted. At the unexpectedly formal reception at the Hyde Park Hotel, the bridegroom's father, Lord Bath, remarked, 'Marriage will tame Valentine. I'm hoping it will, anyway.' It was noted that Lord Valentine's interests now included the running of a dance-hall in Peckham.

On March 27, it was announced that Paul Getty had installed a telephone coin-box for the use of his house guests at Sutton Place. 'A lot of people in the house want to make phone calls, often long distance ones. It mounts up to a pretty substantial sum and I thought it was business-like to install a coin-box' explained the multi-millionaire. 'After all, I am not running a free phone service for anyone who comes here.'

The same day, huge crowds watched Elizabeth Taylor leave the London Clinic. A Rolls-Royce belonging to her husband Eddie Fisher took her to London Airport where an ambulance was waiting to take her out to an American-bound aircraft, accompanied by her private oxygen cylinder and breathing mask. Rumours circulated that the film star's illness had cost 20th Century Fox over £1,400,000.

On April 2, young Lady Beatty gave birth to a baby boy at a National Health hospital near her Buckinghamshire home, Chicheley Hall. 'It all happened so quickly' said her fifty-six-year-old husband 'that we dared not risk taking Lady Beatty to London. So our doctor got her into the local nursing-home.'

On April 13, reluctant peer Lord Stansgate, better known as Anthony Wedgwood Benn, was present in the gallery of the House of Commons to hear his plea to remain an MP voted down. He did, however, win support from Conservative MP Viscount Lambton, heir to the seventy-seven-year-old Earl of Durham, who later defied his party chiefs to speak in Mr. Wedgwood Benn's favour at a public meeting in Bristol.

On April 21, the Queen celebrated her thirty-fifth birthday in the mud and rain at the Badminton Horse Trials. In the royal party was Mr. Antony Armstrong-Jones, who wore a new riding mackintosh and carried a combined shooting-stick and umbrella.

Four days later, thirty-year-old Dominic Elliot, an old friend of Princess Margaret, now working for an advertising agency in Holborn, was found riding to and from his office on a bicycle. 'It's a very handy way of getting to work' he said. 'It takes about the same time as the tube and it's much more pleasant.'

On April 30, it was reported that Mr. David Ormsby-Gore, soon to be appointed British Ambassador in Washington, was already giving consideration to the domestic arrangements at the Embassy. 'I don't know what silver there is in the Embassy, but it is apparently quite common to supplement it with one's own.'

On May 4, the Rev. William Bryn Thomas, former vicar of Balham and a doctor of philosophy, was defrocked for 'open and notorious sin'. Sad organ-music was played before the ceremony at Southwark Cathedral conducted by the elegant Bishop of Southwark, Dr. Mervyn Stockwood, who later signed the deposition order with a red pen. 'I still hold my certificate of ordination with the Non-Conformist Church' said the plucky Mr. Bryn Thomas. 'My unfrocking does not prevent me from preaching in their churches.'

The following day, the Queen and Prince Philip were received by Pope John at the Vatican. The Queen, who wore a Hartnell gown of black lace and a headdress of black lace and tulle incorporating a tiara, presented the Pope with an ebony walking-stick tipped with rhino horn.

On May 18, it was revealed that Lady Anne Fitzalan-Howard, eldest daughter of the Duke of Norfolk, was doing social welfare work in the heart of London's Dockland. 'I feel I am doing something worthwhile. And I find it fascinating to meet people in their homes from a different type of society to the one in which one has been brought up.'

On May 22, Lady Maclean, whose son Donald had fled to Moscow ten years earlier, spoke of her son at her flat in South Kensington. 'I still hear regularly from Donald and his wife. They and my grandchildren lead a perfectly normal and ordinary life in Russia. They seem very happy. But I don't think there is any chance they will ever come to Britain.'

On May 24, it was announced that a wealthy American named Madame Montgomery de Brabant had rented Inveraray Castle for three months at £180 a week. A staff of ten and the services of the Duke's piper were thrown in with the house. It was said that the Duke of Argyll was spending the summer in Italy.

On May 30, Mr. Jimmy Goldsmith and Mrs. John Aspinall gave a party in a dome-shaped marquee in

Sussex Place, W.2. Guests, who included the Earl of Carnarvon, Lord Ednam, Dominic Elwes and the Maharajah of Jaipur, danced to the music of a seventeen-piece band. Beforehand, there had been angry protests from a local resident, Mrs. Basil Lindsay-Fynn. 'I think this is a shocking situation' she said. 'Lorries coming back and forth and noisy workmen in our lovely gardens.'

The following day, celebrities flocked to the Derby. Cigar-smoking property man Jack Cotton watched the race from his private box. 'It's all just a spot of fun for me' he said. 'I really don't know a darned thing about horses.'

On June 4, the new American President, John Kennedy, flew into England in a red and silver Boeing 707. He was met at London Airport by Mr. Macmillan and escorted in a thirteen-strong motorcade to 4 Buckingham Place, home of Mrs. Kennedy's sister, Princess Lee Radziwill. The next day, Mr. Kennedy, son of a former American Ambassador to Britain, attended the christening of Princess Radziwill's daughter at Westminster Cathedral. After dinner at Buckingham Palace that night, he flew back to America. The beautiful Mrs. Kennedy remained in England for several days, dining the following night with Mr. and Mrs. Jakie Astor, Cecil Beaton and Mr. and Mrs. William Douglas-Home.

On June 8, royalty and high society gathered in Yorkshire for the wedding of the Duke of Kent and Miss Katharine Worsley. After the service in York Minster, there was a reception at the home of the bride, Hovingham Hall, where a marquee had been erected on Sir William Worsley's private cricket pitch. The bridal couple later flew off to their honeymoon at Birkhall near Balmoral in a private plane well-stocked with champagne and smoked salmon sandwiches.

On June 16, there was an exciting international incident when twenty-three-year-old Rudolf Nureyev, star dancer with the Kirov Ballet of Leningrad, broke away from his party and ran through Le Bourget Airport shouting in English: 'I want to stay in France. These men are kidnapping me. I want to be free.' He was immediately granted political asylum.

On June 20, the Marquess of Tavistock and Miss Henrietta Tiarks were married at St. Clement Dane's in the Strand. A crowd of 1,000 onlookers gathered outside the church to see the bridegroom arrive with his best man, Lord Chelsea, in a sleek green Aston Martin followed by the bride in her father's blue Rolls-Royce. Several Green Line buses were hired to transport the guests, who included the Duchess of Argyll, Earl and Countess Beatty, Miss Sharman Douglas, and Douglas Fairbanks, to the reception at Claridge's. Absent from the ceremony was the bridegroom's stepmother Lydia Duchess of Bedford.

The next wedding of interest took place on Saturday July 1 when twenty-one-year-old Auberon Waugh married Lady Teresa Onslow, daughter of the Earl and Countess of Onslow, at the Church of our Lady of the

Twenty-one-year-old Auberon Waugh with his bride Lady Teresa Onslow

Assumption in Warwick Street. One of the bridesmaids, who wore dresses of gold crystal organza, was six-year-old Princess Antonia of Prussia, great-granddaughter of the Kaiser.

The following weekend, Lord and Lady Astor gave a house-party at Cliveden where the guests included John Profumo, Secretary of State for War, and his wife, actress Valerie Hobson. On the evening of July 8, Lord Astor, in a dinner-jacket, led his guests through the garden to the swimming-pool where they encountered Lord Astor's osteopath, Dr. Stephen Ward, who for the past five years had rented a cottage on the estate. Swimming in the pool, with no clothes on, was a friend of Ward's, nineteen-year-old Christine Keeler.

Meanwhile, finishing touches were being put to Mr. Basil Mavroleon's new £400,000 luxury yacht, *Radiant II*. On July 24, it left London on its maiden voyage. 'I can't pretend I need a holiday' said Mr. Mavroleon. 'I am an old war horse. I love work.' Also on board the 580-ton vessel was Commander Michael Parker, former secretary to the Duke of Edinburgh.

On August 14, the Prime Minister Harold Macmillan left London by train to shoot grouse with the Earl of Swinton at Masham Hall and then with his nephew the Duke of Devonshire at Bolton Abbey, where he had spent part of his honeymoon forty years earlier.

Three days later, Dr. Michael Ramsey, who had recently replaced Dr. Fisher as Archbishop of Canterbury, was found holidaying with his wife at an inn in Devonshire. 'We enjoy the quiet homely atmosphere. I like the food. It's good, plain stuff. It suits me. And I like a drop of cider with it. It rounds off the meal.'

On August 18, an angry letter was published in *Tribune* from thirty-one-year-old playwright John Osborne which included the phrase 'Damn you, England'. It was noted that the playwright was in the process of acquiring an old water-mill at Hellingly in Sussex in which to hide away from the world.

On August 22, it was announced that Goya's portrait of the Duke of Wellington, acquired from the Duke of Leeds for £140,000 the previous year, had been stolen from the National Gallery. 'No theory is too crazy to be impossible' said an official. 'It would be quite impossible to dispose of such a masterpiece.'

On August 24, forty-one-year-old Lord Ednam married twenty-eight-year-old actress Maureen Swanson. 'We have waited a long time to get married' said Maureen. 'Now I am going to give up my career.' It was noted that Lord Ednam's father, the Earl of Dudley, did not attend the ceremony. He was playing bridge at the St. James's Club at the time.

At the beginning of September, the thirty-five-year-old Marquess of Blandford, whose name was now romantically linked with Mrs. Tina Onassis, was found staying with Tina's brother-in-law Stavros Niarchos on his 3,000-acre Greek island of Spetsopoula. On September 11, they were joined by Lord Blandford's father, the Duke of Marlborough. 'I do not know Mr. Niarchos well' he said, 'but I have met him shooting.'

On September 12, eighty-nine-year-old Earl Russell and his wife were each sentenced to a week's imprisonment for their Ban-the-Bomb activities. Emerging from Brixton a week later, the great philosopher declared, 'It provided me with a much needed holiday. I had roses in my private hospital cell and read detective novels and a history book.' Lady Russell, who had served her sentence in Holloway, remarked, 'I really was treated exceptionally well. My fellow prisoners were delightful.'

On September 24, attention turned to John Osborne's newly-acquired water-mill in Sussex where the young playwright had recently been joined by Mrs. Penelope Gilliatt, wife of the best man at Princess Margaret's wedding. 'Mrs. Gilliatt will be staying here for some time' said Osborne.

On September 30, twenty-two-year-old heiress Katherine Dowsett, whose runaway romance with Chelsea playboy Edward Langley had made headline news two years earlier, was married to Old Etonian Michael Barclay. Uniformed and plain-clothed officers guarded the church at Greatford in Lincolnshire against the possibility of gate-crashers.

On October 3, it was announced that father-to-be, Antony Armstrong-Jones, had accepted an earldom. After hours of discussion with Princess Margaret, he had chosen the title Snowdon. 'I think it's splendid' said his former stepmother actress Carol Coombe. 'I just love the title. I'm just about to send a telegram off to the dear boy.'

On October 11, delegates to the Conservative Conference at Brighton were diverted by the sight of Lord Hailsham, Minister of Science, complete with goggles, flippers and snorkel swimming in the sea. 'I hope he's all right' remarked Lady Antonia Fraser, who was also braving the waves with her husband Hugh.

On October 23, 100 photographers burst into the Greek church in Paris where the Marquess of Blandford

The Marquess of Blandford and his bride Mrs Tina Onassis

was getting married to Mrs. Tina Onassis, both wearing coronets of flowers. The Duke of Marlborough, who was noticed staring at the ceiling during the ceremony, remarked afterwards, 'It was very nice – quite amusing.'

The death of Augustus John on October 31 caused widespread grief. One of those who was affected by the event was playboy Edward Langley who was found the following day drunk on Chelsea Embankment. After being fined 7s.6d. at Marlborough Street Court, he explained: 'A couple of artist friends and myself got together and we were upset about Augustus John's death.'

On November 2, twenty-two-year-old ballet dancer Rudolf Nureyev, who had defected from Russia in dramatic circumstances earlier in the year, made his London debut at a matinée of the Royal Academy of Dancing at the Theatre Royal, Drury Lane. He was given an hysterically enthusiastic reception.

On November 3, Princess Margaret gave birth to a baby boy. Lord Snowdon toasted his son in champagne, while in Wales the baby's grandfather, Mr. Ronald Armstrong-Jones, invited local villagers to his home Plas Dinas where he set off a special rocket to celebrate the event.

The same day the Marquess of Blandford and his new wife arrived in England. They were met at London Airport by the Marquess's butler-chauffeur and driven to his home at Charlbury near Blenheim Palace. That afternoon, the new Marchioness took part in a shooting-party and a day or two later she was formally introduced to the tenants and staff at Blenheim. 'It is a comfort to me to know that one day Tina will be Châtelaine of this vast and unwieldy place' said the sixty-four-year-old Duke of Marlborough.

On November 13, Mr. Aristotle Onassis arrived in London, booked into Claridge's and expressed a hope that he would see his ex-wife during his visit. 'Our relationship has always been most friendly and as far as I know, we are still on the best of terms.'

On November 27, a thief broke into Fort Belvedere, home of Mr. and Mrs. Gerald Lascelles, and stole a fur-coat and jewels, including a diamond brooch that had once belonged to Queen Mary. 'I can't understand it' said Mr. Lascelles. 'I was sitting in my library with my three King Charles spaniels. Normally they give the alarm at the slightest sound.'

Meanwhile, a new nurse, Verona Sumner, had been recruited to look after the infant Viscount Linley and the baby's parents were in the process of moving into much larger accommodation in Kensington Palace: a suite of some twenty rooms, currently in a very poor state of repair.

On December 19, Lord Linley was christened by Dr. Ramsey, Archbishop of Canterbury, in the Music Room at Buckingham Palace, watched by eighty-two guests. Among the godparents was Lady Elizabeth Cavendish, at whose house Princess Margaret and Lord Snowdon had first met four years earlier. A special 15 lb. christening cake was served bearing an inscription of the baby Viscount's coronet.

On December 22, forty-three-year-old Lord Derby was fined £5 for causing a collision by ignoring a halt sign. He had been spared prosecution on a more serious charge by claiming that the bonnet length of his Rolls-Royce had restricted his vision. A spokesman for the Rolls-Royce Company said afterwards, 'The visibility from our cars is quite satisfactory.'

1962

On New Year's Day, it was announced in the *London Gazette* that the Queen and Prince Philip had appointed a royal muffin-man, seventy-five-year-old Edward Tong, who operated from a small bake-house near Reading. Asked how perfect muffins should be made, Mr. Tong explained, 'The bakehouse must always be the same temperature and each muffin individually made.'

On January 5, it was announced that Lord Snowdon, currently on holiday in Antigua with Princess Margaret, had been appointed an artistic adviser to the *Sunday Times*, now owned by Canadian Roy Thomson. It was said that he would work closely with his old Cambridge friend, Mark Boxer, editor of the newspaper's colour magazine.

Meanwhile, Princess Margaret and Lord Snowdon had been criticised in the House of Commons for the heavy cost of the repairs being carried out on their new twenty-room flat, 1A Kensington Palace, most of which was being paid for by the Ministry of Works.

On January 23, it was announced that thirteen-year-old Prince Charles would be going to Gordonstoun the following term. 'My heart bleeds for him' commented seventeen-year-old Lord Rudolf Russell who had run away from the school two years earlier. 'My only recollections are of complete horror.'

On January 31, some trinkets belonging to the late Prince Aly Khan and not required by his family were sold at Christie's for £1,386.

At the beginning of February, the filming of the epic *Cleopatra*, now taking place in Rome, was suddenly surrounded by rumours of a romance between co-stars Elizabeth Taylor and Richard Burton. Miss Taylor dismissed the rumours as 'nonsense' and Mr. Burton stated that he was already happily married 'and hope to remain so forever'.

On February 15, the Duke and Duchess of Windsor were shown indulging in a new dance called 'the Twist' in a Paris nightclub.

On February 20, the sixty-nine-year-old Duke of Leinster was found in a cottage in Kent designing hand-knitted skating clothes for children. 'I have no formal artistic training but I find it easy to create these clothes. The idea came to me because I love to see women well dressed' said Ireland's premier Duke, whose life had been far from uneventful.

The following day, it was learned that the Duke of Norfolk was advertising for an extra gamekeeper to help run his estates at Arundel in Sussex. Said the Duke's head keeper, Mr. Garrett, 'I could really do with another three men. There is much more poaching from motor-cars now.'

On March 3, Miss Jane Ormsby-Gore, nineteen-year-old daughter of the new British Ambassador in Washington, was found working in an Islington antique shop run by twenty-three-year-old Christopher Gibbs. 'Jane is a good friend of mine' said Mr. Gibbs. 'She is helping me for six months.'

On March 6, the Queen, Princess Marina, Princess Margaret and the Earl of Snowdon were present at Covent Garden to witness the last performance of *Giselle* at Covent Garden starring Russian dancer Rudolf Nureyev. Owing to a mix-up over tickets, Princess Marina was placed in the Royal Box and the Queen in the Grand Tier.

On March 15, it was disclosed that the Earl of Snowdon's green Mini-Cooper was to return to the factory for further work to be done on it. 'Lord Snowdon's car will be coming into the works within the next few weeks' said designer Mr. Alec Issigonis. 'He wants it hotted up slightly. This is not something we would do for anyone else.'

On March 29, fire broke out in the Earl of Derby's private kitchen in the grandstand at Aintree racecourse. The Earl's domestic staff, who had come over from Knowsley Hall for the day, raised the alarm and two fire-engines raced to the scene.

On Sunday April 8, Prince Philip took the Queen and Prince Charles out for a ride in his new 100-mph convertible Alvis, which had recently been acquired for £3,110 and was said to be fitted with disc brakes. On the Queen's lap was a favourite Corgi.

On April 11, attention turned to Sotheby's where thirty-five paintings from the collection of eighty-eight-year-old Somerset Maugham were to be auctioned. The paintings, which included works by Picasso, Matisse, Monet and Gauguin raised £523,880. After the sale, which took place in the evening, Maugham's companion and private secretary Alan Searle, rang through to the aged writer at his villa at Cap Ferrat with details. 'He seemed rather dazed' he said. 'After all, it is a great lot of money for a single gentleman of his age to come into.'

Shortly after the sale, it was announced that Maugham's daughter, Lady John Hope, wife of the Minister of Housing, was taking steps to claim her share of the proceeds. 'I don't know anything about this' she told reporters. 'It's all in the hands of the lawyers.'

Meanwhile, a new cathedral had been built at Coventry, featuring a backcloth to the altar by Graham Sutherland. The consecration service on May 25, attended by the Queen, Princess Margaret and Lord Snowdon, was enlivened when the Lord Mayor of Coventry fainted. The Lord Lieutenant of Warwickshire, Lord Willoughby de Broke, helped him back onto his seat and the Mayor later blamed the incident on his heavy robes, weighing some 32 lb. and containing no pocket in which smelling salts could be hidden.

The same day, Lord Rothermere gave a party at his palatial house in St. James's to celebrate the eighty-third birthday of Lord Beaverbrook. Among those present were the Prime Minister Harold Macmillan, Sir Winston Churchill, the Earl of Rosebery, the Hon. Vere Harmsworth and Mr. Roy Thomson, who were all photographed together in a room hung with Reynolds and Goyas.

On May 30, it was announced that Eaton Hall, Cheshire, colossal Victorian home of the Dukes of Westminster, which had been occupied by the Army for many years, was to be pulled down. 'The place is full of dry rot' said Colonel Gerald Grosvenor, heir to the Dukedom. 'It would be impossible to put it right. The cost would run into many thousands.'

On June 5, the Duchess of Argyll appealed unsuccessfully to the House of Lords that her private diary, seized by the Duke of Argyll for use in his battle against her, should be regarded as confidential.

On June 6, there were chaotic scenes at the Derby when six jockeys, including the Queen's jockey Harry Carr, were injured and one horse had to be destroyed. A subsequent enquiry conducted by the Duke of Norfolk, the Earl of Halifax and Sir Humphrey de Trafford, criticised owners and trainers for allowing unqualified horses to compete in the race.

On June 14 it was announced that the twenty-two-year-old Marquess of Tavistock, currently travelling home to England on board the *Queen Mary* had failed his final examinations at Harvard. 'I hope to sit the exams again at the American Embassy in London' he announced from the ship.

On June 28, the ninety-nine-year-old Marquess of Winchester died in the Princess Grace Clinic in Monte Carlo.

A few hours later, Sir Winston Churchill was admitted to the same hospital following a fall in his room at the Hotel de Paris. An emergency operation was performed and the following day, a RAF Comet ambulance flew him home to London where another operation to pin his broken thigh was performed at the Middlesex Hospital. 'You'll be happy to know the old man is all right' said one of the surgeons involved.

During his convalescence, Sir Winston was visited by Field Marshal Montgomery, who insisted on discussing current affairs with his old comrade. 'I was delighted to discover that he was against us going into the Common Market' said Monty afterwards.

On July 13, there was a ball at Blenheim Palace to celebrate the coming of age of Lord Charles Spencer-Churchill, younger son of the Duke of Marlborough. Earlier in the day, Lady Anne Tennant, Mrs. Maurice Macmillan and other guests visited the Brompton Road salon of hairdresser John Olofson to have their tiaras professionally put in place.

The following day, the Queen lunched with bearded washing-machine tycoon John Bloom at a charity race meeting at Lingfield Park. The Rolls Rapid Handicap, sponsored by Bloom, was won by Spartan General, owned by Mr. Freddie Laker, proprietor of the Channel Air Bridge Company.

On July 19, twenty-four-year-old Lord Londonderry gave a party for 300 friends at Londonderry House,

Londonderry House, Park Lane, the last great town house to come under the auctioneer's hammer. It was sold for £500,000 to Mr. Isaac Klug and subsequently demolished

Park Lane, which was soon to come under the auctioneer's hammer. Guests, who included the Duke and Duchess of Rutland, Lord and Lady Beatty and Miss Patricia Rawlings, were entertained by Benny Goodman. 'We wanted to give the old house a wake' said young Lady Londonderry. 'It was a wonderful, gay night. But, for us, sad too.' A week later, the house was sold for £500,000 to Mr. Isaac Klug, director of the Budget Property Company. Planning permission had already been granted for shops or a hotel to be erected on the site.

Meanwhile, much interest had centred upon sixty-six-year-old Nubar Gulbenkian's action against the BBC in the High Court. Gulbenkian claimed that the BBC had broken a promise by failing to hand over a tele-recording of his recent 'Face to Face' interview with John Freeman. Each day of the hearing, cold lunches of lobster, quail, truffles, smoked salmon and other delicacies were brought in by waiters from the Caprice Restaurant and carried at shoulder height to a private room at the Law Courts. On July 27, Gulbenkian was awarded only £2 damages, but stated he had achieved his real objective which was to publicise his criticisms of the Gulbenkian Trust set up under the will of his father.

July ended with sixty-five-year-old Sir Oswald Mosley back in the news, being kicked, punched and flung to the ground at meetings of his new political party the Union Movement, held in various parts of the country on successive days. The grimmest of these occasions occurred on July 31 in the East End of London when the violence was such that several of Sir Oswald's friends feared there was a plot to kill him.

On August 8, the Bishop of Bath and Wells, the Rt. Rev. Edward Henderson, in crash-helmet and dog-collar, went Go-Karting at Castle Combe in Wiltshire. 'Splendid, splendid' he declared after completing three laps of a special racecourse.

On August 12, Harold Macmillan left by train for the Earl of Swinton's grouse moors at Masham in Yorkshire, accompanied by his personal detective, two secretaries, two despatch-boxes, two guns and a typewriter. 'After studying the reports, I have hopes there will be fair game' he said.

On August 21, Princess Margaret broke the tradition of a lifetime by celebrating her birthday at Abbey Leix in Ireland, home of Lord Snowdon's sister, Lady de Vesci, instead of Balmoral.

The same day, Sir Winston Churchill left Middlesex Hospital after fifty-four days' treatment for his broken thigh. He carried a cigar and wore a suit of medium pale-grey Prince of Wales check. That night at 28 Hyde Park Gate, there was a dinner-party followed by a showing of the film *Rob Roy* and a member of the staff at the house said that Sir Winston was 'in the pink'.

At the beginning of September, Mayfair gambler John Aspinall was found cruising around the Greek islands and Black Sea on board the magnificent yacht the *Sister Anne* owned by Mrs. Reginald Fellowes which in 1935 carried the Prince of Wales and Mrs. Simpson on a Mediterranean cruise. Mr. Aspinall's guests included Lady Annabel Birley and her brother, the twenty-four-year-old Marquess of Londonderry.

On September 7, it was revealed that the fifty-seven-year-old Earl of Longford was learning to swim in the pool at Dolphin Square. 'All the family can swim except me' he said. 'I've always funked it. But when my wife installed a swimming-pool at our Sussex home, I decided I must learn.'

On September 12, Admiralty clerk William Vassall, son of a curate at St. James's, Piccadilly, was arrested and charged with offences under the Official Secrets Act.

On September 21, seventy-six-year-old Lord Astor of Hever, chief proprietor of *The Times*, announced that he was going to live abroad. 'If I remained domiciled in this country, my death will mean that almost the whole of my American property would disappear in death duties and my family would be involved in serious financial consequences.' Lord Astor and his wife would move to a villa at Cannes and would be accompanied by their butler Mr. Albert Bursby, who had served them for thirty-five years.

At the end of the month, a Rolls-Royce driven by ninety-five-year-old millionaire Gilbert Beale, head of Carter's Tested Garden Seeds, plunged into the Thames at Pangbourne. Mr. Beale and his passengers, who included eminent surgeon Mr. H. P. Winsbury-White, were rescued from the £8,500-car a few seconds before it sank. 'Mr. Beale was absolutely calm, most commendable' said Mr. Winsbury-White. 'I found it quite horrifying.'

On October 9, Dame Edith Sitwell's seventy-fifth birthday was celebrated with a concert at the Royal Festival Hall in her honour. Sixty-year-old Sir William Walton flew over from his home on the island of Ischia to conduct the orchestra. Dame Edith, who occupied the Ceremonial Box with her brothers Sir Osbert and Sacheverell, wore a Tudor-style robe of scarlet satin, gold shoes and a gold hat.

On October 22, William Vassall's conviction for spying for Russia was quickly followed by an explanation from the secretary of the Bath Club in Brook Street, Mayfair, as to how the Admiralty clerk had become a member of this exclusive institution. 'He was never elected' said Mr. Peter Frend. 'He became a member of the Conservative Club in 1950 and only became a member of our club when the Conservative merged with us in 1951. This is how he slipped in.'

On November 5, the opening of the Clermont Club at 44 Berkeley Square, was noted. The house had been converted into a gambling club by veteran interior decorator John Fowler, under instructions from thirty-five-year-old Mr. John Aspinall. At the opening party, eighty-one-year-old Lord Esher remarked, 'Takes me back to my boyhood when a town house was a town house.' Simultaneously, the basement of the house was being turned into a nightclub by Aspinall's friend Mark Birley. He had chosen the name 'Annabel's' for the premises in honour of his wife, grand-daughter of the late Lady Londonderry.

On November 6, Dame Margot Fonteyn was partnered for the first time by Mr. Rudolf Nureyev. That evening they danced together at Covent Garden in a performance of *Les Sylphides*. Shortly afterwards, it was announced that twenty-three-year-old Nureyev, said to be earning £15,000 a year, was suffering from a strained ankle but had ignored the advice from an orthopaedic surgeon to take a rest. 'Nureyev is a law unto himself' said a Covent Garden official.

On November 12, Cecil Beaton left London for Paris where he planned to work on costumes and scenery for the film version of *My Fair Lady*. 'London is too suffocating, too insular' he explained. 'Paris has the right atmosphere for my ephemeral art.'

On November 24, two disastrous By-election results for the Conservative Party did not cause the Prime Minister Harold Macmillan to alter his plans to spend three days pheasant shooting at the Earl of Home's country seat, Castlemains in Lanarkshire. Here, he appeared in his usual knickerbockers and gaiters, on top of which he wore bell-bottomed waterproof trousers.

On November 29, Princess Alexandra announced her engagement to thirty-four-year-old company director, the Honourable Angus Ogilvy, grandson of Mabell Countess of Airlie, Lady of the Bedchamber to the late Queen Mary. Mr. Ogilvy, who was said to hold twenty-nine directorships, lived in a house in Culross Street, behind the American Embassy.

On December 9, the Duke of Beaufort broke his nose while out hunting in Gloucestershire. It was noted that four months earlier, the sixty-two-year-old Duke had broken his leg in a fishing accident in Scotland. 'I must admit I have been rather unfortunate this year' he said. 'I broke my nose once before – I'm not letting it hinder me. I'm going on as if nothing had happened.'

Two days later, it was revealed that the elegant Viscount Lambton, Tory MP for Berwick-on-Tweed, had been wounded on the ear by a fellow shot while out shooting in Yorkshire with Prince Stanislaus Radziwill, brother-in-law of Mrs. Jackie Kennedy. 'It's all very irritating' he said after returning home and cancelling all his engagements.

On December 18, young Lord Chelsea, heir to the great Cadogan estates stretching through Chelsea and Belgravia, announced his engagement to Lady Philippa Wallop, daughter of the Earl and Countess of Portsmouth, who was currently working on a glossy magazine. Said Lady Portsmouth: 'My daughter and Lord Chelsea have known each other on and off for years but they have only been going out together for a matter of months.'

On December 28, it was announced that eighty-eight-year-old Somerset Maugham was endeavouring to legally adopt his secretary-companion fifty-year-old Alan Searle, and would be using his great fortune to set up a trust fund to aid young and struggling authors. Said Maugham's daughter, Lady John Hope, 'I cannot understand why my father has taken such an action. It makes no sense at all.'

The New Year was welcomed with a medieval fancy-dress party given by the fun-loving Mr. and Mrs. Anthony Kinsman at Crosby Hall in Chelsea. Bunty Kinsman was dressed as a unicorn while her husband wore a fur cover from a baby's pram explaining that he was 'a middle-aged wolf'.

On January 2, the Earl of Buckinghamshire, former Deputy Speaker in the House of Lords, died and the title passed to his second cousin, sixty-one-year-old Mr. Fred Hobart-Hampden, who was employed by Southend Corporation as a £9 a week gardener. 'I knew I was the heir but the old Earl never had anything to do with me and I never met him' he said.

On January 13, a storm blew up over a religious item on the new late-night television programme *That Was The Week That Was*, compèred by twenty-three-year-old Mr. David Frost. Joining in the criticism was Frost's clergyman father. 'I think it was very clever but I knew David was running into trouble' he said. 'He has his own Christian principles but I don't think you should satirise doctrines.'

On January 23, twenty-seven-year-old Raymond Bellisario appeared in court at Ascot in Berkshire charged with leaping out from behind some bushes in Windsor Great Park and taking informal photographs of the Queen, Princess Anne and a groom riding in the park. He was discharged but ordered to pay fourteen shillings costs.

The same day, Elizabeth Taylor left the London Clinic after treatment for a twisted knee. Waiting for her in the nearby Devonshire Arms public-house was her new friend Richard Burton.

On January 31, it was announced that an emerald was missing from the famous Exeter Salt Cellar, a piece of royal jewellery kept in the Tower of London and used at Coronation banquets. 'The stone must have fallen out during cleaning' said an official. 'This has happened before and the missing stones have always been found.'

That night, Prince William of Gloucester celebrated his twenty-first birthday with a party for 400 friends at St. James's Palace. 'I don't want people to come along in evening dress' he said. 'The whole thing will be much more informal than that.' The Queen Mother and the Princess Royal mingled with the Prince's friends from Cambridge and Chelsea.

On February 1, the seventy-four-year-old Duke of Sutherland, one of the great hosts of the pre-war years, died in Nassau. His body was flown home and a funeral was held in the drawing-room of his Scottish seat, Dunrobin Castle. The dukedom passed to his distant relation, the Earl of Ellesmere.

On February 14, forty-six-year-old Harold Wilson was elected leader of the Labour Party following the death of Hugh Gaitskell. Mrs. Wilson remarked, 'People keep asking me what kind of curtains I am going to have at Downing Street and all that sort of thing. But I can't possibly say. I must wait until it happens.'

On February 24, the fifty-eight-year-old Marquess of Bath, the seventy-year-old Duke of Leinster and other less illustrious figures, set off on a walk from London to Brighton. Lord Bath, who was in the middle of a health cure and was living only on yoghurt and fruit-juice, dropped out of the walk after thirteen-and-a-half miles, retiring to bed with pneumonia.

The following day, Nicholas Luard, twenty-five-year-old owner of the new magazine *Private Eye* and The Establishment nightclub, married Miss Elizabeth Longmore at St. Margaret's, Westminster. After the ceremony, there was an unexpectedly formal reception at Claridge's where the presence of Edward Adeane, son of the Queen's Private Secretary, and James Butler, son of the Home Secretary, R. A. Butler, was noted. After a two-day honeymoon in Paris, the couple flew home to face a libel action over an article in *Private Eye* from fifty-one-year-old Randolph Churchill.

On February 26, the Earl of Snowdon attended the royal première of a sentimental cockney film *Sparrers Can't Sing*, starring Barbara Windsor, which was held at the ABC Cinema, Mile End Road. Princess Margaret was confined to her room at Kensington Palace with 'flu. 'My wife was really looking forward to seeing this film and is most upset that she could not be here' said Lord Snowdon. 'I do apologise on her behalf.' After the film, there was a party for the cast at the nearby Kentucky Club owned by famous East End boxing twins, Ronald and Reginald Kray.

On March 3, the news broke that Kim Philby, cleared of being 'the Third Man' in the Burgess-Maclean affair in 1955, had disappeared in Beirut where he had recently been working as correspondent of the *Observer*. 'It will probably be very difficult to find him' remarked David Astor, the newspaper's editor.

Meanwhile, the long-awaited Argyll divorce case had opened in a sombre Edinburgh court-room. The case dragged on for many days and on March 14, the judge, Lord Wheatley, announced that he would deliver his judgment at a later date.

The Duke and Duchess of Argyll at the time of their lengthy divorce case

On March 21, twenty-three-year-old Lance Callingham, Old Harrovian son of the energetic Lady Docker, was married at Caxton Hall to twenty-five-year-old Miss Lynn Aldridge. Sir Bernard and Lady Docker arrived at the ceremony in a black and turquoise Rolls-Royce. 'I'll be glad when this is all over' remarked Lady Docker, who wore a brown mink coat.

The following day, the Minister for War, Mr. John Profumo, told the House of Commons that there had been no impropriety in his relationship with the beautiful Christine Keeler, whom he had met two years earlier at Cliveden with Lord Astor and who was now being sought as a witness in a trial at the Old Bailey. That afternoon, Mr. Profumo and his wife, former actress Valerie Hobson, were in the Queen Mother's party at Sandown Races and in the evening they were found dancing together at Quaglio's Restaurant off Jermyn Street.

On March 24, Aristotle Onassis visited Paul Getty at Sutton Place and was photographed sitting cross-legged at his feet. 'It was a sort of business lunch' said Getty, 'but as we are old friends, I'd say it was more of a social occasion.' The startling photograph was taken by Lord Lambton's daughter Lucinda, who was keen to make her name as a freelance Press photographer.

On April 17, there was another gathering of multi-millionaires at a party to celebrate the opening of the newly-built Hilton Hotel. Paul Getty, Charles Clore, Nubar Gulbenkian, Conrad Hilton and the Duke of Bedford mingled with lesser mortals like Dr. Beeching and Labour MP George Brown while a Guards band played 'Who Wants To Be A Millionaire?'

Three days later, the Queen gave a much publicised ball at Windsor Castle to celebrate the marriage of Princess Alexandra and the Hon. Angus Ogilvy; thirty-six turkeys, fifty ducks and twenty-four hams were consumed and 1,600 bottles of non-vintage Grand Marc champagne were drunk. Prince Charles and Princess Anne watched the festivities from a gallery in the Castle's famous Waterloo Room. Among the glittering gathering of aristocracy and foreign royalty was found the controversial Minister of Transport, Mr. Ernest Marples. It was noted that on his way to collect his fiancée before the ball, Mr. Ogilvy crashed his Jaguar, badly damaging its radiator grill.

On May 1, eighty-eight-year-old Sir Winston Churchill put on white tie and tails, the blue ribbon of the Garter and the badge of the Order of Merit and attended the Royal Academy banquet at Burlington House. Earlier in the day, he had announced that he would not be standing for Parliament at the next General Election.

On May 8, after two months' consideration, Lord Wheatley delivered in his judgment in the Argyll divorce case. He took 40,000 words to say that he had found the Duchess guilty of adultery, savagely attacking her morals in the process. 'Her attitude towards the sanctity of marriage was what moderns would call enlightened' he said. After the verdict, the jubilant Duke announced that there would be a celebration bonfire at Inveraray Castle, a plan he did not go through with. In Paris, the forty-nine-year-old Duchess said, 'It has been a horrible time for me. I just want to get away for a while and think.'

The following day, the Duchess flew home under the name Mrs. Campbell and was met by scores of Press photographers at London Airport. The assistance of the police was required to get her to her Rolls-Royce which took her to her house in Upper Grosvenor Street, Mayfair. 'Her Grace is exhausted' a maid told reporters. 'She will probably have a light meal served in bed later. She will not be going anywhere tonight.'

On May 22, property millionaire Bernard Sunley gave a lunch-party at the Coq d'Or in Stratton Street which was attended by Socialist Leader Harold Wilson, his colleague George Brown, Mr. Charles Clore and others. One of the guests observed, 'When the Tories are in power, they behave like Socialists. When the Socialists are in power, they behave like Tories.'

On June 5, Mr. Profumo issued a statement that he had lied to the House of Commons and resigned both as Minister of War and as an MP. The Prime Minister was in Scotland at the time and was found setting-off on a pleasure-steamer with Lady Dorothy to the island of Iona.

Three days later, on Saturday June 8, society osteopath Dr. Stephen Ward was arrested at Watford and charged with living off immoral earnings. He appeared in court wearing sky-blue slacks, slippers and no socks and was remanded in custody.

On June 17, Charles Clore gave an eve-of-Ascot dance at which Margaret Duchess of Argyll made her first public appearance since her divorce.

On June 18, Mr. and Mrs. Profumo returned from a secret country location to their house in Chester Terrace, Regent's Park, where they were visited that evening by Mr. Profumo's brother Philip and Mr. Randolph Churchill. The butler at the house, Mr. Stanley Briscoe said, 'Mr. and Mrs. Profumo are very happy together tonight. They have enjoyed themselves tremendously at the dinner-party and now they are tired and preparing to go to bed.'

The same night, twenty-one-year-old boxer Cassius Clay appeared at Wembley Stadium in contest with Mr. Henry Cooper and beat him in the fourth round. In front-row seats at the fight were Elizabeth Taylor and Richard Burton.

The following day, a Buckingham Palace spokesman admitted that fourteen-year-old Prince Charles had ordered a glass of cherry brandy at a pub in Stornoway during a recent excursion from Gordonstoun School. 'I cannot say what action will be taken until I know the full circumstances' said the Prince's headmaster, Mr. Robert Chew.

At the end of the month, it was announced that thirty-two-year-old tycoon John Bloom had purchased a 375-ton yacht, the *Ariana III*, for £330,000. Said to be the largest yacht built in Britain since the war, it had a lift linking its master-bedroom to the bridge.

On July 1, Kim Philby, who had disappeared in January, re-emerged in Moscow. In the House of Commons, Lord Privy Seal Edward Heath was now asked if Philby was in fact the Third Man. 'Yes, sir' he replied in a quiet voice. Colonel Marcus Lipton, who had named Philby as the Third Man eight years earlier, commented, 'Even now, I doubt whether the whole story has come out. The truth is only beginning to be told.'

On July 3, Dr. Stephen Ward was released from custody on £3,000 bail. He left Marylebone court by taxi and was later found in a Chelsea restaurant eating scampi and salad and drinking coffee from a glass cup. 'I shall probably stay in London for a while then off to the country for a complete rest' he said.

Two days later, there was a charity concert in the Gold Library at Cliveden at which guitarist Segovia gave a recital. 'We have had an excellent sale of tickets. In fact, a complete sell-out' said one of the organisers. 'I don't think it has anything to do with Cliveden being written about recently.' After the concert, Lord Astor praised Segovia. 'I must say I've never heard Segovia before. I'm absolutely enchanted. He really is terribly good.'

On July 11, the seventy-five-year-old Dowager Duchess of Northumberland, Mistress of the Robes to the Queen Mother, was the victim of a daring robbery outside her Eaton Square home. Five thieves snatched a diamond tiara and pearl necklace which she had just collected from her jewellers and was intending to wear at a banquet that night at Claridge's in honour of the King and Queen of Greece. Later that day, the Queen Mother called to comfort her.

On July 22, the opening of Dr. Stephen Ward's trial at the Old Bailey coincided with the opening of an exhibition of his drawings at the Museum Street Galleries in Bloomsbury. Portraits of many members of the Royal Family were included. After a tiring day sitting in the dock at the Old Bailey, Ward arrived at the Private View that evening in a bubble car.

On July 31, the trial took an unexpected turn when it was announced that the defendant had taken an overdose of nembutal tablets and had been taken to St. Stephen's Hospital, Fulham Road, where he was said

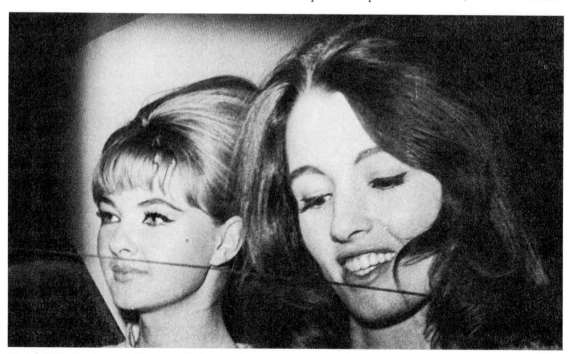

Mandy Rice-Davies and Christine Keeler, chief prosecution witnesses at the Old Bailey trial of society osteopath Dr. Stephen Ward

to be grievously ill. That evening, Miss Mandy Rice-Davies, a key witness at the trial, was present at the première of *Cleopatra* at the Dominion Cinema, Tottenham Court Road. 'Whatever he has done or admitted' she said, 'he never deserved to get into this awful mess.'

The same day, the Peerage Act had become law and Lord Stansgate, who had been fighting for this legislation for many years, had signed away his peerage and returned to being Mr. Anthony Wedgwood Benn.

On August 3, Stephen Ward died without having ever regained consciousness. It was revealed that he had left fourteen suicide notes, in one of which he had written, 'I'm sorry to disappoint the vultures.' His friend Lord Astor later issued an unusual epitaph praising Ward's gifts of healing. 'Those who were fortunate enough to have been treated by him will remember him with great gratitude. His readiness to help anyone in pain is the memory many will treasure.'

On August 8, a brilliantly organised gang of men stopped the Glasgow–London mail train at Cheddington in Buckinghamshire and got away with £2,500,000 in cash, causing a wave of sneaking admiration across the country. 'I don't feel any admiration for these gentlemen at all' said Mr. Bevins, the Postmaster-General. A list of men the police wished to interview was soon issued, one of whom was antique-dealer Bruce Reynolds, who was thought to be somewhere in the South of France. 'He knows it like the back of his hand' said a detective.

On August 9, the beautiful Baroness von Thyssen, who the previous year had been voted one of the world's best-dressed women, was refused admission to the restaurant at the Dorchester Hotel because she was incorrectly dressed.

On August 30, Mr. Marks, seventy-seven-year-old manager of Wilton's restaurant, complained that oysters were no longer being consumed by the Royal Family. 'We've supplied the Royal Household since the time of King William IV but since the Duke of Windsor left, they haven't eaten any at all.'

On September 1, Old Etonian missing diplomat Guy Burgess died in Moscow's Botkin Hospital. 'I didn't even know he was in hospital until his housekeeper phoned to say he was dead' said his old comrade, fifty-year-old Donald Maclean, interviewed on the landing outside his flat. Burgess's mother, seventy-six-year-old Mrs. Eve Bassett was said to be seriously ill in her flat in Arlington House and had no comment to make.

In the meantime, Princess Margaret, now expecting her second child, and Lord Snowdon had left for a holiday with Stavros Niarchos on his private island Spetsopoula. Also in the party were the Marquess and Marchioness of Blandford and the Princess's private detective, Chief Inspector Fred Crocker. Niarchos placed his helicopter and fabulous 697-ton yacht *Creole* at the disposal of his royal guests. It was noted that the island had been well stocked with Scottish grouse.

On September 20, thirteen-year-old Princess Anne was one of the new pupils at Benenden School. 'The girls all look so alike in their uniforms that I don't know whether I shall be able to pick out Princess Anne when I come next' the Queen told the headmistress, Miss Elizabeth Clarke.

On September 21, orchids grown by Mr. Charles Clore in his greenhouses on his country estate were awarded the Gold Diploma at the Newbury Agricultural Show. At the same show, Clore's Aberdeen Angus bull came first in its class.

On September 26, Lord Denning's racily written report on the Profumo affair was published. It was revealed that Lord Denning had interviewed 160 people in the course of his enquiry, including Margaret Duchess of Argyll. Over 100,000 copies were sold within twenty-four hours. Mr. Profumo was in the north of Scotland at the time and said he had no comment to make.

On October 2, property tycoon Bernard Sunley was slapped on the face by an actress at the première of *A Funny Thing Happened On the Way to the Forum* at the Strand Theatre. Two policemen were called and Sunley, president of a £26-million investment trust, was taken away and later fined £10 for insulting behaviour. 'If the young woman cares to phone me up' said Sunley, 'I'll be happy to buy her lunch and we can talk things over.'

On October 8, eighty-one-year-old Lord Rosebery announced that he had named one of his yearlings

Cheddington. 'The Great Train Robbery was not far from my estate at Mentmore' he said. 'As Cheddington's sire is called Hook Money, I just couldn't resist the name.'

The same day, the Prime Minister Harold Macmillan entered King Edward VII's Hospital for Officers for an operation to remove a prostate obstruction. A hot line between his room and 10 Downing Street was quickly installed by the GPO. One of his first visitors was Lord Dilhorne, the Lord Chancellor, who brought a bouquet of red roses.

Two days later, Macmillan announced his resignation as Prime Minister from his hospital bed. Within a few hours, Lord Hailsham had declared that he would resign his peerage and no less than five other candidates had emerged as possible successors.

On October 13, the newly discovered pop group, the Beatles, appeared on a television programme broadcast from the London Palladium. Police were called when fans broke down a door to the back entrance. 'I haven't seen anything like this since 1955 when Johnny Ray was here' said the stage doorman, Mr. George Cooper.

On October 18, the sixty-year-old Earl of Home, one-time Parliamentary Private Secretary to Neville Chamberlain, became the new Prime Minister. His eighty-one-year-old mother, the Dowager Countess of Home, declared, 'I am quite amazed. I was sure it was going to be Mr. Butler. There was nothing unusual about him as a boy. On the contrary; he was a very shy and retiring boy.'

On November 1, eighty-year-old Elsa Maxwell, the greatest party-giver of the first half of the twentieth century, died in New York. It was noted that she had made her last appearance a week earlier at the 'April in Paris' Ball in New York in a wheelchair.

On November 4, the Queen Mother met the Beatles following the Royal Variety Command Performance at the Prince of Wales Theatre. The Queen Mother, who wore a double-tiered crinoline gown of silver and gold, was informed that the Beatles' next date was at Slough. 'That's near us' she responded.

On November 22, the assassination of the American President John Kennedy sent waves of shock and horror throughout the world. Among the many tributes that poured in was a message from eighty-eight-year-old Sir Winston Churchill. 'This monstrous act has taken from us a great statesman and a wise and valiant man. The loss to the United States and to the world is incalculable.'

On November 28, there was a reception at the Carlton Tower Hotel following the marriage of power-boat enthusiast Lord Bingham, heir to the Earl of Lucan, and Miss Veronica Duncan. The following day, the couple flew to Paris where they caught the Orient Express for Istanbul where they spent their honeymoon.

On December 8, twenty-four-year-old Rudolf Nureyev, wearing long black boots, a leather coat and fur hat, was knocked down by a motor scooter in Chelsea. He was taken to St. George's Hospital suffering from cuts and bruises.

On December 16, Mrs. Richard Burton was granted a divorce on the grounds of her thirty-eight-year-old husband's 'cruel and inhuman treatment.' Marriage between Mr. Burton and Miss Elizabeth Taylor was expected to follow soon. 'I don't think they will wait very long' said a friend.

December 28 saw the last edition of the television programme *That Was The Week That Was*, which had been condemned by many people in authority, including the Lord Chancellor, Lord Dilhorne. 'Those responsible for it have got to the stage of being unable to distinguish between what was humorous and what was offensive and rude. I gave up watching it some time ago. It became such a bore.'

1964

On January 1, sixty-nine-year-old Harold Macmillan reported for work at his family publishing company of which he had taken over as chairman after resigning as Prime Minister. On his first day, he arrived late, visited the Carlton Club at noon and went on to lunch with a friend. He was back in the office at 3.30 pm smoking a cigar, dictated a few letters and left at 5.00 pm.

On January 21, Eton reassembled with a new headmaster, Mr. Anthony Chenevix-Trench. 'I think that being known as an Old Etonian can be an embarrassment, a cross a boy has to bear probably all his life' he said. 'There is much to be done but I realise making changes in such a historic place as Eton must be difficult.'

On January 22, a joint statement was issued on behalf of Somerset Maugham and his daughter Lady John Hope to the effect that their differences had been settled. The great writer was no longer attempting to revoke his gifts to his daughter and he had also paid the costs of her lawsuits. Three days later, on January 25, he was able to celebrate his ninetieth birthday in a happy atmosphere. Over 3,000 letters and birthday cards poured in.

Meanwhile, Bobby Kennedy, thirty-eight-year-old American Attorney-General, had arrived in England on a private visit. On January 25, a plane of the Queen's Flight took him to Chatsworth to visit the grave of his sister, the Marchioness of Hartington, who had died in a plane-crash in 1947.

Also visiting England were the Duke and Duchess of Windsor. At the end of the month, the sixty-seven-year-old Duchess, whose existence was still not officially acknowledged by the Royal Family, entered the London Clinic for 'a face operation'.

On February 7, the Beatles flew off to America where their tour was to be marred by unseemly scenes at a ball at the British Embassy in Washington, drawing humble apologies from the Ambassador's wife, Lady Ormsby-Gore.

The same day, nineteen-year-old Mandy Rice-Davies flew in after appearing in cabaret in Munich. She was accompanied by Baron Pierre Cervello, French-born heir to a Jamaican sugar fortune, who had given her a diamond ring. 'I don't want to talk about our wedding plans' said Mandy. 'Pierre has problems – like getting a divorce – which must be solved first.'

On February 12, Mr. and Mrs. John Bloom celebrated the third anniversary of their wedding with a party at the Jack o' Clubs in Soho. Among those present were Lord Thomson of Fleet, Sir Isaac Wolfson, pop singer Adam Faith and Vera Lynn. Towards the end of the evening, singer Dorothy Squires gave an impromptu cabaret.

On February 19, Prince Andrew's fourth birthday was celebrated with a party in his nursery at Buckingham Palace. Tables groaned with iced cakes and jellies and guests included three-year-old Viscount Linley, the Earl of St. Andrew's, baby son of the Duke and Duchess of Kent, four-year-old Philip Astor, grandson of Lord Astor of Hever, and three-year-old Henry Tennant, son of Colin Tennant.

At the end of the month, Princess Margarethe of Sweden announced her engagement to thirty-nine-year-old Haileybury-educated British businessman, John Ambler, who was said to own a flat in Wilton Crescent and a freight company in the East End of London.

On March 10, the Queen gave birth to her fourth child, attended by veteran midwife Nurse Helen Rowe. RAF Lightning jets screamed overhead to pay tribute to the baby boy, later christened Edward.

Two days later, twenty-three-year-old Mrs. Diana Wolfe Murray, daughter of the Prime Minister Sir Alec Douglas-Home, gave birth to a baby in a public ward in Westminster Hospital. 'I felt that she should have her own room but she absolutely insisted that she should go into the wards' said her husband, an executive in a whisky firm.

On March 19, Harold Wilson, Leader of the Socialist Party, met the Beatles at the Variety Club luncheon at the Savoy Hotel. 'We are all proud of the creation of a new musical idiom in world communications' he said, naming the Beatles Show Business Personalities of the Year. Mrs. Wilson watched the ceremony, sipping tomato juice.

On March 26, it was revealed that several rooms in the Wyatville Wing at Chatsworth had been given a face-lift. The Duchess of Devonshire had chosen 130 yards of oyster-coloured watered silk instead of wallpaper. 'It was the sort of job you can take a pride in' said interior decorator Albert Greenwood.

At the end of the month there was much excitement over the first outpourings from a floating broadcasting station named Radio Caroline. 'Although we are piratical in a sense' said one of the backers, thirty-year-old Jocelyn Stevens, 'we are not breaking the law. We have been advised by the best British legal brains.'

On April 6, seventy-year-old Harold Macmillan caught a 12 lb. salmon while fishing in the River Blackwater on the Duke of Devonshire's Irish estate. 'What a game fish. It gave me a tough time and a great thrill' remarked the former Prime Minister. 'It's thirty years since I last held a rod.'

On April 15, it was announced that Maureen Marchioness of Dufferin and Ava, had purchased five acres on the north coast of Sardinia where land was now fetching £8,000 an acre and was planning to build a villa there.

On May 2, the legendary Nancy Lady Astor died aged eighty-four while staying with her daughter, Lady Ancaster, at Grimsthorpe Castle in Lincolnshire. In her will, Lady Astor left careful instructions regarding the appointment of an official biographer in order that she should be presented to the world as she wished.

On May 7, twenty-five-year-old Earl of Shaftesbury announced that he would attempt to climb the 22,930-foot Dorje Lhagpa mountain in Central Nepal. 'This peak is a very tough nut to crack' he declared.

A few days later, twenty-one-year-old Viscount Feilding announced that he was to start parachute jumping. 'It's all very rather exciting but frightening as well. I don't think I want any spectators at my first jump' he said. 'You can't really stop sons doing what they want to do,' commented his father, the Earl of Denbigh.

On May 25, actor David Niven arrived in England in acute pain after a road accident in Switzerland. 'I swerved to miss an old boy who was pushing a barrow' he explained. 'At the time it didn't seem that any damage had been done but the following day my back just seized up.'

On June 3, the usual crowds flocked to the Derby. Among those present in Lord Derby's box was twenty-three-year-old pop singer Billy Fury who had recently purchased a race horse Anselmo for £8,500. The horse came in fourth and Mr. Fury, in grey topper and tails, received congratulations from the Queen and Queen Mother.

On June 10, the death of eighty-five-year-old Lord Beaverbrook caused widespread grief. Among the hundreds of mourners at the memorial service held later at St. Paul's cathedral were Lady Churchill, Paul Getty, Lord Brownlow, Godfrey Winn and Margaret Duchess of Argyll. Eighty-two-year-old Lord Rosebery began his address with the words, 'We are here to pay tribute to one of the most remarkable men who has lived in our time.'

On June 16, the Queen appeared at Ascot in a white straw hat and white silk dress speckled with navy-blue spots. Five carriages and three Daimlers were required to transport her guests down the course, among whom was the twenty-seven-year-old Aga Khan.

On June 22, Mrs. Dorothy Cavis-Brown fell asleep while umpiring a match on number three court at Wimbledon. 'I have had a very exhausting time just lately' she said after being woken up by a ball-boy.

On June 29, financier Kenneth de Courcy, who had recently been sentenced to seven years imprisonment for fraud, broke away from two prison officers at his solicitor's office, where he had been taken to discuss his appeal, and disappeared among the alley-ways of Lincoln's Inn. Two days later, he was recaptured at Fareham in Hampshire. 'I decided to escape on the spur of the moment. It was not premeditated' he said.

On July 6, Princess Margaret attended the charity première of the Beatles' film *A Hard Day's Night* at the London Pavilion. Among those selling programmes at the cinema was the Princess's goddaughter, sixteen-year-old Marilyn Wills. At the private party afterwards at the Dorchester Hotel, Princess Margaret told George Harrison's mother 'It was a lovely film. You have a talented son.'

On July 9, the engagement of the young Marquess of Dufferin and Ava and Miss Lindy Guinness, daughter of banker Loel Guinness, was toasted with champagne at the Marquess's modern art gallery in Mayfair.

'When I told my family about the engagement, they shrieked with surprise' said Lindy.

The same day, Deputy Labour Leader George Brown's new fawn Jaguar was involved in a collision with a bus at the junction of Knightsbridge and Sloane Street.

On July 15, twenty-three-year-old Winston Churchill married Miss Minnie d'Erlanger. After the ceremony at Kensington Registry Office, the couple posed for photographers with the bridegroom's grandfather Sir Winston Churchill in his garden at 28 Hyde Park Gate. A reception was held later at the Hyde Park Hotel at which the bridegroom cut the wedding-cake with the ancient Sword of Ramillies, carried in battle by the first Duke of Marlborough.

On July 17, the headlines blazed the news that John Bloom's company Rolls Razor Limited, had gone into voluntary liquidation. The thirty-three-year-old tycoon was informed of his fellow directors' decision while cruising in the Black Sea. He issued a statement saying, 'I am extremely depressed at the news I am receiving from London. I am returning to try to sort matters out.' Back in England two days later, he plunged into desperate discussions with his advisers at his flat in Aldford House, Park Lane. A spokesman emerged to say, 'Mr. Bloom is inside with a number of gentlemen. I cannot disturb him.'

On July 27, Sir Winston Churchill paid a farewell visit to the House of Commons of which he had first become a member in February 1901. He was supported to his seat by Conservative MPs Captain Lawrence Orr and Sir Rolf Dudley-Williams. He left after forty-five minutes.

On August 20, sixty-two-year-old Tallulah Bankhead, the toast of London during the 1920s, arrived in England to play the part of a woman with homicidal tendencies in a film called *Fanatic*. Later in the day, Tallulah slipped and fell down the steps of the Ritz Hotel.

On August 26, a near distaster befell Princess Margaret, currently on holiday with Lord Snowdon at the Aga Khan's new holiday development in Sardinia. While cruising to the island of Sofia, her host's yacht *Amaloun* hit a rock and showed signs of sinking. The Princess and her companions jumped into the sea where they lingered until they were picked up by fishing boats,

On September 5, John Bloom, whose collapsed Rolls Razor Company had now become the subject of a Board of Trade enquiry, flew off with his wife for a short holiday in America. 'John suddenly decided he needed a rest' said a colleague. 'I don't think he will be doing any business over there.' It was noted that Mr. Bloom had shaved off his famous beard.

The following day it was revealed that Dame Margot Fonteyn was taking driving lessons on a housing estate in North London. 'I have always wanted to learn to drive but I have never had the time' she said. 'She is a wonderful pupil' said her instructor.

On September 14, the Prime Minister Sir Alec Douglas-Home flew to Balmoral to tell the Queen the General Election date. He travelled in a scarlet and black Heron of the Queen's Flight and was sustained with smoked-salmon sandwiches and coffee during the flight.

On September 17, headlines blazed the news that fifteen-year-old Prince Charles and his cousin, seventeen-year-old Crown Prince Carl Gustaf of Sweden, had upset a paddle boat containing three cameramen at the exclusive Asteria Beach Club near Athens, where they were staying for the wedding of the young King of Greece.

On September 28, it was announced that fifty-seven-year-old Viscount Astor had cut short his holiday in Northern Italy and returned to Cliveden following a mild heart attack. 'It was of the mildest possible kind' he said, 'but I have got to keep very, very quiet.'

The country had meanwhile plunged into the throes of the General Election. Among those playing an active part in the campaign was eighty-one-year-old Earl Attlee, who had recently moved from his Buckinghamshire home to a flat in the Temple. 'I'm not so much in touch with things as I once was' he said on October 7, 'but I am doing what I can to ensure a Labour victory.'

On October 9, attention was diverted away from the Election to the marriage of wealthy twenty-three-year-old Lord Eliot, heir to the Earl of St. Germans, and Miss Jacquetta Lampson, daughter of the late Lord Killearn. At the ceremony at St. Margaret's Westminster, Lord Eliot was eccentrically dressed in grey

Edwardian frock-coat and blue cravat but it was noticed that he had shaved off his beard. A reception was held afterwards at the House of Lords, which was attended by eighty-one-year-old Princess Alice Countess of Athlone.

On October 15, seventy-two-year-old Lady Diana Cooper was fined £17 at Maidenhead for overtaking a queue of cars on the near-side in her Austin Mini. Lady Diana expressed her surprise in court that the off-duty constable who had reported the incident 'could be such a sneak'.

The same day, the country went to the polls and voted the Labour Party to power with a slim majority. A foretaste of Socialist social life was provided by a party given that night by Mr. Cecil King in his opulent ninth-floor suite at the *Daily Mirror* building. Jaguars, Bentleys and Rolls-Royces brought guests to the party, who included Lord Robens, chairman of the Coal Board, Sir Billy Butlin and Lord Cobbold, ex-Governor of the Bank of England. As news of the Labour victories filtered in, red and blue rockets were let off from the roof of the building.

THE LATE SIXTIES
1964–1969

With the fall of the Conservative Government, a revolutionary new era was ushered in with wide-reaching social repercussions. The deb season became unimportant, the classless classes emerged and the Selective Employment Tax and other Socialist legislation made life increasingly difficult for the Old Guard, an increasing number of whom went into exile for tax purposes. The success of the Beatles and the Rolling Stones coincided with the arrival of a youth-oriented culture and a new pop aristocracy of actors, artists, singers, fashion photographers, interior decorators and men's outfitters from a wide mixture of social backgrounds. The rigid standards of the past were relaxed. Kenneth Tynan said 'fuck' on television, homosexuality between consenting adults was legalised and vast quantities of mind-bending drugs were consumed. In this new environment, media people seemed to be the leading lights and David Frost confirmed this impression when on January 7, 1966, the Prime Minister Harold Wilson, the Earl of Longford and Dr. John Robinson, Bishop of Woolwich paid court to him at a breakfast at the Connaught Hotel. It was not long before socially-active aristocrats such as the Earl of Lichfield shed their titles and joined in the swim. In apparent contrast to these goings-on, was the resolution of the young Lord Strathnaver, great nephew of the late Duke of Sutherland, to become a policeman. The anachronistic activities of the young Earl of Lucan and his friends at the Clermont Club also struck a different note. However, by the end of the decade, the new pop aristocracy had also shown a measure of respect for old-fashioned British values by acquiring stately homes, Rolls-Royces and even flats in Mayfair's Albany.

1964

On October 16, forty-eight-year-old Harold Wilson took his wife Mary, sister Marjorie and sons Robin and Giles to Buckingham Palace, where he accepted the Prime Ministership from the Queen. He then moved triumphantly into 10 Downing Street, while Sir Alec and Lady Douglas-Home left quietly by the back door. It was announced that the Wilsons would continue to sleep at their semi-detached home in Hampstead Garden Suburb for the next week or two.

On October 21, the Labour victory was partly forgotten at the Westminster Abbey wedding of the young Marquess of Dufferin and Ava and twenty-two-year-old Lindy Guinness at which the bride wore the Dufferin and Ava shamrock tiara and a dress of white silk gaberdine made by John Cavanagh. Among the 1,800 guests were Princess Margaret and Lord Snowdon, the new Lady Dartmouth, formerly Lady Lewisham, Paul Getty, David Hicks, the Duke and Duchess of Bedford and a number of unnamed 'beatniks'. A reception took place at the Café Royal where closed-circuit TV had been set up to enable guests to watch the cake-cutting ceremony.

The Queen's first concession to the new Socialist regime came on October 29 when it was announced that she would be giving up the use of the eight-coach Royal Train, including a special children's coach built in 1955 for the use of Prince Charles and Princess Anne. It was announced that in future the Queen would travel in four special coaches which would be tacked onto an ordinary train.

Meanwhile, a row had blown up over the theft of an exercise book belonging to fifteen-year-old Prince Charles from his classroom at Gordonstoun and said to contain essays on democracy, the monarchy and publicity. On November 4, it was announced that the book, olive green in colour, had been retrieved, though not before copies had been made and offered to Continental publishers.

240

On November 12, the Wilson family moved into 10 Downing Street together with their Siamese cat Nemo, who was said to be the first cat at the house since Sir Winston Churchill left in 1955. 'I only hope he settles in at Downing Street' remarked Mrs. Wilson. Among the Wilsons' other possessions were a harmonium, a portable TV and a twin-tub washing-machine.

The following day, seventeen empty crates of champagne were taken away from the house by the Downing Street dustmen. 'The bottles probably came from the champagne buffet the Prime Minister gave for the Olympic contestants last Saturday' said a spokesman. A dustbin man was seen gulping the last drops from one bottle.

The Queen leaves the House of Lords after the State Opening of Parliament. The Duke of Norfolk follows at a discreet distance

On November 20, it leaked out that forty-six-year-old property millionaire Max Rayne had contributed £250,000 towards the purchase of Cézanne's *Les Grandes Baigneuses* for the nation. 'There's no denying its importance as a painting or the wonderful opportunity of getting it for Britain' said Mr. Rayne, who already had a fine collection of paintings of his own.

On November 26, twenty-one-year-old Mick Jagger, lead singer with the Rolling Stones pop group, was fined £10 at Tettenhall, Staffordshire for driving without insurance. Jagger's solicitor explained to the court that the Rolling Stones were 'not long-haired idiots, but highly intelligent university men'.

At the end of the month, Sir Winston Churchill celebrated his ninetieth birthday at his house in Hyde Park Gate. The Pope sent a message of congratulations and the Queen sent a bunch of lilies. After visiting his famous patient, Lord Moran, himself eighty-one years old, said, 'I have found him very well, in good spirits and tremendously looking forward to his party.' That evening, Randolph Churchill, Winston Churchill, Jr., Sarah Lady Audley, Mr. and Mrs. Christopher Soames and other relations were cheered as they arrived for a family dinner-party and Sir Winston waved from a window to the waiting crowds.

In the meantime, Margaret Duchess of Argyll had taken legal action to prevent her ex-husband publishing the secrets of their married life in the *People*. On December 4, Mr. Justice Ungoed-Thomas granted an injunction to the fifty-year-old Duchess, describing the contents of the articles as 'wholly objectionable'. As a result of this publicity, the sixty-one-year-old Duke was asked to resign from White's Club, where he had been a familiar figure since the early Fifties.

On December 10, it was announced that the seventy-year-old Duke of Windsor was to enter the Methodist Hospital at Houston in Texas for an operation to correct a ballooning artery. The Duchess moved in with him, occupying an adjoining room. 'I have been overwhelmed with phone calls from around the world' said the Duke. 'I want to say how much I appreciate the sentiment of all these people.' Said the director of the hospital's cardiographic unit, 'The Duke is in superb general health.' While he was in hospital, the Duke received flowers from both the Queen and Princess Margaret.

On December 21, it was noted that Mr. Brian Epstein, manager of the Beatles, had acquired a five-storey house in Chapel Street, Belgravia. 'It looks rather small from the front' he said, 'but it sticks a long way out at the back like 10 Downing Street.'

Shortly after Christmas, a hundred teenage friends of Prince Charles and Princess Anne attended a party in the Crimson Room at Windsor Castle where dancing took place to music from Prince Charles's tape-recorder. During the course of the evening, the Queen and Prince Philip looked in on the festivities.

On December 30, the première of *The Yellow Rolls-Royce* at the Empire Cinema Leicester Square was attended by Paul Getty and his legal adviser Miss Robina Lund, the new Socialist Foreign Secretary Patrick Gordon Walker and Shadow Cabinet Ministers Edward Heath and Duncan Sandys. Mr. Heath was accompanied by an old friend, Mrs. June Osborne. 'I think we met at Lady Birley's when he was Chief Whip' she said later. 'I really think he ought to go out with the ladies more.'

1965

The Prime Minister Harold Wilson saw in the New Year with a gathering of neighbours on the Scilly Isles where he owned a holiday bungalow named Lowenva. It was noted that the Wilsons' Siamese cat, Nemo, had been transported from 10 Downing Street to spend the festive season with its family.

On January 7, well-known East End boxing twins Ronald and Reginald Kray were arrested and charged with demanding money with menaces from wealthy baronet's son, Hew McGowan, owner of a newly-opened Soho nightclub called 'The Hideaway'. Although the thirty-one-year-old twins were able to offer sureties of £18,000, bail was refused.

On January 15, it was announced that Sir Winston Churchill had had a stroke and was fighting for his life at 28 Hyde Park Gate. His doctor Lord Moran issued a statement that the former Prime Minister was 'slipping into deeper sleep and is not conscious of pain or discomfort'. Among the visitors at his bedside was the Prime Minister Harold Wilson. Film and television crews began a day and night vigil in the quiet cul-de-sac.

On January 19, Princess Margaret and Lord Snowdon dined with Cecil Beaton at 8 Pelham Place to meet Rex Harrison and Audrey Hepburn, co-stars of the film version of *My Fair Lady*, for which Beaton had designed the sets and costumes.

The following day, details were disclosed of the divorce settlement between Baron von Thyssen and his beautiful English wife, Fiona. It was reported that Baroness von Thyssen would receive something between a quarter and half a million pounds, according to whether she remarried, and was to keep all the jewellery her husband had given her.

On January 24, the death of Sir Winston Churchill caused intense international grief. The State Funeral six days later at St. Paul's Cathedral was attended by President de Gaulle, ex-President Eisenhower and many other Heads of State. Also there was Sir Winston's great friend of the past few years, Aristotle Onassis, who stayed at Claridge's where a suite was permanently reserved for him. A notable absentee was seventy-seven-year-old Viscount Montgomery, who was on a cruise to South Africa after an operation. 'It is no good going to the funeral of an old friend and ending up dead yourself' he announced.

Following the funeral, a curious accident befell the Duke and Duchess of Gloucester. On their way back to their Northampton home, their Rolls-Royce, with the Duke at the wheel, the Duchess beside him and his chauffeur and valet in the back, suddenly left the road, crossed a footpath, jumped a four-foot ditch, crashed through a thorn hedge and somersaulted into a field. The Duchess was later treated for a broken arm in Bedford Hospital but reported to be 'in excellent spirits'.

On Feburary 2, the Duke of Norfolk, who had been in charge of Sir Winston Churchill's funeral service, flew off with his wife for a holiday in Cannes. The Duke wore a loud check overcoat and smiled benignly at reporters at London Airport.

On February 10, junior Socialist Minister, Lord Snow, explained in the House of Lords why he had sent his son to Eton. 'It's perfectly simple' he said. 'It seems to me that if one is living in a fairly prosperous home, it is a mistake to educate one's child differently to those one knows socially.'

The following day, also in the House of Lords, Lord Boothby asked if the government intended to keep the Kray twins in custody for an indefinite period. 'I might say that I hold no brief for the Kray brothers' he added. In the uproar that followed his question, Boothby shouted 'We might as well pack up.'

The same day, much publicity attended the marriage of Beatle Ringo Starr and hairdresser Maureen Cox at Caxton Hall. The couple left afterwards for a house in Brighton, which had been loaned to them by show-business solicitor David Jacobs. 'You will appreciate' said the butler at the house, Mr. Minton, 'that they are on their honeymoon and do not want to be disturbed.'

On February 23, the remains of Sir Roger Casement, who had been hung for treason in 1916, were exhumed from Pentonville Prison and returned to Ireland where he was given a belated State Funeral. 'It is a commonsense solution with which I hope the House will agree' said Prime Minister Harold Wilson in the House of Commons.

On March 8, millionaire Nubar Gulbenkian appeared with his famous eyebrows and moustache brushed downwards, rather than up. 'This is all part of the sacrifices I make for Lent every year' he explained. 'I also give up my cigars – oh how I miss them – and suck chewing-gum instead.'

On March 9, female impersonator Danny La Rue celebrated the first anniversary of the opening of his club, located off Bond Street and numbering Princess Margaret and Lord Snowdon and other fashionable figures among his patrons.

On March 15, an historic meeting took place between the Queen and the Duchess of Windsor at the London Clinic, where the Duke of Windsor had been undergoing a series of eye operations. This was the first time that the Queen and the Duchess had met since an encounter in 1936 at the Royal Lodge at Windsor when the Queen was ten years old. 'It was a very pleasant visit indeed' said a spokesman. 'The Queen, the Duke and the Duchess spent the time talking in their sitting-room.'

The following day, it was announced that a racecourse commentary service, known in bookmaking circles as 'the Blower', had been installed at Clarence House for the benefit of the sixty-four-year-old Queen Mother. 'She cannot always get to the races' said a spokesman, 'and she does like to follow her horses' progress.'

On March 28, the sixty-seven-year-old Princess Royal died suddenly at Harewood House. This much loved member of the Royal Family had been seen a few days earlier touring the Ideal Home Exhibition and had also visited the Duke and Duchess of Windsor at the London Clinic.

On April 5, famous boxing twins Ronnie and Reginald Kray were acquitted at the Old Bailey on charges of demanding money with menaces from Soho clubowner Hew McGowan. 'Definitely it's the quiet life for us now' said Ronnie as the twins made their way through crowds of reporters and photographers to a bronze-coloured Jaguar which carried them off to celebrate their acquittal at their parents' humble home in the heart of the East End.

A fortnight later, Reginald Kray married twenty-one-year-old Frances Shea at St. James's Church, Bethnal Green. It was described as 'the East End wedding of the year' and was attended by famous boxers Kid Lewis and Terry Spinks, among others. Photographs were taken by fashion photographer David Bailey, who wore a blue velvet suit and arrived in a blue Rolls-Royce. After the ceremony, the bride and groom were transported in a maroon-coloured Rolls to the reception at a hotel in Finsbury Park.

On April 28, Alan Clore, undergraduate son of property tycoon Charles Clore, celebrated his twenty-first birthday with a party for forty friends at Annabel's, the fashionable new nightclub started by Mark Birley two years earlier. 'When my son passes his exams – that is when he will get his present' said Clore senior.

On May 3, *A King's Story*, film version of the Duke of Windsor's autobiography, had its première in London. Among those present were Lady Churchill, who had recently been made a life peeress, and Lady Alexandra Metcalfe, whose late husband 'Fruity' Metcalfe had acted as best man at the Duke of Windsor's wedding in 1937.

On May 5, it was announced that former Army officer twenty-six-year-old Lord Lichfield, godson of the Queen Mother, had taken up photography. One of his first commissions was a portrait of the grandchildren of the Duke of Marlborough photographed in the room at Blenheim Palace where Sir Winston Churchill was born. It was noted that the young Lord had recently purchased a green Aston Martin.

A few days later, rumours circulated that property-developer Harry Hyams, currently involved in a skyscraper development at St. Giles's Circus, had purchased Ramsbury Manor in Wiltshire. Mr. Hyams refused to comment on the story saying that he abhorred personal publicity. 'The image of the property man is of a land speculator and a shark' he said. 'While this nasty image is perpetuated, I do not wish it to spill over into my private life.'

On May 31, three-year-old Viscount Linley, sixth in succession to the throne, entered Great Ormond Street Hospital for Children for an ear operation to be performed by plastic surgeon Mr. David Napier Matthews.

That night, young Viscount Gormanston and interior decorator David Mlinaric were refused admission to Annabel's because they were wearing pale-coloured suits. 'All we stipulate is that a dark suit and ties are

Publicity shy property developer Harry Hyams, third from left, at the Annual General Meeting of Wimpey's

worn' said a spokesman for the club.

On June 10, financier Clarence Hatry, whose companies had crashed in dramatic circumstances in 1929 but who had later made a comeback, died in Westminster Hospital at the ripe old age of seventy-six.

On June 11, the award of the MBE to the Beatles caused a storm of protest. One of the first to voice his anger by handing his own MBE back was ex-Squadron Leader Paul Pearson, who had been decorated for his part in sea-rescue operations in the Channel during the war. 'I know the war is old hat and I've got nothing against the Beatles, but . . . they have been amply rewarded already. All they do is exploit a basic jungle rhythm for money.' The storm gathered momentum over the next few days, causing Beatle Ringo Starr to remark, 'The whole matter is becoming a drag.'

On June 15, much attention was focused on a three and a half foot wide black-and-white tulle hat worn at Ascot by a certain Mrs. Gertrude Shilling, wife of a clothing manufacturer.

On June 21, a special train was laid on to carry guests to a twenty-first birthday celebration at Chatsworth for the Marquess of Hartington, heir to the Duke of Devonshire. Among those who made use of this facility were Princess Margaret and Lord Snowdon, Lord Charles Spencer-Churchill, younger son of the Duke of Marlborough, and his American fiancée, Gillian Fuller.

At the end of the month, attention turned to Bagnor Manor in Berkshire where Princess Margaret's old friend Billy Wallace had begun breeding ornamental pheasants. 'They have been a bit depressed by the weather' he remarked, 'so their plumage isn't as good as it was.'

On July 14, the news broke that Lady Jane Vane-Tempest-Stewart, a Maid of Honour at the Coronation and a leader of the Chelsea Set, had been secretly married to millionaire property magnate Max Rayne. Lady

Jane revealed that she had changed her religion three or four months earlier.

The same day, American statesman Adlai Stevenson collapsed in Upper Grosvenor Street within a few yards of the newly built glass-and-concrete American Embassy. His companion, the beautiful Mrs. Ronnie Tree, attempted to give the statesman the kiss of life but he died before reaching St. George's Hospital.

On July 22, three of the Rolling Stones were fined £5 each after being found guilty of insulting behaviour at a Stratford East London filling station after a pop concert. It was alleged that the pop stars, Mick Jagger, Bill Wyman and Brian Jones had urinated against the boundary wall of the filling station 'without taking steps to conceal this act'.

Later that day, Lord Harlech, father of Julian, Jane and Victoria Ormsby-Gore, gave a sensational party at his mother's house in Notting Hill Gate. Guests included Princess Margaret and Princess Alexandra and noisy music went on till five in the morning drawing angry complaints from neighbours.

At the end of July, Sir Alec Douglas-Home was replaced as Leader of the Opposition by forty-nine-year-old bachelor and former grammar-school boy Edward Heath, who subsequently posed for photographs over a cup of tea in his flat in Mayfair's Albany.

Prime Minister Harold Wilson at a press conference in the Scilly Isles

On August 10, the Prime Minister Harold Wilson was found lounging in the sand-dunes of the Scilly Isles dressed in sandals and short trousers with his suntan peeling from his face. 'I could be back in London very quickly' he assured reporters. 'I only hope to have time to change my shirt and pants.'

On August 18, East End-born fashion photographer David Bailey married actress Catherine Deneuve whom he had met for the first time two months earlier photographing her for *Playboy* magazine. At the ceremony at St. Pancras Registry Office, the bridegroom wore green corduroys, pale-blue woolly sweater and Cuban-heeled boots. The best man, Mick Jagger, was in an open-necked blue shirt, denim suit and white shoes and was accompanied by his new girlfriend, Chrissie Shrimpton.

Another unconventional wedding took place on September 2 when twenty-two-year-old Viscount Feilding, known to his friends as Rollo, was married to Miss Judy Cooke. At the ceremony at St. Paul's, Knightsbridge, the bridegroom's cousin, artist William Feilding, wore dinner-jacket trousers with his tail coat. Emerging from the church, the bridegroom lit a cigarette, and after the reception, the couple drove off in a red Chevrolet Stingray.

Five days later, Lord Snowdon was found in the Scottish village of Ballater near Balmoral wearing knee-length tweed knickerbockers, long leather boots and a brown velvet anorak.

On September 15, thirty-seven-year-old Billy Wallace announced his engagement to Miss Elizabeth Hoyer Millar, daughter of Lord Inchyra, whom he had known for some sixteen years. 'It was a tremendous surprise' said Elizabeth's sister Annabel. 'We never dreamed there was anything romantic between them. I thought he was determined to carry on enjoying his bachelordom.'

Later that day, a new nightclub called 'The In Place' opened, backed by Mrs. John Bloom, whose husband's famous washing-machine empire had crashed the previous year. The opening party was attended by newly-emerged celebrities such as David Frost, Lionel Bart and Frank Norman, author of the popular musical of five years earlier *Fings Ain't What They Used To Be*.

Meanwhile, old established nightclub owners were complaining about the restrictions on expense account entertaining proposed by Chancellor of the Exchequer Jim Callaghan. 'Mr. Callaghan's decision to tax entertaining is a death knell to the whole entertaining business' said Mr. Bertie Green, owner of the Astor Club in Berkeley Square.

On October 1, the coming-out of Lady Charlotte Manners, daughter of the Duke of Rutland by his first marriage, was celebrated with a ball at Belvoir Castle. Among the 600 guests, who danced to the music of the Nottingham Beat Group, was the sixty-eight-year-old Duke of Marlborough, who was staying nearby with Earl Fitzwilliam at Milton Hall.

On October 4, the Duke of Beaufort disclosed that the proposed M4 motorway would cut through his estates, ruining some of the best hunting country in the world. 'The M4 and other motorways are the greatest nightmare to Masters of Foxhounds' declared the sixty-five-year-old Duke.

The same day, Rhodesian Prime Minister Ian Smith arrived on board a VC 10 airliner for eleventh hour talks with Mr. Wilson.

On October 10, after talks between the two Prime Ministers had broken down, great excitement was stirred up when the plucky Rhodesian leader drove to Hatfield House, the Rhodesian flag fluttering from the bonnet of his car, to lunch with veteran Tory statesman, the Marquess of Salisbury, who had declared himself unable to support Mr. Heath's 'We support the Government' line.

Five days later, the seventy-two-year-old Marquess made a dramatic speech at the Conservative Party Conference in which he asked delegates to oppose all ideas of sanctions, economic or military, in the event of a declaration of independence by the Rhodesian government. The speech was described in certain quarters as 'the last stand of the House of Cecil.'

On October 17, Lady Churchill, now eighty years old, was knocked down by a football in Hyde Park and was treated for a broken arm and injured ribs. 'It's not too serious and I don't expect to make many calls' said Royal surgeon Sir Herbert Seddon after visiting his patient at her new home in Princes Gate.

On October 19, Billy Wallace and his fiancée Elizabeth Hoyer Millar, threw a pre-wedding party at the

Savoy Hotel. Among the 750 guests were the Dukes of Gloucester, Marlborough, Fife, Devonshire, Rutland and Atholl, Conservative Leader Edward Heath, the Marquess of Salisbury, publisher George Weidenfeld and Cecil Beaton. 'There is no special technique for capturing a confirmed bachelor like Billy' saïd Miss Hoyer Millar. 'It just needs patience.'

The wedding took place two days later at the parish church of St. Peter's, East Lavington in Sussex. Among the congregation was the bridegroom's old friend Princess Margaret, who had lunched beforehand with Mr. Robin Douglas-Home, who had a country home nearby. It was said that this marriage marked the final disintegration of 'the Margaret Set' whose activities had filled the newspapers for many years.

The same day, twenty-three-year-old Christine Keeler was married to a twenty-four-year-old engineer named John Levermore. 'Christine is just like any other girl and they are both very much in love' said her mother. 'That other business was two years ago and since then she has tried to keep out of the spotlight.'

On October 28, Sir Winston Churchill's old home 28 Hyde Park Gate and the house adjoining it, were sold for £102,500 to Dr. Leonard Simpson, chairman of the department store Simpson's of Piccadilly. 'My head is a jumble of colour schemes, alteration plans and furniture' remarked his wife.

On November 13, critic Kenneth Tynan unleashed an uproar when he used the word 'fuck' on television. The fatal word was spoken during a discussion with Robert Robinson on a late-night programme broadcast live. In the furore, Wolverhampton housewife Mrs. Mary Whitehouse announced that she had written to the Queen asking her to ensure that the word should never again be used on the BBC. Postmaster General, Anthony Wedgwood Benn, was also deluged with complaints. 'I heard the programme but it is not my responsibility' he said.

Millionaire financier Charles Clore beckons his chauffeur after a wedding at St. John's Wood synagogue

On November 18, sixty-one-year-old Charles Clore celebrated his acquisition of Selfridges department store at a cocktail-party at the Carlton Tower Hotel. A garland of pink orchids was placed round his neck.

On December 6, thirty-eight-year-old Mark Watney, a popular and well-known West End figure who had once been tipped as a possible best man at the wedding of Princess Margaret, was found shot dead in his Mayfair flat. 'I am staggered by this' said his friend Jocelyn Stevens. 'I saw him only last week at a dinner-party. He looked fine. He was an enormously popular, gay, lively and generous man.'

On December 16, ninety-one-year-old Somerset Maugham died in his four-poster bed at his villa at Cap Ferrat overlooking the Mediterranean. 'I have lost my greatest friend' said Mr. Alan Searle who had looked after the famous old writer for the past thirty-four years.

Meanwhile, a romance had blossomed between thirty-seven-year-old oil heiress Olga Deterding and bachelor television interviewer Alan Whicker. On December 19 the couple sailed off together on board the liner *Andes* for a cruise to the Canary Islands and West Africa. 'I admire her very much and I am very fond of her' said Whicker.

Shortly after Christmas, the Kildare Hunt Ball was enlivened by the presence of Jane Ormsby-Gore, daughter of Lord Harlech, and twenty-three-year-old Sir Mark Palmer, who had acted as a page of honour to the Queen at the Coronation. Miss Ormsby-Gore wore a garment she described as 'an old family nightdress'.

Mr. and Mrs. Harold Wilson danced into the New Year at a gathering at the St. Mary's Golf Club in the Scilly Isles. It was noted that the forty-nine-year-old Prime Minister had recently undergone cosmetic dental treatment.

On January 5, it was revealed that Chelsea playboy Edward Langley, whose amorous adventures had made headline news some years earlier, was working on his memoirs. 'Quite brilliantly written' commented his prospective publisher, Ralph Stokes of Tandem Books. 'And, of course, he does have the background.'

On January 7, television personality David Frost gave a breakfast-party at the Connaught Hotel, which was attended by the Prime Minister, the controversial Bishop of Woolwich, Dr. John Robinson, the Earl of Longford and seventeen other illustrious figures. Kidneys, bacon and eggs, and caviar with sour cream were served, followed by champagne. 'This was a private party' said Frost, 'and I hope a chance for a few friends who don't always meet to gather and chat.'

A few days later, there was a fancy-dress party at Christie's to celebrate its two hundredth anniversary. For the evening, the famous saleroom had been converted into the style of nineteenth-century Deauville by young interior decorator David Mlinaric and was thronged with guests including Billy Wallace, Jane Ormsby-Gore, George Harrison and Mick Jagger. One of the few people present to wear a dinner-jacket was Sir Isaac Wolfson.

On January 27, an exhibition of paintings by Cecil Beaton opened at the Lefevre Gallery, among which was a portrait of Mick Jagger. 'I saw him on television and he inspired me' said Beaton. 'He looks like someone who has sprung out of the woods.' A few days later, Beaton departed for Barbados suffering from exhaustion.

On February 13, it was announced that John Bloom, now being sued for vast sums by his old company Rolls Razor, had sold his 310-yacht *Ariana III* which he had purchased at the height of his success in 1963. The yacht's new owner was Mr. Charles Revson, head of the famous American cosmetics firm.

Former washing machine tycoon John Bloom after the collapse of his company

On February 22, Mr. Michael Tree announced that he was selling Mereworth Castle, his famous Palladian-style home in Kent, which had been the setting for some remarkable parties over the years. 'In a nutshell, I can't really afford to remain at the castle. Costs have risen greatly in the seventeen years since I inherited it. My father had to sell his lovely country house, Ditchley Park, Oxfordshire for the same reason.'

At the end of the month, a three-month-old tiger was found prowling and sauntering around the Clermont Club in Berkeley Square. The animal belonged to the club's owner, thirty-eight-year-old John Aspinall. On February 25, it was stated that the tiger had been taken from the club to its owner's house in Lyall Street, Belgravia. 'Honestly, I hope we have seen the last of him' said a member of the club's staff. 'He could scratch someone's ankle off.'

On March 1, a Bentley belonging to the Hon. Richard Wrottesley, flamboyant twenty-three-year-old heir to Lord Wrottesley, was found upside-down in the snow outside the Palace Hotel, St. Moritz. 'Fortunately no harm was done to the car' said its owner cheerfully.

On March 8, it was announced that Lord Mountbatten had installed a lift at Broadlands, his stately home near Winchester, for the benefit of the elderly members of his domestic staff.

The same day, Lord Astor died suddenly while on holiday at Lyford Cay, Nassau. His title and family trusts and property, valued at £100 million, passed to his fourteen-year-old son, now at Eton. Soon afterwards, it was announced that the Astor family would be moving out of Cliveden, their famous Thames-side home since 1893.

On March 17, Prince Stanislaus Radziwill and his wife gave a party at their house in Buckingham Gate to celebrate the twenty-seventh birthday of Rudolf Nureyev. 'We are very fond of the ballet and he has become a good friend of ours' said Princess Radziwill, sister of Mrs. Jackie Kennedy.

On March 18, Richard Wrottesley gave 'a wake' at Crockford's Club for his broken romance with Miss Nicola Hutton-Potts. 'I didn't think it was a time to start crying into my champagne' he said, as 100 friends tucked into a lobster-and-champagne dinner at the club's premises in Carlton House Terrace.

Meanwhile, the country had plunged into the General Election campaign. Conservative leader Edward Heath was found balancing on a skateboard and photographed in the bedroom of his Albany bachelor flat with his pyjamas neatly laid out on his double bed.

On March 22, the Prime Minister Harold Wilson was hit in the eye by a stink bomb while he was addressing a meeting at Slough. 'It's all right. I shall survive' he said and Mr. Heath announced that he was 'immensely sorry' about the incident.

On March 31, the Labour Party romped home with its majority increased to ninety-seven. Mr. Wilson returned in triumph to 10 Downing Street the following day.

On April 3, it was announced that fifty-one-year-old Group-Captain Peter Townsend, who had been living abroad for the past thirteen years was returning to England with his twenty-five-year-old wife and young family. The Group Captain was to join a public relations company run by his old Fighter Command colleague Colin Hodgkinson. 'Peter has unrivalled knowledge of Europe' he declared. 'He will join my board of directors and be responsible for expanding our business there.'

Two days later, attention turned to Longleat where a 100-acre encampment containing fifty lions and lionesses was being opened to the public. 'Providing motorists heed our warning notices, they are in no danger' said the sixty-one-year-old Marquess of Bath.

On April 10, novelist Evelyn Waugh died suddenly at Combe Florey House near Taunton, where he had lived for the past ten years. A requiem mass was held later at Westminster Cathedral which was attended by, among others, Lady Diana Cooper, still a dazzling beauty at the age of seventy-three.

Later in the month, a story blew up over the publication of Lord Moran's account of his dealings with Sir Winston Churchill, who had died sixteen months earlier. The *Lancet* accused the elderly doctor of breaking the time-honoured bond of confidence between doctor and patient and there was an angry letter in *The Times* from Sir Winston's son Randolph.

On May 3, it was announced that the Duke of Edinburgh had acquired a specially constructed glass-roofed Reliant Scimitar sports car.

That night, many of the young men attending Queen Charlotte's Birthday Ball at the Grosvenor House had shoulder-length hair. 'I dislike the idea that people should make fun of long hair' said one of the youths in question, seventeen-year-old Old Etonian Peter Gore-Booth. 'I like it and will keep it.'

On May 12, East End born fashion photographer Terence Donovan moved into a Mayfair flat next door to the old home of Sir Bernard Docker. 'Mayfair is my favourite part of London' he said. 'A lot of my friends are living here.'

On May 17, it was revealed that the young Lord Lucan was attending a golf school in Lowndes Square, Belgravia. 'Lord Lucan is capable of hitting with enormous power' said the school's proprietor Mr. Leslie King. 'His swing is inclined to get a bit rough but if I had the pick of all the titled people who come to my school, I would select Lord Lucan as the one potential champion.'

On May 25, the Derby was won by Lady Zia Wernher's Charlottown. Seventy-three-year-old Lady Zia was carrying the Derby Cup when she called later at King Edward VII's Hospital for Officers where her daughter, Mrs. Harold Phillips, was recovering from an operation for a slipped disc. 'These are our only celebration plans for the evening' she said.

On June 2, Nubar Gulbenkian celebrated his seventieth birthday with a party at the Hilton Hotel, where guests were served with champagne from Mrs. Gulbenkian's family vineyards at Rheims. 'I've flown in more than a hundred pounds of caviar from Moscow' said the flamboyant host. 'It's the first of this year's crop. But I've had trouble with my Havana cigars. The customs have impounded them. I managed to get one barrel through though.'

On June 7, ex-officer Norman Baillie-Stewart, who had made headline news in 1933 when he had been charged with treason and imprisoned in the Tower of London, died in Dublin aged fifty-seven. It was noted that he had completed his autobiography a few weeks earlier. 'He wrote it because he wanted to clear his name for the sake of his two children' said his publisher Leslie Frewin.

On June 11, it was announced that fashion designer Mary Quant had been awarded the OBE in the Queen's Birthday Honours. 'I can hardly believe it' she said. 'But what's it going to be like curtsying in a mini-skirt?'

Two days later, tycoon Charles Clore gave his traditional pre-Ascot Party, held this year at the Hilton Hotel. Maureen Marchioness of Dufferin and Ava, Margaret Duchess of Argyll and many other glittering figures were found circulating on a revolving dance-floor. It was revealed that at the last moment Mr. Clore decided against having peacocks strutting in gilded cages to amuse his guests.

In the Queen's Ascot house-party at Windsor Castle were Prince Rainier and Princess Grace of Monaco. Princess Grace appeared at the races dressed in a black cocktail dress adorned with pink and white flowers.

On June 22, a new nightclub named Sybilla's, named in honour of beautiful twenty-two-year-old Chicago-born heiress Sybilla Edmondstone, opened in a basement in Swallow Street, with Beatle George Harrison and twenty-five-year-old baronet Sir William Pigott-Brown as backers. The opening party was enriched by the presence of veteran club owner Al Burnett, who had been in the nightclub business for many years and had been an acquaintance of the late Mrs. Meyrick, famous nightclub owner in the Twenties.

On July 3, Margaret Duchess of Argyll was spotted photographing the anti-Vietnam demonstrators outside the American Embassy from a window of her house in Upper Grosvenor Street. Around her neck was a string of huge pearls.

On July 13, long-haired Viscount Weymouth, heir to the Marquess of Bath, announced that he had contracted an 'anti-marriage' with seventeen-year-old Ceylon-born Tania Duckworth, who would now be sharing Lord Weymouth's Kensington home. 'We intend to have children and bring them up in our religion' the Viscount explained. 'This is called Theistic Humanism.'

Three days later, John Osborne and actress Jill Bennett were found together at Miss Bennett's house in Princes Gate Mews. 'They are here together' said Osborne's secretary, 'but obviously nothing can be said about marriage. He is not even divorced.'

On July 19, the bouncy Dominic Elwes was ordered to leave a Spanish Caravel jet at London Airport after a row with the crew. It was revealed that the trouble had begun after Elwes had mislaid a file of papers on the plane and had then refused to fasten his safety-belt.

The following day, Mr. Nubar Gulbenkian flew home from a holiday on the Riviera to find that his distinctive-looking wickerwork covered taxi-cab had been removed by the airport police after lingering too long in a restricted area.

On July 31, Frank Sinatra and his wife Mia Farrow flew in on board a Hawker-Siddeley 125 executive jet. On landing at Northolt, the couple transferred to a Mark 10 Jaguar with smoked-glass windows and radio-telephone, which carried them to a flat in Grosvenor Square.

On August 11, John Lennon apologised in New York for saying that the Beatles were more popular than Jesus Christ. It was said that the remark had particularly upset the inhabitants of the Bible Belt of Memphis, Tennessee. 'It is not my purpose in life to insult people's religion' Lennon explained.

At the end of August, the usual gathering of celebrities at Deauville included the twenty-nine-year-old Aga Khan, still a bachelor, the glamorous Susy Volterra, Charles Clore, buried behind a copy of the *Financial Times*, and the handsome Earl of Lucan. During his holiday, Lord Lucan was spotted at the baccarat tables at the resort's Casino by film director Vittoria de Sica as a possible person to play opposite Shirley Maclaine in a new film. 'He wants me to go for a film test' said the Earl on September 5. 'I reckon the chances of passing it at about 50 to 1.' The test did indeed prove unsuccessful. 'The trouble was that before the cameras, he just froze up' explained a friend of the Earl.

On September 14, the flamboyant Richard Wrottesley was charged with wilfully damaging a cell at Notting Hill Police Station where he had been placed after being found drunk in the neighbourhood earlier in the day. He pleaded guilty to the offence and was fined £3. Back in his Regency-style flat in St. James's Street, he described the lunch-party which had preceded these adventures. 'We had quite a lot of drink. I began by drinking Bloody Marys. Then I consumed about one and a half bottles of some excellent wine, followed by a quantity of port.'

Three days later, the beautiful Mandy Rice-Davies, now twenty-one years old, was married to airline steward Rafael Shaul, whose family was said to own a chain of discotheques in Israel. It was stated that Mandy was preparing to become a Jewess. 'It isn't really a case of changing my religion because I never had one before' she said.

Meanwhile, Princess Margaret's friend Colin Tennant had constructed a dazzling modern mansion in Tite Street, Chelsea, on the site of the former home of Victorian artist, James Whistler. 'I've only just moved into my bedroom' said Lady Anne Tennant on September 21. 'The other house was completely knocked down as we were slowly sliding into the Thames.'

On September 24, Jane Ormsby-Gore, eldest daughter of Lord and Lady Harlech, married Mr. Michael Rainey, owner of a fashionable Chelsea outfitters named 'Hung on You'. The bride had broken the news to her parents only the day before.

On September 27, there was a sensation at Quaglino's when a man entered the famous restaurant carrying a baby and presented it to one of the diners. A blood test later proved conclusively that the unfortunate diner in question could not possibly have been the father of the child.

The following day, it was announced that Sir Bernard Docker was selling a gold cigarette-box, cigar-piercer, silver champagne-bucket and silver cocktail-shaker. Asked if he was giving up smoking and drinking, Sir Bernard replied, 'Certainly not. That would be a great mistake. Mr. Wilson has deprived us of most of our pleasures but not, thank goodness, those two.'

On October 3, twenty-four-year-old Sir Mark Palmer, former Page of Honour to the Queen, was found working in a bookshop in Mount Street wearing high-waisted Victorian trousers and a frogged jacket. 'I'm just filling in for a day or two' he explained.

On October 7, Sarah Lady Audley, actress daughter of the late Sir Winston Churchill, appeared in cabaret at the Ritz Theatre Club at Brighouse in Yorkshire. After singing 'A Nightingale Sang in Berkeley Square', 'I

Love Paris' and other numbers, she finished her act standing on a grand piano.

At the end of the month, it was announced that Mr. and Mrs. Dominic Elwes, whose sensational elopement eight years earlier had enthralled the public, had parted company. 'There is no chance of a reconciliation' said Tessa, now working with interior decorator David Mlinaric.

At the beginning of November, it was stated that Princess Margaret and Lord Snowdon's long search for a country home had ended and a cottage on Lord Snowdon's mother's estate at Nymans in Sussex was now being converted and modernised for their use.

On November 19, the Duke and Duchess of Windsor were found staying at Schloss Enzesfeld near Vienna, where the Duke had spent the first few months after his Abdication thirty years earlier. The Duke was in a three-piece check suit and the Duchess was in plaid stockings.

On November 24, the marriage took place at St. Margaret's, Westminster between Miss Bunty Lampson, daughter of the late Lord Killearn, and Chelsea outfitter Ian Ross. The bride wore an old Victorian wedding-dress and the bridegroom was in a striped frock-coat with velvet collar and cuffs designed by Tara Browne, youngest son of Lord Oranmore and Browne. The reception afterwards was attended by Princess Alice of Athlone, formally attired.

On December 1, the Prime Minister Harold Wilson was in his familiar Gannex macintosh when he stepped on board the warship *Tiger* at Gibraltar for a three-day conference with the rebel Rhodesian leader, Ian Smith. Accompanying the Prime Minister during these abortive talks was the toothy Mrs. Marcia Williams, who had worked as his personal political secretary since 1957.

While these talks were carrying on, the ever newsworthy multi-millionairess Barbara Hutton, now fifty-four years old, was carried onto a plane at Tangiers bound for Mexico City, surrounded by rumours that her

Multi-millionairess Barbara Hutton during a tour of Europe with her seventh husband, Prince Doan Vinh de Champacack

seventh marriage was about to be dissolved. 'I don't know if I'll come back' she said. 'I'm very ill, you know.'

On December 18, tragedy struck the newly emerged 'Swinging London' when twenty-one-year-old Tara Browne died at the wheel of his light-blue Lotus Elan when it hit a parked car in Redcliffe Gardens, Chelsea. It was noted that Tara had been living for the past few weeks at the Ritz Hotel.

The following day, a bill to legalise homosexual acts between consenting adults in private passed through the House of Commons on its second reading, in spite of bitter protests by Captain Walter Elliot and other MPs. 'It will not cleanse the national bloodstream' said fifty-six-year-old Captain Elliot, Tory MP for Carshalton. 'It will corrupt and poison it.'

On December 28, eighteen-year-old Prince Charles gave a dance-party in the Waterloo Chamber at Windsor Castle, which was described as his 'first grown-up party'. Among the guests was the Prince's life-long friend, nineteen-year-old Marilyn Wills who had recently been dismissed from her job as a cook with Searcys due to pressure of the newly-introduced Selective Employment Tax. 'I am looking for another job as a cook' she said. 'I love it. It means cooking for all types of receptions.'

The New Year was greeted by Margaret Duchess of Argyll, her son Brian Sweeny and her former husband Charles Sweeny at a party at Annabel's in Berkeley Square. Prohibited from entering the club that night was Beatle George Harrison because he was not wearing a tie. 'We went round to Lyons Corner House and celebrated the New Year there' said his manager Brian Epstein the following day.

On January 3, headlines blazed the news that the Earl of Harewood, first cousin of the Queen, was being sued for divorce on the grounds of his adultery with Miss Patricia Tuckwell, by whom he had already had a child and with whom he had been living in a house in Hamilton Terrace, St. John's Wood. After the initial impact of the announcement, interest quickly faded, which was interpreted as a sign of a more liberal attitude towards divorce on the part of the Press and public.

On January 18, thirty-seven-year-old bachelor Old Etonian Jeremy Thorpe was elected leader of the twelve-strong Liberal Party, following the resignation of the handsome Jo Grimond the previous day.

On January 24, Princess Margaret and the Earl of Snowdon lunched with their bankers, Coutts, in the Strand. It was noted that the couple arrived and left separately, the Princess in a Rolls-Royce and her husband in a black mini-car. A few days later, when the Princess entered Edward VII's Hospital for Officers for a check-up, Lord Snowdon was said to be abroad. 'We don't know exactly, but we think somewhere far afield, probably Japan' said a spokesman.

On February 6, the unsmiling Soviet Premier Alexei Kosygin arrived in London and was driven to Claridge's where an entire floor had been taken over for his use. That night, he dined with Mr. Wilson at 10 Downing Street, off turtle soup, fillet of sole, saddle of Welsh lamb, with celery and potatoes, and lemon soufflé. During the visit, it was revealed that the Imperial Russian banqueting service was to be sold at Christie's. The 1,742-piece service had been shipped from Russia in forty-six cases.

On February 12, Mrs. Neville Chamberlain, widow of the former Prime Minister, died aged eighty-four at her home, 8 Chester Square. A memorial service was held later at Westminster Abbey attended by, among others, Conservative leader fifty-one-year-old Edward Heath.

The same day, police raided a party at the home of Rolling Stones guitarist Keith Richard at West Wittering in Sussex and took away substances for analysis at Scotland Yard.

On February 23, Mick Jagger and his new girlfriend, singer Marianne Faithfull, turned up to see a new ballet at Covent Garden five minutes after the arrival of Princess Margaret. It was noted that Jagger wore a black sombrero and embroidered jacket and no tie and Miss Faithfull was in floral pantaloons.

On February 27, thirty-six-year-old Lord Snowdon flew into New York from Tokyo and gave a Press conference denying rumours that his marriage was on the rocks. 'How do these things get started?' he said. 'Nothing has happened to our marriage. When I'm away, and I'm away quite a lot for my paper, I write home and I telephone like other husbands in love with their wives.'

On March 10, there were smiles all round when the couple were reunited at Kennedy Airport and flew off together for a holiday at the Nassau home of Mr. and Mrs. Jocelyn Stevens, where one of the other guests was Lord Snowdon's fellow photographer, the twenty-seven-year-old Earl of Lichfield, who preferred to be known professionally as Patrick Lichfield.

On March 25, a new era began at the National Portrait Gallery with the appointment of nattily dressed thirty-one-year-old Dr. Roy Strong as Director. He soon staged the first photographic exhibition ever held there.

On April 2, it was announced that Sir Bernard and Lady Docker were to move to Jersey, where they had purchased a four-bedroom house near St. Helier. 'There are lots of reasons for the move' seventy-year-old Sir Bernard explained. 'Income tax is only four shillings in the pound and there are no death duties. We shall of course have our yacht *Shemara* down there. Jersey will be a very good base from which to go cruising.'

On April 9, the twenty-first birthday of Charles Clore's daughter, Vivien, was celebrated with a party at the top of the Hilton Hotel. Mr. Clore, in midnight-blue dinner-suit, received guests who included Sir Isaac and Lady Wolfson, Max Rayne and his wife, the former Lady Jane Vane-Tempest-Stewart, and the eligible Lord Irwin, heir to the Earl of Halifax.

Five days later, Mr. Clore and his daughter were present at a party at Claridge's following the première of the James Bond film *Casino Royale*. Among others present on this occasion were the white-haired Earl Beatty, Lord Butler, Dominic Elliot and Princess Alexandra and Angus Ogilvy. Festivities went on till 4.30 in the morning.

On April 29, Cecil Beaton placed an order for three suits with the Pierre Cardin shop in London, two to be of corduroy, one of mohair.

On May 6, it was announced that sixty-seven-year-old Lord Glenconner had resigned most of his directorships and passed on his 7,000-acre Peeblesshire estate to his son, Colin Tennant. Lord Glenconner had built a new tax-free home for himself on the island of Corfu.

On May 10, Mick Jagger and Keith Richard appeared in court at Chichester charged with offences under the Dangerous Drugs Act following the raid on a party at Richard's Sussex home earlier in the year. Jagger was charged with illegally possessing four amphetomine tablets and Richard with allowing his house to be used for the smoking of Indian hemp and both were sent for trial at West Sussex Quarter Sessions.

The same day, Rolling Stone Brian Jones was arrested at his flat in Courtfield Road, South Kensington, and charged with possessing fifty grains of cannabis. After being released on £250 bail, the pop star was driven away from the court in a new silver-grey Rolls-Royce.

On May 24, the Duke of Bedford celebrated his fiftieth birthday with a party at his London home near Regent's Park, which was attended by television personality David Frost, the controversial new model Twiggy, composer Lionel Bart and multi-millionaires Paul Getty and Charles Clore.

May 25 saw the unveiling of John Lennon's re-painted Phantom V Rolls-Royce. At the cost of £1,000, the huge car had been covered with scrolls, flowers and other psychedelic decorations. 'Of course we have no power to prevent this' said a Rolls-Royce spokesman. 'Mr. Lennon can do what he wishes with his car – but this is most unfortunate.'

On May 30, Lady Harlech, mother of the trendsetting Ormsby-Gore children, died in a car-crash in North Wales. Family friends Mrs. Jackie Kennedy and her brother-in-law Senator Robert Kennedy flew to England for the funeral service.

On June 5, the Duke and Duchess of Windsor were met at Southampton by Lord Mountbatten and driven to his country house, Broadlands. Two days later, the Duchess of Windsor was at last formally recognised by the Royal Family when she appeared with them at the unveiling of a plaque to Queen Mary outside Marlborough House. Under the gaze of Press reporters and television cameras, the Queen and the Duchess were seen smiling and chatting together. After the ceremony, which was also attended by the newly-divorced Earl of Harewood, the Queen left for the Derby and the Windsors went off to lunch with the Duke and Duchess of Gloucester at St. James's Palace, where the former Prince of Wales was greeted by his old valet, Mr. Amos.

On June 12, Lady Illingworth gave a house-cooling party at her forty-two-room mansion in Grosvenor Square where she had lived since her marriage in 1931 and which had recently been acquired by Mr. Maxwell Joseph, who was to build a hotel on the site. Dispensing champagne at the party was Lady Illingworth's butler, Mr. Baldry, who had worked at the house since 1925.

On June 28, the Queen, the Queen Mother, Harold Macmillan and other representatives of high society gathered at St. Martin-in-the-Fields for the wedding of the Marquess of Hartington, heir to the Duke of Devonshire, and Miss Amanda Heywood-Lonsdale. 'I could have worn something unconventional' said the twenty-three-year-old bridegroom, 'but it would have been rather a bore and might have offended some people.' Miss Catherine Tennant, youngest daughter of Lord Glenconner, arrived at the ceremony too late to be admitted and peeped into the church through a keyhole.

Meanwhile, Mick Jagger and Keith Richard had been sentenced to various terms of imprisonment for drug offences. On June 30, they were released from custody on £7,000 bail each and were collected from their

Mick Jagger signs autographs on his way to court in Chichester

respective prisons, Wormwood Scrubs and Brixton, in a light blue Bentley with smoked-glass windows. In a pub near his solicitor's offices, Jagger, in a yellow flounced shirt and green tie, sipped vodka and lime juice and remarked, 'It will take a few days to readjust.' Both convictions were later quashed by the Court of Appeal.

On July 4, Cecil Beaton's home at Broadchalke in Wiltshire was ransacked by burglars. 'All they seem to have left me with is my dirty laundry' said the royal photographer.

On July 7, the frail-looking Francis Chichester was knighted by the Queen after his heroic 28,500-mile solo voyage round the world in his yacht *Gipsy Moth IV*. At the ceremony at Greenwich, the Queen used a sword of Sir Francis Drake, who had been knighted on the same spot 387 years earlier. Lady Chichester wore a controversial red trouser-suit, spotted headscarf and sandals.

On July 9, the young Marchioness of Dufferin and Ava, gave a joint birthday-party for her art-dealer husband Sheridan and artist David Hockney, which was attended by Princess Margaret and Lord Snowdon. The most startlingly dressed guest was Lord Dufferin's twenty-seven-year-old shirtmaker Michael Fish, who wore a gold and mauve lamé jacket and a gold mini-skirt.

The same day, Conservative leader Edward Heath celebrated his fifty-first birthday on board his newly acquired yacht *Blue Heather*. 'He's really bitten by the sailing bug' said his stepmother Mrs. William Heath. 'It is the one way he can get relaxation.'

On July 12, it was announced that Princess Margaret and Lord Snowdon were building a house on the Caribbean island of Mustique, where they had been given a plot of land as a wedding-present seven years earlier by the island's owner, Colin Tennant.

On July 21, the Bill permitting homosexual acts between consenting adults finally passed through the House of Lords. 'This is no occasion for jubilation and certainly not for celebration' said the Earl of Arran who had helped bring about this legislation.' Any form of ostentatious behaviour now or in the future would be utterly disgraceful.'

Five days later, Canon Hugh Montefiore caused an uproar when he suggested at a churchman's conference at Oxford that Jesus Christ might have been a homosexual. The suggestion drew an immediate rebuke from the Archbishop of Canterbury, Dr. Ramsey. 'There is no evidence whatsoever to support Canon Montefiore's reported ideas' he declared.

On July 27, it was announced that the expansion of air travel had forced the Cunard Company to sell the thirty-three-year-old liner *Queen Mary*. The purchaser was the Vice-Mayor of Long Beach, California, who planned to turn the stately ship into a museum.

A few days later, it was discovered that Colin Tennant was selling part of the art collection which had recently been handed over to him by his father, Lord Glenconner, including portraits by Romney and Zoffany. 'You can say they are surplus to my needs' he explained.

In the middle of August, attention turned to Sardinia where holidaymakers included Aristotle Onassis on board his yacht *Christina*, Princess Margaret and Lord Snowdon and actor Peter Sellers and his gorgeous new wife Britt Ekland. Staying at Mrs. Ian Fleming's villa on the island was the Socialist Home Secretary, Roy Jenkins.

On August 18, sixty-seven-year-old Lord Boothby announced his engagement to thirty-four-year-old Sardinian beauty Wanda Sanna. 'Don't you think I am a lucky boy?' he said posing for photographs with his fiancée at his flat in Eaton Square.

On August 24, John Lennon, Paul McCartney and George Harrison attended a lecture on transcendental meditation given by the Maharishi Mahem Yogi in the ballroom of the Hilton Hotel. McCartney said afterwards, 'This has been one of the most illuminating and exciting experiences I've had.' Said Lennon, 'It takes a time to come down to earth after an experience like this.' The following day, all four Beatles left for the Welsh mountains to attend a course of transcendental meditation conducted by their white-robed hero.

On August 27, while the Beatles were still in Wales, their thirty-two-year-old manager Brian Epstein was found dead in the bedroom of his Chapel Street, Belgravia home. 'It is a terrible shock' said Paul McCartney in Bangor. 'We are going straight to London.'

On September 9, it was revealed that John Osborne had purchased the sixty-year lease of a house in Chelsea Square. Said his close friend actress Jill Bennett, 'John has bought this new house for both of us. We do live together. We just want to be happy. There's nothing wrong in that is there?'

In the middle of September, Jane and Michael Rainey and their baby Saffron were found staying in a barn near the ancient Christian landmark of Glastonbury Tor in Somerset. It was noted that Mrs. Rainey, daughter of Lord Harlech, wore a multi-coloured Turkish bridal gown. During the course of their stay, the barn was raided by police and two of their friends were arrested and charged with drug offences.

September 20 saw the launching of the new Cunard liner *Queen Elizabeth 2*. It was noted that the crockery on board the ship had been designed by the thirty-seven-year-old Marquess of Queensberry, Professor of Ceramics at the Royal College of Art.

On October 8, Prince Charles arrived at Trinity College, Cambridge in a small red chauffeur-driven Mini and was greeted by the Master of the College, Lord Butler. It was reported that the heir to the throne, who was to study Archaeology, would occupy a small flat in the college consisting of a sitting-room, bedroom and kitchen equipped with a sink and gas-ring.

On October 9, the much publicised 'breathalyser' was introduced by the Minister of Transport Barbara Castle. One of the first people to refuse to use this unreliable contraption was Mrs. Julian Amery, daughter of former Prime Minister Harold Macmillan, after being stopped while driving in Belgravia.

On October 13, Richard Burton and Elizabeth Taylor flew in on board their recently acquired £360,000 Hawker Siddeley executive jet. 'We played dominoes during the flight. I am not nervous of flying. I love it' said Miss Taylor.

On October 17, there was a memorial service for Brian Epstein at the London Synagogue, St. John's Wood. All the Beatles wore suits. Also there were their lawyer David Jacobs, singer Cilla Black, Bernard Delfont and critic Kenneth Tynan. The rabbi spoke of Epstein as 'this extremely capable young man with a great gift for discovering extraordinary talent and helping it on its way'.

The following day, the Beatles were in less formal attire at the première of John Lennon's film *How I Won the War*.

On October 30, Brian Jones, in striped blue suit and lace shirt, pleaded guilty to possessing cannabis and permitting his South Kensington flat to be used for reefer parties. Sentencing him to nine months' gaol, the magistrate said 'I would be failing in my duty if I failed to pass a sentence of imprisonment, The offences to which you have pleaded guilty are very serious.' The Rolling Stone was taken to Wormwood Scrubs but was freed on bail the following day pending his appeal.

On November 6, twenty-five-year-old Richard Wrottesley flew off to America with Miss Georgina Clifton, daughter of wealthy landowner Colonel Peter Clifton. 'We're eloping' said Wrottesley. 'Georgina and I are very much in love but her father won't agree to our getting married.' The following day, it was announced that they had married in Las Vegas.

A few days later, Mrs. Jackie Kennedy was found touring Cambodia with Lord Harlech, former British Ambassador in Washington, whose wife had been killed in a car crash earlier in the year. Rumours circulated that the couple were contemplating marriage.

On November 16, one of the seven judges of the 'Miss World' contest at the Lyceum Ballroom in the Strand was the high-spirited sixty-two-year-old Marquess of Bath.

The Honourable Richard Wrottesley

Leading fashion designer Michael Fish arrives at a London wedding

On November 25, Prince Charles took the weekend off from Trinity College Cambridge to go shooting on the Duke of Grafton's 11,000-acre estate at Euston Park, Norfolk. It was reported that the Prince's party shot 314 pheasants, several woodcock and a few hares.

At the beginning of December, twenty-eight-year-old East End-born actor Terence Stamp was found installed in a flat in Mayfair's Albany. 'It knocks me out I'm so happy with it. I wake up in the morning and think of all the great men who have lived here' he said, adding 'I will not bring in floozies and give all-night parties.'

On December 12, Brian Jones's nine-month prison sentence for possessing cannabis was replaced by the Court of Appeal with a £1,000 fine and three years' probation. 'No permitted fine could really hit this young man's pocket' grumbled the Lord Chief Justice, Lord Parker. Jones left the court in a brand new Rolls-Royce Silver Cloud and went straight to his dentist to have two teeth extracted.

On December 20, nineteen-year-old Prince Charles flew off with both the Prime Minister Harold Wilson and the Leader of the Opposition Edward Heath to attend a memorial service for the Australian Premier Mr. Holt. Only two bunks were provided on the plane and Mr. Heath suffered the indignity of sitting up all night in a standard aircraft seat.

On December 27, Prince Philip drove from Windsor Castle to King Edward VII's Hospital for Officers to have a cyst removed from his right wrist by the Queen's orthopaedic surgeon Mr. Henry Osmond-Clarke. Three days later he emerged to rejoin the Royal Family at Sandringham.

Interior decorator David Mlinaric

1968

The New Year was greeted by an oddly assorted group of celebrities at Annabel's in Berkeley Square. Revellers included the tall Lord Charles Spencer-Churchill, the Sultan of Johore, actor Stanley Baker and television personality John Bird. In the small hours of the morning, they were joined by Princess Margaret and Lord Snowdon. It was noted that Lord Snowdon wore a white polo-neck sweater with his dinner-jacket.

On January 2, it was announced that twenty-year-old Lord Strathnaver, great nephew of the late Duke of Sutherland, wished to become a policeman. 'I have been for a preliminary interview before a panel of three big brass' he explained. 'If I am accepted, I want to be with the Metropolitan Police Force. Apart from Scotland, it's the only place I know. I look forward to pounding the beat.'

On January 9, it was announced that photographer David Bailey and his film-star wife Catherine Deneuve

Painter David Hockney and photographer Patrick Lichfield

had parted. 'It's just that things are a bit difficult and I am not seeing him much at the moment' said Miss Deneuve in Paris.

On January 12, the Prime Minister and Mrs. Wilson were found lunching at L'Epicure restaurant in Frith Street, Soho. At the same establishment was the Poet Laureate, Mr. Cecil Day-Lewis. 'It was quite a surprise to see Mr. Wilson' he said, 'but I've no intention of writing a poem about this particular occasion.'

On January 29, former tycoon John Bloom was arrested and charged with falsifying the account of one of his companies which had crashed four years earlier. After a night in the West End Central police station, he was released on bail of £75,000. He was driven away from the court wearing a 'shortie' camel-hair overcoat and large bowler-hat.

On February 8, Richard Burton and Elizabeth Taylor flew in and spent the next few weeks living on a lavishly-equipped 200-ton yacht, the *Beatriz of Bolivia*, moored on the Thames near Tower Bridge. The excuse for this luxury was that it enabled the couple to keep their pet dogs with them which would otherwise have been subjected to quarantine regulations.

Princess Margaret and the Earl of Snowdon leaving the King Edward VII Hospital for Officers where the Princess had her tonsils removed

At the end of the month, it was revealed that, following an anonymous tip-off, four policemen had raided Lady Diana Cooper's home in Little Venice and searched her bedroom for a hat-box which they had been wrongly informed contained cannabis. 'It's like living in Germany or Russia to have this sort of search of your home' said seventy-five-year-old Lady Diana, who later received an apologetic visit from Sir John Waldron, Deputy Commissioner of the Metropolitan Police.

On March 7, Dr. Emil Savundra, head of the former Fire, Auto and Marine Insurance Company was convicted of mammoth fraud and sentenced to eight years imprisonment. After the verdict, his sari-clad wife was driven home by Rolls-Royce to her Thames-side house at Old Windsor. 'We're broke' she said. 'There's nothing left. There are no secret numbered bank accounts in Switzerland or anywhere else.'

On March 18, at the auditions for the Berkeley Dress Show, much attention focused on the gorgeous-looking sixteen-year-old débutante Jayne Harries, daughter of self-made millionaire Welsh businessman William Harries.

The following day, a fifty per cent increase in the Selective Employment Tax caused dismay in London's clubland. 'Obviously it's going to cost us quite a few thousands' said secretary of the Junior Carlton Club. 'We may have to do some paring down of staff.' At the Constitutional Club in St. James's Street, a spokesman observed, 'Most clubs are already working on minimum staff.'

On March 25, it was stated that a noisy party at Blades, fashionable new tailoring outfitters at the end of Savile Row, had disturbed Conservative Leader Edward Heath, who had a flat in the nearby Albany. 'I am very, very sorry about the incident' said the proprietor of Blades, Mr. Rupert Lycett Green. 'I am going to write a humble note of apology to Mr. Heath.'

On April 1, thirty-eight-year-old Liberal Leader Jeremy Thorpe announced his engagement to twenty-nine-year-old Caroline Allpass, who was working in the Impressionist Department at Sotheby's. It was reported that Mr. Thorpe had popped the question in the revolving restaurant at the top of the Post Office Tower.

The same day, the Duke of Bedford was fined £50 and banned from driving for six months following an incident on the M.1 motorway when he had overtaken on the inside. He had been identified by his tell-tale personalised number plate 'DOB 1'.

On April 8, King Freddie of Buganda, who had two years earlier entertained the Queen Mother, Princess Margaret and Lord Snowdon at his palace in Kampala, was found living in a tenement flat in Bermondsey and was now dependent on National Assistance. 'I'm glad to say the odd friend slips me a fiver now and then' he said.

On April 10, the sixty-eight-year-old Duke of Beaufort was involved in an ugly incident while out hunting with his famous pack of hounds in Gloucestershire. 'I told them to get off my land' said farmer Colin Robertson. 'When the Duke intervened, I rapped his knuckles with the flat end of a spade.'

A few days later, the Duke suffered the added misfortune of being informed that his private railway station at Badminton was to be closed down. In future, he would have to drive to Swindon or Bristol to catch the London train.

At the end of April, it was announced that thirty-nine-year-old David Hicks, son-in-law of Earl Mountbatten, was to open a shop in New York selling furnishings he had designed.

On May 3, thirty-eight-year-old bachelor Viscount Furness, whose mother Thelma Lady Furness had been one of the Prince of Wales's intimate friends before the war, turned up at the preview of the Royal Academy Summer Exhibition in top-hat and morning-coat. 'Not too long ago, everybody attended this occasion dressed as I am' he explained. 'It is a tradition. I don't see why we shouldn't stick to it.'

On May 7, it was revealed that Lord Mountbatten had sold his seven-bedroom house in Wilton Crescent to the Republic of Singapore and was moving into its small mews cottage.

The following day, famous clubowners Ronald and Reginald Kray were arrested at their East End home and taken to West End Central Police Station in Savile Row, where thirty-six hours later they were charged with conspiracy to murder, grievous bodily harm, demanding money with menaces and other offences. A huge escort of police motorcyclists later accompanied the twins from Bow Street Court to Brixton Prison where, over the next few months, they were to receive visits and messages from many friends in the show-business and sporting worlds.

On May 16, Richard Burton purchased the famous Krupp diamond, almost an inch square, at Sotheby's in New York. A spokesman on behalf of the actor explained, 'Miss Taylor was very anxious to have the diamond and Mr. Burton was very anxious that she should have it. It isn't a present for a special occasion. Mr. Burton doesn't give presents for special occasions. He gives presents because he likes giving them.' Miss Taylor added, 'I have a lust for diamonds, almost like a disease.'

On May 20, Sir Bernard and Lady Docker arrived in London from Jersey on board their yacht *Shemara* announcing that they must at last part with this famous vessel, which had been built for Sir Bernard some thirty years earlier. 'I will be very sad to see her go, but she is much too large for us now' said fifty-nine-year-old Lady Docker.

The following day, Brian Jones was arrested following the discovery of 144 grains of cannabis in a ball of wool at his Chelsea flat. On this occasion he was fined only £50 and was told by the magistrate 'You really must watch your step.'

On May 29, the Queen, Princess Marina, the Duchess of Gloucester, the Duke of Norfolk and the elderly

Earl of Rosebery were present at Epsom to see Lester Piggott achieve his fourth Derby win, this time on Sir Ivor, owned by American Raymond Guest. Much controversy was excited by the fact that many of those present had turned up for the first time in lounge suits. 'I personally hope that top hats and tails will always be worn on these occasions' remarked beautiful racegoer Patricia Wolfson.

On June 6, fifty-seven-year-old Randolph Churchill died at his Suffolk home where he had been working on a five-volume biography of his father Sir Winston Churchill.

On June 8, it was announced that Cecil Beaton was selling four paintings at Sotheby's in order to meet his income-tax demands. 'It's sad, but I have to do it' he said.

On June 15, Elizabeth Taylor wore her newly-acquired diamond ring at the wedding of Mr. Simon Hornby and Miss Sheran Cazalet in Kent. Walking up the path to the church, the film star casually removed her white glove and showed off the monster diamond to the gaping villagers.

On June 18, sixteen-year-old débutante Jayne Harries was refused admission to the Royal Enclosure at

Millionaire's daughter Jayne Harries in white lace 'micro' dress at entrance to Royal Enclosure at Ascot

Ascot because she was wearing a white crêpe trouser-suit. Fifteen minutes later, after quickly changing in the back of her father's Rolls Royce, she turned up in a white 'micro' dress and no objections were raised. 'It really is ridiculous that I can't wear what I like' she said afterwards.

Later in the week, Mayfair hairdresser 'Teasy Weasy' Raymond, a racehorse owner of thirty years' standing, was also refused admission to the Royal Enclosure. 'My wife was simply dying to see the race from the Enclosure because all her friends are there' said Mr. Raymond. 'Maybe it's simply not the thing to be a hairdresser.'

On June 24, headlines blazed the news that Beatle John Lennon had transferred his affections from his wife Cynthia to thirty-four-year-old Japanese sculptress Yoko Ono, with whom he recently made a film exclusively featuring bare bottoms.

At the beginning of July, Prince Charles was found cruising on a yacht off Malta with eighteen-year-old Sibella Dorman, daughter of the island's Governor-General, who had accompanied him earlier in the year at the Trinity College May Ball. During this holiday, dramatic photographs of the Prince having his back applied with suntan oil by his young friend were taken by the resourceful young photographer Raymond Bellisario.

The remainder of the month was occupied by the exciting elopement of much-publicised sixteen-year-old débutante Jayne Harries and a twenty-four-year-old hairdresser, Gavin Hodge. 'My parents just couldn't understand how I could be in love with Gavin' said blonde-haired Jayne as the couple flew off to Lisbon on

July 16. 'Her parents don't think I'm socially acceptable because I'm a hairdresser' said Gavin.

Two days later, self-made millionaire William Harries and his wife followed the runaway couple to Portugal in a private plane. 'I'm prepared to give my permission for them to marry providing I can see them and see for myself that they are happy' said Mr. Harries.

The following day, a reunion took place between the two couples and all four flew on together to Gibraltar where, on July 23, the marriage between the runaway couple took place. It was noted that Jayne had now dyed her hair black. 'We are absolutely thrilled that this chapter is ending so happily' said Mrs. Harries. 'The more I see of Gavin, the more I like him' said Mr. Harries. 'He has character and ambition.'

On August 7, Harold Wilson's golden labrador, Paddy, set off from London in a specially reserved First Class carriage accompanied by a security man. The Prime Minister and his wife joined the train at Exeter and the party travelled on together to the Scilly Isles.

On August 9, it was announced that publicity-shy property tycoon Harry Hyams, who was said to have built up a fortune of twenty-seven million pounds, was in the process of purchasing the Dockers' yacht *Shemara*. A figure of £270,000 was mentioned for the sale.

On August 16, thirty-five-year-old Senator Teddy Kennedy, whose brother Bobby had been struck down by an assassin's bullet nine weeks earlier, visited ex-Prime Minister Harold Macmillan at his Sussex home. 'He came on his own and the two of them talked privately' said a member of Macmillan's staff. Many people hoped that Teddy would enter the Presidential race, but he had resolutely refused to become a candidate.

In the middle of August, the Duke and Duchess of Kent were found on holiday at Porto Rafael on the Sardinian coast. The Duke was in yellow bathing-trunks and the Duchess in a floral bathing-cap. It was said that the Duchess's holiday reading matter included the recently published diaries of Chips Channon.

On August 27, the Duke of Kent's mother, sixty-one-year-old Princess Marina, died suddenly at her home in Kensington Palace. At the funeral at St. George's Chapel, Windsor, three days later, the Duke of Windsor wore the same tail-coat that he had worn at his own wedding thirty-one years earlier.

On September 10, twenty-six-year-old Sir Mark Palmer, a former page to the Queen, appeared before Glastonbury Magistrates charged with the possession of hash. After being fined £20 and having his antique Moroccan pipe confiscated, Sir Mark drove away from the court in a horse and trap. It was noted that he wore a gold silk waistcoat and yellow velvet trousers.

The following day, the Queen's great-aunt, eighty-five-year-old Princess Alice, Countess of Athlone, was found boarding a number 9 bus in Kensington High Street.

On September 17, an old-fashioned note was struck when Mr. Christopher Soames, newly-appointed British Ambassador in Paris, set off from Victoria Station to take up his appointment. He was accompanied by his wife and daughters, Emma and Charlotte, and his pet pug, Jim, and labrador, Shingle. The party was seen off at the station by Lady Spencer-Churchill and Mr. Soames's mother, Hope Lady Dynevor.

At the end of September, the English social scene was enriched by the presence of American film star Zsa Zsa Gabor. During her visit, she lunched at Blenheim Palace with the Duke of Marlborough and strained her right arm when she fell from a black Arab stallion in the Blenheim park.

On October 2, photographs of the Queen in bed were published, exciting much indignation in certain quarters.

On October 11, it was noted that East End-born photographer David Bailey and fashion model Penelope Tree, eighteen-year-old daughter of former MP Ronald Tree, were now constant companions.

On October 15, thirty-six-year-old Robin Douglas-Home was found dead in his Sussex home. A bottle of pills was found at his side and an inquest later decided that he had taken his own life.

Two days later, it was announced in New York that thirty-nine-year-old Jackie Kennedy, widow of the late President, was to marry multi-millionaire Aristotle Onassis. The ceremony took place three days later on Mr. Onassis's private island of Scorpios and the couple sailed off for a honeymoon cruise on the famous yacht *Christina*. In London, Lord Harlech commented: 'Mrs. Kennedy has been a very close personal friend of mine for fourteen years. I hope she will be very happy.'

East End-born photographer David Bailey and millionaire's daughter Penelope Tree

Meanwhile, police dogs had sniffed out 219 grains of cannabis in a flat occupied by Mr. John Lennon and his friend Yoko Ono. The couple were subsequently fined £150 each for possessing the drug and obstructing the police in their execution of a search warrant.

On October 29, tax exiles Sir Bernard and Lady Docker were found staying in a double room at the Great Western Hotel at Paddington Station. 'We are not the rich people we were once' said seventy-one-year-old Sir Bernard, who was now drawing his Old Age Pension.

On November 5, eighteen-year-old Princess Anne, attired in a mini-cocktail-dress, attended a reception in London in honour of the medal-winning Olympic Equestrian Team. Among those whom she met for the first time on this occasion was brilliant twenty-year-old equestrian Mark Phillips.

On November 14, the newly-wed Mr. and Mrs. Aristotle Onassis flew into Heathrow on board a Hawker Siddeley executive jet but were refused the use of the Brabazon VIP lounge at the airport, which Jackie had frequently used in the past as former First Lady of America.

On November 28, the wealthy Duke of Buccleuch, brother of the Duchess of Gloucester, was taken from his Border Country home to a hospital in Wigan where an operation was performed to relieve an arthritic hip. It was noted that, unlike many of his fellow dukes, the seventy-three-year-old Duke had not sold a single acre of his estates.

The following day, the famous Cunard liner *Queen Elizabeth* left Southampton for the last time. The thirty-year-old vessel was off to Florida where it would be converted into a convention centre. In the meantime, it was noted that Cunard's new liner *Queen Elizabeth 2* had run into mechanical troubles during its trial run and a cry had gone out from the great vessel, 'Send tugs immediately.'

On December 3, it was announced that the Duke and Duchess of Windsor were selling their country home near Paris, the Moulin de la Tuilerie. 'The Duke and Duchess just want to be free to go where the sun is shining' said their secretary John Utter. 'They have a house in Paris. Why should they want two houses in the same climate?'

On December 15, show-business solicitor David Jacobs hung himself in the garage of his home near Brighton, where Ringo Starr and his wife had spent their honeymoon three years earlier. 'He bore so many burdens for so many well known people – perhaps in the end the strain caught up with him' said a friend.

Meanwhile, the Duke and Duchess of Windsor's circle of friends had continued to expand. Shortly before Christmas, they were found dining at a fashionable restaurant on the old Ile de St. Louis in Paris with Richard Burton and Elizabeth Taylor. 'They have always enjoyed the company of show business people' explained the faithful Mr. Utter. 'And then what with Mr. Burton being Welsh and the Duke's old connexions – Prince of Wales and all that – there was lots of common interest.'

1969

Heiress Jayne Harries, whose runaway marriage to hairdresser Gavin Hodge had filled the newspapers the previous summer, saw in the New Year at the fashionable Alvaro's restaurant in King's Road, Chelsea.

On January 13, antique dealer Bruce Reynolds, the last of the participants in the Great Train Robbery to be rounded up, pleaded guilty to his role in the crime and was sentenced to twenty-five years' imprisonment. It was noted that Mr. Reynolds had recently been voted an honorary life membership of the Students Union at Southampton University.

In the middle of January, Old Etonian Richard Collins, twenty-two-year-old son of Canon Collins of St. Paul's Cathedral, began training with the Bolshoi Ballet Company in Moscow. 'I don't think my father was terribly proud of my ballet dancing, but when he saw I was serious, he gave me all possible support' he said.

On January 16, eighty-three-year-old Lady Churchill dined with the Conservative Leader Edward Heath at his Albany flat.

At the end of the month, Princess Margaret flew off for three weeks' holiday in Barbados staying with Lord Snowdon's uncle, theatrical designer Oliver Messel. Also heading for Barbados was the Princess's valiant old great-aunt, Princess Alice, Countess of Athlone, who was travelling by banana boat.

On February 9, Richard Burton appeared in a 'shortie' mink overcoat, which had cost him £3,000.

On February 24, the newly-elected American President Richard Nixon arrived in England. The following day, he lunched at Buckingham Palace with the Queen, Prince Philip, Prince Charles and Princess Anne off poached salmon, lamb cutlets, and loganberry ice before making his way to the House of Commons to watch Prime Minister Harold Wilson answering Questions. During this brief visit, a spokesman commented on 'a personal chemistry' at work between the American President and the British Prime Minister.

Meanwhile, upper-class gypsy Sir Mark Palmer had been spending the winter with his horse and caravan parked at an Elizabethan manor, Stargroves, in Berkshire, recently acquired by his friend Mick Jagger. 'We'll be going back on the road any day now' Sir Mark announced on February 26. It was noted that the young baronet kept a picture of the Mother and Child in his wagon.

On March 4, the famous East End twins, Ronald and Reginald Kray, whose friends and acquaintances were said to include Judy Garland and photographer David Bailey, were found guilty of murder and were each sentenced to thirty years' imprisonment. 'In my view, Society has earned a rest from your activities' said Old Bailey judge, Mr. Justice Melford Stevenson.

Also missing from the social scene at this time was the flamboyant oil millionaire Nubar Gulbenkian, who had been struck down by a heart attack in the South of France and was to spend many months in hospital.

On March 12, the Queen paid a private visit to Trinity College, Cambridge and lunched with Prince Charles in his rooms, off mushroom soup and fried chicken, without meeting Lord Butler, Master of the College, or any of the dons.

On March 17, the sixty-five-year-old Duke of Argyll confirmed rumours that he was going to live abroad for tax reasons, handing over the running of Inveraray Castle to his son, the Marquess of Lorne. 'I have sent a memo to everyone on my estates informing them of my decision' he said.

On March 20, the marriage took place in Gibraltar of John Lennon, now bearded and long-haired, and his Japanese friend Yoko Ono. A few days later, the couple announced from the Hilton Hotel, Amsterdam, that they were going to bed for seven days. 'It's spring and it's a nice thing to do. It's a happening' said Yoko, who wore a voluminous white night-dress for the event. It was noted that Lennon had recently acquired an English stately home, Tittenhurst Park near Ascot.

On April 7, six paintings by Picasso and nineteen other masterpieces valued at £300,000 in all, were stolen from the Kensington flat of art critic Sir Roland Penrose, who had been a life-long friend of Picasso. 'My only concern now is that the stolen works will not be destroyed' he said.

The same day, it was announced that the fifty-year-old Earl of Derby had become chairman of a Soho-based theatrical agency with several pop groups on its books. 'Lord Derby is very interested in young people and the development of the business' said a spokesman.

On April 15, Princess Anne attended the new musical *Hair* at the Shaftesbury Theatre, the first act of which closed with a controversial nude sequence. At the end of the show, the Princess, dressed in a purple trouser-suit, danced on the stage with the cast and other members of the audience. The Princess's escort on this occasion was twenty-year-old David Penn, son of Lieutenant-Colonel Eric Penn, Comptroller of the Lord Chamberlain's Office.

April 20 saw the arrival of the new American Ambassador, fun-loving multi-millionaire Walter Annenberg. With him came his magnificent art collection which included paintings by Van Gogh, Gauguin, Renoir and Monet. It was stated that the Ambassador's official residence, Winfield House, was being given a another face-lift and Mr. and Mrs. Annenberg would reside temporarily at Claridge's.

On April 25, twenty-four-year-old Michael Pearson, heir to the wealthy Lord Cowdray, won £16,000 in a backgammon tournament at the Clermont Club, beating the favourites, businessman Jimmy Goldsmith and the playboy Earl of Lucan. 'It's a nice amount of ready cash to have' said Pearson, celebrating at a restaurant he owned in Belgravia.

At the end of the month, it was announced that Billy Wallace's butler, Dunning, had left him after ten years' devoted service, and taken a butling job in the City of London looking after the directors of the Spillers Company. 'We gentlemen in service need a bit of security like anyone else' said Dunning. 'It's a good life but it has always seemed that people outside were getting all the benefits.'

At the Royal Academy Summer Exhibition, which opened on May 2, attention was focused on Ruskin Spear's striking portrait of politician Enoch Powell, whose recent announcements on racial matters had had considerable impact. 'I did it entirely from newspaper photographs' said Mr. Spear. 'I've never met Mr. Powell personally.'

On May 4, the new Cunard liner *Queen Elizabeth 2* left Southampton on its maiden voyage to America. In the course of the crossing, blood was seen on the bows of the vessel and rumours that she had hit a whale were denied by the Cunard authorities.

On June 4, it was noted that for the first time in several years, the Aga Khan's box at Epsom was occupied for the Derby. On this occasion, the handsome thirty-two-year-old potentate was accompanied by a new friend, the startlingly beautiful ex-model Sarah Croker-Poole, whose marriage to Lord James Crichton-Stuart, brother of the Marquess of Bute, had recently been dissolved.

On June 7, it was announced that Mayfair hairdresser 'Teasy Weasy' Raymond would be permitted to enter the Royal Enclosure at Ascot. 'Bravo, is all I can say' said Mr. Raymond. 'I have had a tremendous amount of correspondence with the Duke of Norfolk.'

On June 8, headlines blazed the news that Brian Jones was leaving the Rolling Stones. 'We no longer communicate musically' he said. 'The only solution is to go our own separate ways – but we shall still remain friends. I love those fellows.'

On June 17, Mr. and Mrs. Jack Heinz gave an elaborate fancy-dress party at their as yet unfurnished Berkshire home which was attended by Somerset Maugham's daughter Liza, now Lady Glendevon, Lady Antonia Fraser, Mr. and Mrs. Billy Wallace, Mr. Paul Getty, Margaret Duchess of Argyll, Fiona Baroness von Thyssen, Mr. and Mrs. Walter Annenberg, the Marquess and Marchioness of Milford Haven, the Earl of Lichfield, Princess Joan Aly Khan and many others.

The next big social event was a dance at the British Embassy in Paris on June 28 given by Sir Christopher and Lady Soames. Among the 900 guests were Princess Anne, Princess Alexandra and Prince Michael of Kent. A representative of Olofson's hairdressing establishment in Brompton Road flew to Paris to attend to many of the guests' hairstyles.

Missing from this glittering occasion was twenty-year-old Prince Charles, who was now deeply involved in preparations for his Investiture as Prince of Wales.

This historic ceremony took place on July 1 at Carnarvon Castle witnessed by Miss Tricia Nixon, daughter of the American President, and almost the entire Royal Family, with the notable exception of the Duke of Windsor, who had been through the same ordeal in 1911 and preferred to watch the event on television at his home in Paris. The thirty-nine-year-old Earl of Snowdon played a particularly important role in the proceedings dressed in a tunic of dark hunting green and a belt of black corded silk, which he had designed himself. The Royal Family's host on this occasion was the elegant sixty-two-year-old Sir Michael Duff, Lord Lieutenant of Carnarvonshire, whose stately home Vaynol had been the setting for great festivities over the years.

On July 3, former Rolling Stone Brian Jones was found dead in the swimming-pool of his Sussex home. Fellow members of the group absorbed their grief in a massive concert two days later in Hyde Park, which was attended by almost half a million fans and at which Mick Jagger wore an elaborate white dress designed by Mr. Michael Fish.

On July 11, Elizabeth Taylor appeared in a yellow caftan and her famous Krupp diamond at the Eton-Harrow match at Lord's cricket ground.

On July 21, the American landing on the moon was celebrated with a kedgeree and scrambled eggs breakfast at the Savoy Hotel, which was attended by the Minister of Transport, Richard Marsh, Russian ballerina Ulanova, Sir Lew Grade, Dr. Robert Stopford, Bishop of London, and artist David Hockney. 'It just seems so inevitable' drawled Hockney. 'I fell asleep as those fellows were getting out of their spaceship.'

On July 30, it was announced that the Chancellor of the Exchequer Mr. Roy Jenkins had been made an honorary member of the exclusive Pratt's Club whose premises were in a basement off St. James's Street and which had been a stronghold of the Conservative Party for many years.

At the opening of Cowes Week on August 4, much attention was concentrated on Mr. Heath's new £7,000 fibreglass sloop *Morning Cloud*. It was noted that the boat was equipped with ship-to-shore telephone with which Mr. Heath could keep in touch with the Tory Central Office.

On August 12, disturbances broke out in Northern Ireland causing the Prime Minister to cut short his holiday in the Scilly Isles and fly to London in an Andover of the Queen's Flight. While troops attempted to instil order in the troubled area, it was revealed that Earl Mountbatten, now sixty-nine years old, was staying at his romantic gothic castle of Classiebawn in County Sligo, with members of his family. 'We arrived here before the real trouble began but we're not allowing it to spoil our holiday' said the former Chief of the Defence Staff.

Meanwhile, extensive alterations had been carried out to the yacht *Shemara* which property tycoon Harry Hyams had purchased for £290,000 from Sir Bernard and Lady Docker earlier in the year and the famous vessel was now ready to sail off to an unknown destination. 'The new owner has not told us where she is going' said a spokesman at a Southampton shipyard.

On August 25, millionairess Olga Deterding announced from her suite at the Ritz Hotel that her four-year-old romance with television interviewer Alan Whicker was over.

On September 11, Old Etonian author Jeremy Sandford, whose TV play *Cathy Come Home* about homeless families had had considerable impact, was fined £70 for permitting cruelty to eighty-six sheep and twelve horses on his Welsh farm. 'We are prepared to accept that you are devoted to animals. Unfortunately, devotion is not always enough' said the magistrate. 'I am a very sad man' said Sandford. 'This is the end of my romantic dreams about farming.'

In the middle of September, the London scene was enriched by the presence of Sir Oswald and Lady Mosley who had been living at their beautiful house near Paris for many years. During their visit, seventy-two-year-old Sir Oswald gave a dinner-party at his London hotel for Lady Mosley's sister, the Duchess of Devonshire, and had discussions with politicians of many different political colours.

On September 19, the marriage took place in Norfolk of interior decorator David Mlinaric and eighteen-year-old Martha Laycock, whose grandmother Mrs. Freda Dudley Ward had been an intimate friend of the Prince of Wales some forty years earlier.

Meanwhile, several hundred squatters had moved into 144 Piccadilly, an empty 100-room mansion, the former town house of Lord Allendale now owned by the Amalgamated West End Development and Property Company. On September 21, the squatters were ejected by a carefully-planned commando-style police assault and many arrests were made.

On October 1, the thirty-two-year-old Aga Khan and his new friend Miss Sarah Croker-Poole were found lunching together at the Mirabelle Restaurant in Curzon Street. Gossip columnists predicted the imminent announcement of their engagement.

On October 10, thirty-seven-year-old former washing-machine tycoon John Bloom pleaded guilty at the Old Bailey to two charges of falsifying the accounts of one of his companies which had crashed five years earlier and was fined £30,000. 'No doubt you have learned that the worship of the golden calf is as idolatrous and evil today as it was in olden times' said Judge Bernard Gillis. Celebrating his freedom afterwards at a flat in Hyde Park Square, Mr. Bloom declared 'I miss my big yacht. I miss my Rolls-Royce. Otherwise, I am comfortably off.'

On October 24, Richard Burton paid over £500,000 at Cartier's in New York to buy his wife the world's most expensive diamond. 'It has not been bought for a special occasion' said a spokesman for the couple at the Dorchester Hotel. 'It's just a bauble.'

The Aga Khan and his bride, the former Lady James Crichton-Stuart

Richard Burton and Elizabeth Taylor. Elizabeth wears a million dollar diamond in her cleavage

Four days later, Londoners witnessed the glitter and pomp of the State Opening of Parliament. The forty-three-year-old Queen arrived at Westminster in the Irish State Coach and gave her Speech from the Throne wearing heavy scarlet and ermine robes and the massive Imperial Crown. She was accompanied by Prince Charles, resplendent in the uniform of Colonel-in-Chief of the Royal Regiment of Wales.

The same day, the wedding of the decade took place in Paris when the Aga Khan, spiritual head of some twenty million people, was married to Miss Sarah Croker-Poole. A solemn religious service was followed by a glittering reception at the Aga's floodlit thirteenth-century home on the Île de la Cité. Among the 600 guests were Princess Margaret, Lord Snowdon and the Earl of Lichfield, who had been flown from London after the State Opening of Parliament in the bridegroom's private Gulf Stream jet.

On November 9, the Duke of Edinburgh caused a stir by stating on American television that the Royal Family would go into the red next year and might have to leave Buckingham Palace. 'We have had to sell a small yacht and I shall have to give up polo fairly soon, things like that' he said. In the confusion that followed these remarks, the Prime Minister announced that a Select Committee would be appointed to look into the Royal finances.

On November 13, Mr. John Profumo made his first public appearance since his resignation as a Minister and MP six years earlier. Opening an art exhibition by prisoners in the East End of London, where he was now working as an assistant warden at Toynbee Hall, he said 'Rehabilitation is a long, lonely, hard haul.'

On November 14, Prince Charles's twenty-first birthday was celebrated with a large party at Buckingham Palace at which Yehudi Menuhin played a Mozart violin concerto and rockets were let off into the night sky. Harold and Mary Wilson were among the 500 guests.

At seven o'clock the following morning, the Prince flew off with twenty-year-old Lady Leonora Grosvenor, elder daughter of the Duke of Westminster, for a weekend's shooting on her family's Cheshire estate, where the vast rambling Eaton Hall had recently been demolished and replaced with a smallish concrete-built house. The following day, Lady Leonora issued a denial that she and the heir to the throne were contemplating marriage. 'Rumours that the Prince and I are to become engaged are completely unfounded and untrue' she said.

On November 20, eighteen-year-old heiress Jayne Harries confirmed rumours that she and her husband, hairdresser Gavin Hodge, had parted. 'My marriage to Gavin is completely over. I should never have married. Marry again? No fear' she said from her three-bedroom home in Cadogan Lane, Belgravia.

On November 25, Beatle John Lennon announced that he had withdrawn from 'the Establishment game' and was returning his MBE to the Queen. 'It was an embarrassment to me' he said. 'It was a humiliation. I don't believe in Royalty and titles.' The medal was subsequently transported to the headquarters of the Orders of Knighthood in Buckingham Gate by a white Mercedes.

On December 1, it was announced that Mr. Michael McCrum was to take over as Headmaster of Eton. 'I have only been there once' he said. 'I found Eton's public image wildly wrong. In reality, it is extremely dynamic and exciting. The boys are nice and unspoilt.'

On December 11, the marriage took place between fifty-one-year-old widower Lord Harlech and thirty-three-year-old American journalist Pamela Colin. At the ceremony at the Grosvenor Chapel, Mayfair, former Prime Minister Harold Macmillan, now seventy-five years old and leaning on the shoulder of his son Maurice, diverted attention from the harlequin leather boots, maroon-coloured crushed velvet trousers and ankle-length cloaks worn by Lord Harlech's children.

On December 16, Noel Coward celebrated his seventieth birthday in London. That day he lunched at Clarence House with the Queen and Princess Margaret, who were standing in for the Queen Mother who had been struck down by an illness. In the evening, there was a televised banquet at the Savoy Hotel, where the guests ranged from the sixty-nine-year-old Earl Mountbatten of Burma to the aged musical comedy star June, Lady Inverclyde, who had been a friend of Coward's since the Twenties.

On December 21, Mrs. Jackie Onassis arrived with her two children, John-John and Caroline, to spend Christmas with her sister Princess Lee Radziwill at her hill-top Berkshire home. It was noted that sixty-three-year-old Mr. Onassis would spend Christmas on Greek soil.

On Christmas Eve, the sixty-nine-year-old Duke of Beaufort had a fall while out hunting, injuring his back and neck. He was taken to a nursing-home in Bristol where a bulletin was issued saying that he was 'reasonably comfortable'.

The decade ended with sixty-one-year-old Lady Docker complaining about her fellow residents on the island of Jersey where she had been living with her husband for the past two years. 'They're the most frightfully boring, dreadful people that have ever been born' she said, declaring her intention of leaving the tax-haven as soon as possible. 'With the money we get for the house, we will buy a yacht and then we'll be on the move. We'll pull up anchor and float away.'

SOURCES OF ILLUSTRATIONS

INDEX